Canada's Air Forces
ON EXCHANGE

(Above) Canadian Forces pilots have enjoyed many US Navy, US Marine Corps and RAAF F/A-18 Hornet exchanges, while pilots from various Allies have flown Canada's CF-18s. Here, a 433 "Ti-Pic" Squadron Hornet shares the ramp with USN VFA-83 "Rampagers" Hornets at Burlington, Vermont on May 6, 1989. They were taking part in "Maple Leaf", a US/Canada fighter exercise. (Larry Milberry)

(Title page) RCAF fighter pilots on exchange in the 1950s-60s flew the RAF's impressive Gloster Javelin all-weather interceptor. Javelin FAW.9 XH885 "R" of 60 Squadron is seen in all its glory during a sortie from Tengah, Singapore. On November 15, 1964 XH885 was destroyed at Tengah when it caught fire upon starting. (*Flight* via Roger Lindsay)

Canada's Air Forces
ON EXCHANGE

Larry Milberry

CANAV Books

Canada's first C-17 Globemaster III has its national markings applied in the factory at Long Beach, California, June 2007. Several Canadians were on C-17 exchanges in 2007, and delivery of Canadian Forces C-17 No. 1 was slated for the summer of that year. Canada's four C-17s will be operated by 429 Squadron at Trenton. (Boeing)

ISBN-13: 978-0-921022-18-3
ISBN-10: 0-921022-18-2

Design by Robin Brass Studio
Proof reading by Ralph Clint
Photo scans by Matthew Milberry

Printed and bound in Canada by Friesen Printers, Altona, Manitoba

Published by CANAV Books
Larry Milberry, publisher
51 Balsam Ave.
Toronto, ON M4E 3B6
Canada

www.canavbooks.com

Library and Archives Canada Cataloguing in Publication

Milberry, Larry, 1943-
    Canada's air forces on exchange / Larry Milberry.

Includes bibliographical references and index.
ISBN 0-921022-18-2

    1. Canada. Royal Canadian Air Force--History. 2. Canada. Canadian Armed Forces. Air Command – History. 3. Combined operations (Military science) – History – 20th century. 4. Canada – Armed Forces – Foreign countries. 5. Canada – Military relations – Foreign countries. I. Title.

UG635.C2M546 2007   358.4'1460971   C2007-903200-1

(Facing page) One of the early RCAF pilots to fly the F-86 on exchange was F/O James E. Hanna, who served with the 58th FIS at Otis AFB in 1951-52. In this group of 58th pilots seen at Otis in November 1951 are Lt O'Neil (USN), Capt Gaines, Capt Ernest Craigwell, Jr., F/O Hanna (RCAF) and Capt Ray Connolly (USMC). (Hanna Col.)

Contents

Capts Don Elphick and Bob Worbets were the only RCAF pilots to fly the
Convair F-106 Delta Dart operationally. Here, F-106 59-0100 of their
squadron, the 49th FIS, lands at Griffiss AFB, NY on July 11, 1986. Later a
QF-106 target drone, '0100 was shot down by an AIM-120 on July 1, 1994.
(Larry Milberry)

Preface

Exchange postings among military allies foster dialogue in ideas, reveal new technology, doctrine and tactics, strengthen international bonds, and build long-lasting friendships at the personal and unit levels. Rarely has this topic been studied – this is the first Canadian book covering the topic. For the purposes of this book, an exchange generally involves a member of Canada's military serving with a foreign air arm in peacetime for two or three years (here, "peacetime" means all but times of world war). Combat usually isn't part of the exchange experience, and the individual on exchange often has a foreign counterpart in Canada. Sometimes, Canadian airmen have had exchanges requiring top secret clearance. A few have been involved in leading-edge R&D, as with F/L Alan M. Robb flying RAF Lightnings in development of the Red Top missile, or S/L E. Lloyd Graham on a US Navy team developing advanced anti-submarine warfare systems.

I also cover postings that may fit better under the heading "secondment" or "on loan", as when RCAF personnel were attached to Allied units on technical or aircrew courses, but without foreign counterparts in Canada. Such was the case when F/L Albert Carter and F/O Arthur Fleming did parachute training with the US Army at Chanute Field, Illinois in 1924; or when Canadians attend foreign test pilot schools, staff colleges, or work in technical detachments, e.g. at McDonnell Douglas in St. Louis during CF-18 production.

Examples also are given of briefer visits by Canadians to foreign units to observe, study, train, even socialize. For example, there is the unit exchange, where a squadron may visit a foreign base for a few days or weeks. Sometimes squadrons become "twinned", thus developing closer connections professionally and socially. In earlier decades, RCAF representatives also regularly attended international commercial technology shows and public airshows to gather the latest "gen", something that continues today. Air attaché postings are mentioned in the way in which they include intelligence gathering as unofficial "secondary duty". I also include Canadian "ex-pats" flying abroad, e.g. aircrew joining the RAF after they had been released by the RCAF in the infamous "500 cut", and ex-RAF members who emigrated to Canada to find work in the RCAF. Excluded are age-old NORAD and NATO postings, e.g. to regional NORAD HQs or to USAF AWACS at Tinker AFB, or NATO AWACS at Geilenkirchen. Inevitably, such history will be covered by others.

Canada's Air Forces on Exchange brings onto the stage some remarkable new material. Exchanges commenced soon after the First World War, as with William Barker, Canada's renowned fighter pilot and recipient of the Victory Cross. Who would have expected to find this heroic figure with the RAF in war-ravaged Mesopotamia in 1925? Happily, like those following on such postings, he produced excellent reports and photos (ironically, these closely mirror another Iraqi escapade 80 years later). Following Barker, the interwar years fill with exchanges, for this was a time when Canada eagerly sent men abroad to absorb as much as possible about technology and to see how policies, doctrine and tactics were developing internationally.

While *Canada's Air Forces on Exchange* includes a wide range of subject matter, it is only the tip of the iceberg. Each sub-heading, be it fighters, transports, maritime aviation or training deserves a book of its own. In the fighter world, alone, dozens of Canadians have had exchanges on F/A-18s with the US Navy, US Marine Corps and RAAF, F-15s in Alaska, F-16s from Holland to Hill AFB, Tornados in the RAF and Germany, Mirages in France, with Eurofighters and F-35s on the horizon. Clearly, the topic of exchanges represents a fruitful field in Canadian historical research. Students are invited to explore it more academically, e.g. by defining categories more finely.

Over the years of working on this project, I followed the same system developed while researching *Aviation in Canada* in the 1960s-70s. Piles of official documents were sifted, archives visited and many face-to-face interviews completed (a method upon which, sad to say, Canadian history academics often look askance). For any interview, my subject would have his important resources on hand – log books, official personal documents, correspondence, scrap books, photographs, maps and memories. From each such meeting evolved a profile, moving from a subject's early training to his first posting, onward until it was evident from his success why he would make a good exchange candidate. To complete the history loop, the subject's later career usually is summarized. When possible, the rough manuscript was proof-read by the man involved. Besides such attention to "getting it straight", much letter writing was done, along with endless telephoning, faxing and emailing. One wonders what else possibly could be done to gain the approval of Canada's "real" historians.

As to the style of this book, political correctness is not in the picture, e.g. for measures CANAV uses Imperial, which remains common in global aviation. We have been to school, so can compute back and forth between Imperial and Metric. Benefit? Our pages are not cluttered with unsightly conversions. Neither will you find them disturbed by footnotes. While the academics revel obsessively in their footnotes, the CANAV style is to plug "footnotable" material into the text, where it best belongs, thus avoiding supercilious, obtrusive footnotes. Also, whether one uses such a term as "mission" or "operation"; "First World War", "World War One" or "WWI"; or "aeroplane", "aircraft" or "plane" does not bother CANAV – life is too much fun to have a stroke over nothing. According to convention, our captions name people from the left, unless explained otherwise. To get the most out of *Canada's Air Forces on Exchange*, be sure to have your basic tools handy – atlas, dictionary, internet, essential reference books, e.g. *RCAF Squadrons and Aircraft 1924-1968* or *Canadian Airmen and the First World War*.

As with any CANAV effort, hundreds enthusiastically assisted as I put in 20+ years researching this subject. Sad to say, however, my work on helicopter exchanges fell apart in 2006. Without explanation, several people, mainly serving members, dropped out, taking much of that chapter with them. When I tracked down possible replacement candidates, these were interested, but soon faded. Well, who wouldn't smell a rotten egg somewhere, eh! With a publishing deadline looming, I salvaged a bit of rotary-wing material and pushed on. This explains the

While stationed at Camp Borden in 1924, F/L Carter and F/O Fleming, completed a US Army parachuting course at Chanute Field. This photo from Fleming's album shows drogue chutes deployed and parachutes flaring as jumpers prepare to leap from between the wings of a Martin bomber. (CANAV Col.)

absence of a chapter honouring all those who have had rotary wing exchanges over the decades. The only other research snag relates, predictably, to DND Public Affairs, who failed to come through when I sought assistance.

Now to the stellar list of solid citizens who assisted. Armed with my wish lists, Hugh A. Halliday tracked down official documents at the Canadian War Museum, DND Directorate of History and Heritage, DND Joint Imaging Centre, and Library and Archives Canada. Herb Smale of VP International answered many queries about maritime exchanges. Aviation historian Roger Lindsay (chronicler of Venom, Javelin and Lightning history) was my chief UK assistant. Ralph Clint laboured with proof-reading, so that our rate of typos and other minuscule errors is minor. Matthew Milberry scanned the photos used in the book. Robin Brass, who guided my first book through McGraw Hill-Ryerson some 30 years ago, laid out the pages which you see before you. Otherwise, our list of top-notch supporters includes: Michael Adams, W.B. Allen, Martin O. Aller, Fred Allport, Roger Arsenault, Frank Augusta, George R. Ayres, Stuart Baines, David Bashow, Joseph Baugher, Jean-Guy Beaumont,

Don Bergie, Bill Bland, Floyd Bosko, John E. Bossons, Jeff Brace, John Bradley, Robert T. Brinkhurst, David Brown, R.T. Brown, Grant Bruckmeier, Dave Burton, Tom Byrne, Bert Campbell, Don Carney, Bill Carr, Nan Carruthers, Tony Cassanova, Paul Charles, J. Robert Chisholm, Garth Cinnamon, Andrew Cline, Brian Cluer, Chris Colton, George Conway-Brown, Gordon Cooper, Carl Cottrell, Michael V. Cromie, Dave Cummings, H. Ray Cutt, D.C. Deagnon, Jack Deakin, D.V. "Dan" Dempsey, Peter Desmedt, Gordon L. Diller, Wilfred L. Dobbin, T.E. Dodd, Brad Dolan, Mike Dooher, Peter Dunda, Guy Dutil, Jess Eisler, Ann Elphick, Robert J. Endicott, Ron Fentiman, Don Fair, Doug Fenton, Helen Finseth, John Foote, Jerald M. Fryer, Noel Funge, Morris D. Gates, Denis Gauthier, Donald Gerlinger, Richard Girouard, Lou Glussich, John E. Goldsmith, Edward Gosden, Perrin Gower, Jr., E. Lloyd Graham, Bob Grandin, Ping Green, James W. Gregory, Stephen Gulyas, John "Pogo" Hamilton, James E. Hanna, R.M. Haskins, Christopher M. Hasler, H.E. Hemming, Howard Hewer, Pete Howe, Russell E. Hicks, David Huddleston, Iain Huddleston, John Hudson, Lloyd Hunt, David F. Ives, Russ Janzen, Gorm Jensen, Vic Johnson, R.J. Jolley, James G. Joy, Bill Kalbfleisch, Herb Karras, Ken Kee, Hans Kimm, Francis G. Kincaid, G.R. "Sky" King, Gerald R.W. King, Stella Krantz, Harvey Kuszmaniuk, Janet Lacroix, Romeo Lalonde, Michel Legault, Charlie Leake, L. Anthony Leicester, Gary Liddiard, Barry Lumley, Ian A.H. Macfarlane, Mike Mahon, Orv Malcomson, Don Marion, Errol Martyn, Jock Mackay, R.G. "Bob" Middlemiss, Carl and Sonia Mills, Paul Minert, Mike Mirza, Stuart Mohr, Paul Molnar, Donald T. Monk, Ian Morrice, Hank Morris, Fred Mueller, Harry A. Mueller, J.J.M.

May to September 1952, F/O Claude LaFrance flew Sabres with the 39th FIS (USAF) in Korea. On August 5 he shot down a MiG-15. From August 1 to 31, 1956 LaFrance was on exchange with a French squadron at Dijon. There he checked out on the Dassault Super Mystère (below). After flying 33 sorties for 32:30 flying hours, he concluded that the RCAF Sabre, which he was flying at 441 Squadron, was NATO's superior day fighter. (PL-48390 DND, ECP Armées F61-116-R26)

Capt Dolan with his navigator S/L Colin Jones (right) and ground crew during their combat tour at Dhrahan, Saudi Arabia in February 1991. (Dolan Col.)

In 2001 Capts Jeremy Reynolds and Jean Maisonneuve were the first CanForces pilots to fly the Boeing C-17 transport on exchange. Both gained invaluable operational experience with the USAF in Iraq and Afghanistan, before Canada ordered its own C-17s in 2006. Below, C-17 03-3121 begins a demonstration air drop during the 2006 airshow at Edwards AFB. (Jeff Wilson)

Canadian Forces fighter pilots have had numerous RAF and Luftwaffe Tornado exchanges. Capt Brad Dolan flew the Tornado F.3 on exchange with 29 Squadron during the First Gulf War. Here, an F.3 refuels from an RAF VC-10 tanker while en route to the Persian Gulf theatre on August 11, 1990. (Dolan Col.)

Mueller, W.W. Nesbitt, W.T. O'Gorman, Garnet W. Ovans, Jack Parkinson, Wallace R. Peel, Dave Penney, W.D. Peterson, Frank Phripp, Ernie Poole, Preston (UK) City Council, John H. Ralph, Chuck Reed, Merv Reid, Jeremy Reynolds, Doug Rivoire, Alan M. Robb, C.M.V. Roff, Bill Ross, Kurt Saladana, Robert A. Saunders, Harvey Schaan, Rayne D. Schultz, Douglas G. Scott, Lisa Simkins, Mark Simkins, Darrel G. Smith, Rogers Smith, William B. Sparks, W. Don Stewart, E.H. Stone, Larry Sutton, E.D. "Don" Tack, Brodie Templeton, Claude Thibault, David J. Thompson, Donald T. Thompson, Terry Thompson, Ernie Throne, Ron Van den Voort, Bill Van Oene, Pierre J. Verhelst, J.E. Vernon, Chops Viger, Greg Vincent, W.H. Vincent, John Waldie, Duke Warren, Gordon W. Webb, F.C. Weir, Don Weixl, Eric Welin, Kevin Whale, Wilf White, Allan G. Williams, C.A. Winegarden, R.W. Worbets, Bill Worthy, Glen Younghusband, Gordon Zans. Sad to say, but some of these great citizens passed on during the long grind towards publication.

LARRY MILBERRY, June 2007

CHAPTER 1

Early Days

First World War Aftermath

The exact figure is unknown, but it is thought that more than 22,000 Canadians may have served as flying and ground crew among British air elements during the First World War. Their great deeds are recorded in many books and countless journal articles. Immediately after the war ended in November 1918, most returned home. A handful, however, stayed on with the nascent Royal Air Force. Of these, a few even lost their lives fighting "the Reds" in Russia in 1918-20.

Two Ontario men, Lt James D. Vance of London and Lt Harry A. Yates of Ingersoll, were among the RAF's post-WWI Canadians. Vance flew Handley-Page heavy bombers, was shot down in January 1918, served time as a POW, then was repatriated. In 1919 he and Yates were with 86 Wing, transporting VIPs between London and Paris for the Versailles Conference. Suddenly, they were tasked to rush a Foreign Office diplomat from England to Egypt – there was fear in the region of an Arab revolt.

Having decided to attempt a record for their Cairo trip, on June 21 Vance and Yates departed Lympne on the English Channel in Handley-Page O/400 No. F318. They reached Paris in 1:50 hours. Next day they made Lyons in 3:40 hours, but expected RAF service personnel were not present to assist. Used to wartime adaptability, the crew got on its way, Vance later noting how "we filled the machine ourselves, assisted by local Chinese kindly loaned to us by the French". Next stop was Istres (Marseilles) where they found the field very rough ("rocks are scattered all over the aerodrome"). Finally, they made Pisa, hav-

D9717 – a typical HP O/400 "Paralyser". Britain's leading WWI bomber, the O/400 used two 360-hp Rolls-Royce Eagle VIII engines. General specs included: wing span 100', length 62' 10", empty weight 8500 lb, bomb load 2000 lb, gross weight 14,000 lb and maximum endurance 8 hours. Production totalled about 650 Paralysers, on which many Canadians crewed in 1917-19. (RE64-103 DND)

Barker's detailed report of his Iraq sojourn includes photographs. Shown above left is a Vickers Vernon on the Cairo-to-Baghdad air mail service, the vast RAF aerodrome (above) at Hinaidi near Baghdad, and (inset) D.H.9 bombers of 6 Squadron at the RAF field near Kirkut. At left is seen the aftermath of a D.H.9 raid on dissident Iraqis. Of the latter, Barker noted in his captions, "… bombing a hostile chief's HQ … between Basra and Baghdad … subdued the chief in question [and] convinced a large number of wavering chiefs." (DHH)

(Below left) Barker's 1925 photo showing the legendary Golden Dome of Samara in the distance and "the old Arab fort (mud) in foreground". In February 2006 pitiful madmen blew up the dome, 1200-year old religious cultural treasure that it was. (DHH)

Barker was struck by the geographic wildness of the northern Iraq hinterland and, perhaps, by the unlikelihood of Britain ever controlling it. Seen below is the area around Rawandiz, northeast of Mosul and near today's Iranian border. (DHH)

percent at least, and it is doubtful whether great weights could be readily taken to that altitude.

c) The Fleet's A.A. guns could come into action and, in addition, capital ships at full speed could alter course considerably during the flight of the bomb.

I am, however, firmly convinced that bombs of three or four thousand pounds, not intended for penetration, would make a shambles of the deck and destroy the Central Gunnery Controls and do other damage to the signal arrangements which would reduce the efficiency of a capital ship by at least 50%. I do not, however, think that bombs in themselves will sink the modern capital ship ...

On this same posting W/C Barker was despatched to the Middle East and Mesopotamia, about which he submitted to Ottawa a field report dated July 13, 1925. Ideally, the best concepts and practices described in such reports were passed to RCAF units, where they might be applied to improve training and operations. Barker began by describing the weekly RAF air service between Cairo and Baghdad, a topic of interest to Ottawa, then experimenting with air mail. To help with navigation across the desert, a furrow had been ploughed, which a pilot could follow. Barker noted: " ... having been done several years ago [the furrow] is hardly visible in spots now and, in bad weather or in sand storms, is easily lost altogether." Along the way were several rough emergency landing fields.

On March 12, 1925 Barker set off from Cairo for Baghdad in an RAF Vernon transport. The first leg (0630 to 1130 hours) was to Ziza, 12 miles from Amman. After refuelling, they left for Ramadi (63 miles from Baghdad), but the pilot lost the furrow and had to return after three hours. Next day they tried again, the Vernon carrying 10 hours (4800 lb) of fuel. They made Ramadi after 7.5 hours, then pressed on to Baghdad. The worst part of the journey was the stench of kippers, cases of which were piled around Barker. In Baghdad, Barker was thoroughly briefed. On March 16 S/L Corballis, CO of 55 Squadron, arranged for him to go to Mosul, a 3-hour flight in a D.H.9 bomber. Here, Barker met the regional police chief, then the D.H.9 flew to Kirkuk to have its damaged propeller changed. He returned that evening to Mosul. On March 17 he set off in a Bristol Fighter to visit such frontier locations as Erbil, where the RAF was in action against Sheik Mahmoud. They returned to Mosul later that day, Barker commenting: "Flying over mountains is always uncomfortable,

but in this particular case they reach over 13,000 feet ... landing is not only impossible but, in all probability, the natives would be dangerously hostile ... The machines are very much overloaded and a forced landing would be serious." He also observed that the RAF had suffered casualties in Iraq, with aircraft shot down by rifle fire – marksmen often were on the heights looking down on passing aircraft. "Only a week ago a Bristol Fighter was shot down in flames", Barker lamented.

Barker also reported on the RAF in Iraq, listing squadrons (Nos.1, 6, 8, 30, 45, 55, 70), stations (Hinaidi/Baghdad, Kirkuk, Mosul) and aircraft (D.H.9, Bristol Fighter, Snipe, Vernon). He noted how aircraft had to fly overloaded, since regulations stated that many spares be carried, lest a machine go down. A D.H.9, for example, had 132 lb of spares, everything from a wheel, to flying wires, spark plugs, nuts and bolts, wrenches, oil can, funnel and canvas covers (RAF experience in Iraq was that all these spares rarely were useful). Then there was a desert survival kit including blankets, first aid kit, 5 gallons of water (57 lb), 9 lb rations per man, revolver with 50 rounds and a Lewis gun. Barker observed that the Vernon was a multi-purpose machine, flying the mail, transporting troops 15 at a time, and bombing unruly tribes. He also reported on RAF aero engines in use and considered the D.H.9's Liberty to be the best.

Barker described Iraq as 600 x 250 miles in extent. Here, his report seems a prophesy of what the US would face after its 2003 invasion of Iraq. Policy originally had been set in collaboration with France in 1918. Included was the need to expel the Turks, liberate indigenous locals, establish a national government run by Iraqis and secure the region's oil fields. In 1922 responsibility for military affairs passed from the War Office in London to the Air Ministry, so that the RAF might test its capabilities, build experience and prove its worth as an Imperial asset.

Barker described the natural difficulties of the region, and how tribesmen were well-armed and "accustomed to continual warfare", adding that "Air action is the ideal way of dealing with these offenders. It is swift and sure. Not only can the tribes be quickly punished, but their camels and livestock are easily destroyed from the air." The distribution of RAF squadrons in Iraq meant that any point could be attacked by air within four hours of orders being issued. However, Barker admitted how "political considerations sometimes delay the swift application of air action."

British forces in Iraq in 1925 (by then much reduced since 1918) also included armoured cars, two battalions of troops (one British, one Indian), a battery of artillery (Indian), a company of sappers/miners, 5000 Levies (local Christian militia under British control) and 6000 Iraqi soldiers (under local control), two armoured trains and three river gunboats. Barker noted how Britain hoped to hand over civil and military control to the Iraqis by 1929. He next described each aircraft type. The Snipe, armed with .303 machine guns and 4 x 20-lb bombs, was ideal for strafing and for attacking caves head on. The Snipe and D.H.9 were useful in liaison, mainly in picking up and delivering messages. The D.H.9 had a 450-lb bomb load, the Vernon 2500. Barker also summarized intelligence, transportation and communications in Iraq, noting that "Every evening all wireless stations report to HQ … should any fail to report, aircraft visit the area and report on the situation."

The most common type of air operation was the "routine demonstration". This saw the RAF over-flying a region to remind the population in the mountains and near the frontier "that they are under observation … it exercises a very quieting influence on them." Another tactic was leaflet dropping (still used in psychological warfare), the problem being that few tribesmen could read in any language. Should air strikes be needed, Barker categorized these as burning crops using incendiary bombs, shooting and bombing flocks, bombing irrigation channels and works, bombing buildings and inhabitants, and bombing and machine gun attacks on the general population. He concluded that "the first four methods are normally sufficient to achieve success".

To illustrate the usefulness of air power, Barker cited how, in November 1923, the British conducted punitive raids in a rebellious area along the Euphrates. After a final order to comply with government terms was refused, the RAF attacked. After one day all the rebellious sheiks had surrendered. In May 1924 similar raids were made against Sheik Mahmoud in north Iraq – 28 raids on 101 flights in two days. The sheik capitulated. One target had been a tobacco factory in Sulaimaniyah, the sheik's source of personal wealth. Barker emphasized the economy of the air element – how Britain had been able to pare costly ground forces in Iraq, saving some £2 million annually. Air action also left tribesmen frustrated at being rarely able to score against their enemy, for there were no armed columns to harry and plunder.

Barker described a case where the RAF conducted a full-out air action. This occurred on August 14, 1924 after Wahabi tribesmen attacked Ziza. The raid was confirmed early on the 14th by D.H.9 and armoured car recce. At 0900 three D.H.9s attacked, then three armoured cars pursued the tribesmen. Having refuelled and re-armed at Amman, the D.H.9s were in action again by 1130. One D.H.9 and four Bristol Fighters attacked the retreating tribesmen at 1530. All aircraft were hit by rifle fire, two aircrew being wounded. Recce flights on the 15th and 16th found no trace of the Wahabi. It later was determined that they had planned to take Amman. The sudden use of airpower, a 1925 version of America's 2003 "shock and awe" strategy, made short work of this threat. No British were lost in this action, but some 40 innocent locals died, along with 500 Wahabis and many of their camels. The RAF had expended 40 x 20-lb bombs and 9260 rounds of .303. Barker also noted the value of air transport in rushing troops and supplies to distant locations. In May 1924, for example, riots exploded between Christians and Muslims in Kirkuk. Reinforcements were flown in within eight hours, while at least five days would have been required by land. Barker reported that "the situation was quickly got in hand and peace was restored." Barker's return trip to Cairo was from March 19-21. For the whole excursion he entered these flying times:

Route	Hours Aloft
Cairo–Baghdad	15:30
Baghdad–Mosul	3:05
Mosul–Kirkuk	1:00
Kirkuk–Mosul	1:10
Mosul–Frontier	3:30
Mosul–Baghdad	2:55
Baghdad–Cairo	13:35
Total	40:35

CHAPTER 2

The Interwar Years

Southampton Flying Boat Exchange

The RCAF exchange process seems to have begun in earnest in 1927, lapsed in the early 1930s (likely for fiscal reasons), then surged again. Many RCAF personnel would be abroad in these years, gaining invaluable experience and enriching RCAF HQ with a flood of new information. F/L Earl Leslie McLeod, for one, would serve at RAF Station Calshot, Southampton. At the same time, F/L F.J. Mawdesley (pilot), F/L N.F. Mossop (Equipment Branch) and F/L R.J. Grant (Engineering Branch) had UK exchanges. In a 1983 memoir McLeod wrote:

At the Conference of Prime Ministers of the Commonwealth, held in 1926, it had been decided that there would be an exchange of officers between Commonwealth countries. Great Britain had asked for an officer with as much experience as possible in flying boat and seaplane flying. I had the privilege, therefore, of being the first officer to be selected for exchange service. My opposite number, from the RAF to the RCAF, was Flight Lieutenant J.A. Sadler. In the meantime, up until March 1927, I continued flying on a photographic survey near Ottawa and on other routine flying.

In March 1927 F/L McLeod sailed from Halifax for the UK in the company of several interesting Nova Scotians, with whom he played a lot of bridge. Once at Calshot, he was pleased to meet some officers with whom he had served in the RNAS in 1917-18. He soon was busy: "I found myself involved in station duties immediately – parades, naval co-operation flying, bombing practices, navigation, naval code books, etc. On March 4th, 1927 I took delivery of

G/C McLeod at his desk at RCAF HQ in London in 1940. Greatly experienced on flying boats, it was natural that in 1938 he receive command of 4 (FB) Squadron (Vedettes and Vancouvers) at Jericho Beach, BC. (PL-4302 DND)

Southampton Flying Boat No. 1125, put it through its acceptance tests, and kept it for my own use, almost exclusively, during the time I was in England." In a report describing activities between December 9, 1927 and March 9, 1928 he explained his duties as flying boat instructor, stated his flying time (50 hours, 10 minutes) and added:

The five months "Coastal Reconnaissance Course" which commenced in September, with twelve pupils, was completed on February 29th, and a new Course with eleven pupils commenced on March 6th. A final Cruise was carried out by the last Course during the period February 20th to 25th, four boats taking part. Navigation practice was carried out throughout the Cruise, each boat flying independent courses. Felixstowe and Falmouth were used as Bases for re-fuelling and for mooring for the night, and practice flights were made from these Bases. The various duties assigned to pupils throughout the Cruise were carried out exceptionally well. On February 21st, officers on the Cruise visited Martlesham Experimental Air Station, and had the work of the Station described to them.

Later, McLeod admitted that he had an ulterior motive in choosing the route during a later training exercise: "I wished to visit the native island home of my grandparents before I returned to Canada. The flight … was a pilgrimage for me." Immediately after taking part in Armistice Day ceremonies at Stranraer on November 11, No. 1125 was beset by a gale. McLeod and a fellow officer boarded from a rowboat, then tended the aircraft through the day, when it sometimes

During the 1930s RCAF exchange pilots flew the RAF's Southampton flying boat. This was excellent experience for the Canadians, who soon would be making the transition at home to the Stranraer. (RAF)

"kited" in the gale (i.e. became airborne). The Southampton reached Calshot on November 20.

The Schneider Trophy speed trials were held at Calshot in 1928. Part of the experience for McLeod was to deal with re-porters and photographers, who especially sought access to Lt. Samuel M. Kinkead who was in charge of speed runs. On March 12 Kinkead took off in the record-breaking Supermarine S.5 sea-plane: "I happened to be on the look-out on the top of Calshot Castle, when Kinkead, racing just off the water, a short distance away … nosed steeply down into the Solent. I and Squadron Leader Ray Collishaw were representatives, as Honorary Pall Bearers, at the funeral." Also during his exchange, McLeod had a month of annual leave. In this he delighted, taking his car across the English Channel, then driving to Switzerland to mountain climb and visit friends. His tour ended in March 1929, when he was promoted to squadron leader and appointed to com-mand RCAF Station Vancouver. Eventually, McLeod rose to be an RCAF air commodore.

While most Canadians in the RFC and RNAS came home at war's end, others remained with the nascent RAF. Included was Raymond Collishaw of Nanaimo, the great ace with some 60 kills. In early postwar years he fought the Bolsheviks in Russia and native tribes in Persia. Retired from the RAF in 1943, A/V/M Collishaw settled in his native British Columbia. In this July 1918 photo Collishaw chats with Capt Arthur T. Whealey of Toronto, one of his Camel pilots on 203 Squadron. (LAC PA2789)

In 1933 RCAF HQ posted Sgt J.D. "Jack" Hunter on a technical course to RAF Cranwell. Next, he flew Virginia bombers with 7 Squadron at Worthy Down and Catfoss, his task being to learn the Smiths Automatic Pilot's Assister, an early auto pilot. When he returned to Canada, he flew this system in an RCAF Bellanca on aerial photography. Jack joined Canada's newly-formed Department of Transport in 1937. He rose to oversee the DOT aircraft fleet. In this photo from June 1995, Jack (right) is with aviation author Fred Hotson. (Larry Milberry)

The Great Mawdesley

In 1934 F/L F.J. Mawdesley was on exchange, flying Singapore flying boats with 210 Squadron at Pembroke Dock, Wales. Having joined the RCAF in 1924, Mawdesley had flown on many humanitarian missions and forestry operations. He was nominated (but not selected) for the 1929 McKee Trophy, Canada's premier aviation award. He led a Northwest Territories expedition in 1930. Flying a Fairchild 71, that summer he covered some 15,000 miles on survey duties. In 1932 he flew a Vancouver flying boat supporting the Imperial Conference in Ottawa. This involved RCAF detachments taking priority mail from ocean liners off Newfoundland, then relaying it to Ottawa.

From December 3-12, 1934 Mawdesley, commanding Singapore K3594 "H", participated in a 210 Squadron "Home Cruise" exercise prior to delivering four flying boats to 205 Squadron in Singapore. They visited several harbours from Oban, Scotland to Felixstowe on the English Channel. The exercise covered everything from flight planning

to formation flying, navigation, communications, mooring, meteorology reporting, fuel and quarters, maintenance, even preparing meals in flight. Before departing, the weight and balance sheets for "H" noted: tare (empty) weight 19,608 lb, crew 1280, equipment 1601, baggage 260, fuel for longest leg 4812 (625 gal), oil 324, spares 150, gross weight 28,035. Some 1896 miles would be flown at an average of 85 knots.

On January 15, 1935 the Singapores departed. Preparations were more detailed than in training, especially since so many countries would be visited or overflown. There even were rules for personal cameras ("must not be used when flying over foreign territory"). Mawdesley's crew comprised three additional pilots, two fitters, a rigger, a wireless telegrapher and a civilian from the Royal

The inimitable "Mawdie" in a snapshot from early RCAF years. (CANAV Col.)

(Below) One of the RAF's stalwart Short Singapores, a type on which several RCAF exchange officers gained valuable interwar experience. (*The Aeroplane*)

As a senior flying boat man, F/L Mawdesley flew the RCAF's early Stranraers and commanded 4 (FB) Squadron. Shown is "Stranny" 916/QN-P of 5 (BR) Squadron stationed at Dartmouth early in WWII. (LAC WRF-158)

ficer than the inimitable "Mawdie". The route would carry the Singapores to such destinations as Naples, Athens, Baghdad, Karachi, Rangoon and on to destination by March 2. Sad to say, on February 15, K3595 crashed in bad weather near Messina, Sicily, killing all nine men aboard.

Mawdesley, who would have learned much at 210 Squadron, returned to Canada in 1935. Not surprisingly, he later was involved in accepting and delivering Canada's first Stranraer flying boat in March 1938. Early in the war he commanded 4 (Flying Boat) Squadron at RCAF Station Jericho Beach. Later he commanded RCAF Station Dafoe, Saskatchewan. In 1944 G/C Mawdesley received the Air Force Cross in recognition of his exceptional service. "Mawdie" left the RCAF in 1945 but not as a happy man. Drink and gambling would defeat him. In 1968 he died impoverished in New Jersey and, reportedly, lies in a pauper's grave.

F/L Costello

On April 4, 1935 F/L Martin "Max" Costello reported on exchange to 210 Squadron (Short Singapore IIs) at Pembroke Dock. Since he first had to qualify on large flying boats, from May 6 to June 15 he was on course at Calshot. At this time 210 was preparing to re-equip with Singapore IIIs, but this was a slow process. Meanwhile, 230 Squadron had moved from Basra to Pembroke Dock, and was exchanging older Rangoons for Singapore IIIs. Costello was on two interesting flights: July 16 (taking official photographers over the Fleet to record a Royal Review) and July 24 (flying the Prince of Wales from the Channel Islands to Calshot). Late in September 1935 a 210 detachment was established at Gibraltar with two Rangoons, delivered September 25-28 via France, Spain and Portugal. Excerpts from 210's Movement Order note:

Aircraft of "A" and "B" Flight will remain … not more than ¼ mile of each other … When ashore all ranks will wear No. 1 Tunic, Cap and Slacks. This order will not be deviated from without the express permission of the Officer Commanding the squadron … At foreign Ports of Call, the RAF Ensign will be hoisted immediately

Aeronautical Establishment (to deplane in Karachi). Maps (42 lb per aircraft) were carried for every leg. So were detailed data as to radio frequencies and meteorological reporting. Contingency planning included a possible forced landing: "If the crew … appear to be in immediate danger, the Senior Officer in the air may order another aircraft to land for the purpose of taking off the crew, but only when the risk of doing so will not jeopardize the lives of further personnel … Aircraft in the formation will be detailed to assist in attracting the attention of ships." Each man also was assigned secondary duties, F/L Mawdesley covering officers' accommodation and social duties. For the latter he was the ideal choice, for the RCAF had no more sociable an of-

During WWII G/C Costello served in Eastern Air Command in the U-boat war, then was station commander at RAF Castle Archdale, home to RCAF Sunderland squadrons. Postwar, Air Commodore Costello commanded Tactical Air Command, then Maritime Air Command. (PL-117408 DND)

on landing. It will be lowered when the mooring lights are lit at nightfall and hoisted again when mooring lights are extinguished in the morning.

F/L Costello crewed in Rangoon K2809 as second pilot to S/L A.F. Lang. Patrols from Gibraltar, chiefly in co-operation with the Royal Navy, included searches for foreign submarines. Work was considered so secret that Costello was not allowed to pass copies of the Operations Orders to the Canadian Liaison Officer in London. From Gibraltar he would log 70:45 flying hours. He returned to England as captain of Rangoon S1435 on March 18, 1936. Next day he was attached to the Marine Experimental Establishment at Felixstowe. However, he was assigned immediately as captain on Singapore K6911 ferrying to 205 Squadron in Singapore. The operation (which also included K6910) was delayed when the factory failed to release K6911 on schedule, but an itinerary finally was arranged:

Date	Routing
April 27	Felixstowe to Plymouth
April 29	Plymouth to Gibraltar (1030 miles)
April 30	Gibraltar to Malta (980 miles)
May 2	Malta to Aboukir, Egypt (920 miles)
May 6	Aboukir to Lake Habbaniyah, Iraq (800 miles)
May 8	Lake Habbaniyah to Basra (300 miles)
May 9	Basra to Rasal Khaimah (650 miles)
May 10	Rasal Khaimah to Karachi (650 miles)
May 12	Karachi to Raj Samand (370 miles)
May 12	Raj Samand to Gwalior (165 miles)
May 13	Gwalior to Allahabad (248 miles)
May 14	Allahabad to Calcutta (477 miles)
May 18	Calcutta to Mergui (900 miles)
May 19	Mergui to Singapore (830) miles)

This schedule was followed until May 12 when K6910 was delayed two days at Karachi with engine trouble. F/L Costello proceeded to Calcutta, conducting surveys at the intermediate bases. Both boats left Calcutta on the 19th, had a weather delay along the Malay coast, then reached Singapore on May 23. After handing over his aircraft, Costello visited Hong Kong, did a bit of flying from RAF Station Kai Tak, then boarded a steamer for England. A January 31, 1937 report describes the end of his exchange. As of the previous July 17 he was re-attached to the MEE, equipped with 3 Supermarine Scapas, 1 Stranraer, 1 Singapore, 1 Short Knuckle Duster, 2 Saunders Roe Londons and 2 Blackburn Perths. Costello ruefully observed:

It will be noted that among these there are no entirely new types. With the exception of the civil type of Short Empire Boat, there has been no new design of flying boat tested in England since the Stranraer and London were first produced in 1934 ... The Stranraer was being put through service trials; the older flying boats were being used in a variety of tests, including variously shaped engine cowlings and propellers. One [Scapa] was fitted with accelerometers to measure stresses on different parts of the airframe during take off and landing ... One Perth had 18 hull pressure recorders to determine pressures on the bottom surfaces on landing. A second Perth was routinely refinished with different paints to test their resistance to corrosion.

Having been involved in Stranraer testing (of 44 test hours flown at Felixstowe in 1936, he logged 32), Costello reported how "the aircraft is superior in performance to any type of service flying boat." Even so, he lamented its cramped interior and lack of robustness, compared with a London. Among tests was a climb to altitude that ended at 21,000 feet "as the crew were not equipped with oxygen". Several climbs to 16,000 feet were made, times to altitude being only 19-20 minutes. Costello felt that, when loaded to 22,000 lb ("overload" weight), a Stranraer could take a further 1000 lb "in good conditions of sea and weather". In general, he was mildly critical of RAF flying boat operations:

CHAPTER 4

RAF Exchanges
in Canada

Taylor Comes to Grief

While the RCAF had exchanges in the UK, RAF men were in Canada, learning of the RCAF's training, organization and administration, and of its specialized operations in the North, especially regarding mapping and photography. Of all this, little has been published. In 2002, however, a case was brought to light by Hugh A. Halliday. F/L Lancelot F.J. Taylor was born in New Zealand in 1909. He is believed to have trained with the New Zealand Territorial Air Force in the 1920s, then moved to England. He graduated in 1930 from Canterbury University College and was commissioned in the RAF in 1931. He gained experience on many types, from Atlas to Audax, Bulldog, Gauntlet, Osprey, Singapore and Wallace. He flew the Bulldog at 32 (F) Squadron at Biggin Hill, and the Horsley at 36 (TB) Squadron in Singapore. By 1937 he had flown 1400 flying hours. That May he was posted on RCAF exchange. Assigned to No. 6 (TB) Squadron, then flying Blackburn Sharks at Trenton, he also would fly such types as the Fairchild 71, Shark and Vedette. Sadly, Taylor's exchange would end in tragedy. On November 20, 1937, while flying Fleet Fawn 237, he crashed fatally into a building at Trenton's seaplane base.

Adjusting in Canada

Such RAF exchange postings were interrupted 1939-45, but quickly resumed afterwards. Personnel involved would form

F/L Lancelot F.J. Taylor in December 1927, while a flight cadet in New Zealand. Then, his headstone in a cemetery on the western edge of Trenton, Ontario. (Errol Martin/RNZAF Museum, Larry Milberry)

their own impressions of Canada and the RCAF. Figures for 1956 give an idea about exchanges in this era. There were 5 RAF and 12 USAF officers attached to RCAF Air Defence Command, 2 RAF and 3 USAF with Air Materiel Command, 3 RAF and 1 USAF at Air Transport Command, 2 RAF in Maritime Air Command, 1 each RAF and USAF in Tactical Air Command, 19 RAF and 8 USAF in Training Command, 4 RAF and 7 USAF at AFHQ. There also was an Australian officer with RCAF CEPE.

Exchange officer reports, as submitted to their home HQs, are historical snapshots, summarizing procedures, operations and curricula at scattered locations. As a courtesy, officers often left copies with RCAF HQ. These are valuable, even if the RCAF might have taken exception to views expressed (as the RAF might have done earlier, when reading the reports of such Canadians as Barker and Lewis). Some of these narratives can be witty and illuminating. F/L J.M.B. Edwards (RAF), writing about 4 FTS at Penhold in 1955-56, had mixed feelings about the Harvard: "No one at 4 FTS suffers under any illusions as to the suitability of this ancient masterpiece as a basic trainer. The oldest aircraft at 4 FTS first saw service in 1941 and has … 8000 airframe hours … Considering this, serviceability is very good." F/L J.G. Roberts (RAF), who served in Air Transport Command in 1947-48, commented on such topics as ATC's evolution from Group to

Command, and the introduction of the North Star. He also experienced northern ops with 435 Squadron. Apart from operational anecdotes, he had revealing comments about the difficulties of service life, including finding accommodation for his family in a tight housing market. In 2006 F/L Ken Mude, DFM, on exchange at RCAF Station Greenwood, reported on the same topic. An RAF signaller (RCAF equivalent to radio officer), in August 1955 he joined 405 Squadron. There, he found transition to the P2V-7 easy, for he recently had been on the RAF P2V-5: "I soon fit in, while relishing several improvements, especially the RCAF's advanced radar system." Of the housing and social scene, he recalled:

In this period RAF married quarters came fully equipped with furniture, kitchen equipment, bedding and so on. All one needed to set up home right away were personal effects, a fridge and washing machine. In contrast, RCAF married quarters came only with a fridge and stove, everything else being provided by the exchange officer and shipped at government expense on transfer between stations.

On arrival in Canada I first was briefed by the UK liaison staff in Ottawa, then travelled with my wife, Eileen, and 4-year old son, Ken, to Greenwood, arriving with only personal and private effects. Initially, we spent a few days in a small motel near Aylesford, until I found a two bedroom apartment in a converted farmhouse about 15 miles from Greenwood. We quickly adjusted to the local scene and customs.

Postwar, F/L Ken Mude was a radar specialist on Neptunes at RAF Topcliffe. Here he is with a crew at Greenwood. Behind are unknown, Bruce Cunningham, John Gridley (nav) and unknown. In front are Ken, unknown, Eric Boyd (RO), Don Miller (nav) and FSgt A. Campbell. Upon returning to the UK, F/L Mude had postings to St. Mawgan evaluating ASW equipment, at Londonderry with the Joint Anti-Submarine School and at Coastal Command HQ in Northwood. S/L Mude left the RAF in 1973, working first with Computing Devices, then at RAE Farnborough. (Mude Col.)

Aircrew from the RAF, USAF, USN, etc. invariably came from solid backgrounds. Here is FSgt Ken Mude during his RAF stint 1940-45. From August 1943 to February 1945 he was a radar operator on 502 Squadron (Coastal Command), stationed at Chivenor. On March 15, 1944 his crew encountered seven German E-boats, two of which they engaged. This operation resulted in Mude receiving a DFM. The whistle near his collar was used to signal, e.g. if down at sea in darkness. The elephant pendant was a personal good luck charm. (Mude Col.)

(Below) Halifax GR II HR686 "J2" of 502 Squadron in which FSgt Mude's crew shot it out with the E-boats. HR686 went missing on a sortie of October 3, 1944. (Mude Col.)

CHAPTER 5

Postwar with the RAF

Staff and Flying Exchanges

After WWII many Canadians enjoyed exchanges, secondments and other forms of duty in the RAF, RN, British Army, Canadian High Commission in London, etc. Aircrew began on wartime equipment like the Spitfire or Halifax, then came the early jets, more advanced types like the Javelin, and on to today's Nimrod and Tornado, with the Eurofighter on the horizon. In such books as *Sixty Years: The RCAF and CF Air Command 1924-1984* and in *Canada's Air Forces at War and Peace*, Vol.3, the postwar experiences of RCAF exchange test pilots (Eddie Gale, Russ Janzen, Frank Phripp, etc.) are recounted. Also covered is S/L Chris Hare, attached to RAF Transport Command Development Flight January 1949 to June 1951. There he did experimental transport and "met" flying that brought him an Air Force Cross. So many others followed that it would take volumes to cover the story. Typical was S/L Ian A.H. Macfarlane. Having joined the RCAF in 1940, he instructed in the BCATP, then flew Cansos and Liberators on both Canadian coasts. Post-war, he was on Cansos with 13 (P) Squadron at Rockcliffe, then sailed aboard SS *Aquitania* for the UK in February 1948 to join 540 Squadron, flying Mosquito PR.34s at Benson. In September he led a Mossie section during the Battle of Britain flypast over London. Besides Mosquitos, he briefly flew PR Spitfires, then had a stint with an RAF photo interpretation unit. He converted to Lancasters at Kinloss and, from October 1949 to March 1950, flew PR Lancasters with 82 Squadron in Takoradi, Gold Coast, then Nairobi, Kenya.

By studying reports sent home by those on exchange, one learns much of air forces, politics, world geography, even human nature. W/C Frank William Hillock, at RAF Waterbeach in 1952-53, submitted reports both witty and astute. He arrived at a time when rationing remained in effect. To meet needs, most RAF stations kept a farm, and ran an annual gardens competition. Waterbeach's farm was dedicated to pigs, but an egg producing

scheme was introduced under Hillock. Most staff were civilian, with an RAF corporal in charge. In December 1952 Waterbeach held a night aircrew evasion exercise. Men were dropped from trucks 25 miles from a finish line, while RAF police and civil authorities created a security screen. Those apprehended were subjected to authentic grillings by interrogators. Noted Hillock, "This is probably the last large scale exercise that will be held, due to the number of complaints received from farmers about damage to property and the possibility of spreading foot and mouth and other livestock diseases."

Postwar RCAF exchanges also included ground postings. In 1947-48 W/C Richard W. Desbarets was at Halton, an RAF technical training station. There he reported on pay and personnel administration, comparing RAF and RCAF methods. W/C Albert R. Sinclair's reports in 1953 dealt with RAF efforts to introduce automated pay accounting. In 1959-60 S/L Arthur A. Kinchen provided feedback to Ottawa on courses, publications and experiments associated with the Joint School of Nuclear and Chemical Ground Defence at Salisbury. W/C J.W.C. Galvin, serving at RAF Staff College at Bracknell from 1963-65, had a variety of duties, e.g. monitoring RCAF men on course, instructing, suggesting syllabus changes to include more "North American" content, and reporting to Ottawa on trends in RAF staff training.

S/L I.A.H. Macfarlane, whose RAF exchange was on Mosquitos and Lancasters. Returning to Canada, he had postings at AFHQ and RCAF Staff College. Before retiring in 1972, he commanded 404 Squadron. (PL-104378 DND)

W/C Albert R. Sinclair and W/C J.W.C. Galvin had non-flying RAF exchanges. (PL-57059, PL-128225 DND)

Air Ministry Tour

In 1947-48 S/L Barry H. Moffit was on exchange in the Directorate of Personnel Services at the Air Ministry in London. Born in Toronto in 1920, he joined the RCAF to fly PBY-5s with 5 (BR) Squadron in Eastern Air Command. Moffit received the AFC in January 1943 then, on May 4, 1943, while operating from Torbay, attacked and sank U-630 south of Greenland. For this good show, he was awarded the DFC. On exchange, S/L Moffit was to analyze problems in recruiting and aircrew training. For this he visited several establishments, including (April 19, 1948) RAF Flying Training Command HQ. There, G/C Stephenson complained about the poor calibre of aircrew recruits, grumbling about the RAF "only getting what it is paying for". Also visited were such flying stations as 3 FTS at RAF Feltwell, 2 FTS at RAF South Cerney, 6 FTS at RAF Ternhill and 1 ANS at RAF Topcliffe. At these the list of recruiting and training shortcomings was lengthy.

Moffit addressed the basic recruiting philosophy: "Recruiting literature glamourizes the pilot and only makes fleeting remarks about the value of the navigator in

present-day aircrew." One brochure was entitled "Career with a Future". Those "in the know" scoffed at it, explaining how the RAF was offering aircrew candidates little for their futures. Specifically influencing morale was how the RAF suddenly released 400 aircrew. Meanwhile, trainees had little hope of receiving a commission (most would be no more than corporals and sergeants). Moffit recommended that, if nothing else, a few from each class be commissioned, and some should immediately be granted permanent commissions.

Another form of discouragement among postwar aircrew was the slow rate of promotion. Moffit bluntly recommended speedier promotions. He criticized cadets' low pay, pointing out that any good prospect would be better off by following a civilian career. "Lack of decent pay has no doubt dissuaded many suitable young men from volunteering for aircrew ... Is it not best to have a small, well-paid, efficient and contented Service?" he lamented. He also argued that the RAF offer improved benefits, once a man returned to civilian life: "If the Service must take the five most important years of an individual's life, it must give him some compensation other than a small gratuity." Moffit recommended that the RAF offer men leaving the service a range of courses to help ready them for civilian jobs.

Meanwhile, a situation existed in the postwar RAF whereby airmen could withdraw from training at will, and return to civil life. Moffit urged an end to this, suggesting that anyone withdrawing from a program be obliged to complete the 5-year term to which he originally had agreed. The topic of marriage was touchier. Moffit was stern in recommending that married men not be accepted as aircrew recruits, and that no one be allowed to marry whilst training: "As these recruits spend almost two years on intensive training requiring a lot of private study in evenings and on weekends, it is not possible for them to lead normal

W/C Barry Haig Moffit, DFC, AFC in a portrait from August 1954. Born in Toronto in 1920, he was awarded the AFC for his work on 5 (BR) Squadron. His AFC citation states: "His efforts ... have been untiring and he has set a consistently high standard for the other members of the squadron." On May 4, 1943 Moffit sank U-630, this resulting in a DFC, although he had been recommended for a DSO. Following his exchange, in 1949-50 W/C Moffit commanded 412 Squadron at Rockcliffe. In 1954-57 he commanded 404 Squadron at Greenwood. Later duties involved diplomatic service in Poland. This great Canadian passed away in Stoney Creek, Ontario in July 1992. (PL-100764 DND) married lives." He disapproved of having "ex-regular airmen" in aircrew training ranks, claiming that these men (referred to in the RCAF as "retreads") resented discipline. He called them "barrack room lawyers" who lolled about concocting ways to shirk their duties: "They definitely are an undesirable influence on direct entry cadets." He suggested limiting retreads to the rank of corporal. As to syllabi, it was agreed that introductory courses in this period were too difficult, academically. Moffit suggested rewards, e.g. special certificates of merit and merit pay, to encourage cadets to master their studies.

RAF cadet quarters generally being sub-standard, Moffit urged station commanders to improve facilities, especially messes; suggested that food standards be raised, and that more competent cooks be hired. He also recommended visits "to and from squadrons to meet pilots or crews, hear of their work and examine their aircraft, and talks on operations by wartime aircrew could do a great deal towards building up enthusiasm, handing on experience and lore, thus giving an aim and incentive beyond the completion of the training course." On a different level, Moffit addressed the state of RAF training aircraft. The vintage Tiger Moth and Harvard needed replacement, but the government was dilly-dallying.

RAF Transport Command

In this period the RAF was rebuilding old ties through a special Hastings unit, 24 (Commonwealth) Squadron. The hope was that Commonwealth members interacting in one unit would strengthen far-flung relations. In 1954 the squadron was manned chiefly by Australian, British, New Zealand and South African personnel. Canadian representation was seldom more than two men. Meanwhile, in the 1950s the British Empire, though in retreat, still had outposts in what were almost client states. F/L R.E. Austin, an RCAF navigator with 24 Squadron, reported in 1955 on route conditions between Britain and Singapore. In this era Habbaniyah, Iraq was the largest RAF air station. Of it, Austin wrote: "Because of its location, one might say 'smack' in the middle of the desert, the amenities which exist there for the personnel are rather surprising … a golf course, swimming pools for all messes, a riding course, tennis courts, etc. During the summer months the temperature will reach 120 degrees F. or better … standing in the breeze is not recommended …" On April 18, 1956 Austin was aboard a Blackburn Beverley operating Abingdon-Istres-Toulouse-Bordeaux-Abingdon. He was impressed by the huge and docile machine. As navigator, however, he occupied the least comfortable position, in line with the engines, getting the full benefit of their vibration. Indeed, during take-off he reckoned the discomfort to be worse than riding in an RCAF "Noisy Star"!

Reports from the field often were written in the third person, diminishing the roles their authors played in events. F/L Douglas Roland Pearce, DFM, did not even mention that he was the navigator on Hastings TG613 (99 Sqn), flying UK–Singapore on July 22, 1953. Not long after leaving Idris, Libya, the Hastings lost three engines and ditched in the Mediterranean. Both wings tore off on impact and TG613 sank in moments, but there were no deaths among the six crew plus

Postwar, the Handley Page Hastings was the backbone of long-range RAF transport operations. First flown in 1946, it replaced the York, then itself was replaced by the Britannia. All-up weight was 80,000 lb, similar to the RCAF North Star. RAF Sabre pilot Sgt G.H. "Check" Collison, photographed these Hastings at Goose Bay in July 1953.

F/L D.R. Pearce, DFM, of Edmonton survived a Hastings ditching in the Mediterranean. While a wireless operator on the Halifax with 78 Squadron in 1943, FSgt Pearce received the DFM. In recommending him for this gallantry award, his station commander at Linton-on-Ouse noted: "The calm and gallant way in which this Non-Commissioned Officer carries out his duties, has been a fine example to his crew." When down in the Mediterranean, Pearce's crew certainly would not have argued about that! (PL-101620 DND)

passengers. Two of five dinghies were damaged, another floated off to be lost. After 3½ hours two USAF Albatrosses arrived, but could not land due to seas. A Lancaster with Lindholme survival gear dropped five SAR canisters of which three were retrieved, as a USN Neptune flew top cover. The seas finally abated and an Albatross landed. Towards midnight the destroyer HMS *Barfleur* took on survivors, then stood by until sunrise, when the Albatross departed. *Barfleur* then sailed for Malta. Like a good staff officer, F/L Pearce devoted seven paragraphs to the incident, but 10 more analyzing procedures and equipment used to transmit distress signals, and the rescue itself. In this, he was recognized with a Queen's Commendation for Valuable Services in the Air. The citation vividly described his role:

On the morning of the 22nd July 1953, Flight Lieutenant Pearce was the signaller on Hastings flying from Idris, in Libya, to Habbaniyah in Iraq. Some one and one half hours after take off from Idris a state of emergency arose owing to the failure of two engines, followed shortly by a failure of a third engine. Flight Lieutenant Pearce was ordered by the captain to send out a distress message. He had his wireless equipment set up on the distress frequency and despatched a distress message with admirable expedition. On receiving an acknowledgment from a ground station, he clamped his key and then rendered very valuable assistance to his captain by fitting the safety waistcoat and adjusting his straps whilst the captain was fully occupied in feathering engines and controlling the aircraft. When the aircraft came to rest on the water, Flight Lieutenant Pearce displayed

coolness and efficiency in the way in which he made his exit from the cockpit through the astro dome and in assisting other crew members to escape. Once in the dinghy, Flight Lieutenant Pearce took charge of the dinghy radio and radar equipment, and operated them to the limits of the equipment performance.

Radio officers F/L D.R. Pearce and F/L Arthur D.J. Delmotte, attached to 99 Squadron (Hastings) from 1952-54, flew as far afield as Australia, the Cocos Islands and Japan, but also were on Ex. Snowdrop (April 1953), moving an airborne regiment from the Suez Canal Zone, then dropping it in Cyprus. Three years later the RAF would be doing the same thing in reverse, dropping troops into Suez in October–November 1956. F/L Harold A. Spikings (navigator), while on exchange with 24 (C) Squadron, was not allowed (by RCAF HQ) to fly in the Eastern Mediterranean during the Suez War. The RAF had to find other things for him to do – he did squadron "adj" duties and spent three weeks at 242 OCU, when practically everyone else was away. Spikings was at last cleared for duties in March 1957, flying on the Hastings from May 29 to August 6, supporting British nuclear testing on Christmas Island during Op. Grapple.

F/L Donald Harrison was a Bomber Command veteran, having flown the Halifax and Liberator on 178 Squadron in North Africa. Postwar he flew North Stars with 426 Squadron, then was on Hastings at RAF Upavon. He had a front-row seat in September and October 1956 during Op. Buffalo – four atomic

F/Ls Delmotte and Spikings, whose RAF exchanges took them to distant parts of the world. (PL-97662, PL-142516 DND)

tests at Maralinga, near Woomera, a secret base in the Australian desert. His main duty was transporting men and equipment to and from the test site. Here is his description of the test of October 11, which involved a bomb dropped from a Valiant (documents declassified in 2003 note that Britain considered the Hudson Bay Lowlands near Churchill, Manitoba as an A-bomb testing zone, but chose Australia for climate reasons).

Our crew was to pick up a VIP at Adelaide and fly him to Maralinga, so we arrived just prior to the test and had a very excellent observation point. By 2:00 p.m. everyone was cleared from the actual runway area and the bomber took off. Without trying to be dramatic, I am sure that the crew were not the only ones getting the aircraft into the air … The main spectator observation points were in clearings approximately eight miles distant and five miles away from the target. The public address system had a VHF receiver connected to it so that the crew of the bomber could be heard. We had been instructed to have our backs to the target, eyes closed and covered with our hands until after the flash, then we could turn and watch.

It was a perfectly clear day, surface wind practically nil, upper wind southerly. The bomber made a dummy run and then announced that it was coming in on its bombing run. His height appeared to be approximately 40,000 feet … The crew called out their height and bomb gone. The seconds were counted down to zero. Perfect timing. The flash was sensed, and we turned around, heard the explosion, and saw the familiar mushroom-shaped cloud develop.

When Ottawa became more cautious about allowing RCAF exchange officers to participate in sensitive operations, F/L R.T. "Dick" Brown (nav) and F/L C.H. "Chuck" Parent (pilot), RCAF crew on exchange flying the Britannia with 511 Squadron in 1963-64, wrote in one of their reports to AFHQ about the difficulties for both guest aircrew and their host caused by this policy: "The frequent emergencies that have arisen during the past two years require the Britannia force to be at full operational strength at all times. This strength is reduced on No. 511 Squadron approximately 10 percent during every emergency because of exchange positions. When authority is received to proceed on a given emergency, it is often too late. As a result the squadron is unnecessarily understaffed during a time of great need."

The Britannia

In 1960-61, as the RCAF was preparing for the Canadair CL-44 Yukon, F/L Donald T. Thompson (pilot) and F/L James L. Braiden (nav), were posted to 511 Squadron at RAF Lyneham to learn how RAF crews converted to the Bristol Britannia, and to gain long-range, turboprop experience. Thompson, who had earned a private pilot's licence in Charlottetown in 1948, joined the RCAF at Victoria in May 1951. He won his Wings on the AT-6 Texan at Centralia, Ontario, did advanced training at Saskatoon on the B-25, passed the North Star OTU at RCAF Station Lachine in Dorval, and was posted to 426 Squadron in December 1952. In July 1954 he became a captain on the North Star. He completed several trans-Pacific trips on Operation Hawk, supporting the UN in Korea, and had a 3-month stint as 426 detachment commander at Shemya in the Aleutians. In late 1955 he was posted to 412 Squadron at Uplands then, in December 1959, joined 511 Squadron, replacing F/L Gerry Fosberg, who had been on Hastings at 24 Squadron at RAF

For his RAF exchange F/L Donald T. Thompson flew the Britannia. When he left the Canadian Forces in 1972, he joined Transport Canada in the air carriers branch. Later, he spent 12 years with Wardair, flying the 747 and Airbus A310. He retired in 1991 to settle in Gravenhurst, Ontario. (Thompson Col.)

(Right) RCAF navigator F/L J.L. Braiden's RAF exchange was on Britannias at Lyneham. His final posting was to Air Transport Command in Trenton. Sadly, on April 23, 1966 he lost his life when 121 KU Albatross 9302 crashed near Hope, BC. (PL-115101 DND)

From 1959-75, 99 and 511 squadrons operated Britannias from Lyneham and Brize Norton. Here sits XM496 "Regulus" at Dorval *circa* 1960. Retired in 1975, it later served with Aerocaribbean of Cuba and Trans Air Cargo Zaire. Grounded at last in 1997, it joined the Britannia Aircraft Preservation Trust at Kemble, UK. (Canadair 47141)

Colerne. Thompson spent his first five months at the Britannia OTU, his first flight on the new type being on August 9, 1960.

In this period a Britannia crew comprised captain, co-pilot, flight engineer, navigator, signaller and loadmaster. In November 1960 Thompson began the operational part of his exchange, initially flying Lyneham-El Adam (5:50 hrs) and on to Aden (6:30). He quickly appreciated what an improvement the Britannia was over the North Star – it was bigger, pressurized, carried more and flew farther, higher and faster. On a normal operation Thompson and his crew would operate Lyneham–Aden, lay over, press on to Gan in the Maldives, then to Singapore. Longer trips were to Hong Kong, even Maralinga. Thompson also flew trans-Atlantic to Fredericton supporting the British Army at Gagetown, New Brunswick, and to Namao, near Edmonton, supporting similar training at Wainwright, Alberta. Missions of 10-12 hours were typical. For his tour, which ended in August 1962, Thompson logged some 850 flying hours. He now was posted to ATC operations at Trenton, then converted to the Yukon, which he flew for three years at 437 Squadron. In 1968 he attended CF Staff College in Toronto, flew the 707 with 437 Squadron, left the military in 1972 to fly with Wardair, then retired from aviation in 1991.

"Ex Pat" on Britannias

Having grown up on a farm in McCreary, Manitoba, Ronald N. Plessis joined the RCAF in 1955 at age 18. After flight training at Moose Jaw ("from tractor to Harvard" is how he recalled this period) and MacDonald (T-33), in March 1957 he was posted to the Air Navigation School at Winnipeg as a staff pilot on Expeditors and Dakotas. Next, he got into the maritime world, starting with the Neptune OTU at Summerside. In August 1959 he began an Argus tour at 404 Squadron. Flying such a complex, modern airplane was great experience, although Plessis did not find the life of a long-range maritime pilot to be terribly exciting. Nonetheless, it did have its moments, as when a crew was on the carpet for smuggling a load of booze back from the Azores. Plessis' opinion of his CO, W/C Macfarlane, rose a notch when he remarked to Plessis how he thought this to be a pretty good squadron skit. On another occasion, however, when Plessis mentioned to the boss that he didn't think so much of high rank as he did of a man's character, the CO told him that he could forget about ever getting his permanent commission. Years later, however, after Plessis had a look at his service records, he found that W/C Macfarlane had always given him a fair review.

His short term commission expired and with about 1000 hours

on the Argus, F/O Plessis was out on the street looking for work. He thought of going back to the farm, but also checked out flying options. TCA wasn't hiring, but the RAF was, so in October 1961 Plessis signed a contract with them in Ottawa. He quickly accepted Britannias when offered, especially since the RAF gave him an immediate promotion from flying officer to flight lieutenant. He, his wife, Bibiane, and children, Leonard and Melanie, soon were in the UK, where Ron started with technical courses at Bristol and at Smiths Instruments. OTU at RAF Lyneham followed – simulator sessions, then his first flight on type on March 16, 1962. F/L Plessis was immediately struck by the scale and professionalism of the RAF, commenting in 2006: "They were playing for real. The Britannia fleet alone totalled 23 aircraft at Lyneham."

Flight cadet Ron Plessis while training on Harvards over the summer of 1956. (Plessis Col.)

Posted to 99 Squadron, F/L Plessis soon was into the routines of Air Transport Command, his first trip commencing on May 20, 1962. They flew to El Adem, Aden, Bahrain, back to Aden, down to Nairobi, Aden again, then El Adem and home on the 26th. Such gruelling operations were normal, an ATC crew day being 19-hours for a front-end crew of two pilots and an engineer – no double crews in those days. Frequent missions were conducted to far off Singapore via Gan in the Maldives, as were trans-Atlantic trips to Fredericton and Edmonton. Besides regular skeds, Plessis had many special flights, as to Mauritius during unrest there. With rebellions in Aden and Malaya, other missions rushed home troops wounded in action. December 3-20, 1963 Plessis and crew were on an exercise in Australia. On the return flight on the 19th they logged 11:30 hours non-stop between Perth and Gan.

On the whole the Britannia gave good service to the RAF, although Plessis was not in love with its Proteus engines. These were prone to icing up and flaming out. One Lyneham aircraft had all engines quit on this account while over East Africa. Happily, it got safely down after numerous attempts to relight the engines. The "Brit" also was prone to electrical snags.

Meanwhile, F/L Plessis was not the only ex-RCAF pilot flying Britannias at Lyneham. Others whom he met were F/Ls Bud Bird, Dave Collingwood, Anthony Gallow, Bob Henderson, Jack May and "Doc" O'Connor.

Since life on a Britannia squadron meant that crews were away for lengthy periods, things were not ideal for a young service wife and mother. Mrs. Plessis also was sometimes frustrated by the lack of information as to her husband's comings and goings. One day she was informed that he would not be home for several days. Almost at that moment he walked in the front door!

Early in 1965 F/L Plessis was promoted to captain on the Britannia. As he neared the end of his tour, the squadron showed its appreciation by giving Plessis a round-the-world "going away present" – a training trip that departed Lyneham for Gander in Britannia XL637 on April 14, 1967. They proceeded to Chicago O'Hare, Travis AFB, Honolulu, Wake Island, Guam and Singapore. Here they switched to XL659 for the leg to Gan. Gan to Bahrain and Cyprus again was in XL637, then they completed the trip in XL659, landing home on April 25, having logged 72:35 hours.

The Plessis family now settled in Winnipeg, but flying jobs were scarce. Ron spent a few weeks delivering milk, then talked to Transair, which was hiring. When he showed up for a DC-3 ride, the check pilot sat him in the left seat. Plessis was surprised, since he hadn't flown the DC-3 for many years. "Don't let that bother you," joked the Transair pilot, "it's been a lot longer than that for me." Plessis soon was on the Transair prairie milkrun, flying the DC-3 and Viscount, but when the chance came later in 1969, he jumped to CPA. There he worked his way up from DC-8 second officer to captain on the DC-10 by the time he retired in November 1996. Over the decades he had logged some 21,700 hours. (In modern days, ex-Canadian Forces pilots still work as "ex-pats". This occurs especially when jobs are scarce at home, but another incentive is the exceptional pay offered by some nations. Few are surprised in the 2000s to hear that former CF-18 pilots from Cold Lake, or Hawk pilots from Moose Jaw have left the CanForces to instruct in places such as Bahrain or Saudi Arabia.)

A&AEE Exchange

Having joined the RCAF in 1954, T.E. "Ed" Dodd trained as a long-range navigator at the ANS in Winnipeg, then took the navigation course at 2 (M) OTU in Summerside. His first posting was to 407 Squadron on Lancasters. Finished there, he instructed at 2 (M) OTU, attended the SPEC-N course in Winnipeg 1962-63, then was on staff until 1968 at CNS, instructing on the Aerospace Systems Course. In 1968 F/L Dodd replaced F/L E.D. Fonstad at the RAF Aircraft and Armament Experimental Establishment at RAF Boscombe Down (his opposite number was an RAF officer on exchange at AETE, Cold Lake). Dodd, his wife and

Exposed as they were to new cultures in distant Australia, the UK, or the US, children absorbed much during their fathers' exchanges. Here, "air force brats" Melanie and Leonard Plessis ham it up at Lyneham. (Plessis Col.)

five children settled into a mansion-like home in Salisbury. For the next three years his job was testing navigation equipment being developed for military and commercial aviation. Typical was a long-range nav aid (mainly for commercial airliners) known as DECTRA, an airborne system designed to cover the North Atlantic. DECTRA employed ground-based transmitters in Scotland, Iceland, Newfoundland and the Azores. After trials aboard the A&AEE's Comet IV "flying laboratory", Dodd recommended that the system not be adopted, the chief reason being DECTRA's obsolescence in view of the appearance of Litton INS and LORAN-C, which gave greater world coverage. Meanwhile, DECTRA was being studied in the US; Dodd spent some time there assisting with FAA trials in Atlanta. In that period he flew four times (26 flying hours) on a test bed DC-6B.

On November 27, 1996 Ron Plessis flew his last trip as a DC-10 captain with Canadian Airlines International. (Plessis Col.)

(Right) The Dodd family departing by train for Trenton to meet their Yukon flight for overseas. With their parents, Joyce and Ed, are David, Susan, Jim, Ian and Ronald. (Dodd Co.)

Besides DECTRA, Dodd also had projects evaluating Doppler radar and LORAN-C, and operated the DECCA Omnitrack, one of the first airborne digital computers, a huge piece of electronics with only 4K of memory. Nonetheless, Omnitrack, which even had a "moving map" display, could perform most of a navigator's usual tasks. Experiments were done with a Sperry INS concept that was tied in with Omnitrack and Doppler. F/L Dodd also evaluated the moving map display in a Wessex helicopter.

While at A&AEE F/L Dodd did most of his flying on the Comet, eventually logging some 600 flying hours. On a typical mission the Comet had a flight crew of six, plus a trials crew of 10 to 15. In 2005 he noted: "On away trips we always carried our own ground maintenance crew of up to eight techs. Such trips often included equipment demonstrations to foreign military and civilian interests, so we would bring along company reps and officials from the British Board of Trade." In 1971 Ed Dodd returned to Canada. He was replaced at A&AEE by Capt Jim Ward, the last from Canada to hold this exchange. Capt Dodd now joined 405 Squadron on the Argus, and had a tour with MP&EU at Summerside.

F/O Leicester (right) in his RCAF days with W/C Michalski, CO of No. 1 Instrument Flying School at Centralia. (Leicester Col.)

(Below) Tony Leicester's Anson sits almost crushed by another which landed atop him at Carberry. (Leicester Col.)

A "Brit" in the RCAF

While RCAF aircrew flew as "ex pats" in the postwar RAF, over the years many "Brits" served as members of the RCAF, one being L. Anthony "Tony" Leicester, whose book *Flights into the Night* recounts his wartime days. Having joined the RAF in 1941, he trained initially on Tiger Moths, then sailed for Canada aboard the *Louis Pasteur*. Posted to RCAF Station Carberry, Manitoba, he completed service flying training on Ansons. While landing one day, LAC Leicester had an Anson crash atop his. Happily, both pilots were uninjured. Leicester was absolved of blame, and left Carberry with his Wings in January 1942.

Once home, Leicester completed his training on Wellingtons, then flew operations in India-Burma. Back in England, he flew with RAF Transport Command. Upon being demobbed in 1946, he emigrated to Canada. After a period in Toronto, where he worked for a paper company, he joined the RCAF in 1948. Posted initially on Dakotas with 111 KU in Winnipeg, he next spent four years instructing on Expeditors at No. 1 Instrument Flying School at Centralia. Other postings followed, including to 412 Squadron in Ottawa and 115 ATU at El Arish. Along the way, F/L Leicester produced some valuable technical "pubs", including the RCAF *Instrument Flying Instructor's Manual*, and compiled *Flying Orders for the RCAF*, Vols.I and II.

F/L Leicester's final RCAF posting was in Base Operations at Trenton, from where he retired in 1968. He moved to the island of San Salvador in the Bahamas, where he and his wife managed an out-island hotel for some years. Back in Florida, Tony wrote boating articles and completed his memoir. In 2007 he was working on a book about the Bahamas.

CHAPTER 6

USAF Tours

Weather and Transport Assignments

Post WWII the RCAF had much to learn from the United States, where R&D and the introduction of new aircraft and systems were booming. Many USAF transport exchanges arose, with Canadians crewing on such USAF types as the C-54, C-97, C-130, C-141 and on to today's C-17. F/L Douglas G. Scott's exchange was with the 55th Weather Reconnaissance Squadron. Having joined the RCAF in November 1943 at age 17, Scott was held at No. 1 Manning Depot in Toronto until age 18. While at No. 3 Initial Training School at Victoriaville, Quebec, his class learned that there would be no new pilot trainees. Scott soon found himself at Rivers, Manitoba on its final navigation course (Crs.114), after which he was back home on the farm. Still wanting to be a pilot, he earned his private pilot licence, re-enlisted in the RCAF and reported to Manning Depot in Toronto on March 1, 1948. Training on Harvards and Expeditors began at Centralia on May 1, leading to Wings in late January 1949. After 2 months at AAS in Trenton, Scott was commissioned and posted to 426 Squadron at Lachine. He converted to the North Star, then began operations, which would include 19 Korean War trips.

In early 1952 F/O Scott took the FIS course at Trenton, then had tours on Harvards and Expeditors at Gimli and Moose Jaw. He also taught instrument flying at Centralia. In late 1955 he was posted to 408 Squadron at Rockcliffe, flying Lancasters on aerial photography, ice reconnaissance, geodetic survey, and special "Air Romp" missions, which assessed Soviet "scientific" camps on the polar ice in Canadian waters. In December 1957, 408 sent Lancaster KB976 with a double crew under W/C Jim Mitchell to Ladd Air Force Base at Anchorage, Alaska. This was a liaison trip to discuss Arctic operations with the 55th WRS, flying WB-50s. Then, in the fall of 1958 F/L Scott was sent on exchange to the 55th. Following a final air test in KB976 on October 17, 1958 he was off to the MATS OTU at West Palm Beach, Florida. In February 1959, having qualified on the WB-50, he joined his new squadron at McChord AFB near Tacoma, Washington (the 55th had moved from Fairbanks). Scott's first mission was a conversion flight under Capt Watson on February 20.

With four 28-cylinder, 3750-hp P&W R-4360 engines the WB-50 was bigger, faster, and far more comfortable than the Lancaster. A crew varied from 8 to 12 men (6 to 10 in a

A standard Boeing WB-50D (49-313) of the 55th Weather Reconnaissance Squadron, McChord AFB. The B-50, descendant of the B-29 and first flown in 1945, was one of the USAF's most versatile postwar workhorses, serving as a bomber, weather recce and spy plane, aerial tanker and trainer. The last B-50 retired in 1965. (D. G. Scott Col.)

Lancaster). On ops, all weather missions had code names, as with Tacoma to Honolulu – "Lark Uniform", Honolulu to Fairbanks – "Loon Hotel", Fairbanks loop over the Arctic Ocean to Fairbanks – "Ptarmigan", Fairbanks to Tacoma – "Stork Golf", a loop south of Hawaii – "Petrel Kilo", and one off the west coast – "Loon Kilo". Missions ran 11 to 14 hours. The meteorological crewman worked in the bomb-aimer's nose position. Observing instruments and outside conditions, he collected data at frequent intervals. Periodically, a "met" instrument package would be dropped, which would return data at various altitudes. Also, to track the results of atomic tests, air sampling was conducted. Most tracks were flown daily and other squadrons were monitoring other areas around the world, producing an overall picture of conditions across the northern hemisphere. Tracks were flown at standard millibar levels, rather than at such and such an altitude. Starting out, standard missions were flown at 700 mbs (10,380 feet) until about half time, then a climb was made to 500 mbs (18,000+) for the rest of the flight. Special missions were flown at 300 mbs (30,000+). A typical deployment lasted 7–10 days as with this sample: Day 1 – Lark Uniform, Day 2 – day off, Day 3 – Petrel Kilo, Day 4 – off, Day 5 – Loon Hotel, Day 6 – off, Day 7 – Ptarmigan, Day 8 – off, Day 9 – Stork Golf which ended back at home base. Petrel Kilo lasted 10 or more days. At that time the "Discoverer" series of "scientific" satellites was being flown. Recovery of a returning satellite was accomplished by a C-119 under-flying the satellite and snagging its parachute with a cable and hook trailing behind. Visual conditions were required for a catch, so Petrel Kilo missions commenced 10 days before a scheduled satellite launch. Using their data, military forecasters would recommend whether or not a satellite should be launched.

On June 21, 1959 F/L Scott, by then an aircraft commander, took his 10-man crew on a Lark Uniform. For the first hour all went well, then the engine-fire master warning light illuminated. The engineer confirmed that a light for No. 3 engine was on and he and the right scanner verified smoke and flame from No. 3. It was promptly feathered, the fire died and the return to McChord was uneventful. Flight time – 2:20 hours. The crew changed aircraft, then flew a routine Loon Kilo to Hawaii, adding a further 13:50 hours to their work day. After two crew rest days, a Petrel

F/L Scott's crew for the June 29, 1959 mission. Standing are CWO Peters (weather tech), Capt Rex Price (nav), Lt V.C. Stewart (nav), SSgt Murdoch (FE) and SSgt Cole (radio op). In front are F/L D.G. Scott (aircraft commander), TSgt Hank Veenkant (FE), Lt Reg Wackford (co-pilot), A1C Hernandez (crewman) and SSgt Caracausi (dropsonde). (all, D. G. Scott Col.)

Kilo was flown (12:50 hours). Two days later came a Loon Hotel up the centre of the Pacific to Nome and Fairbanks (13:20).

On June 29 the crew departed Fairbanks in WB-50 48-108 for a Ptarmigan mission over the Alaska mountains to Point Barrow, then on a NNW track over the Arctic until about 900 nm from Fairbanks. Suddenly, came a very loud "Chunk" – distinctly metallic, extremely startling and accompanied by wild buffeting. Scott closed the throttles and looked out to see No. 2 engine trying to tear itself from the wing. He activated the feathering circuit and the propeller stopped in 15 to 20 seconds. As he unplugged the autopilot and started a turn towards Fairbanks, he asked flight engineer TSgt Hank Veenkant for climb power. Nos. 3 and 4 set up properly, but Veenkant discovered that No. 1 prop wouldn't give the RPMs required, so that engine was limited to cruise. By the time the aircraft was on its Fairbanks heading, it was stable, but descending about 50 fpm. There was no temptation to increase Nos. 3 and 4 beyond climb power – the R-4350 was known to fail if over-worked. Doug Scott describes what ensued:

Damage assessment had begun while the propeller was feathering, but several crew were talking at the same time. That was quickly quelled and rational analysis began. We realized that the cause of the emergency was losing 17 inches of one blade of the 16-foot diameter No. 2 propeller. The blade tip had entered the fuselage almost half way up, exiting at the front of the left bomb bay door. On its brief transit it severed electric cable bundles, one structural "I" beam, one elevator cable, besides shattering the valve controlling the front bomb bay doors. Both doors hung open, the left one being unrestrained. This increased aerodynamic drag, but the loss of an elevator cable didn't matter – as a combat aircraft, the WB-50 was double rigged. However, the severed electrical cables were another story, as the entire bundle for No. 1 engine was cut. Not only was propeller control lost but, with the exception of manifold pressure, all its instrument wires were cut. Had trouble developed with No. 1, it would not have feathered.

As the flight progressed and fuel was burned, the WB-50 levelled at 9400 feet and cruising altitude (10,000) was regained at an indicated speed of 180–185 knots. Eventually, power on Nos. 3 and 4 engines could be reduced. An early call for search and rescue revealed that there was no equipment to escort us. However, another WB-50 from the 55th, piloted by Lt "Slim" Slemmons, was a welcome sight near Umiat, about an hour and a half from Fairbanks. Early in the descent we lowered the landing gear and, as feared, the left main gear did not come down. Having been relieved on the panel by SSgt Murdoch, TSgt Veenkant went into the rear bomb bay and completed the manual procedure for lowering the gear.

As the flaps would not deploy, Scott approached at 175 mph (135 was normal). On touch down, he gave the brakes a quick

jab, to see if they would work. Then, he let the aircraft roll free for about a mile of Eielson AFB's 13,000 foot runway. When the brakes finally were needed, they were firmly applied to the point of smoking. Flight time for the mission turned out to be 9:40 hours. In his statement to the investigation board, F/L Scott praised his crew for "the quiet and panic-free manner" in which they did their jobs. Lt Reg Wackford, an experienced WB-50 co-pilot, ably had assisted on the flight deck, navigator Capt Rex Price provided the return heading and all further guidance, and radio operator Sgt Cole handled long-range communications.

Throughout the emergency two things relieved the tension. In one, before the incident, Lt Wackford had gone aft for a rest, so weather observer CWO Peters, idle for a few minutes, had settled into the co-pilot seat for a different perspective. With the emergency, Peters stood up and leaned over the yoke and instrument shroud in an effort to see what was happening on the left side of the aircraft. Just as smartly, Wackford resumed his seat, did up his parachute and shoulder harnesses, thus neatly trapping Peters between Wackford's legs, the seat and the yoke, but Peters extricated himself smoothly. Half an hour later, when some stability had been established, Scott reached down in front of his seat and picked up the sandwich he had been eating,

Some of the damage caused when the prop tip smashed through the WB-50 – bundles of wire and a structural support have been sliced.

before he had been so rudely interrupted. By the time things had settled down for the crew at Eielson, F/L Scott received a message ("green signal") from LCol Harvey P. Hall, his CO in Sacramento:

Unclas from Det 1, 55th WRS 2-G-7. For Flight Lt. Douglas Scott. Regret that I did not see you personally to express my admiration for the manner in which you and your crew handled the loss of part of a prop blade and resulting damage to aircraft. You displayed a very high degree of airmanship and coolness under stress, which undoubtedly resulted in saving the aircraft. Pass to your crew congratulations on handling this emergency in such a professional manner.

In the post-flight inspections it was found that two torsion members in No. 2 engine mount were broken, indicating that quick feathering was indeed fortuitous. Also, when the aircraft departed Eielson for repairs at McClellan AFB, Sacramento, it was airborne only about 10 minutes when No. 3 engine failed. The crew then realized that using more than climb power at the time of the prop failure likely would have precipitated engine failure, so the WB-50 would not have made Eielson. In his summary to a USAF board of enquiry, F/L Scott wrote:

F/L Doug Scott being honoured by the USAF for his good show. The USAF Distinguished Flying Cross hangs from his breast pocket. On the left is BGen Norman Lewis Peterson, commander in 1949 of the 108th Air Weather Group at Westover AFB. Born in Houston in 1911, he first was an Army Air Corps pilot, but in 1940 earned a Masters degree in meteorology with his thesis "The Origin and Movement of Tropical Hurricanes". He worked in "met" through WWII. In 1958 he commanded the USAF Air Weather Service. MGen Peterson retired in 1968 and died in 2005. On the right is F/L Scott's CO, LCol Harvey P. Hall. He too would face one fearful WB-50 mission – a January 1958 "Loon Echo" when his aircraft suffered a grave fuel leak. Hall successfully brought his crew home. As to F/L Scott, later postings included a year flying the Caribou and Otter with 116 ATU in El Arish, Egypt. Subsequently, he flew the Yukon for almost 5000 hours. After leaving the CF in 1971, he flew in corporate and commercial aviation until retiring 1993.

Immediate retarding of all four throttles until the cause of the buffeting was identified. Minimum delay in identifying and feathering the faulty engine. Maximum co-operation by all ground radar facilities. The reassurance provided by the intercepting aircraft. The decision to return to Eielson where the runway length would cover many troubles. The complete co-operation of Eielson airfield facilities. Above all, the quiet and panic-free manner with which the crew members proceeded with their jobs.

F/L Scott finished by recommending that flapless landings be included in WB-50 training. In July of 1959 the McChord detachment of the 55th WRS moved to McClellan AFB to amalgamate with that detachment. Then, in April 1960 Scott was assigned to a desk as Assistant to ops officer LCol McKibban. He checked out on the squadron's C-54, used for liaison and transport with the Hawaii and Alaska detachments. On May 3, 1960 a parade was held to award LCol Hall (who had started his military career with the RCAF in WWII) a squadron efficiency award, and F/L Scott the USAF DFC. Meanwhile, MATS commander LGen William H. Tunner extended a "well done" to F/L Scott and crew for their "superior judgment and airmanship". Tunner's sentiments were echoed in a statement by MGen H.H. Bassett, USAF Weather Service Commander.

With an 11:50 hour "Lark X-Ray" mission in WB-50 "264" on December 28, 1960, and a C-54 flight on January 29, 1961, F/L Scott's exchange ended. He had logged 1178:05 hours on the WB-50, 324:10 on the C-54. This position was filled successively by: F/Ls George McCormick (1961-63 – WB-50), Len Halpin (1963-65 – C-130 and WB-47), and Joe Bourgeois (1965-1967 – WB-47 and WC-135). McCormick flew normal weather operations, while Halpin and Bourgeois flew many air sampling missions.

Triple Exchange: Gordon W. Webb

Raised in Hamilton, Ontario, Gordon W. Webb joined the RCAF in 1941. He completed elementary flying training on Tiger Moths at Goderich, Ontario; service flying training on Ansons at Centralia; then converted in the UK to the Whitley and Halifax. P/O Webb joined 432 Squadron for a Halifax tour (26 ops), then moved to 405 Squadron to fly 46 Pathfinder ops on Lancasters. For this good work he qualified for the Pathfinder Force Award. In 1944 F/L Webb, DFC and Bar, was posted home. He had his sights set on flying Dakotas but, upon reporting in at RCAF Station Hagersville, learned that he was slated for a trans-Canada Victory Bond tour. This was a turn-off, but the RCAF left him no option, so Webb returned to Civvie Street. In 1946, however, he was back in uniform. After refresher flying at Trenton and a pilot-navigator course at Summerside, he went on exchange in 1947 to Strategic Air Command to fly recce B-29s at Ladd Field, Alaska. The details of these missions remain a mystery.

Returning to Canada in 1949, F/L Webb joined 426 Squadron at Lachine. When the Korean War erupted in June 1950, he served with 426, flying North Stars to Japan and supervising pilot training. Then, when a C-97 exchange opened at MATS Continental Division HQ, Kelly AFB, Texas in 1951, F/L Webb took it. Following the C-97 aircraft commander course at Kelly, Webb came to enjoy the big transport. Since it was pressurized, gone was the aggravation of bashing through rough weather at 9000 feet in a North Star. With reverse propellers, a C-97 could make better-controlled landings, it cruised faster and its R-4360 engines gave ample power. More than most big aircraft, however, the C-97 had to be flown strictly "by the book". In 2005 Webb commented: "It was just a wonderful airplane. You couldn't have had a better transport in those days."

The typical C-97 Atlantic mission from Kelly usually carried about 80 passengers. It flew first to Westover, Massachusetts, then on to Lages in the Azores and Rhein-Main near Frankfurt. From Rhein-Main there might be a trip down the Frankfurt–Berlin air corridor. At Rhein-Main a crew such as Webb's would train in a simulator that replicated this route. They learned how to recognize when the Soviets were tampering with beacons, putting out false signals and trying to decoy aircraft out of the corridor, where they would be fair game for Soviet fighters (several Allied planes were shot down along the Berlin corridor). Webb also made several C-97 trips to Japan, operating first to Travis AFB near San Francisco, then Honolulu, Wake Island and Haneda (Tokyo). Passengers and cargo would be carried outbound, while Korean War casualties often were on board for the return.

At Kelly, F/L Webb received a briefing and familiarization flight in the sole Convair XC-99, the transport version of the B-36. In another case, he was asked by RCAF HQ to glean what he could about the Fairchild C-119, which recently had been ordered for the RCAF. On this score the MATS Continental Division Commander agreed that Webb go on temporary duty to Mountain Home AFB, Idaho to check out on type. Next, he flew to Korea to spend three weeks as a co-pilot with a USAF squadron. There he experienced first hand a variety of C-119 combat missions and had all his questions answered. Later, he reported in detail to AFHQ about the C-119. Home in 1953, he served at Lachine as senior ATC pilot training officer. In 2005 he explained how the best thing that he brought to this job was what

Gordon W. Webb, DFC and Bar. His DFC resulted from his service as a Pathfinder Force pilot on 405 Squadron. In part, the citation for the Bar to his DFC notes, "Under a calm and quiet manner, he has a fine offensive spirit in action, which inspires confidence in his entire crew." Webb surely would have been a welcomed member on each of his three USAF squadrons. (via G.W. Webb)

The one-of-a-kind Convair XC-99 (based on the B-36). F/L Webb flew one XC-99 mission from Kelly AFB, Texas. In 2007 the XC-99 was destined for restoration by the USAF Museum at Wright-Patterson AFB, Ohio. (CANAV Col.)

1955-58. A tour in AFHQ followed, at the end of which Air Marshal Hugh Campbell was retiring. Campbell asked Webb if there was a posting that he would like, to which Webb replied "McGuire ".

McGuire AFB in New Jersey is a famous MATS base and Webb, after a brief OTU at Tinker AFB in Oklahoma, soon was there flying Douglas C-118s with the 1611th Air Transport Wing. This tour (1967-70) was typical MATS in that a crew never knew where it might be headed, Webb recalling: "One night we landed in a tornado-like rain storm in Seoul, Korea. Nine days later we were on approach to Bahrain in a sandstorm. Once we had the aircraft safely on the runway, my co-pilot and I looked at each other with that 'all in a day's work' expression." Returning one day from Rio de Janeiro, Webb's radio officer reported that "Air Force One", en route to Japan with Secretary of State Dean Rusk, had been ordered home. Webb's C-118 then was directed to land at Kelly AFB. Everyone soon learned what was up – President Kennedy had been assassinated. Webb recalled that the streets of San Antonio that night were virtually deserted.

Another time, Webb landed at the USN base at Rota, Spain, where the American commander explained that Webb could not go on to Madrid – the Spanish area commander insisted that no foreign nationals (other than Americans) could land at

he had learned at Kelly about standardization. In this period the RCAF still had captains flying according to their personal styles. A first officer had to get to know each captain's idiosyncrasies, a poor situation that lead to accidents. At Kelly, however, Webb learned "the MATS way", with everything prescribed. Included were check lists, which were not then widely used in the RCAF.

C-97 cockpit procedures were disciplined. In a let-down, for example, everything was prescribed – speeds, rates of descent, use of flaps, landing gear, etc. It was a smooth, professional operation with no room "to wing" anything. In 2005 Webb summarized the MATS policy: "In unusual circumstances, of course, pilots were expected to use good judgment and experience, and adjust accordingly. Under normal conditions, however, they were expected to follow tried and tested procedures." From ATC HQ, Webb flew the North Star and C-5 with 412 Squadron

A typical MATS C-118 as flown and much enjoyed by S/L Webb during his third USAF tour. (Wilf White)

Rota without his prior approval. After realizing that Webb was the aircraft commander, and that delaying his mission while awaiting approval would cause trouble at higher levels, the USN officer relented. From McGuire, W/C Webb returned to an ATC training slot at Trenton. An NDHQ posting followed, then he retired in 1975 as perhaps the only RCAF officer with three flying exchanges to his credit. For several years he worked in urban affairs for the City of Ottawa, from where he retired in 1987. Thereafter, Gord Webb was active as a volunteer, coaching the blind at golf and curling.

MATS Navigator

On a MATS exchange at the same time as F/L Webb was F/L John E. Goldsmith, DFC, AFC. Having joined the RCAF in 1942, he became a navigator, then excelled in Bomber Command, especially on 156 (Pathfinder) Squadron. Postwar, he was with an RCAF meteorological flight in Yarmouth, then 168 (T) Squadron and 13 (P) Squadron at Rockcliffe. Navigating on 13 Squadron Cansos, he assisted in the lengthy and historic project to pinpoint the North Magnetic Pole 1947-49, receiving the Air Force Cross for this good work. He next crewed on North Stars with 426 Squadron, then was posted on exchange to MATS Pacific Division HQ at Hickam Field, Hawaii.

Arriving in Hawaii in July 1951, F/L Goldsmith crewed with the 1266th Air Transport Squadron on C-97 missions to Japan supporting the Korean War. Homeward bound, aircraft often carried casualties. As did F/L Webb, Goldsmith found the C-97 a dream. As to getting around in MATS, he noted, "We used astro navigation along with LORAN facilities and there were few navigating difficulties." Since the Pacific routes averaged 12–14 hours per crossing, the C-97's crew rest area had bunks. From February 1952 Goldsmith was on a C-54 detachment in Haneda, flying supplies into Pusan and Taegu, Korea, then taking out the wounded. By this time, he was doing check rides on MATS navigators flying the Pacific. In 2004 he commented about this to historian Carl Mills:

F/L John E. Goldsmith, DFC, AFC. In this 1949 RCAF portrait he also wears his Pathfinder Force and Operations wings. (PL-110550 DND)

USAF navigators were required to take a check ride every six months, or when a pilot made an adverse report about a navigator's performance. There was a requirement for six check navigators in the Pacific Division. When they became short by one, they asked me to apply. To qualify, you had to have passed a recent check ride, have 3000 hours or more as a navigator, pass a written test, and pass an oral test given by a panel of a minimum of three check navigators. I started this duty in February 1952 and remained on it for the last half of my 14-month tour, flying the C-54 and C-97.

Commenting about life at Hickam, in 2006 Goldsmith recalled:

In Hawaii my wife, son and I had a large, comfortable bungalow overlooking Pearl Harbor. It was better than the RCAF housing that we had lived in. The Officers' Clubs at Hickam and Pearl Harbor were first class with low-cost food and drinks. My squadron mates and neighbours treated us like family members. The USAF had resorts on Oahu and we were made very welcomed there. I consider this to have been the happiest period of my military service.

With MATS, F/L Goldsmith logged 272 hours on the C-54, 695 on the C-97. Back in Canada in 1953, he had several key postings, including commanding 425 AW (F) Squadron on CF-100s. Important NORAD ground postings followed, until LCol Goldsmith retired from the military in 1973 and, eventually, settled in Sidney, BC.

Tactical Aviation

In 1952 RCAF HQ, then studying integrated airborne operations, posted F/L Sydney R. Wallis, DFC, to the 316th Troop Carrier Group at Sewart AFB at Smyrna, Tennessee to compare RCAF and USAF tactical transport operations. Wallis had joined the RCAF in 1942. A navigator, he completed 30 ops with 427 Squadron. The citation for his DFC notes: "His outstanding ability and determination to remain in hazardous gardening areas until precise mining could be guaranteed has set a very high example, and has enhanced the record of the squadron as a whole." Little wonder that RCAF HQ was confident in sending Wallis on a postwar exchange. On March 24, 1952 he submitted a report that must have pleased AFHQ, noting how, at the 316th, he had taken part in planning, briefings and field activities during Ex. Southern Pine. He described the force structure from the top, i.e. from the 18th Air Force down to the 314th Troop Carrier Wing at Sewart with its elements, e.g. the 316th Troop Carrier Group comprising the 36th and 37th Troop Carrier Squadrons and 16th Assault Squadron (L). The

F/L Sydney R. Wallis, DFC, in a 1960 portrait. (PL-128519 DND)

36th and 37th flew C-119s, while the 16th was a specialized unit to evaluate the shortcomings of glider operations and solutions thereto.

Having suffered frightful glider losses in WWII, the US military sought a more battle-worthy transport plane. As Wallis explained, a new aircraft would be able to take off and land in a short distance on unprepared strips with heavy loads, then depart with casualties. In this regard the USAF had supported the Chase Aircraft Co. of New Jersey. In the late 1940s Chase designed the YG-18A and the larger, 60-man XG-20 metal

gliders, but the air force suddenly abandonned gliders. Chase then powered the XG-18A with two Wright R-1820 engines, re-designating it the YC-122. The 16th Assault Squadron, Wallis' home unit at the 314th, was equipped with these (only nine YC-122s were built). Next, Chase powered the XG-20 with R-2800s, turning it into the XC-123. Kaiser-Frazer took over Chase and, with the outbreak of war in Korea, the USAF placed large orders for C-119s and C-123s. Failing to live up to its commitments, however, Kaiser-Frazer lost the C-123 contact, which was acquired by Fairchild in Maryland. Now began the distinguished career of the C-123, while the innovative days of Chase were lost in the cobwebs of history. S/L Wallis wrote about the task of the 16th AS (L):

In the initial stages of an airborne assault the paratroopers are dropped. This drop is followed by the heavy equipment drop, this in turn is followed by a … landing by assault aircraft. With the first of the paratroopers there will be an air force officer and two airmen, all fully trained in forward control … it will be their responsibility to see that a landing strip with the minimum number of obstructions is prepared and properly marked. They will also set up temporary radio communications … [the C-122s] will follow the heavy drop … When the aircraft are unloaded, they will be reloaded immediately with any casualties … The 16th Assault Sqn with the C-122 … has

A Chase YC-122s in a fine William J. Balough, Sr. period photo. (via David W. Menard)

A typical 426 Squadron North Star as flown by Maj Ralph. (PL-88328 DND)

operated successfully in a number of exercises and displays … In each case the Landing Zones used have been practically unprepared strips … on an average size of 2000' × 60' and the time spent on the ground for five aircraft was approximately six minutes.

In the two days of "Southern Pine" YC-122s made 45 sorties onto rough strips delivering everything from a 40-mm anti-aircraft unit to ten 105-mm howitzers, 24 3/4-ton trucks, 4 motorcycles, 87 troops and 4 tons of supplies, while evacuating 83 "casualties". Wallis reported 100% results. He also took part in exercises at Eglin AFB, Florida, and Lawson AFB, Georgia. He pointed out how USAF standard operating procedures for airborne assault were being developed from work done at the 16th. Coincidentally, his exchange came as the RCAF was phasing out assault glider training (then based at Rivers), and as a new RCAF tactical transport was being studied (the C-119 was ordered in 1951). Ironically, within a few years Canada would lead in fixed-wing battlefield transports with the DHC-4 Caribou. Adopted by the US Army, it proved indispensable during the war in South Vietnam.

A Yank on North Stars

Transport exchanges were a two-way street – US military personnel had RCAF exchanges since North Star days, and to this day crew on Canada's C-130s. Born in Wisconsin on August 27,

1921, John H. "Jack" Ralph attended the University of Wisconsin, then joined the US Army Air Force in December 1941. He passed through the training system on Fairchild PT-19s, then Vultee BT-13s and Curtiss AT-9s, an advanced twin on which he earned his Wings at Lubbock, Texas in August 1942. Ralph now joined the 307th Heavy Bomb Group, flying B-24s in Ephrata, Washington. This was an experience, since there still was no B-24 conversion unit. "Sprogs" such as Lt Ralph had to learn on the job – a few lectures, study the pilot's notes, then "get out there and fly".

In October 1942 the 307th transferred to Hawaii, where it flew patrols until January. While deployed to Midway Island, Ralph flew on a successful 26-plane Christmas Eve raid against the Japanese at Wake Island. In February 1943 the 307th moved to Guadalcanal in the Solomons, there to take a beating on daylight ops, losing crews almost every day, mainly due to a lack of long-range escort fighters. When Ralph got his own crew in April 1943, most on the 307th already had been shot up, shot down or ditched at least once. Eventually, the 307th switched to night bombing, sending out B-24s as single intruders, a tactic also proven in the Indian Ocean by the RAF. Meanwhile, the Japanese bombed the 307th several times a week. After 70 missions Jack Ralph returned to the United States in October 1943, first to instruct on the B-17 and B-24 at Biggs Field at El Paso. Next came a posting to Air Transport Command on the C-54, beginning with conversion at Homestead, Florida. This course

Maj Ralph was recalled in 1952 to a job in war planning at Westover, Massachusetts. By then he had logged about 700 hours on North Stars. He now occasionally flew the C-118, but remained in the war planning world in the Pentagon, in Japan with 5th Air Force, and at SAC HQ at Offutt AFB, Nebraska. In 1969 he retired as LCol Ralph, settling first in Universal City, Texas, then in Enid, Oklahoma. He passed away on May 19, 2005. In part, his obituary noted: "He was a graduate of the Air War College and a command pilot with more than 10,000 flight hours. His awards included the Distinguished Flying Cross, the Air Medal with seven clusters, the Asiatic Pacific Campaign Medal with four stars, the Meritorious Service Medal and the Joint Services Commendation Medal."

Typical 426 Squadron Operations Flown by Jack Ralph

Date	Route	Time
13-8-1951	Dorval–Churchill	6:30
14	Churchill–Resolute Bay	5:45
15	Resolute Bay–Churchill	6:00
	Churchill–Coral Harbour	2:30
15	Coral Harbour–Churchill	2:30
16	Churchill–Dorval	5:40
21–9–51	McChord–Elmendorf	8:30
22	Elmendorf–Shemya	7:50
26	Shemya–Haneda	9:35
29	Haneda–Shemya	10:10
30	Shemya–Elmendorf	6:45
	Elmendorf–McChord	no data
16–11–51	Dorval–Gander	4:25
	Gander–Lages	6:00
17	Lages–North Luffenham	6:40
	North Luffenham–London	0:50
20	London–Keflavik	5:50
	Keflavik–Dorval	11:05

Security Issues at Sewart

In 1960-61 F/L William J. Finseth was posted to Sewart AFB from where he reported on C-130 operating and technical problems, and on USAF plans for larger transports such as the C-141. At the same time he was instructing on the C-130B simulator. Finseth was mainly associated with the 774th Troop Carrier Squadron, part of TAC's Composite Air Strike Force, which used C-130Bs to support the USAF in troubled foreign

areas. In one report F/L Finseth mentioned US concerns about nuclear weapons, noting diplomatic problems that could arise for exchange officers:

It is common knowledge that foreign nationals are not permitted access to atomic equipment. From time to time Sewart aircrews may become involved with such equipment … CASF exercises and missions, in most cases, involve "emergency war plans", which are classified "not releasable to foreign nationals". In such instances it is not possible for the Exchange Officer to participate in any way, and he may find himself unemployed when his assigned squadron is deployed on a CASF mission. Such a situation developed during the past six months and it was at that time the writer became employed in the Flight Simulator …

This problem has been discussed with senior officers from both Sewart and Canadian Joint Staff (Washington), and it was decided in each case that it would not be possible for this exchange officer to participate in such actions. In view of Canadian and American foreign policies differing slightly on some occasions, there could be situations arise where it would not be in the best interests of Canada to have [an officer] appear on some foreign scene at an inopportune moment.

F/L Bill Finseth, who specialized in tactical air transport and whose USAF exchange provided valuable insights for the RCAF. Here he is congratulated by Air Commodore R.J. "Reg" Lane for having earned the USAF Outstanding Unit Award. (PL-146250 DND)

RCAF Exchange/Liaison Officer Postings, June 1963*

Officer	Trade	Posting
Adams, F/O W.H.	AE	Air Defence Systems Directorate, F-104 program, WPAFB, Ohio
Allport, F/L F.T.S.	Pilot	Advanced Squadron, CFS, RAF Little Rissington
Benton, S/L W.D.	Telecom	Communications Services, Scott AFB, Illinois
Bonnyman, F/L F.W.	Telecom	RAF Bomber Command Development Unit, RAF Scampton
Brabbs, F/L R.J.	Telecom	USAF Rocket Research Facility, Fort Churchill, Manitoba
Bradley, S/L I.W.	Supply	Sacramento Air Materiel Area, McClellan AFB, California
Bradley, F/L J.A.	Navigator	4757th Air Defence Weapons Wing, Tyndall AFB, Florida
Brinkhurst, F/L R.T.	Pilot	231 OCU, RAF Bassingbourn
Brown, F/L K.W.	Telecom	Electronic Systems Division, Hanscom Field, Massachusetts
Brown, F/L R.T.	Navigator	511 Squadron, RAF Lyneham
Buchan, S/L W.J.	Pilot	MATS HQ, Transport Operations, Scott AFB, Illinois
Cardin, S/L L.P.R.	AE	Production control, Mobile Air Logistics Area, Brookley AFB, Alabama
Carney, F/L D.E.	Pilot	4757th Air Defence Weapons Wing, Tyndall AFB, Florida
Chilton, F/L R.H.	Armament	F-105, Eglin AFB, Florida
Chivers-Wilson, S/L J.A.	AE	USAF Missile Test Center, Patrick AFB, Florida
Chisholm, F/L J.R.	Pilot	111 Sqn, RAF Wattisham
Christmas, S/L B.	Pilot	Staff Flying Training Wing, Randolph AFB, Texas
Conway-Brown, S/L G.E.	Navigator	3535th Observer Training Wing, Mather AFB, California
Cooper, F/L C.E.	Navigator	Coastal Command ASW Development Unit, RAF Ballykelly
Doyle, S/L G.I.	Pilot	USAF HQ, Operations/Intelligence
Dundas, F/L R.H.	Pilot	2 FTS, Syerston, Notts.
Fellows, S/L F.G.	Pilot	USAF HQ, Air Defence Command Operations
Funge, F/L N.T.	Navigator	58 (PR) Squadron, RAF Wyton
Galvin, W/C J.W.C	Pilot	Staff, RAF Staff College, Bracknell
Garland, S/L J.W.	AE	USAF ADC HQ, Directorate of Aircraft Engineering, Colorado Springs
Gates, S/L M.D.	Navigator	Staff, RAF Flying College, Manby
Goosens, F/L J.A.G.	Navigator	Bloodhound Mk.2 training squadron, RAF North Coates
Halpin, F/L L.J.	Navigator	58th Weather Reconnaissance Squadron, McClellan AFB, California
Hamilton, F/L E.E.	Pilot	Air Fighting Development Squadron, RAF Binbrook
Harris, F/L T.M.	Pilot	Aeronautical Systems Development, WPAFB, Ohio
Hart, F/L H.A.	Pilot	Pilot Training School, Reese AFB, Texas
Heal, S/L J.A.	Telecom	"Project Advent", Fort Monmouth, New Jersey
Heath, F/L D.P.	Pilot	RAF Directorate of Air Intelligence, London
Hill, F/L G.M.	Telecom	Hanscom Field, Massachusetts
Holgate, S/L H.F.	Telecom	RAF Coastal Command, Northwood
Hudson, F/L J.R.	Navigator	120 Squadron, RAF Kinloss
Johnson, F/L J.P.	Supply	SAGE Office, Hanscom Field, Bedford, Massachusetts
Jolley, F/L R.J.	Pilot	60th FIS, Otis AFB, Massachusetts
Kazakoff, S/L M.	Telecom	Directorate of Communications, USAF HQ
Kincaid, F/L F.G.	Pilot	USAF Fighter Gunnery School, Nellis AFB
Lathey, F/L J.H.	AE	Aeronautical Systems Development, WPAFB, Ohio
Litt, A/S/L R.G.	Pilot	Pilot Instructor School, Randolph AFB, Texas

Continued over >

Officer	Trade	Posting
MacDonald, F/L G.H.	Armament	USAF Rocket Research Facility, Fort Churchill, Manitoba
MacDonald, S/L J.M.	Telecom	Hanscom Field, Bedford, Massachusetts
MacFarlane, F/L G.	Armament	Engineering Development Center, Arnold AFB, Tennessee
Machen, F/L	Fighter Controller	Computer Programming Section, ADC HQ, Colorado Springs
Mahon, F/L M.J.V.	Navigator	60th FIS, Otis AFB, Massachusetts
McFadden, F/L J.E.	Radio Op	USAF Academy, Colorado Springs
McKay, W/C J.	Pilot	Fighter Command HQ, SAS Branch
McRay, F/L	Armament	Engineering Development Center, Arnold AFB, Tennessee
Meurling, F/L A.F.	CE	USAF Air Training Command HQ, Randolph AFB, Texas
Miller, F/L A.G.W.	Telecom	Hanscom Field, Massachusetts
Nason, F/L C.H.	Navigator	RAF Flying College, Manby
O'Gorman, F/L W.T.	Navigator	RAAF Townsville, Australia
Olien, S/L L.C.	Navigator	USAF HQ, Operations/Intelligence
Olson, S/L B.W.	Pilot	USAF HQ, Special Training Devices
Olson, W/C E.L.	Telecom	Plans and Operations, Hanscom Field, Massachusetts
Parent, F/L C.H.	Pilot	511 Squadron, RAF Lyneham
Pasco, F/L A.	Pilot	RAF Coastal Command HQ, St. Mawgan
Pederson, S/L L.M.	Pilot	School of Land Air Warfare, Old Sarum
Pfaff, F/L R.W.	Telecom	HQ Signals Command, Medmenham
Pickering, F/L A.	Pilot	USAF Space Division, Los Angeles, California
Pickering, F/L D.H.	Pilot	Pilot Training School, Williams AFB, Arizona
Pierpoint, S/L J.C.	Pilot	US Navy COMFAIRWING 14, San Diego, California
Pond, W/C L.G.	CE	USAF HQ, Installations Engineering
Rowbotham, F/L W.G.	Pilot	VP-8 Squadron, NAS Norfolk, Virginia
Ruttan, F/L D.A.	Navigator	Air Research and Development Command, WPAFB, Ohio
Scott, F/L J.M.	Supply	Directorate of Data Systems HQ, WPAFB, Ohio
Scott, S/L M.N.	Pilot	USAF HQ, Personnel Planning
Shade, F/L A.J.	AE	Engineering Development Center, Arnold AFB, Tennessee
Stone, F/L E.H.	Pilot	4520th Combat Crew Training Wing, Nellis AFB, Nevada
Thompson, F/L T.R.	Pilot	111 Sqn, RAF Wattisham
Toma, F/L A.	Telecom	USAF Space Division, Los Angeles, California
Truman, S/L L.M.	AE	USAF Air Training Command HQ, Randolph AFB, Texas
Turtle, F/L R.H.	Pilot	314th Tactical Troop Carrier Wing, Sewart AFB, Tennessee
Watson, F/L A.J.C.	AE	Engineering Requirements, Tinker AFB, Oklahoma
Webb, S/L G.G.	Pilot	MATS, McGuire AFB, New Jersey
Webster, F/L J.F.	Navigator	USAF Space Division, Los Angeles, California
Weir, F/L F.C.	Pilot	RAAF Richmond, Australia
Whitaker, S/L D.L.	Nuclear	Joint School of Nuclear/Chemical Ground Defence, Winterbourne Gunner, Wilts.
White, F/L R.A.	Pilot	USAF Space Division, Los Angeles, California
Woodrow, S/L J.H.	AE	Maintenance Engineering Directorate, WPAFB, Ohio
Wray, F/L E.	Navigator	VX-1 Squadron, Key West, Florida
Wright, F/L R.E.S.	Armament	Air Development Command, WPAFB, Ohio

*RCAF HQ File 861-5-3 (DPC) App'x "A"

CHAPTER 7

Flying MAC's Big Jets

C-141 Starlifter

One of the first in the RCAF on a USAF jet transport exchange was Maj David F. Ives. Born on October 1, 1930, he grew up in Red Deer, Alberta. In November 1949 he joined the RCAF, his first flight being at Centralia in a Harvard on January 9, 1950. He graduated with Wings and was commissioned on September 22. He advanced to 2 (M) OTU in Greenwood for the Lancaster OTU, where his initial sortie was in KB957 on January 16, 1951. A Lancaster tour with 404 Squadron ensued, but this was a time when NATO pilot training was expanding, so AFHQ was tapping all commands for instructors.

On April 17, 1952 F/O Ives was posted to Trenton for the FIS course on AT-6s, then instructed at Calgary and Claresholm to 1956. He next was posted to AFHQ in the Directorate of Air Plans and Programs under Air Commodore R.J. "Reg" Lane and G/C Chester Hull. From here emanated staff papers relating to future aircraft for the RCAF. In 1960 Ives was posted to 408 (P) Squadron. By this time the daunting job of mapping northern Canada largely was complete. While 408 still had photo taskings, there were other jobs, e.g. locating, photographing and tracking Soviet ice islands inside what Canada considered its borders. He flew the last such 408 sovereignty mission in May 1963, photographing "North Pole 11", a site near 85°N 130°W. NP11 was difficult to locate in ice fog and a 300-foot ceiling, but F/O Ed Palmer, the navigator, did the job. On reaching NP11, the crew confirmed that it had been abandonned. The option to land was

436th MAW Starlifter 64-0611 at Patrick AFB, Florida at the time of Apollo 17. The 20th MAS, where Maj Ives served on exchange, was part of the 436th. By 2007 the 436th was flying C-5A Galaxies and the last C-141 had retired. Starlifter '0611 went to the bone yard at Davis-Monthan AFB, Arizona in October 2002. (all, Ives Col.)

work. After F/L Middlemiss' CFE tour, for example, he commanded 421 Squadron, while S/L Schultz was posted to CF-100s at 3 AW (F) OTU at North Bay as CFI. Both earned further promotions and commands. Middlemiss pioneered in test flying the F-104 at Edwards AFB, while Schultz went on to win the McKee Trophy and membership in Canada's Aviation Hall of Fame.

Test Pilot: F/L Ayres

Born on December 9, 1924, George R. "Bob" Ayres was the son of Harold P. Ayres, renowned on the Canadian aviation scene as a WWI pilot, pioneer airmail pilot, founder of Canada's first licensed flying school, BCATP in WWII, etc. Bob took his private pilot's licence at Barker Field in Toronto, soloing at age 16 in 1940. He joined the RCAF in 1943 and spent the war instructing. Postwar, he flew in the bush, then re-joined the RCAF in March 1949. He earned his A-1 instructor's category at Central Flying School (the A-1 "ticket" qualified an RCAF pilot to instruct on anything from Harvard to Vampire plus multi-engine types). Ayres now trained RCAF and NATO students at 1 FTS, Centralia. There he led the first RCAF 4-plane Harvard aerobatic team. Late in 1952 F/L Ayres was posted to Chatham for the Sabre course, then flew with 427 Squadron at Zweibrucken, West Germany.

In 1956 F/L Ayres began the year-long course with the ETPS at RAF Farnborough. The ETPS, which began at RAF Boscombe Down in

(Top) F/Os Rayne D. "Joe" Schultz (pilot) and Vernon A. Williams (navigator), while on night fighter Mosquitos at 410 Squadron. On a December 10, 1943 sortie they bagged three Do.217 bombers. Then, 410 Squadron Honorary Colonel Schultz at Cold Lake following a February 19, 1998 CF-18 flight with 410 CO LCol Jim Donihee. (CANAV & Schultz Cols.)

1943, was the world's first dedicated test pilot school (in 1947 it settled permanently at Farnborough). Previously, test pilots had been self taught, a process at which many died. The survivors tutored upcoming pilots on an *ad hoc* basis, which was far from desirable, especially in WWII with the great volume of testing being done. Thus did the RAF set out to get test flying onto a professional footing, the ETPS leading the way. F/L Ayres first flew at the ETPS in D.H. Devon XA879 on February 20. Henceforth, life got hectic, Ayres recalling in 2006 how ETPS seemed like the equivalent of a couple of years of intensive university study, but with no time off. "Classroom subjects," he explained, "included theory of aerodynamics, theory of flight, physics, mechanics, aircraft structures, piston and turbine engines, data reduction, and reporting.

Sir George Gardner explained in his introduction to the 1961 ETPS yearbook: "Only men of the highest calibre are picked for training. Not only must they be good pilots, but they must be technically sound, fearless, and men of the highest integrity." Flying assignments were demanding, each taking hours of preparation. Students were expected to adapt effortlessly to each new aircraft with no more instruction than what could be derived from the RAF standard pilot operating instructions. The only aircraft where a briefing was offered were larger types such as the Varsity. Ayres explained further:

(Top left) F/L Frank Phripp, DFC, was one of the first RCAF pilots on the RAF ETPS course. Here he is *circa* 1960 as wing commander i/c CEPE Air Armament Evaluation Detachment at Cold Lake. Then a historic view in the bare bones ETPS common room in 1945. Pilots are looking busy for the camera. (All, Phripp/CANAV Col.)

F/L Phripp photographed the unusual aircraft at Boscombe Down and Farnborough. Here is the diminutive Gloster G.40, Britain's first jet aircraft. Then, an early Meteor F.1. In 1999 Phripp reminisced how "The Meteor ... climbed smartly and, once level, impressed any pilot with its speed. With the nose pushed down a little, it really moved. Then, around 400 mph, the controls started to get heavy. The steeper the dive, the heavier they became, warning the pilot to back off."

RAF war prizes with the Foreign Aircraft Flight: the Heinkel He.162 "People's Fighter" and Messerschmitt Me.262 "Stormbird". (All, Phripp/CANAV Col.)

(Below) A German glider in which ETPS staff and students had fun in 1945-46. Then, a Messerschmitt Me.163 "Komet" rocket fighter, which flew at Farnborough only as a glider, towed by a Spitfire.

Early RCAF at the ETPS

Course	Years	Canadian Students
2	1944-45	S/L E.L. "Shan" Baudoux, DSO, DFC
		S/L Roger Mace[1]
		S/L Ian Somerville, AFC
3	1945	S/L E.B. Gale, AFC[2]
		F/L C. Frank Phripp, DFC
5	1946-47	F/O James F. Fewell
6	1947	F/L L.S. Lumsdaine, DFC[3]
7	1948	S/L C.L.T. Sawle[4]
		F/L Paul A. Hartman, DFC, AFC
8	1949	F/L Bruce Warren, DFC[5]
		F/L J.H. "Jack" Phillips, DFC
9	1950	F/O Douglas E. Biden, DFC
		F/L G.A. "Bud" Heck
10	1951	F/L O.B. Philp, DFC
11	1952	F/O J.F. "Jack" Woodman
12	1953	F/L J.C. "Jack" Henry
13	1954	F/O R.W. Smith
		F/O S.R. "Reg" Kersey
14	1955	F/L E.A. "Ted" Strutt
		F/L E.N. "Norm" Ronaasen[6]
		F/L John H. Waldie
15	1956	F/L James E. Hanna
		F/L A.L. "Larry" Nelson
		F/L George R. Ayres
16	1957	F/O Robert J. Cockburn
		F/L Alex Bowman
		F/L Lorne B. Pollock
17	1958	F/O J.W. "Willie" Hough
18	1959	F/L R.A. "Bud" White

1. Killed in flying accident (Lancaster) 16-12-44
2. KIFA (Mustang) 25-5-46
3. KIFA (CL-41) 28-3-66
4. KIFA (Meteor) 30-8-48
5. KIFA (CF-100) 5-4-51
6. KIFA (Canadair Challenger) 3-4-80

(Right) A newspaper clipping (source unknown) mentioning RCAF men at the ETPS in 1946-47, although S/L Foster is thought to have been a Canadian in the RAF.

Train Test Pilots In British 'School'

CRANFIELD, Bedfordshire, (CP) —Test pilots of tomorrow—scientifically-trained descendants of men who found out about planes the hard way—are learning their trade over Bedfordshire farms.

They are students of the Empire test pilots' school, drawn from men of half a dozen countries.

"In the past, test pilots just happened," said Air Marshal Sir. W. Alex Coryton, controller of air supplies at the ministry of supply. "Today the test pilot has come into his own. These men are going to aid future aircraft production, and shorten the period required for development of new types of aircraft, by giving designers the benefit of their expert technical advice."

Most pilots are veteran fliers, but now they learn what happens to their aircraft when emergencies arise.

"That's one of the drawbacks of this course," grinned Flt. Lt. S. E. Fewell of Regina, one of two Canadians at the school. "Before, you mightn't know what a close shave you'd had. Now every time anything happens you start figuring out what stresses and so on your aircraft is undergoing."

Fewell and Sqdn. Ldr. W. M. Foster of Guelph will complete the seven-month course in January, spend five weeks at the supply ministry's research centre at Farnborough, Hants, then wind up with a tour of British aircraft plants. They expect to return to Canada in April, to continue their careers in the R.C.A.F.

Another Canadian graduate of the school is Sqdn. Ldr. E. L. Badoux, commanding the flying wing of the R.C.A.F.-R.A.F. winterization experimental establishment at Edmonton.

---

complete assignments independently. Finally, you flew the profiles, manually recording all your observations on the test card on the small clip board on your knee, or by using a voice wire recorder. With everything complete, you compiled a final report including recommendations. In 1956 the ETPS, unlike the USAF or US Navy test pilot schools, had no computers to assist in data reduction – it was all done the old fashioned way – by hand.

There always was the element of risk in learning an aircraft's optimum performance, let alone pushing the limits. In one case Ayres had an assignment in the Canberra. While evaluating asymmetric engine performance, the aircraft got into a difficult spin. On April 17, 1956 he was flying Meteor 7 VW414, the task being to determine limiting Mach number. Flying cautiously at 35,000 feet, he increased speed in small increments on repeated runs, noting any changes in flying characteristics. Suddenly Ayre's mission took a bad turn:

The Meteor entered a high speed stall. Inverted and with the nose pitched up, it tumbled end over end before I regained control at 10,000 feet. By this time both engines were flamed out, and the high "G" forces had caused both engine fire extinguishers to discharge. The Meteor 7 had no ejection seat, so I attempted to open the canopy to go "over the side", but it was jammed. With no more options, I got the engines re-started, but the Meteor was not

F/L John Waldie's log book illustrates how busy and varied life was at ETPS in early post-WWII days. Look at all the types he flew in June 1955 – from the diminutive Sky glider to the hefty Varsity transport and the speedy Hunter. John's care in recording each entry allows one to follow today the history of the aircraft he flew at Farnborough. Note that on June 10 John flew the Pembroke with fellow Canadian Norm Ronaasen. John's RCAF career is briefly outlined in *Canada's Air Force at War and Peace*, Vol. 3. (Larry Milberry)

Sedbergh glider, Sycamore, Tiger Moth, Vampire T.11 and Varsity. He enjoyed each and still recalled their unique traits after more than 50 years. They all flew well, but sometimes might be joked about, as was the Gannett, which students referred to as the "Fairey Battleship", a reflection upon the solid way in which it was built and other such things as its complicated double Mamba engine with counter-rotating propellers. F/L Ayres' last ETPS flight was in a Hurricane on December 18, 1956. In all he logged 220 hours at ETPS. AFHQ posted him to test flying duties in RCAF Station Namao (Edmonton), beginning on February 27, 1957. He would enjoy an intensive career on such projects was cold weather trials on a host of types from the Venom to the CF-100, Argus and Beverley. Since the earliest RCAF and RCN pilots completed the ETPS, Canada continued to post officers there, as well as to the US Navy and USAF test pilots schools at NAS Patuxent River and Edwards AFB. These pilots have contributed much to test flying at CEPE/AETE. Over the decades many had later careers as civilian test pilots with such companies as Avro Canada, Canadair, de Havilland Canada, and Bombardier.

F/L Bob Ayres while testing F-104Gs at Edwards AFB. Then, Mary and Bob Ayres at the ETPS in 1956. (Both, Ayres Col.)

flying normally. GCI vectored another ETPS aircraft to me, which reported signs of aft fuselage structural damage. My escort led me down through cloud and we landed at Farnborough. Gloster later inspected the Meteor, reporting that it was badly bent and would not be repaired.

F/L Ayres' ETPS types included the Ashton, Balliol, Canberra, Chipmunk, Devon, Gannett, Hiller UH-12, Hunter, Hurricane, Meteor 7, Meteor 8, Olympia glider, Pembroke, Provost, Sea Hawk,

(Left) F/L Ayres (upside down) leads Centralia's Harvard aerobatic team. (All, Ayres Col.)

Some aircraft tested by Bob Ayres in the 1950s at Churchill, Manitoba. First, an RAF Venom fires up using cartridge start. On the nose is CEPE's polar bear logo. Then, a Canberra, Bristol Sycamore WT939 and Argus Mk.1 20712.

CHAPTER 10

Bomber and PR Exchanges in the RAF

First on the Canberra

First flown in May 1949, the English Electric Canberra remained a useful RAF type into the early 2000s. A high flying, long range, multi-role jet, it was very "hush-hush" in early days. The RCAF, which was considering a postwar bomber force, monitored Canberra developments. Meanwhile, some at AFHQ were wondering why Avro was struggling to develop the CF-100, when the Canberra would make a suitable all-weather interceptor (the explanation was Liberal government "super minister" C.D. Howe's mission to establish, at any cost, a postwar aircraft industry in Canada).

The first RCAF exchange candidate, once the Canberra reached service in January 1951, was F/L Stephen Gulyas. Too young to serve in WWII, he took flying lessons after the war, going up first in a Welland Flying Club Tiger Moth on July 28, 1946. Having earned a pilot's licence in November 1946, in March 1949 he joined the RCAF. He began training at Centralia where, on May 25, F/O W.H.D. "Wild Bill" Meaden introduced him to the Harvard. He progressed quickly, having a solo check on June 30 with F/O Russ Janzen, then he soloed on July 4. He progressed to AAS at Trenton, thence to PR Lancasters at 408 Squadron. Flying commenced on May 10, 1950 with F/O Sammy Deanes in Lancaster FM215. Gulyas soon was on SHORAN duties in Northern Canada. His log filled with sorties, many in the Arctic.

In November 1952, by when he had logged some 1700 hours, Gulyas was selected for an RAF exchange on Mosquitos.

Many Canadians had RAF and USAF tours on the English Electric/Martin Canberra. First flown in May 1949, this type served in many roles. Here, Canberra T.4 WT478, bomb bay doors agape, overflies Bassingbourn on October 14, 1958. In 1989 WT478 was painted to represent the Canberra prototype. In 1992 it finished its days with 231 OCU at RAF Wyton, then went for scrap. The RAF retired the Canberra after a fly-past by three PR.9s at RAF Marham on July 31, 2006, some 57 years after first flight. (CANAV Col.)

He reported to the Canadian Joint Staff in London then, on November 11, was at 231 OCU at RAF Bassingbourn, near Cambridge. On the 12th he flew a Mosquito with WO O'Connor instructing. On the 18th he flew his first jet – Meteor 7 WH119. Next, he joined 540 Squadron at RAF Benson. Beginning with some Link Trainer exercises, he transitioned to the Meteor 7 and Mosquito PR.34. A syllabus existed whereby pilots first flew 20 hours on the Meteor. In December 1952, the squadron received its first Canberra PR.3s. In this period there were floods in some east coast counties, so Benson flew PR sorties to help assess matters. After one such on February 24, 1953, Gulyas' landing gear would not extend. W/C Hugh Edwards advised him from the tower, then Gulyas landed wheels-up beside the runway.

W/C Steve Gulyas as CO 410 Squadron in Voodoo days. F/O Duncan helps the boss with his parachute. Among the crew listed on the board is F/O Cluer, who later flew Lightnings in the RAF, and F/O Malcomson, who had a USAF exchange. (PL-137499 DND)

Meanwhile, crews kept studying technical publications, taking ground school and familiarizing themselves in a Canberra cockpit procedures trainer. Gulyas flew the new type on March 20, his instructor, F/L Monty Burton, taking WE136 to 45,600 feet, close to the service ceiling. For April, Gulyas' log shows 8:45 hours – Canberra, 9:35 – Mosquito, 5:25 – Meteor and 1:20 – Anson. In an article in *Roundel* magazine (September 1956) he commented about Canberra conversion: "During the first 10 hours of our training, single-engine overshoots and landings, controlled descents and simulated instrument flying kept us in the local area. When the check pilot was satisfied with our progress, he authorized us for cruise-climb cross-countries, which took us over much of northwest Europe."

Route of Canberra WE142

Date	Route	Hours
June 2	Heathrow (London)–Goose Bay	5:15
	Goose Bay–St. Hubert	1:35
June 3	St. Hubert–Uplands	0:35
	Uplands–St. Hubert	0:30
June 5	St. Hubert–Goose Bay	2:50
June 7	Goose Bay–Keflavik	2:50
	Keflavik–RAF Wyton	2:00

For the Coronation of Queen Elizabeth on June 2, 1953 the Canadian Broadcasting Corporation was anxious to obtain "hot" footage, hoping to pre-empt American TV networks. This was a big story, the Toronto *Star* reporting on May 16: "On Coronation Day, June 2, some Torontonians will be preparing meals just about the time television films of the London ceremony arrive at Goose Bay, Labrador. By the time they finish washing the dishes, the films will be in Montreal, 800 miles from Goose Bay." To get the CBC into first place, three RAF Canberras would rush the film "across the pond" on Op. Pony Express. Each would carry film from a different stage – the Royal procession to Westminster Abbey, the Coronation, then the procession back to Buckingham Palace. S/L Kenyon departed first, then F/L Garside, finally the crew of F/L Gulyas and F/O Ron Hiller in Canberra WE142. Meanwhile, a Venezuelan Canberra, chartered by a US network, departed with film but, to the CBC's joy, returned with technical trouble. The "Pony Express" plan was that the Canberras first burn dry their wingtip tanks, then jettison them, something not yet tried by the RAF. This succeeded. At Goose Bay, Gulyas' film was transferred to 445 Squadron CF-100 18137 crewed by S/L Phil Etienne and F/L Russ Baxter. They departed at 1400 hours (local), landing at St. Hubert at 1535. Gulyas and Hiller followed, then everyone attended a reception hosted by Montreal's Mayor Houde.

On June 3 a newspaper headline, datelined Goose Bay, blared "2 Yanks Fight, CF-100 Nearly Hit in

TV Race". The story opened: "Two rival US network representatives fought on the ground and two fighter planes nearly collided in the air yesterday in the frantic relay of television coronation films at this Canadian-US air base." It seems that representatives of CBC and NBC had gotten into a tussle "as boxes of films were unloaded from the first of three Canberra jet bombers to streak across the Atlantic." An RCAF wing commander intervened, as the network men argued about who would get the first film airborne in the fighters they had standing by. Word was that one network despatched its P-51 without receiving permission from air traffic control. Supposedly, the P-51 came close to colliding with 445's CF-100 (some of this likely was media "if you don't have the facts, make them up" hoopla).

Back at Wyton, regular squadron duties continued as with NATO exercises like "Coronet", "Dividend" and "Momentum". In December 1953 F/Ls Gulyas and FSgt Chuck Taylor flew a nav exercise through the Mediterranean. More operational were PR sorties along Warsaw Pact borders. This was dicey business in which several US and UK aircraft had been shot down since 1945. The Canberra, however, could fly to 40,000 feet, then "cruise climb" to 48,000, sometimes a bit higher (cruise climb was done in stages, as fuel was burned). On February 22, 1954 F/L Gulyas and navigator F/L Bob Mullineaux departed Wyton in WE137 with other PR.3s headed for Darwin, Australia. They refuelled at Idris (Libya), Habbaniyah (Iraq), Mauripur (Pakistan), Negombo (Ceylon) and Changi (Malaya). Gulyas proved a keen observer, later describing a leg in *The Roundel*:

After quickly refuelling at Mauripur, we took off for Negombo. Previously, we had encountered no cloud at 40,000 ft., but now we found cirro-stratus at this height. After our letdown at Negombo, the radical change in temperature caused the cockpit to mist up and we were compelled to circle for 10 to 15 minutes until it cleared. By the time we landed and taxied to the apron, the temperature inside the cockpit had reached 120°F. This was our first experience with real tropical climates.

While driving to the mess, Gulyas was amused by a sign reading "Beware of Falling Coco-nuts". En route to Darwin from Java, he and Mullineaux later met cumulo-nimbus towering to 60,000 feet. Somewhere on this leg two Canberras got into trouble. One disappeared, another made a force-landing on an island. Gulyas and Mullineaux had their own crisis – both generators packed in:

This was serious, because flight instruments, compasses, gauges and fuel pumps all depended on power produced by the generators. As we were in cloud and not sure of our position, I decided to transmit a 'Pan-Pan' (emergency) call to Darwin, requesting homing; but Darwin replied that their homer was unserviceable. On the letdown we broke cloud at 10,000 feet. By this time the electricity was so low that our fuel gauges read zero, but Bob estimated that at this height we had 45 minutes' fuel … Ten minutes later we sighted land, and Bob found our position, which was approximately 35 miles northeast of Darwin.

Once WE137 landed, repairs were done and the crew was ordered home – the original high level air sampling task, associated with UK nuclear testing, was assumed by Lancasters. WE137 reached Wyton on April 4. Another unusual operation for Gulyas was supporting the Sultan of Yemen, who was concerned about unauthorized oil exploration in his domain. When suspicious activity was reported, a Canberra would do a recce and unwelcomed visitors would be warned – they'd better disappear or there might be fireworks. Yemen was a serious affair. Gulyas recalled one briefing attended by a contingent of RAF Regiment. These hard-core commandos went out on patrol, but were ambushed and wiped out.

F/L Gulyas made his longest Canberra flight on March 11, 1955 operating Wyton-Lyon-Genoa-Naples-Nice-Paris-LeHavre-Wyton in 6:50 hours. His last

Steve Gulyas, the first Canadian to fly the Atlantic in a jet aircraft, at home in Ottawa in 2002. (Larry Milberry)

flight (Canberra T.4 WT477) was on June 10, then he came home to an AFHQ posting in the Directorate of Air Operations. Now came postings to 410 Squadron on CF-100s, conversion to the Voodoo, RCAF Staff College, RAF College of Air Warfare and command of 439 Squadron (CF-104s) and 434 (CF-5s). Gulyas was Base Commander Cold Lake in 1974, served next in the Directorate of Air Requirements, was Deputy Chief of Staff (Operations) at 4 ATAF HQ in NATO, and Deputy Commander Fighter Group in North Bay, from where he retired in 1984. His career totalled nearly 6600 flying hours, most on jets.

F/L Red Ovans

Having joined the RCAF in 1940, Garnet W. "Red" Ovans of Calgary spent most of his war instructing, then got overseas on Mosquitos with 418 Squadron. While finishing an administrative tour in Winnipeg late in 1954, he was seconded to the RAF, replacing S/L Huchala as RCAF Bomber Command liaison officer at RAF Lindholme. There, Ovans analyzed the Bombing School syllabus, reporting in detail, e.g. about bombing theory, the Mark 14 bomb sight, bombing analysis, and the "GEE H" nav system. Ovans then proceeded to 231 OCU on the Canberra. Here, a student's first weeks were in ground school, covering everything from airmanship to survival, airframe and engines, and aircraft recce. Flying began in July 1955, first on the Canberra T.4, then the B.2. Ovan's course entailed 54:55 hours on 28 sorties. He finally joined 139 "Jamaica" Squadron on Canberra B.2s and B.6s, first at RAF Hemswell, then RAF Binbrook. At this time 139, which comprised 10 crews plus the CO and two flight commanders, was the RAF's only "Marker" squadron, specializing in dropping flares and target indicators as had Pathfinder Group with Mosquitos and Lancasters in WWII. The squadron also trained V-bomber crews in high-level "blind" (i.e. radar) bombing.

Henceforth, F/L Ovans, who soon attained flight commander status, was busy with daily routines. For some months there was little flying (e.g. February 1956 – 8:00 hours). Perhaps a month of poor flying weather? March, however, totalled 27:40 hours,

F/L Garnet "Red" Ovans. Due to Ottawa's "keep a safe distance" policy for exchange officers, he missed out on the Suez War. (PL-77182 DND)

16:45 being at night, while May boomed with 42:25. From March 17-29, 1956 Ovans was at Idris from where 10 Canberras of 109 and 139 squadrons flew marker trials. When night fell, they would depart to find and mark targets at such airfields as Marble Arch and Misurata. Pyrotechnics would be dropped from as high as 10,000 down to 3000 feet, release usually being from a shallow dive at 280 knots. On a typical sortie a Canberra would carry twelve 4.5-inch parachute flares.

In a report, Ovans complained of too many defective flares and TIs. Also noted was how the B.6's highly-touted Blue Shadow nav system fell short. Based on wartime H2S, it used side-looking radar to gather data from 5 to 25 miles to starboard. The system processed the data and provided the navigator with an echo map (on a paper strip) that showed terrain. Blue Shadow's margin of error, however, was in the one-to-three mile range. Still, it was an improvement, especially how it was self-contained aboard the aircraft, freeing a B.6 from ground radar control radio transmissions that were susceptible to enemy jamming. Bomber Command had enough confidence in Blue Shadow to delete the bomb aimer on the B-6 – the navigator assumed his duties. Not surprisingly, Bomber Command posted its top navigators to the B.6.

In view of Blue Shadow's limits, Ovans recommended that two navigators be carried, at least until the "bugs" were worked out. He also suggested that the RCAF consider Blue Shadow in transports flying in high latitudes. Other recommendations included: carrying more flares, dropping a stick of flares by means of a single armament switch, and carrying mixed loads of flares and TIs. Ovans' report of September 1956 gave other details:

During the past year the undersigned and crew attained combat star category [the three categories in Bomber Command Canberra squadrons in order of proficiency were: combat, combat star and select] and were involved in Lone Ranger and special flights to Wunstorf (Germany), Gibraltar, Malta and Nicosia (Cyprus). The crew also took part in a demonstration and flypast for Marshal Bulganin and Mr. Kruschev during April, and for H.M. the Queen

Canberra B.6s of 139 Squadron over Lincolnshire in 1956. Leading is WT371. On November 6, 1956 it was damaged in action during the Suez War. While landing back at Nicosia, it crashed, killing the crew. WJ771 (lower left) served on 109 Squadron in the Suez War, WJ778 with 139. WJ771 was SOC in 1964 following an accident. WJ778 and WJ780 were sold to India in 1969. (via G. Ovans)

in May. In November 1955 the undersigned qualified for a master green instrument rating [equivalent to the old RCAF blue rating] and became the squadron instrument rating officer.

In this period the Middle East was heating up, so the UK strengthened its forces in the region – 139 Squadron deployed to Cyprus. The RCAF, however, could not make up its mind about F/L Ovans. Finally, it instructed him to remain in the UK, clear of Suez. This effectively ended his tour and he returned to Canada in November 1956. Meanwhile, he had strongly recommended to the RCAF "that exchange postings be maintained for at least one pilot and one navigator on a Vulcan squadron", the same on future Victor squadrons. He also wrote an unequivocal commentary about future Bomber Command exchanges:

Recently, due to the serious situation in the Middle East and the possibility of conflict in that area, AFHQ cast some doubt (through AMCJSL) on allowing the undersigned RCAF officer to take part. It should be pointed out that exchange officers in many cases are given positions of responsibility in squadrons and sections and that, if they are not to be allowed to take part in any action the force may be engaged in, their positions will be jeopardized and, in fact, the exchange scheme in general, as far as operational positions are concerned, may be considered of doubtful value from the RAF's point of view. It is therefore recommended that a clear policy be laid down whereby an RCAF officer completely replaces his RAF counterpart irrespective of whether the RCAF agrees with the actions of the RAF or not.

In June 2003 Red Ovans recalled an incident from 139 Squadron days:

It was in the time of the Suez crisis and I had just come home on 72-hour leave from a deployment to Cyprus. On returning with my wife from a shopping trip into Binbrook, I noticed a Land Rover parked in front of our house on the village square. I knew that something was up when our Squadron Commander, Paul Mallory, approached and asked how long it would take me to get back to squadron. My wife reacted instinctively by throwing an egg at the CO!

Late that evening I was instructed to take a Canberra (not my usual aircraft) and Master Navigator Speed (later killed in Turkey), proceed to Bassingbourn, and get some rest. We soon were airborne, but our undercarriage failed to retract. We returned to Binbrook to rectify the problem. As we again set off, we had the same problem, but pressed on to Bassingbourn at low speed. While the landing gear was repaired, we slept. Then, at 0100 we were awakened and advised to take Air Marshal Sir Harry Barnett, Supreme Commander of RAF Middle East, to Cyprus for an 0600 meeting. I then would return with the Air Marshall for an 1800 arrival at Bassingbourn. Our mission was top secret, so much so that we had no flight plan, and the Air Marshal was in an LAC's uniform. We were not to breathe a word to anyone along to way. Off we went but, on crossing the English Channel, we lost GEE H performance. We continued, me referring to a map on my knee. Over Malta it was clear that we were using too much oxygen, so I landed there to replenish our supply.

At Cyprus the Air Marshal was whisked away and I got some sleep. Later in the afternoon we set off for London but, over France, I again noticed an oxygen problem – we were "in the red". I enquired about landing at a USAF base in France, but this was discouraged, considering the delay that would ensue. I had the Air Marshall and Master Navigator Speed switch onto our emergency oxygen supply, as we descended into Manston in Kent. There we requested fuel and oxygen, but the Royal Navy station commander was suspicious. A Canberra with no flight plan with a pilot wearing the "Canada" shoulder flash? That got him thinking, but he relented after inspecting the aircraft, and after I requested that, as one officer to another, it would be better if he saved his questions.

Soon we were flying low-level to Bassingbourn from where Air Marshall Barnett proceeded by car to London, but not before telling me, "Thank you for an interesting trip." No. 139 Squadron would lead the attack in the opening hours of the Suez War, but I missed the whole show. By this time I was slated to stay with the RAF on the V-Force – I would fly Vulcans for a further 2½ years. Sadly, this was cancelled by the RAF on account of Canadian Joint Staff interference. The RAF now set a new rule – no Commonwealth pilots would serve on V-bombers.

On returning to Canada in October 1956, F/L Ovans worked in RCAF accident investigation and flew with CEPE on trials (Argus, Yukon, etc.), until leaving the RCAF in 1968. He returned to Alberta to raise cattle and manage a gas distribution co-op near Cochrane into the 2000s.

Others on the Canberra

RCAF aircrew G.F.J. Jones, Frank Augusta and Merv Reid also flew Canberras. Jones instructed at 231 OCU, perhaps the first in the RCAF to do so. In a 1959 report he noted that OCU took 16 weeks, 4 in school (141 classroom hours for pilots, 173.5 for navigators), 12 flying (44 Canberra sorties for 61 day hours, 25.5 night), emphases being on low-level bombing and photo recce. Back in Ottawa, correspondence officer F/L Barry Lumley wrote to Jones: "Because of the probable employment of the F-104 in the strike and low-level reconnaissance roles, it would be very much appreciated if your next report would give as much detail as possible on employment of the Canberra on the same duties. Any other data that would be useful to 408 Squadron would also be appreciated." Who would dream that, at such an early date, the RCAF getting so specific about the F-104?

Having joined the RCAF in 1942, Frank Augusta served overseas on 429 Squadron. On operations to Duisberg on October 14, 1944 his Lancaster was shot down by flak. His crew escaped, coming down in liberated Belgium. Augusta finished the war flying Dakotas with 435 Squadron. Home in Prince Albert, Saskatchewan, he spent some uninteresting years in the automobile trade, then re-enlisted. He flew CF-100s, then instructed at 231 OCU 1961-63. On March 28, 1963 he took his exchange replacement, Bob Brinkhurst, on a Canberra famil flight. Then, after Brinkhurst had an accident, he remained at Bassingbourn to see that he got back flying OK. Discussing the Canberra in 2003, Augusta concluded: "It was a dream to fly. With its large wing area it had fabulous altitude and manoeuvring qualities." Augusta later flew at CEPE (Uplands), was seconded to fly the NRC North Star, then was a civil helicopter pilot in the Canadian north before retiring in Ottawa.

Surprise Ejection

In 1963 F/L Robert T. Brinkhurst was fortunate to win the 231 OCU exchange. Born in Cut Knife, west of North Battleford, Saskatchewan, Brinkhurst farmed in the area as a young man. Always interested in flying, he considered the RCAF. In 1954 he was 24, but the RCAF age limit was 25. He hustled, was accepted and started ground school at 1PFTS, Centralia, in November 1954. He trained on Harvards at Moose Jaw, then came AFS on T-33s at Gimli, beginning in October 1955. Due to bad weather, some catch-up training was done at nearby MacDonald, where Brinkhurst earned his Wings on February 29, 1955. Following an aircrew survival course, he began CF-100 conversion at Cold Lake, crewing with navigator F/O Yash Paul Singh Gill, an East Indian immigrant. Upon graduation in September 1956, they joined 428 Squadron at Uplands.

His CF-100 tour done, in December 1959 Brinkhurst attended FIS at Portage-la-Prairie, then instructed there into February 1963, when he was notified about his exchange. He sailed for the UK, reported in at OCU on February 23, and commenced flying on March 22. He quickly got the feel of the Canberra which, to him, was a pilot's dream. On July 9, 1963 Brinkhurst was on his final OCU trip in Canberra WT482 with F/L

F/Os Bob Brinkhurst and Yash Paul Singh Gill as a young CF-100 crew on 428 Squadron. (Brinkhurst Col.)

D.J. Cox. They were doing a check regarding single engine/asymmetrics. What ensued is best left to those involved. Their stories were published in the October 1963 journal, *Bomber Command Review*. First is F/L Cox's report:

… I had just demonstrated how to find the minimum safe control speed on one engine at full power, with the undercarriage down, and then it was Bob's turn. He is a big strong chap, no difficulty in reaching and holding full rudder, so I just sat back to watch. It was going well, the Canberra, slightly nose up, was climbing slowly. Bob had full rudder on and was gently applying bank towards the live engine. My attention was divided between looking out, and the airspeed, my feet resting lightly on the rudder pedals, my hands in my lap. The speed was approximately 135 knots, height 1800 feet, when the aircraft started to yaw very slightly. "That's it Bob," I thought, "time to recover," but I didn't get around to telling him.

The noise of the explosion was terrific. It left my ears ringing. The cockpit, briefly, was full of acrid smoke. I felt a sharp pain in my right elbow and my left foot catapulted back towards me. "We've been hit, I thought. We'll have to get out!" It seemed a long time before I realized that Bob wasn't there any more, just a gaping space on my right, no canopy over my head …

I think I throttled back automatically, although by this time

the aircraft was well over on its side and pointing earthwards. As I rolled the wings level, delighted to find normal response, I checked the engine instruments as I increased power and called the navigator, Sgt Brian Webb, on the intercom. Surprisingly, there was no draught, but I had to lower my head to speak to keep out the noise. I was relieved when he answered, and happy to reassure him that the aircraft was still airworthy … Wittering, who were giving us surveillance for the exercise, were informed of the incident and kindly initiated the emergency procedure for me. We had a quick look around for Bob, but saw nothing. All the time I was becoming increasingly anxious to get out of my ejection seat so, perhaps with more discretion than valour, we shot straight off and landed at Wittering.

Now, F/L Brinkhurst's story:

I was flying in the right hand seat of a Mk. T.4 Canberra at approximately 1800 feet during an asymmetric training exercise. As I attained minimum control speed of approximately 135 knots, my ejection seat fired unexpectedly. The noise of the ejection and subsequent wind blast, and the sudden acceleration momentarily confused me. When I realized that I was clear of the aircraft and descending, the seat harness had already automatically released me and I seemed to be in a flat spin facing upwards. The seat was at my left side, attached to me in some unknown manner, which convinced me that the parachute was not going to open automatically. I immediately pulled the outer "D" ring and, although I could not reach the manual override on the seat, I pulled the inner "D" ring, hoping that the parachute would still open. Shortly afterward I felt a slight tug as the parachute opened. Then, almost immediately, so it seemed, I struck the ground with a severe jolt. There was insufficient time to orient myself before landing …

Apart from feeling pain across the toes of my left foot immediately after the ejection, I had no sensation of injuries until I felt the pain in my back as I landed. However, I was able to extricate myself

Canberra WT482 almost was the death of Bob Brinkhurst. The nose section of this aircraft survives with the Stratford Aircraft Collection in Long Marston, UK. (Brinkhurst Col.)

from the parachute harness and stand up without too much difficulty. Noticing the seat a few yards distance, I walked over to it and assured myself that the alternate firing handle had not been fired. I then walked the 50 to 75 yards out of the field in which I had landed. Farm workers from nearby fields had seen me and, as I awaited their arrival, I laid on the ground to ease the pain in my back. My only external injuries were abrasions on both knees, a bruised right forearm and a slight cut on my forehead.

The fact that I had escaped so lightly and the news that the other crew members had landed safely left me in high spirits as I waited the arrival of the ambulance from RAF Wittering. There is no doubt that F/L Cox acted coolly and quickly in regaining control of the aircraft in such a critical asymmetric condition, and in reassuring the navigator, who was about to eject. His instinctive reaction and excellent airmanship saved his aircraft.

In April 2002 Brinkhurst credited his survival to solid RCAF training. Through his years at Portage-la-Prairie, pilots regularly trained in ejection seat procedures, strapping into a T-33 seat and going through the ejection sequence. Having done this so often, when the crunch came, Brinkhurst was ready. A second's hesitation and he would not have made it. He also felt lucky to have landed in a soft field. As it was, he spent five weeks in hospital at RAF Ely. On November 4, 1963 he returned to flying, his first sortie being with F/L Cox. Henceforth, his instructional tour was routine. Meanwhile, RAF Bomber Command investigators discovered what had happened. The trouble had begun at 231 OCU servicing, then done by Airwork, a civil contractor. The *Bomber Command Review* article explains: "The servicing error referred to, resulted in the drogue gun firing, which caused

the drogue line to snag the firing cable and fire the ejection gun. Because of the upset of the sequence of seat operations ... the seat stabilizing drogue could not stream and, although the time release mechanism released the scissors shackle, harness locks, and leg restraint locks, the pilot was not forced out of his seat by the apron, nor was his parachute canopy deployed."

In their investigation the RAF discovered a bent cover plate over the drogue gun timing mechanism. Had the plate been damaged when the seat struck the ground? After tests, this was discounted. The seat would have sustained 150 "g" on landing, while the plate wouldn't bend in the laboratory even at 600 "g". Instead, the cause was traced back six months, when the seat was reassembled and the plate subjected to excessive stress, while nuts were forced into place. Meanwhile, another component had not been properly re-installed. This left the drogue gun susceptible to inadvertent firing, if jolted.

With incorrectly installed seat components, "the pilot forcing back with the pressure of his foot on the rudder pedal [he was using a lot of pressure to keep control at low speed with one engine idle] could move the seat up the rail." The seat only had to move 1½ inches to fire the drogue gun. In summarizing, the AOC No. 1 Group, and the C-in-C Bomber Command congratulated the pilots on the way they reacted to a startling emergency.

Besides routine instructing, F/L Brinkhurst occasionally got away from Bassingbourn. In September 20, 1964 he was in a 4-plane formation to Luqa to celebrate Malta's independence. The Canberras put on a fly-past on the 21st. The following month Brinkhurst, with navigators F/Ls Richards and Russell, flew Canberra B.2 WJ677 on a nav trip to East Africa:

the sun shining to port and starboard, yet we were in the centre band of totality. We continued eastbound until the sun re-emerged. Our cameras captured all of this. We turned for home, where despatch riders were waiting to rush our film to London.

Due to fog, Wyton was below limits for the let-down, so Davis diverted to Waddington. That evening all of Great Britain marvelled at the TV footage of the eclipse brought to them by 58 Squadron. In 1961 the task of surveying migrating wildebeest in East Africa fell to 58 Squadron. Trials (to determine the ideal camera fit and best altitudes) were flown over cattle-raising districts in the UK. On May 8, 1961 Stewart and Davis departed for Nairobi via Idris. Next, Stewart flew by Auster to visit the warden of the wildlife preserve about 150 miles to the southwest. Next day he and Davis flew a recce, which indicated that activity was peaking. On May 14 and 15 they flew two wildebeest sorties. Since fuel permitted, on the 15th they photographed the Nogorogoro crater. Back in the UK on May 17, their film was processed by the PR establishment at Brampton, near Wyton. S/L Stewart flew his last Canberra sortie on July 11, 1961, then returned to Canada to attend RCAF Staff College in Toronto. By this time he had 690 Canberra hours.

F/Ls Gates and Funge

Morris D. Gates of Regina joined the air force at age 18 in 1950. He was on the first course at the RCAF Officer Selection Centre in London, Ontario, then attended the basic air navigation course in Summerside. P/O Gates joined 408 Squadron on Lancasters, doing photo and SHORAN flying from 1951-54. Operations were mainly from such northern detachments as Frobisher Bay, Yellowknife and Churchill. On an October 1954 mission his crew was the first to locate and photograph

"Mo" Gates, whose exchange at the RAF Navigation School included much good Canberra flying. (Gates Col.)

a Soviet scientific ice island (with flag flying) which had drifted into Canadian waters 20 miles from the North Pole. F/L Gates next served with the Air Navigation School at Winnipeg, then did the Special Navigation course there in 1957. A 1959-62 posting at CEPE Uplands followed, Gates' main project being to evaluate Argus navigation and ASW equipment. In 1963 S/L Gates attended RCAF Staff College in Toronto, following which he was on exchange in the UK. In 2005 he recalled:

On completing RCAF Staff College in 1963, I was posted to RAF Navigation School at Hullavington as Chief Navigation Instructor. Before I could get my bags packed, however, my posting was changed to the RAF College of Air Warfare at Manby. There I would be "A" Syndicate Leader of the RAF Specialist Navigation ("SPEC-N") Course, responsible for all course administration, e.g. scheduling and syllabus review. The change of posting had been arranged by W/C Keith Greenaway (RCAF) and W/C "Pinky" Grocott (RAF), each representing his country's advanced air navigation training courses. Their goal was to bring into line the exchange which had begun in 1948, when the RCAF had instituted its own SPEC-N course.

The RAF SPEC-N Course originated at RAF Manston before WWII. During the war it functioned at St. Athan, Wales, with officers on course (all of whom were pilots) being destined for senior navigation responsibilities. The course later moved to 31 ANS (Port Albert, Ontario). In 1943 it returned to the UK, where the first RCAF navigators completing it were S/L K.C. Maclure (originator of the Greenwich Grid Navigation System) and S/L "Gil" Gillespie (first OC of the RCAF SPEC-N Course commencing at Summerside in 1948). The last RCAF graduate was W/C Jerry Wright.

The postwar course (which included 24 students, mainly senior flight lieutenants) began in January with straight academics, before beginning the practical phase, which included visits to industry, to military and civil units in the UK, France and Germany, and to such development formations as the Royal Aeronautical Establishment. Besides teaching advanced navigation, the course also evaluated navigation equipment.

The final field trip was to North America. This began in Ottawa, where the course was briefed as to future RCAF plans, and visited CEPE and Computing Devices of Canada, to be updated on research, and test and development trends. A visit to Winnipeg included a briefing about the RCAF SPEC-N syllabus. The third stop was at the USAF navigation school at Mather AFB,

California. Visits followed to Texas Instruments, General Dynamics, Hughes Aircraft, Wright-Patterson AFB, Sperry Gyroscope, Cape Canaveral and the Pentagon.

While on course, students logged about 60 hours on the Canberra, including sorties to familiarize them with the difficulties of low-level nuclear weapons delivery. They also flew with operational squadrons on several of their visits and there were Arctic familiarization trips aboard a Britannia using grid techniques (25-30 flying hours). During the year, each student selected a navigation subject related to research or operations about which he prepared a 10-page report. The best of these were often the subject of a navigation symposium held at course end attended by command and HQ staff. Upon graduation in December, course members were posted to all commands as squadron and station navigation officers, and to research and trials units. The course was well respected in the RAF and sought after by many. Most graduates eventually attained senior rank.

Besides my duties with the course, I maintained flying currency. When first in the UK, therefore, I attended the RAF Refresher Navigation School at RAF Stradishall, followed by the Canberra OTU at Bassingbourn. I instructed in the air (from a makeshift jump seat beside the pilot), and took part in several "Lone Ranger" sorties to Cyprus, Malta, Gibraltar, Nairobi, Norway, Aden, Tehran, etc. Overall, I logged 300 flying hours, mainly on the Canberra B.2. My exchange proved to be challenging and rewarding by exposing me to new navigation equipment and techniques, and to future aircraft and armament development. I was the first RCAF officer to hold this exchange and was succeeded by S/L Doug Stonehouse. I returned to AFHQ in 1966 to fill the post of Staff Officer Navigation in the Directorate of Air Training in AFHQ.

S/L Gates next worked in personnel in the lead-up to CF unification. In 1972-74 he commanded 404 Squadron on the Argus, was Deputy Commandant at the Maritime Warfare School in Halifax, and Base Commander CFB Winnipeg, where he commanded the parade in 1975 when Air Command came into being. Later postings were to AFCENTE HQ in the Netherlands, and in personnel and administration in Ottawa and Trenton. Colonel Gates retired from the Canadian Forces in 1985. Following this he supported the RCAF Memorial Museum in Trenton and, in 2002, he and Bill Hockney co-authored *Nadir to Zenith: An Almanac of Stories by Canadian Military Navigators* (in 2006 they added volume two to this worthwhile project).

Having joined the RCAF in 1953, Noel Funge trained as a long-range navigator. Upon graduating from CNS in Winnipeg, he hoped for North Stars, but was posted in July 1955 to 408 Squadron. In October 1958 F/O Funge, by then with more than 900 hours (mainly on PR Lancasters), joined 412 Squadron on the North Star and Comet. He left there in April 1961 for 58 Squadron, replacing S/L Don Stewart. With some 4000 flying hours, F/L Funge was one of the more experienced navigators on squadron, and the first RCAF exchange officer there with photo recce experience. In 2005 he discussed his exchange:

The normal operational profile for a 58 Squadron PR.7 was: taxy at all-up weight of 52,000 lb, take off and rotate at 125 knots, climb at

F/L Noel Funge in September 1962 with RAF mates F/O Don Reed and F/L Jim Hainsworth. (Funge Col.)

300 knots, transition to Mach 0.72 to the top of the climb, then cruise at Mach 0.75. Even though the average mission was six hours, there was no auto pilot. At high altitude the range in knots between the limiting Mach speed and the stalling speed became very small, requiring the pilot to constantly be trimming the aircraft. The squadron's war role consisted of high-low-high mission profiles. At the top of the climb, we would jettison our tip tanks and cruise at Mach 0.77 at about 150 nm from the recce target area. Then we would descend, make the photo run at 250 knots, climb back to maximum altitude and return to base at Mach 0.77.

For its alternate mission as a bomber, or for high-level night photography using flash bombs, a PR.7 could carry six 1000-lb stores. To drop bombs at high altitude cruising at Mach 0.75 was an adventure. When the bomb bay doors opened, the eddy currents of the normally smooth airflow caused noise and turbulence. Upon bomb release, particularly in a salvo of six, the aircraft would exceed its limiting Mach, so we had to climb before comfortably resuming Mach 0.75 cruise.

F/L Funge enjoyed a number of deployments from Wyton, most involving Great Britain's plan to update the aerial surveys of its soon-to-be independent colonies. Deployments to East Africa were frequent, if brief, as Funge recalled in 2005:

From Wyton we flew five hours to El Adem, Libya; six hours to Nairobi; then to New Sarum near Salisbury, or Thornhill, near Gwelo, all in Southern Rhodesia. With vast areas to survey, only a few photo lines were flown (always at 40,000 feet) on each detachment. Along the Angolan or Belgian Congo borders, where the jungle below was a featureless green carpet, we employed Green Satin, the standard RAF Doppler computer. This kept us on a steady track.

In September 1962, 58 Squadron was tasked to survey British Guiana. This former colony had not been completely mapped by air, due to diurnal cloud conditions. Two Canberras and six crews, supported by a Britannia, flew to Piarco airport, Trinidad, routing from Wyton via Aldergrove, Goose Bay and Bermuda. Funge noted: "In 12 weeks about 80% of British Guiana was surveyed. Sorties averaging six hours would depart at 0500 in order to begin surveying before the daily cloud build-up. Due to distance and cloud, some areas were not fully covered until the advent of satellites."

While operating from Palisadoes airfield in Jamaica, F/L Funge and his pilot, F/O Bill McGillivray, surveyed British Honduras. In ideal weather they completed the task in about an hour. On another sortie they were despatched to capture a single-frame photo of Antigua from 54,000 feet: "We made several attempts to reach our altitude, but were thwarted by compressor stalls in our Avon engines." This coincided with the Cuban Missile Crisis. On one sortie a crew departed Trinidad on a Bahamas survey. They climbed out between Cuba and Haiti, and soon were on US radar at Guantanamo Bay. With an unidentified aircraft heading north, the controllers watched carefully, although at 50,000 feet the Canberra was too high to be intercepted. Soon enough, however, the RAF crew explained their presence.

When Iraq and Kuwait were in a 1961 border dispute, 58 Squadron was despatched to monitor troop deployments. Although not allowed on these operations, F/L Funge, as squadron nav leader, was involved in photo interpretation at Wyton. Also, since his squadron was part of Bomber Command, all navs were qualified bomb aimers and practiced nuclear weapons release and escape manoeuvres: "As a Canadian I was not permitted to take part in nuclear operations. However, the ever-pragmatic RAF reasoned that, if a war started, every crew had better be ready, so I received the necessary training." 58 Squadron also deployed annually to Luqa to practice high-level bombing and night photo flash releases at the range near El Adem: "The photoflash bomb was roughly the same size and weight and had about the same ballistics as a 1000-lb GP bomb. It took about 50 seconds to fall behind the aircraft to its detonation, which was sufficient to illuminate an area 12 x 12 miles. The camera then was automatically cycled by a photo cell. From 40,000 we used an interval of 45 seconds between releases."

In 1964 F/L Funge completed his exchange and was replaced by F/L Ray Griffiths. In March 1964 he was tasked to set up a training program for pilots, ops staff and photo interpreters on the CF-104 recce squadrons forming at Marville. Next, he served at Rivers, where 408 Squadron had moved in April 1964 upon retirement of the Lancaster. Funge was to assist regarding converting four C-130B to the photo reconnaissance role but, when one of them was written off in an accident, the plan was scrubbed. To be ready to instruct in tactical recce, infra-red sensors and inertial navigation systems for Canada's forthcoming CF-5 fleet, F/L Funge attended the Aerospace Systems Course at

Winnipeg. In 1967, however, the CF-5 recce role was simplified, and Funge joined the Aerospace Squadron at ANS to instruct. A posting in Training Command HQ followed, then he served on C-130Es with 436 Squadron. From 1975-78 he was Chief Air Training Instructor at 426 Squadron, then OC of the Aerospace System Course until 1982. In 2005 he wrote: "My last three years of CF service were as Staff Officer Navigation and Aerospace Training at 14 Training Group HQ. Retiring from the military in 1985, my wife and I moved to Australia, where we established a small business. In 1996 we returned to Canada, settling in Carrying Place, near Trenton." In 2005 Noel Funge was active in the Air Force Association as Ontario Group President, and enjoying amateur radio, a life-long hobby.

Getting Around the Rules: Lincoln Ops

Canadians on RAF postings occasionally participated in work that might raise eyebrows at home. In one case S/L Andrew P. Huchala bombed Mau-Mau terrorist camps in Kenya in 1954, this being in contravention of usual AFHQ policy. Raised in Alberta, Huchala joined the RCAF in1941, serving first as an engine fitter, then remustering to pilot. He flew Halifax bombers on 431 Squadron, where he was awarded a DFC in April 1945. At war's end Huchala remained on strength, serving at various stations until posted to the UK in June 1952, joining 61 Squadron on Lincoln B.2s at Waddington. On August 18 he took command of his squadron, which moved to Wittering in 1955. Huchala helped plan and flew in several large-scale exercises. In December 1952, for example, 61 Squadron joined other units in a bombing and nav exercise at RAF Shaffula in Egypt. War games, vital in Allied training and preparedness, became the hallmark of Cold War days. Huchala's reports about them sound realistic, as per his comments of March 16, 1953 about Ex. Jungle King. The scenario had Russia invading Western Europe. For the 16th Huchala's forces used H2S radar, "window" (radar-jamming aluminum strips), commu-

S/L Andrew P. Huchala in a 1965 portrait. His peacetime exchange is unusual in that it included combat. Huchala flew many aircraft, beginning with the Fleet Finch in 1942 (76:20 hours). Along the way he added such types as the Whitley (79:55), Halifax (511:05), Lincoln (808:40), B-29 Washington (68:20), Canberra (61:53) and Expeditor (1504:20). He left the RCAF in 1961 and passed away in Ottawa in 1998. (PL-133268 DND)

nications jamming and photo recce to achieve success, while the "enemy" opposed with night-fighter Meteors and Venoms:

Photo reconnaissance sorties carried out on 16th March by Canberra and Mosquito aircraft confirmed previous intelligence reports that large numbers of enemy ground attack aircraft, which have assisted his ground forces in reaching the Kiel Canal, were using the airfields of Bremen and Fuhlsbuttel … 42 Lincolns from Nos. 1 and 3 Groups were detailed to carry out concentrated simulated radar bombing attacks on the airfield at Bremen … in an attempt to destroy concentrations of enemy ground attack aircraft known to be there … a force of 24 Washingtons [B-29s] from No. 3 Group was detailed to carry out a similar simulated radar bombing attack on Fuhlsbuttel … where more enemy ground attack aircraft were known to have concentrated.

In March 1954 eight Lincolns of 61 and 144 squadrons left Wittering for RAF Eastleigh, near Nairobi, to relieve other units fighting the Mau-Mau insurrection. As OC 61 Squadron, Huchala led first in war games, flying against an imaginary enemy. Training gave way to operations, although bad weather prevailed. Other than this, targeting on the flanks of Mount Kenya and in the forests of Aberdare proved shaky, due to haphazard intelligence. An exception was a raid of May 11, 1954, Huchala reporting: " … four Lincolns supporting 70 Brigade attacked targets in the area north of the North Keith Saw Mill in Mount Kenya. Harvards also attacked in the same area and, as a result … a gang of terrorists was flushed into the reserve. 20 of them were killed by ground forces and a quantity of arms was recovered."

Huchala complained that there rarely was any decent "intel" available, and target marking by the Kenya Police Reserve Air Wing (flying Piper Pacers) really got him steamed. He called the KPR "unworthy and unable to render support of a proper standard". Huchala gave details about operations from Eastleigh, mentioning, for example, how a Lincoln at all-up weight (73,000 lb) normally would be airborne in 3600 feet. He provides a discourse about wing, propeller and airframe icing, which was a problem in this region of frightful thunderstorms. He also notes how one Lincoln was daily on PR standby at Eastleigh.

S/L Huchala's Lincolns supported other units in the field, e.g. delivering ammunition for Harvards at other bases, and rockets from Khormaksar, Iraq, for anti-Mau-Mau Vampires. His squadron also flew on searches, one for Lincoln RE297 (found crashed by the KPR), one for three lost Harvards (all crash-landed safely), and one for an overdue Rapide. On another operation, a Lincoln flew as weather recce in advance of H.M. Queen Elizabeth travelling from Aden to Entebbe

S/L Huchala flew the Lincoln B.II in East Africa. On February 20, 1946 this example crashed in bad weather near Rearsby Village, Leics. with the loss of all aboard. (CANAV Col.)

on April 28, 1954. Huchala concludes his report: "During the 3-months, No. 61/144 (B) Squadron carried out 311 successful sorties." Bombs dropped included 746 500-pounders and 717 1000-pounders. On June 17, 1954 No. 61 Squadron flew home to convert to Canberras, S/L Huchala taking the course. Now he was attached to Bomber Command at Lindholm, before returning to AFHQ in Ottawa.

Bomber Command Liaison

In the 1950s there were exchanges between the RCAF and RAF whereby one Canadian spent two years as a liaison officer in Bomber Command, while his counterpart served with CEPE Climatic at Namao. During a 1958-59 secondment to Bomber Command, F/L R.E. "Bob" Glunns visited three establishments about which he submitted reports. His duties took him to 230 (Vulcan) OCU at Waddington, 617 Squadron (Vulcans) at Scampton, and Bomber Command HQ at Binbrook. He noted how the OCU was training four crews per course (six weeks of

ground school, six of flying), each of a pilot, co-pilot, navigator plotter, navigator radar and air electronics officer. Generally, there were 16 sorties for 56 flying hours. At 617 Squadron, Glunns noted an establishment of 51 officers, 131 men and 8 Vulcans, each crew flying about 25 hours monthly.

Glunns carefully explained alerts at 617 Squadron: simple, reinforced and general alert/"R-hour". An alert was recognized by the type of warning – Tannoy, siren, etc. For a simple alert a station would go to 1½-hour readiness. At the next level, readiness would see crews "to cockpit readiness … capable of taking off in 15 minutes from the time of despatch of the Executive Order by Headquarters Bomber Command." Finally, matters might reached "R-hour" – with hostilities commencing, by when Bomber Command was going all out. Glunns wrote of the RCAF establishing a bombing force. Although the Canberra B.6 was obsolescent, he recommended a force of 60 to serve in bombing and recce.

One issue seems to be clarified by the Glunns file, i.e. under which authority RCAF officers fell while on RAF exchange. A letter, discovered in the files in RG24 Library and Archives Canada, explains: "Air force officers on exchange duties or courses with the RAF are not attached to the RAF under the Visiting Forces (British Commonwealth) Act 1933, but are on strength of the Canadian Joint Staff London." This letter was received by Glunns from his AFHQ correspondence officer, F/L Barry Lumley.

CHAPTER 11

Flying the Javelin

Javelin Development Squadron

An RCAF exchange officer would be one with an excellent re-cord, strong in airmanship and leadership, and relishing any challenge. Typical of such men was Martin O. "Mo" Aller. Born in Fort William on May 5, 1930, as a boy Mo was fascinated by the aviation scene. Locally, Canadian Car was turning out Hurricanes and Helldivers and test pilots like Al Cheesman and Orville Weiben were local heroes. Aller enjoyed his first flight while in high school – a hop in a little Stinson 105. Meanwhile, his many other interests included playing the bagpipes.

Determined to pursue aviation, Aller joined the RCAF in November 1949, starting at Manning Depot at 1107 Avenue Road in Toronto. Next, he was posted to 1 FTS at Centralia where, on January 9, 1950, he flew in Harvard 3332 with instructor F/O Gordy Jones. He soloed, then moved on, with such instructors as F/Os Mike Dooher and Bill Whitely, men later renowned in the fighter world. Aller stepped up to the Expeditor on October 26, 1950, soloing on November 2. On January 25, 1951 he com-pleted FTS with a flight in Harvard AJ935, then attended AAS. His training totalled 277:20 hours on Harvards and Expeditors in little more than a year.

P/O Aller was posted to 1 (F) OTU at Chatham where, following a few Harvard "famil" flights, on April 24 he flew Vampire 17004. This course ended on June 28, 1951, and Aller was posted to the Canadian Joint Air Training Centre at Rivers in the Tactical and Transport Support School. He flew first at TTSS on July 31 in a Dakota with F/O Collin Dobbin. Busy times ensued – drop-ping paratroops, snatching and towing Hadrian gliders, etc.

First flown in November 1951, the Gloster Javelin was the RAF's front line, all-weather interceptor until replaced by the Lightning in the early 1960s. Here XH756, with RCAF F/L M.O. Aller at the controls, poses for the photographer during a shoot for *Air Pictorial* magazine. Built in 1956 as an FAW.7, XH756 served various squadrons, became an FAW.9, then went to the fire dump at RAF Leeming late in 1966. (Aller Col.)

August 3-11, 1951 Aller crewed on a Dakota searching in the northwest for a missing USAF C-54 (another crew located the plane, crashed on a mountain). Next, he and F/O Clare Gleddie flew a Dakota from Yellowknife searching for bush pilot Johnny Bourassa, lost since June in a Bellanca Skyrocket. The plane was spotted undamaged on September 3, but Bourassa never re-appeared. Aller and Gleddie then searched from Norman Wells for Rev. William Leising in his tiny Aeronca, finding both OK. November 9-11, 1952 he and Dobbin towed a Hadrian behind Dakota 656 from Rivers to Rockcliffe via Armstrong and Kapuskasing, logging 5:20 hours on Day 1, 3:30 on Day 2, 4:05 on Day 3.

On September 2, 1952 Aller flew C-119 22103 with his CO, S/L Ray Churchill. From March to May he was at Centralia for the "green ticket" (instrument flying) course. Returning to Rivers, he switched to the Tactical Fighter Flight, flying Mustang 9567 on July 20, 1953. In this period TFF Mustangs were 9233, 9286, 9287, 9567 and 9594, flying mainly on Army exercises. Other taskings included sorties to nearby Camp Shilo's weapons range to test guns, bombs, rockets, and napalm tanks. Sometimes the RCN would visit with Sea Furies. In his log for November 11, 1953 F/O Aller notes dog fighting with these hot naval fighters. "They tore us up!" was how he recalled the fray. On November 23 he enjoyed his one and only Sea Fury flight.

On December 12, 1953 Aller flew Dakota KN511, searching for a missing Cessna flown by Paul Rickey. Down for six days, Rickey helped when one of his passengers gave birth (the infant died before rescue, *Life Magazine* covered the story). For two weeks in July 1954 TFF, operating from Edmonton's Blatchford

Fort William Flight Cadets In Training

Flight Cadet Martin Aller, left, 20, son of Mr. and Mrs. William Aller, 224 North Marks street, stands in front of his Harvard trainer with fellow Fort William Flight Cadet Kenneth Cheesman, 22, son of Mr. and Mrs. S. A. Cheesman, Ross Apartments. The instructor at Centralia, Ont., with them at the right, is FO. Robert Ayers of Toronto. Flight Cadet Aller, who enlisted with the R.C.A.F. won his wings January 26 at Centralia, where his parents were present. Formerly a tourist guide in this district, Flight Cadet Aller hopes for a post to an air-sea rescue squadron after his training is completed. Flight Cadet Cheesman, who served with the U.S.A.A.F. for two years and was six months on the Berlin airlift as hydraulic specialist, hopes for a post to a fighter unit. He enlisted with the R.C.A.F. last June and is close to winning his pilot's wings. Their 40-week course is followed by twin-engine instruction, then two months in an air armament course before their commission.

A 1950 Fort William "home town news" item featuring flight cadets Mo Aller and Ken Cheesman with their instructor at Centralia, F/L Bob Ayres, who also is featured in this book. Ken Cheesman later flew Sabres, was a bush pilot, a dentist and an avid supporter of the Canadian Bushplane Heritage Museum. Sadly, on June 15, 1997 Ken died in a Beaver crash north of Sault Ste. Marie. (Aller Col.)

Field, supported summer militia training at Camp Wainwright. Illustrating the variety of CJATC flying, Aller flew the Mustang 11 times in August for 12:30 hours, C-119 – 8/22:00, Dakota 8/18:25 and Harvard 1/1:25. On September 23 he flew an RCN Avenger, noting how this fine aircraft "handled like a Dakota".

Some excitement came on June 2, 1955 when F/O Aller dead-sticked 9233 at Rivers after throttle trouble. On June 11 he flew 9233 in the Saskatoon airshow, while F/O Ralph Heard wowed the throngs by dropping a sonic boom with a Sabre. After logging 452 happy hours on Mustangs, Aller was posted to 3 AFS at Gimli on T-33s, his first flight being on August 8, 1955 with F/O Vic Rushton in 21371. He soloed on the 12th in 21293, then advanced to OTU at Cold Lake, flying CF-100 18118 on January-23, 1956, then crewing with navigator Lorne Jokinen.

His course, which ended on April 26, included 94:10 hours on the CF-100, 25:05 – T-33, 23:45 – Expeditor. Aller and Jokinen joined 428 Squadron at Uplands, their tour beginning with a flight in 18518 on May 17 (they later moved to 410 Squadron).

The Aller/Jokinen CF-100 days would be interspersed with some special memories. On January 23, 1957 Aller sat in the back while USAF LCol John W. Bennett, an F-89 Scorpion pilot, flew 18609 (his first CF-100 flight). After lunch they flew 18543. September 9-13 Aller/Jokinen represented 410 at the first annual Air Defence Command rocket meet at the Weapons Practice Flight, Cold Lake. They won the Vincent Trophy for the highest scoring aircrew at 94% (3666.9/4000 points), while 410 took the MacBrien Trophy for best team. December 5-12, 1957 Aller/Jokinen ferried CF-100 18688 for Belgium on Op. Jump Moat, routing Uplands-Goose Bay-Keflavik-Langar-Marville, where the BAF collected '688. They did a second delivery March 5-7, 1958 (Uplands-Goose Bay-Keflavik-Beauvechain.

Now F/L Aller was posted on exchange to the All Weather Development Squadron at RAF Central Fighter Establishment. He was at RAF West Raynham for a famil flight on March 14, flying Meteor 7 WH223 with F/L Frank Gilland, his RCAF predecessor. On August 21 he had a famil flight in Javelin Mk.5 XA660 with Lt Beardsmore, then was assigned to Javelin Mk.8 service trials. In getting used to the new type, on August 27 he twice took Javelin Mk.7 XH748 supersonic. For October 1958 his log shows 12 Javelin sorties, one in a Meteor. Javelin trips averaged 45 minutes without ventral fuel tanks, 1:30 with. Besides West Raynham and Coltishall, Aller operated from Odiham on the Javelin Mk.1 (he would find this mark the nicest of Javelins).

Besides avionics trials, as with ILS (which he was the first to use in the Javelin) in 1959 F/L Aller was a project officer in CFE Trial 316 – "Tactical Trial of the Javelin Mk.8/Firestreak Mk.1 Weapon System". The Mk.8 was the latest Javelin, the chief mods being reheat (i.e. afterburner). It also had drooping leading

With Firestreaks fitted for a trials flight, Javelin FAW.8 XH972 sits at West Raynham. Then, a hangar scene with FAW.5 XA657 and FAW.9 XH756. XA657 later served 5 Squadron in 1962, then was SOS in 1963. F/L Aller recalled two nicknames for the Javelin: "the dragmaster" (hinting at aerodynamics) and "the flying organ", since there was a howling noise from the gun ports. (Aller Col.)

CFE Report, Trial 316

Information

Introduction

1. The Javelin Mk.8 is a development of the Javelin Mk.6, the principal changes being more powerful engines introducing reheat, pitch stabiliser, auto pilot Mk. 12, droop leading edge, Firestreak, and AI Mk.22 [based on the Westinghouse APQ43 radar acquired by the RAF in 1951]. Four aircraft have been delivered to the Central Fighter Establishment for tactical trials by the Air Fighting Development Squadron based at RAF Coltishall.

Authority

2. The trial is authorized by Air Ministry letter BF.231/1277 dated 3rd July 1959.

Priority

3. The trial is allotted Priority "A".

Intention

4. The objects of the trial are (a) To assess the capability of the weapon system. (b) To determine the maximum threat which can be met within the United Kingdom Air Defence environment. (c) To determine the differences in performance and operating techniques between this aircraft and the Javelin Mk.7 Post-mod. 568, introduced by the incorporation of reheat, pitch stabiliser, auto pilot Mk.12, AI Mk.22 and droop leading edge. [With these mods a Mk.7 became a Mk.9. Some 76 Mk.7s were so converted)]

Execution

Control and Direction

5. The Officer in Charge of the trial is Officer Commanding, Air Fighting Development Squadron, RAF Coltishall.

6. The Progress Officer is S/L H. Harrison, AFC, Squadron Leader Trials (Fighter), Central Fighter Establishment, RAF West Raynham.

7. The Project Officers are: S/L R.J. Street, F/L M.O. Aller, F/L A.L. Stevenson.

Conduct of the Trial

8. Manufacturer's figures. Percentage checks of the manufacturer's performance figures are to be made and, by flying specific sorties with and without use of reheat, carrying both two and four missiles, the following data are to be compiled: (a) Climb data including ORP scramble time to 10, 20, 30, 40, 45 and 48 thousand feet, and maximum altitude. (b) Manoeuvrability, acceleration, deceleration and turning performance at 40, 45 and 48 thousand feet, and at maximum altitude. (c) Fuel consumption figures sufficient to construct flight profiles showing radius of action and endurance at 20, 40, 45 and 48 thousand feet, and at maximum altitude, for both good and bad weather at base.

9. Aircraft performance. Comments are to be made on the aircraft's performance with specific reference to: (a) Auto pilot. An evaluation of the AI.12 auto pilot is to be made to determine (i) The operational capability of the equipment within the limits of the clearance. (ii) The reliability of the equipment. (iii) The possibility of making an intercept (to Firestreak release) by use of the auto pilot pitch and turn controls and height lock, acting on navigator's commands without visual references to the flight instruments. (b) Reheat performance. The reliability of the reheat system and its maximum speeds, heights, accelerations and turns are to be investigated and compared with similar Javelin

edges to enhance turn performance at altitude, and improved radar and avionics. Firestreak was the UK's infrared air-to-air missile, in the category of the American Sidewinder. In Trial 316 Aller would fly many sorties investigating missile/aircraft performance. Tactics had to be tried (even lights-out night intercepts). A CFE report detailing Trial 316 suggests the level of responsibility handed to the project pilots (see above):

Exercise Deertrek

One day F/L Aller found himself on escape and evasion – Ex. Deertrek. About this he reported on February 13, 1959: "Participants were equipped only as they might be after bailing out, and were dropped by bus in a strange section of the country just after dark. The object was to evade the police, army militia, etc., and travel 30 miles by foot to a pre-designated safe rendezvous. The above-named officer was caught after 25 miles. The exercise took place over a weekend in October ..." AFDS crews also flew in Fighter Command exercises, F/L Aller taking part in "Mandate". This had three phases: (i) Full GCI of fighters in their loiter lanes. (ii) Jamming by bombers, so the fighters had to position themselves onto targets. (iii) Impediment phase with jamming, atomic fallout, low level attacks, etc. On August 13, 1959 Aller reported on two sorties:

The first, a dawn scramble after an all night wait, was scrambled via a telebriefing line from the runway button. When the pre-briefed

Mk.7 configurations. (c) Pitch stabiliser. The handling qualities of the aircraft at operational heights and speeds with and without the pitch stabiliser are to be compared. (d) Drooped leading edge wing. The effect of the drooped leading edge wing on turn and acceleration performance at operational heights is to be investigated and compared with figures applicable to the Javelin Mk.7. (e) Landing distance. The effect of the higher all-up landing weights on the landing run on dry and wet runways is to be investigated. The suitability of the aircraft for use on 2000-yard runways is to be determined.

10. AI Mk.22: During the trial an assessment is to be made of the following aspects of the AI Mk.22: (a) Search. Pick-up ranges under varying conditions are to be ascertained at altitudes of 40, 45 and 48 thousand feet, and maximum altitude. (b) Lock-on. The maximum and minimum ranges and the limits in elevation and azimuth for achieving and holding lock are to be obtained. The ability of the equipment to discriminate between two targets close together is to be investigated. The effect of cloud and ground returns and the effect of window and ECM is to be reported on. (c) Collimator. The collimator is to be evaluated for stability and accuracy of presentation. If possible, tracking accuracy is to be assessed by use of CGS recorder camera film. (d) Servicing. The serviceability, ease of servicing and the adequacy of the servicing instructions of the AI Mk.22 equipment is to be commented on.

11. Firestreak. Acquisition or drill rounds are to be carried on all tactical sorties, acquisition checks are to be made at both high and low altitudes, in various weather conditions against representative targets. No firing is to take place. Slaving of the missile head at the AI Mk.22 after lock-on is to be checked.

12. Guns. Evaluation of the gun installation is to be made by firing against banner targets at medium altitude. At the same time the accuracy of the AI Mk.22 radar ranging is to be checked.

13. Weapon system. The maximum target performance at high and low level that the weapon system can intercept is to be established, using the figures obtained from the analysis as detailed above.

14. Target. Flying will normally be done against single Javelin targets. However, a certain proportion is to be flown against more representative targets in the form of V-bombers. Some sorties are to be flown against a bomber equipped with AI jamming to ascertain the lock-on capability of AI Mk.22 in these conditions.

15. Recorders. Wirek recorders and G90 cameras are to be installed in the aircraft.

16. Flight recorders and data analysis. In addition to the performance data needed to fulfill the requirements previously mentioned, the following records are required for each interception: (a) Time of arming of Firestreak missile. (b) Fighter and target height, speed and heading. (c) The azimuth, elevation, range and angle-off. (d) The time and position each missiles acquires. (e) The time the firing position is reached. (f) A report on weather conditions, including cloud type and amount. (g) G90 and GGS recorder films. (h) Wirek records.

17. Duration of trial. The exact length of the trial cannot be forecast, but it should be completed in at least six months, if the information obtained is to be of significant value to the user squadrons.

18. Reports. Consolidated reports are to be rendered monthly through the Progress Officer to the Group Captain Operations, Central Fighter Establishment. A report on the performance phase is to be rendered as soon as completed to assist in disseminating information to the user squadrons quickly. This is also to apply to subsequent phases of the trial.

D. Crowley-Milling, Group Captain,
Group Captain Operations,
Central Fighter Establishment

loiter lane was reached, the turn-in was given by GCI. Control on the first target was by GCI, and a successful intercept was made on a Victor bomber doing .86 M at 46,000 ft. A kill was confirmed by taking film from 700-350 yards with the gunsight pipper on the target for a least 5 seconds. The second target, a B-66, was intercepted in the loiter lane without GCI assistance. On the second sortie [at night], VHF electronic and window jamming were encountered. When VHF jamming commenced, another channel was selected and the order to proceed down to the loiter lane was received. No further control was possible because of the confused air situation. A very fast target at 47,000 ft. was chased, but the range could not be closed to gun firing distance before a prohibited ground-to-air missile zone was reached. Range was down to that of Firestreak for some time

before the zone. During the third phase, an accurate count of atomic fallout was kept on each crew member and some were grounded when the maximum count was reached. A scramble after low level targets was unsuccessful.

The impression of the exercise from an aircrew point of view was that it was more realistic in the air, but much slower moving than those experienced in the RCAF … Although there were only two scrambles in three days, the jamming and lack of GCI control in Phase II made for a realistic and interesting sortie. Aircrew scores were good on the first phase, but poorer in the second, when jamming and faster targets were encountered. Scores did not take into account that on a stern attack with a gun-armed Javelin, the fighter aircraft will be under fire for 800 yards before it can fire on the bomber.

FLYING THE JAVELIN   97

FAW.9 XH707 of 23 Squadron launches a Firestreak. (MoD via Roger Lindsay)

Trials 275 and 298

F/L Aller also flew in Trials 275 and 298, the first a preliminary tactical evaluation of the Javelin Mk.7/ Firestreak Mk.1 weapon system from scramble to reaching weapon firing position in the normal Fighter Command sector environment. The system proved effective, with few sorties aborted due to snags. The Javelin handled well with four Firestreaks. On an intercept, GCI would guide the fighter towards a target, which AI radar eventually would acquire. As the fighter closed, the target's IR signature would illuminate an enunciator light in the pilot's cockpit. When in range, the light, which flickered at first, shone steadily, indicating that the pilot could fire.

Trial 275 showed that a target could not easily break lock-on by evasive action. However, if it throttled back, it could do so by lowering jet pipe (IR) temperature. Should more than one target be ahead, there was no way of knowing which would be pursued by a Firestreak. Although radar jamming could deter a pursuer, should a Firestreak launch within parameters, it was not affected by jamming. A pursuer was to plan for two minutes to arm missiles. These had to be fired between Mach 0.7 and Mach 1.3 within +3G and -1G. Firestreak controls were locked for the first second of flight. The engine burned for 1.6 seconds, boosting the missile to Mach 1.6 above launch speed. A Firestreak could withstand 15G using pneumatically-powered flight controls.

On a test sortie, ideal conditions for best "KP" (kill probability) included: co-ordinate fighter and target at similar speeds and

Of this photo Mo Aller notes: "Cockpit of Mk.I Javelin XA623 outfitted for Trial 794 - evaluation of roller blind flight instruments driven by a central air data computer and offset TACAN. Standby mechanical flight instruments on top, roller blind instruments below." Delivered in January 1956, XA623 went to the A&AEE to be evaluated by the USAF. It joined the AFDS in early 1960 and was sold for scrap in March 1963.

height, fire missiles at 20° off-angle, and have the target evade at 2G. At 5000' ASL a Firestreak was found to fly under control for 1900 yards, 35,000' – 4200 yards, 45,000' – 4350 yards. Closest range for a kill at 5000' was 850 yards, 1050 yards at altitude. Should a target be above the Javelin's 48,000-foot ceiling, the pursuer could "snap-up" – pull up and launch from below to hit a target as much as 5000 feet above. Lethality was predicted within a 40-foot radius of detonation. Other results from Trial 275 determined that ground clutter could adversely affect KP, so a Firestreak should not be fired downward. Also, instead of its target, a Firestreak might chase the sun or moon, if fired within 5° of either. Cloud or contrails also could reduce KP. The missile seeker head seemed to be immune to fogging up or icing.

Trial 298 further evaluated the Mk.7/Firestreak. This time, some Mk.7s would have standard armament of four 30mm Aden cannons, others would have two or four Firestreaks, plus two cannons. More technical questions were resolved on this trial. For example, at maximum takeoff weight of 42,000 pounds (with ventral tanks and total fuel of 10,700 lb), takeoff distance for the Mk.7 was 900 yards with a specific wind, temperature, etc. As with any fighter, manoeuvrability was limited at altitude, F/L Aller's report of February 13, 1959 noting re. 50,000 feet: "The aircraft [clean] is very touchy to fly at this height." Such data were summarized and passed on to operational squadrons.

Javelin Pros and Cons

Having flown various Javelins, F/L Aller compared the Mk.7 (no reheat) and Mk.8 (reheat, but 1529-lb higher AUW), plus the Mk.9. The latter was a Mk.7 converted to reheat (the first Mk.9 flew in May 1959). Climbing to 40,000 feet, Aller reported that the Mk.8 was 33 seconds faster than a Mk.7. However, it used 620 lb more fuel in reheat. From there to 45,000 feet, a Mk.8 was 3 minutes, 55 seconds faster, but used a further 485 lb fuel. As to 48,000 feet, Aller reported: "A tanked Mk.7 [i.e. equipped with ventral tanks] cannot climb to 48,000 feet from takeoff. A Mk.8 can. However, an untanked Mk.7 can climb to 48,000 feet from takeoff taking two minutes, 31 seconds longer, but using 895 lb less fuel than a Mk.8."

Aller observed that a Mk.8 was limited in bank to the onset of buffet, "because a suitable position has not yet been found for the wing stall warner flag. It appears unlikely to be found." Other figures showed that a Mk.8 closed the gap from M.80 to V-max (i.e., maximum speed – M.94) at 40,000 feet in 1:24 minutes, while a Mk.7 took 1:32 minutes from M.80 to its V-max (M.925). At 48,000 feet a Mk.8 closed from M.80 to V-max (M.93) in 1:48 minutes, compared to a Mk.7 from M.80 to its V-max (M.905) in 3:54. A Mk.8 climbing to 40,000 feet from takeoff had a range (with a "bad weather fuel allowance") of 641 nm, while a Mk.7 could fly 833 nm in similar conditions. Thus did the Mk.8 have 192 nm less range than a Mk.7. F/L Aller's conclusion? "In a loiter environment the Mk. 8 and Mk.9 can be considered as having virtually no loiter time available", while a Mk.7 could intercept a target 100 nm further out than a Mk.8. He added that a Mk.8 would have a higher maintenance

AFDS personnel in 1960: John Sorsby of Sperry, S/L Pete Kingston (pilot, Javelin flight commander, who also had a USAF exchange in Turkey flying the F-86D), F/L Jock Stevenson (nav), F/L Nick Thurston (nav), F/L Chris Bryce (pilot), F/L John Reynolds (pilot), F/L Roy Jones (nav), F/L Pete Borrett (pilot) and F/L Aller.

penalty in such things as changing cracked exhaust cones and tire/brake wear. As to converting Mk.7s to reheat, he advised: "The large amount of money to be spent converting Mk.7s to Mk.9s for the questionable value of the performance increase and range decrease may have better uses." His final comment was as blunt:

In the unjammed air defence environment the Javelin Mk.7/Firestreak Mk.1 weapon system is capable of intercepting and destroying a target flying at .85 TMN at 50,000 feet. This is more than adequate to meet the Badger/Beagle component of the threat. While it would appear that the performance increase of the Javelin Mk.8 and Mk.9 may raise this a few thousand feet, any threat performance increase is likely to be a large one, which will put any Javelin out of the picture.

Another report by F/L Aller covers "Windscreen Hot Air Dispersal". The system bled air from the compressor of each engine, directing it to an outlet at the base of the windshield. Having flown with this several times, Aller noted in his report of November 15, 1958:

A typical page from F/L Aller's log book in 1959.

This has proven to be a very effective rain dispersal system. On one flight, before starting up, the windscreen was almost completely opaque with rain. After turning the unit on, the windscreen completely cleared in a few seconds and remained so as long as the system was on. The return to base via GCA under conditions of low ceiling and rain was made much easier, having the extra visibility afforded by the system. It has been found effective up to 400 K …

This is the crowning touch to make an aircraft really all-weather. As well as providing extra in-flight visibility, it also simplifies taxying in precipitation, especially at night. Frost or ice is also easily removed. It is felt that this rain dispersal system would be readily applicable to all RCAF jet aircraft.

RCAF and RAF: General Impressions

In his February 13, 1959 report F/L Aller compared RAF and RCAF details. His squadron mates at the AFDS were "first class officers and keen to fly". Since their sorties usually were shorter than in a CF-100, flying times were less. Also, it seemed more likely that RAF crews be grounded in poor weather or for unserviceabilities. On the other hand, they flew from shorter runways and "with closer fuel tolerances". Aller found AFDS Javelins less serviceable than the average CF-100: "Radio communications in the Javelin is poorer than … in T-33s or CF-100s. The Javelin suffers from fading due to the aerial locations and blanking by the airframe. The tone of the radios under good conditions is still noisier than the CF-100."

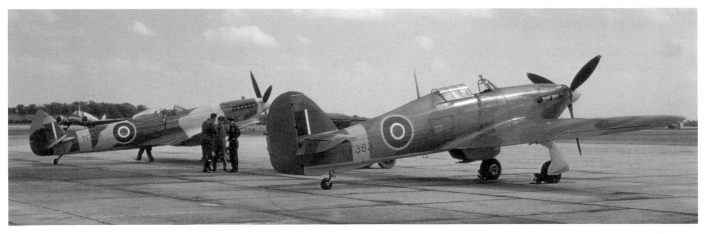

F/L Aller enjoyed everything about his exchange. Not surprisingly, when these lovely RAF vintage fighters appeared one day at Coltishall, he dashed for his camera!

F/L Aller found RAF fighters of the 1950s challenging, yet pleasant to fly. A Javelin was faster than a CF-100, cruising at .85M compared M.80, but supersonic only in a power-dive. Service ceiling was comparable, a Javelin being on the edge at 48,000 feet. According to *RCAF EO 05-25F-1* of January 1, 1958, the CF-100 Mk.5 (the highest-flying CF-100) had a 45,000 ceiling, although a few pilots, picking their airplane and flying conditions, reached about 50,000 feet. (As years pass, memories blur – one former CF-100 pilot reported that going to 60,000 feet in a CF-100 was a piece of cake, when it was impossible!) F/L Aller concluded that the CF-100 had better AI radar, with lock-ons possible at 40 miles, compared to 15 for a Javelin. With places such as West Raynham having only a 6000-foot runway, a Javelin clearly had ample takeoff performance.

On July 21, 1960 F/L Aller finished at CFE. That day he took up XA556 with Mr. Langrish in the back seat, logging the flight as "T294 FCC TACAN" – a flight control computer/tactical air navigation avionics sortie. Aller ended with 325:20 hours on Javelins, 57:40 on Meteors. Except for one trip, his tour had been unevent-

Mo Aller at home in Ottawa in 2001. (Larry Milberry)

ful. That occurred on May 7, 1959, while night flying with his favourite navigator, F/L Jeff Bingham. In the worst of weather their radios failed. They descended in the clag, looking for a landmark. Spotting USAF Sculthorpe, Aller turned on instinct for West Raynham, groping along at 2000 feet and guzzling fuel. Entering the circuit, he flashed his landing lights, indicating "Nordo" (no radio) to the tower, then landed. Another memorable flight was in XH756 on March 4, 1960. That day F/Ls Aller and Broughton posed for an RAF photographer, their Javelin sporting four Firestreaks. One of these photos was the cover on *Royal Air Force Flying Review* for February 1961.

On Squadron with Javelins

While F/L Aller flew in test and development, H.E. "Hank" Hemming had a regular squadron exchange. Having grown up in Ottawa, he joined the RCAF in September 1949. He trained at No. 1 FTS at Centralia, his first flight being with F/O Williams on November 14, 1949. He finished at Centralia on August 10, 1950 with 245:35 hours on Harvards and Expeditors. After Air Armament School, he was posted to the FIS at Central Flying School. In November he was back at Centralia instructing, his first student being F/C Norquay. Then came a dizzying list of sprogs, including F/Cs Goldie, Hallowell, Holtby, Husch, Morton and Villeneuve, all destined for exemplary RCAF careers. In January 1952 Hemming returned to the FIS, flying such types as the Beech T-34, Mustang, Vampire, Dakota and Mitchell. On April 14, 1953 he flew the T-33 for the first time, taking up 21005 with F/O Scott. By the end of 1953 his log already showed nearly 1700 hours.

One day at Trenton, Hemming asked his boss, W/C C.H. Mussells, about getting an operational posting on fighters. The influential Mussells soon had something arranged. On October 6, 1955 Hemming made his first flight on the CF-100 at OTU in Cold Lake, going up with instructor Frank Augusta, then crewing with F/O Andy Wojciechowski. Upon

Hank Hemming as a young RCAF fighter pilot. (PL-65257 DND)

graduation they were posted to 433 Squadron at North Bay under W/C Mike Dooher, but later moved to 414. In July 1958 Hemming got word that he was posted to night fighter Meteors at RAF Waterbeach. After some leave, he joined 25 Squadron, flying first on a famil ride in Meteor T.7 WA615 with P/O Ritchie. Now he crewed with F/L Larry Parakin, RCAF, the two flying initially on September 19 in Meteor N.F.14 WS752. Although fine to fly, the N.F.14 was obsolete. Years later Hemming recalled its takeoff numbers as: liftoff at 120 knots, safe on one engine at 140, manoeuvrable at 160. The cannon-armed N.F.14 had a vintage AI radar that would acquire a target at 10-12 miles. In December 1958, 25 Squadron converted to the cannon-armed Javelin Mk.7, Hemming checking out on XH905 on February 3,

1958 (XH905 later was lost upon colliding off Cyprus with a Canberra). For his first month Hemming flew 18 times for 27:50 hours and was in love with the Javelin, considering it "a beautiful aircraft to fly".

Hemming later flew the Javelin Mk.9 with Firestreaks. In February 2002 he described a usual intercept. GCI would vector a Javelin in a head-on approach. The fighter would pass the target, then do a sweeping turn to re-approach, using radar. When in range, Firestreaks could be "fired", then the pilot might press in close to attack with cannon. This was excellent training, although real combat would have been dangerous – Soviet bombers had remotely-aimed cannons that could hit a Javelin at long range. Other activities at Waterbeach included Op. Halyard – standby at the end of the runway. Javelins would wait to scramble, at which moment the engines would come to life and the aircraft would be airborne within two minutes. Such sorties lasted 1:00 to 1:35 hours. Another exercise sent Javelins on low-level (250 feet ASL) sea patrols, practicing lest low-flying Soviet bombers ever encroach. Since the Javelin had short endurance, low patrols were flown on one engine at 250 knots to preserve fuel.

Since 25 Squadron was dedicated to the defence of Cyprus, the task being to maintain a British presence in the eastern "Med", e.g. to warn the Turks about keeping a safe distance from Greece and Cyprus, or to keep an eye on Egyptian military activities. Hemming and Parakin first went to Cyprus in July 1960 in XH880. They flew from Waterbeach to Istres, France on the 27th (1:30 hours), thence to Luqa

Carrying Firestreaks, FAW.9 XA880 of 25 Squadron sits at Weathersfield during a May 1960 open house. Hemming/ Parakin ferried XA880 to Cyprus in July 1960. (Roger Lindsay)

(1:20). Next day they flew to El Adem (1:20), then Nicosia (1:10). The deployment lasted to September 3, when they flew home. On September 22, 1960 Hemming scrambled with AI observer Sgt Garfoot, intercepting a USAFE B-66, then a RAF Canberra. Such targets often were above 40,000 feet (on one sortie Hemming coaxed his Javelin to 52,000).

F/L Hemming's last Javelin sortie was on November 10 in XH880 with F/L Hustwayte (Parakin had returned early to Canada), a one-hour scramble intercepting a Valiant. He returned to Canada, first to AFHQ, then (1965) to fly C-130s with 436 Squadron at Uplands. After three years he took a SAGE exchange posting with the 4626th Air Base Squadron at Topsham AFB, Maine. Topsham, in the Bangor Air Defense Sector, directed NORAD fighters and Bomarcs. While he went to work in a bomb-proof bunker every day, he also did practice flying from NAS Brunswick in USAF T-33s, C-47s and Cessna U-3s. In 1969 Hemming had hopes of a CF-104 tour, but Ottawa was cutting back in NATO. Instead, he "flew a desk" at NDHQ, but returned to the C-130 in 1977. By the time he left the military, he had more than 4000 C-130 hours. He then enjoyed a long career with Transport Canada in Ottawa.

Javelin Navigator

Robert Alexander Saunders, born in Stratford, Ontario on April 20, 1929, was raised in Ottawa. In high school he excelled at sports, then played football for the Ottawa Rough Riders in 1949. The team was undefeated in its 12-game schedule, but lost to the Montreal Alouettes in the 2-game, total points eastern final, so missed the Grey Cup final. Through the season, Saunders earned $75 per game so, instead of sticking with football, chose the RCAF. Indoctrination was at Manning Depot in Toronto, from where he was posted to CNS at Summerside. After introductory lectures, he flew his first exercise on March 23, 1950 in Dakota 963. Saunders graduated on November 7, having logged

Hank Hemming at home in Ottawa in March 2002. After leaving the CF, he joined Transport Canada, where he flew the Citation, King Air and Twin Otter. Having logged more than 15,000 flying hours, he retired in 2003. (Larry Milberry)

Alex Saunders as a youthful football player in Ottawa, then as a Javelin AI navigator. (Both, Saunders Col.)

161:40 hours. Next came a short bomb aiming course at AAS – in early postwar years the RCAF still needed air gunners for its maritime patrol Lancasters.

On January 26, 1951 Saunders joined 408 Squadron, flying initially on Lancaster FM207 on March 7. The squadron was preparing for its summer SHORAN detachments. As close to northern break-up as possible, crews set off for Yellowknife. For June 1951 F/O Saunders' log shows 87:10 hours flown in FM212 and FM215. His flying dropped to 62:50 hours in July (he was hospitalized for 10 days with a skin condition). Things returned to normal in August with 103.45 hours. September 5 to 30, 1951 Saunders was on the search for Dr. Albert Hudson and Toronto Maple Leaf hockey star Bill Barilko, lost on a Hudson Bay fishing trip. Flying on FM207, '217 and '218,

Saunders logged 34:50 hours on this fruitless task (years later the lost plane was found). Op. Bug of October 1951 involved sampling the atmosphere over the Pacific. Filters installed atop a Lancaster collected air tainted by Soviet nuclear tests. For Op. Bug, Saunders flew from Sea Island on October 1, 2, and 3. On March 31, 1952 he navigated FM208, flown by F/O Steve Gulyas, from Resolute Bay to Rockcliffe in 10:30 hours, then came an interlude navigating North Star 17510 from Dorval to and from Japan from April 4-21. This grind added 93:05 hours to his log.

F/O Saunders last flew with 408 on September 16, 1953, navigating FM217 on a weather recce from Rockcliffe to Sable Island and home in 10:30 hours. He now was posted to the CJATC, beginning flying on October 25 in photo Dakota KN511. He would fly often at Rivers, although his main job was lecturing in the Joint Air Photo Interpretation School. Since the CJATC also had C-119s, he devised a mount for a 9 x 9-inch aerial camera in the C-119 belly escape hatch. Whenever possible he crewed on C-119s, as on February 13, 1955 during a search for a missing B-47 in northern Manitoba. He was promoted to flight lieutenant in June 1955, while deployed to 4 ATAF at Trier, France, where he was augmenting 4 ATAF's photo interpretation unit during Ex. Carte Blanche.

In July 1957 Saunders was posted to CF-100s, training first on Mitchells in Winnipeg. His first CF-100 flight was in 18144 at Cold Lake on May 28. Being a senior navigator, he crewed with W/C W.M. Middleton, 425 Squadron's CO. They began operations at St. Hubert on August 8. In July 1960 Saunders was posted to Javelin F.A.W. 5s at 72 Squadron, RAF Leconfield. For this he crewed with F/L G.B. "Gerry" Smith, RCAF, whom he met aboard SS Sylvania as they sailed for England. Saunders and Smith began with the Javelin course at 228 OTU at RAF Leeming – four sorties for 4:10 hours. Saunders first flew at 72 Squadron on September 8 with S/L New, logging the trip as "Close and battle formation, cine and mutual PI's" (practice intercepts). F/L Saunders soon adapted to Fighter Command AI tactics. While the RCAF favoured lead-collision course tactics, the RAF preferred a stern attack. This worked, since a Javelin was faster than a CF-100 (a CF-100, however, had the advantage of range over a Javelin).

Although flying was good at 72 Squadron, there wasn't as much as in the RCAF, e.g. for October 1960 Saunders logged only 21:50 hours. On October 18 there was an emergency. He

Ill-fated Javelin FAW.9 XH791 en route Waterbeach-Istres in July 1961. (Saunders Col.)

was on his second sortie that night when, at 30,000 feet, he could not contact his pilot, F/O Pete Frewer. Since they were in a wide spiral toward the North Sea, Saunders called a mayday. Fighter procedures for such trouble obliged aircrew to eject on passing 10,000 feet, but Saunders persisted in calling on the R/T, rousing Frewer who responded groggily. Saunders convinced him to deploy his emergency bail-out oxygen bottle. Frewer's head cleared, he pulled out at 4000 feet and they landed. It turned out that Frewer had a stuck valve in his oxygen mask. For this good show Saunders was put up for a Queen's Commendation (not awarded).

When 72 Squadron disbanded in June 1961, Saunders and Smith joined 64 Squadron on F.A.W. 9s at Waterbeach. The squadron, however, deployed to Cyprus, so the Canadians were briefly attached to 25 Squadron in order to work up on the F.A.W.9. Saunders later went by Hastings to Cyprus, flying first there with F/L Gribble on June 2. In July he and F/L Ken Pye joined a flight comprising volunteers from several squadrons to ferry new F.A.W.9s to 60 Squadron at RAF Tengah, Singapore. The unit worked up at Waterbeach under F/L Ted Owens. Being more familiar with NDB/ADF procedures that would be encountered en route, Saunders and Pye were in the lead section, flying XA835. In September 2002 Saunders recalled:

On June 19, 1961 Britain relinquished the protectorate status over Kuwait, but would still give military aid. On June 26 Kuwait voted to oppose an Iraqi annexation plan, and on July 1 British troops landed in Kuwait to confront any Iraqi threat. Because of this, and considering the political sensitivities and the position of the UAR, we could not overfly Saudi Arabia, so would follow a route via Turkey and Iran. Meanwhile, Iran was not unsympathetic towards Iraq. Thus, when we flight planned from Tehran to Bahrain, we were told not use "Bahrain" in filing, but a fictitious destination, which simply was "Persian Gulf". This satisfied the Iranians. Nonetheless, one navigator, who had missed the briefing, did enter "Bahrain", causing a fuss with the Iranian Air Force.

Javelin Ferry Flight Waterbeach to Singapore

Date	To	Time
July		
25	Istres (France)	1:20
	Luqa (Malta)	1:25
26	El Adem (Libya)	1:10
26	Nicosia (Cyprus)	1:10
28	Diyarbakir (Turkey)	1:05
	Tehran (Iran)	1:15
29	Bahrain	1:15
	Sharja (Oman)	0:35
30	Masirah (Muskat)	1:00
	Karachi (West Pakistan)	1:20
	New Delhi (India)	1:30
August		
3	Varanassi/Banares (India) – via Hastings	
4	Calcutta (India)	1:10
5	Rangoon (Burma)	1:20
6	Bangkok (Thailand)	0:50
7	Butterworth (Malaya)	1:10
8	Tengah (Singapore)	0:50

Ferrying six Javelins half way around the world was ambitious, but Britain still was capable of such operations in those waning years of empire. The logistics were daunting, e.g. there had to be a friendly landing strip every 500–600 nm with fuel, food and lodging. Even with everything in place, no one was naïve enough to think that an operation would be easy. To begin, one Javelin was lost in a ground fire at Luqa. Then, at New Delhi, Saunders fell ill. He flew the next leg to Varanassi in the support Hastings. After a night's rest he continued with F/L Pye, flying

first to Dum Dum, Calcutta. While climbing out from there at 0535 on August 5, Saunders was watching F/L Owens' Javelin when it exploded. Owens pitched up, then disappeared into cloud. Saunders sent a mayday, then pressed on to Rangoon as lead. Meanwhile, F/L Owens and WO Tony Melton had ejected and descended into jungle in the Ganges delta. The locals were reluctant to enter this area for fear of tigers, but an American with an amphibious aircraft was near by. Co-ordinating with an RAF Shackleton, he taxied through the delta to rescue Melton, but F/L Owens had been killed parachuting into the trees.

The flight pressed on to Rangoon, then Bangkok, RAAF Butterworth and Singapore. Until they reached Butterworth on August 8, the crews had no knowledge of Owens' fate. At Tengah they handed over the Javelins to the OC 60 Squadron. However, before they could depart, there were two days of accident investigation. The ferry crews returned to the UK aboard a chartered Britannia. Saunders' first sortie back at Waterbeach was leading a section of Javelins in formation with some Hunters over Brighton in honour of the Dieppe raid. Normal duties resumed for Smith and Saunders. Since long-range strategic deployment was one of 64 Squadron's roles, there was arduous in-flight refuelling practice with Valiant tankers. Gunnery was also done in the following months, but not using all four Aden cannons. Only one pair was fired (to reduce airframe stress). All crews also did operational readiness standby.

Saunders' tour ended with a final sortie on August 7, 1962. In two years he had logged 282:05 Javelin hours. He returned to a staff job at ADC HQ, St. Hubert. Since his new field of interest was CF-104 pilot training, he took the ground school at Cold Lake. His log shows some flights in NASARR (North American Search and Ranging Radar) Dakotas 656 and KN278 (logged as "DC-104" time), and the occasional back seat ride in a CF-104. In 1964-65 S/L Saunders attended RCAF Staff College in Toronto, then served until 1969 at CF Staff School in Toronto. Next, he worked in NDHQ as the CF Records Officer, then spent a year with the International Commission for Control of Supervision (Paris Peace Treaty) in Saigon. He returned to NDHQ in September 1973, took his retirement in 1975, then was with the Treasury Board Secretariat until 1989. Meanwhile, he was active in volunteer work, mainly coaching amateur football.

Excerpts from F/L Alex Saunders' Diary

Waterbeach–Istres, France Tue 25 Jul 61 Departed Waterbeach after 40 minute delay due to u/s mike on my head set… On approach to Istres we attempted to contact them… RT was difficult to understand.

Istres–Luqa, Malta Tue 25 Jul 61… Turn around at Luqa good… DME had a power failure, so no use from that aid coming in.

Luqa–El Adem, Libya 26 Jul 61… supposed to leave Luqa with XH840 and XH791. XH840 had had a starter change and waited for us. However, after several cartridges had been fired, F/L Botsford had a go and the port side blew up and damaged the starboard engine in the explosion. Category 4. Departure from Luqa good, straight climb out. Leader still having VHF difficulty. Ventrals emptied in 19 minutes. At El Adem we landed on Rwy 33 … a lot of sand, but visibility was still okay.

Adem–Nicosia, Cyprus 26 Jul 61 Another S11 was carried out on the three a/c for cracks in the tail pipes. Departure okay except … a lot of sand blown up by #1 & #2 on take-off affecting visibility for #3. Navigation aids good … Cyprus DMEs poor. Checked through customs–no problems.

27 Jul 61 Took bus to Kyrenia with Ken Pye and Bob Lockhart… Up at 0500. Breakfast 0515. Transport 0545. Met briefing 0600. Take Off 0700.

28 Jul 61… Two a/c failed to start and one had a suspected hydraulic leak… F/L Ted Owens, decided to recall the Hastings which had already departed for Diyarbakir … rest of the day was spent swimming and doing laundry.

Nicosia–Diyarbakir–Tehran 29 Jul 61 All five Javelins departed on time at 0700 hrs and set off … Hastings was there to meet us and turn around took about 1¾ hours. The Turkish Air Force was very hospitable and served us tea. While there I met a Turkish Air Force pilot who had trained in Canada. The flight to Tehran was good … standard of English was good. The hotel accommodation and meals were arranged by BOAC and were fine. I called the Canadian Embassy and was invited to dinner with Mr. Alex Brodie of Trade & Commerce Dept.

Tehran–Bahrain–Sharja 30 Jul 61 Bloody Iranians beat us up a bit – a screw up! Departed Tehran at 1000 hrs and arrived at Bahrain at 1115hrs. Temp was 135°F. Two of the a/c were delayed at Tehran and arrived at 1700 hrs. Use was made of a Canberra as a wx recce a/c… Departure from Bahrain was delayed until the other a/c arrived. At 1700 hrs the first three left for Sharjah … followed an hour later by the other 2. Landing was carried out on a sand strip which was very bumpy. The second pair landed at night. Swimming in a salt water pool … local Sheik flogged a guy this afternoon, poor bugger!

Sharjah–Masirah 31 Jul 61 Departed Sharjah for Masirah at about 0800 hrs. Having to use the temporary runway caused a great deal of dust. At Masirah the reception was very good. This is a very small unit commanded by a RAF S/L. He met each a/c and gave the crew a can of cold beer… The natives are Arabs of the Sultan of Muscat, and appear to be very poorly housed and seemingly kept that way by the local Sheik. Refuelling the 5 Javelins and Canberra weather recce a/c was a time-consuming task because the tender had to be filled from 45 gallon drums by hand and each drum had to be filtered…

Masirah–Karachi 31 Jul 61 Good trip… Reception at the airport was fairly quick and no problems… Capt Michael P. Sullivan [USMC exchange officer, later 2 tours flying F-4s in Vietnam, Marine Aviator of the Year 1974, retired as a major general] and I were singled out by customs and treated to an air conditioned waiting room and offered tea. The special treatment was apparently offered to "former colonials" … accommodation was arranged at the Palace, an older 1st class establishment with recently installed air conditioning…

Karachi–Delhi (Palam) India 1 Aug 61 The departure from Karachi was okay except I nearly lost my camera… Our hotel, the Ashoka, was near the airport and in the midst of foreign embassies. A luxurious place… Mike Sullivan and I visited the U.S. Embassy in the evening… We had planned to hire a car and drive to Agra to see the Taj Mahal, but the monsoon rains prevented that… In the evening I was quite ill from something I had eaten… My treatment at the Ashoka was perfect and my discomfort was overcome quickly.

Delhi–Varanassi (Banares) 3 Aug 61 Got up feeling fine. This leg was made in the Hastings support a/c and took about 2 hours. Pete Botsford and Mac MacMillan took the Javelin (XH835) to keep their hand in and have some relief from being spare crew having lost their a/c in Malta. Upon arrival at Varanassi one Javelin was u/s for radios and was fixed in about 2 hours. The plan then was to proceed to Dum Dum at Calcutta. Three a/c got away and the second section of two had to remain due first to a no-start on one, then generator failure on the other. The no-start was fixed immediately, while the generator necessitated a night stop… The hotel (Clark's) was good … atmosphere was "Empire" revisited. The poverty … is increasing as we go east across India. Appalling! How can a people, who purport to be so sensitive and feeling in their religion, be so much the direct opposite in practice. It is beyond understanding!

Varanassi (Banares)–Calcutta 4 Aug 61 I substituted for Bill Meads (who has sinusitis) and flew with Gerry Shipley … weather conditions were bad and close formation was flown the whole way (45 mins). After arriving and clearing Customs we were driven to our hotel, the Grand (which it is). On the way I guess we saw the poorest human beings imaginable in the world … it was raining a virtual down-pour, yet some seemed too weak to notice. Later, as the rain increased, the street outside the hotel was flooded to about 2 feet… Ken Pye and Bill Meads had to wade in their bare feet … to get

from their cab to the hotel desk! The airmen had to walk to their hotel sometimes up to their necks in water. The amazing part of it was … that all that water drained away in about two hours… In the evening the entire flight was invited to dinner as guests of an American couple staying in the hotel.

Calcutta–Rangoon 5 Aug 61 On leaving the hotel in the morning, carts were being driven by with … bodies of people who had been unable to keep their heads above the water in the monsoon deluge the previous afternoon. Well, this has been a very black day! Ted Owens and Tony Melton crashed in Javelin XH791. We were twelve minutes out of Dum Dum airport climbing through 31,000 feet. I was just taking a fix when Ken Pye drew my attention to what appeared to be ice on Ted's pitot tube looking like a fluorescent tube – a curiosity. He was #1 and we were #3 (on his port side) in a tight 3-plane formation with Gerry Shipley in #2 with Benny Baranowski his navigator. At that instant XH791 pitched up sharply and towards us simultaneous with a "magenta" coloured burst about 2 meters behind and to the right of the rear cockpit. He then pitched forward and down, disappearing with no radio contact at all. I saw two white helmets flash under us as we pulled up and away from

Bound for 60 Squadron and one hop to go – Javelins rest at Butterworth.

them, and then it was gone. We transmitted a MAYDAY and considered it best to press on to Rangoon. The weather could not have been worse – cloud from 2000' to 45,000' … at Rangoon the British Air Attaché met us. Preliminary reports were given and we then went into the city and found a reasonable hotel. In the afternoon 3 of us visited the Schwe Dagon pagoda …

Rangoon–Bangkok 6 Aug 61 Departed Rangoon – no trouble. We are now flying in two sections of two aircraft. Ken Pye is flight commander. Had to delay departure due to heavy rain at Bangkok, reported by wx recce Canberra. Arrival Bangkok no problem … Br. Air Attaché … arranged to meet us for drinks at hotel. His home & then to a night club. What a clip joint. Mike Sullivan & I escaped after 1 drink each and propositions from bar girls. What a bill for one drink each!

Bangkok–Butterworth 7 Aug 61 Departure went well. En route from Bangkok to Butterworth we encountered some serious CB's, but avoided them with the AI radar. Radio compass affected but no problem… Arrived RAAF Butterworth 0945 and well received by Australians. Monsoon hit at about 1030 hrs. Rained for five hours… Met "Red" Henderson in the Officers' Mess reading room. He is now in the RAAF as a Canberra navigator. Quite a surprise bumping into him in Malaya 18 months since I last saw him in St. Hubert. We enjoyed a small "thrash" with the Aussies and good sing song. They found Tony – broken back and badly cut knees, but otherwise okay…

Butterworth–Tengah 8 Aug 61 Good departure from Butterworth in AM. Both sections joined up approaching Tengah and flew past low – 4 out of 6 must have disappointed them. A grand reception, beer in hand down the ladder. Many old 72 Sqn buddies … nice reunion. One last look at our aircraft. Compared to being factory fresh at the start … they are now weather beaten, sand blasted and a bit tired. Most of the camouflage paint is off the leading edges to about 3' back. A few dints from ice and hail, a cracked wind screen. Nice to have made it! Seems we will be sitting about on call for the Board of Inquiry. Tony is here now in Changi Hospital. We'll see him tomorrow …

9 Aug 61 Board of Inquiry is on, much sitting around. Decided to stand by at pool, much better. Went shopping. Leaving tomorrow … Changi, Bombay, UK (Stanstead). As the senior officer of the remaining "ferry flight" I was paraded before the Station Commander RAF Tengah to answer questions related to our time in Bangkok. Apparently some of the officers and men of the ferry flight "busted up" the night club in Bangkok a bit… CO informed me that the Air Attaché had settled the costs with the owner and suggested that some recompense was due. I disagreed and sought refuge in that I was not a RAF officer and, as I had left the scene earlier, I should certainly not be held accountable. I made a stinging rebuttal in pointing out that the Air Attaché had in fact taken us there… Nothing further came of the situation, so "all's well that ends well". We returned to the UK on a BUA charter, mainly hired for British military dependents… At Bombay there was a six hour delay due to an unserviceability of some kind. It was quite a discomfort to all the children and mothers in the un-air conditioned waiting area. About a dozen Ghurkas neatly turned out in blazers and gray flannels sat silent and stoic through the whole time … great to land back close to home at Stanstead. So ended our epic… Unknown to me, our wives had not received a casualty notice about who was not involved in the crash of XH791 and were still in an anxious state …

XA660, shown in 137 Squadron markings at RAF Leeming, was the first Javelin flown by F/L M.O. Aller, once he began his RAF exchange in August 1958. (Air-Britain via Roger Lindsay)

Supersonic Lightning

First Exchange

Several RCAF pilots were on the English Electric Lightning interceptor. First flown in August 1954 as the experimental P.1, this was Britain's first design capable of supersonic speed in level flight. In April 1958 the Lightning Mk.1 flew – 50 feet long, 34-foot wing span, all-up weight 40,000 lb, twin 30-mm cannons in the nose plus two Firestreak AAMs. Engines were two Rolls-Royce Avons each of 11,250-lb thrust (14,430 in reheat), enough to assure Mach 1.7 (Mach 2 exceeded on January 6, 1959). The first Canadian on Lightnings was F/L Terry Thompson. Born in Edmonton, he worked in banking after finishing high school. In 1951 he joined the RCAF, training as a radar operator. In 1953 he remustered to pilot, earning his Wings in February 1954. He flew CF-100s with 409 Squadron in Comox, then went on exchange in 1961, converting to the Lightning and serving with 56 Squadron at RAF Wattisham, Suffolk. In 1963 he was part of his squadron's "Firebirds" aerobatic team. Thompson describes this period in his 2004 biography *Warriors and the Battle Within*.

Lightning Weapons Development

Also on Lightnings was Alan Marwood Robb. By scrutinizing his records, we can see how he won such a dream posting. The son of a dentist, Al Robb

grew up in Winnipeg. On December 31, 1949 he joined the RCAF and the following April was on Course 17 at Centralia. There he chummed with such flight cadets as Len Bentham, Ralph Biggar, Garth Cinnamon, Denny den Ouden, Swede Evjen, Bob Morgan and Wes McEwen – lads who would make their names on Sabres. F/C Robb first flew on March 6, 1950 in Harvard 3034 with F/O Wilson. He departed Centralia with 230 hours, was at AAS in Trenton in December/January, then advanced to Chatham. There he flew Vampire 17066 on March 5, 1951 – his first jet. OTU ended on May 21, Robb being posted to 410 at St. Hubert. At Dorval on June 20 he made his first Sabre flight.

In October, 410 embarked for North Luffenham in the UK – home of newly-formed

No. 56 SQUADRON

"The Firebirds"

ROYAL AIR FORCE
FIGHTER COMMAND

Squadron pilots: F/Ls Terry Thompson, Robert Offord and Henryk Ploszek. Then, the cover of 56 Squadron's 1963 "Firebirds" demo team brochure. (Thompson Col.)

XM147, carrying Firestreaks, was the Lightning on which F/L Robb soloed on September 23, 1964. Roger Lindsay photographed it at Mildenhall in May 1969, when it had the name "Felix" and the emblem on the tail of Wattisham's Target Facilities Flight. XM147 went for scrap in 1994.

No. 1 (RCAF) Air Division. Arrived in Scotland, Robb's first task was to test Sabre 19149 at Renfrew (Glasgow) on December 8, 1951, then he delivered it to "North Luff". Daily routines now occupied 410. July 1952 was a typical month for Robb – 18 sorties for 21:15 hours. There were constant exercises – "Ardent", "Coronet", "Fabulous" with 410 fighting Meteors and Vampires, and intercepting B-29s, B-45s, B-50s and Canberras.

Pilots at 410 became notorious for their capers, including (so the legend goes) F/Os Haran and den Ouden rousting the Duke of Edinburgh from his horse during a low-level "exercise" over Sandringham, a Royal estate. For their sins, Haran served a month as orderly officer; den Ouden got 15 days. Legend also tells of an RAF wing commander at Linton-on-Ouse chiding 410 about Sabres not being truly supersonic. Figured 410, "we shall see." On November 28, 1952 the matter was settled as 12 Sabres appeared over the wingco's base. They peeled off one by one, put the 'drome in their gun sights, then "boomed" the place – 12 times. The wingco was humbled, yet, like any good RAF type, was decent about things. Even though there was broken glass in local green houses, 410 was off the hook. Another time, 410 was on E&E. Al Robb and Frank Sylvester paired in the challenge. After dark they were accosted by a policeman, split and ran, "Sly" fording a river, which stymied his pursuer. Taking refuge in a horse barn, Robb could see himself riding triumphantly to the

exercise "safe point" aboard a great steed, but reason prevailed and he returned on foot. The first RCAF Sabre aerobatic team, formed at 410 in October 1952, included Grant Nichols (lead), Al Robb and Garth Cinnamon (wingmen) and Len Bentham (box). By the end of July 1953, Robb's log showed nearly 800 hours, 387:45 on Sabres. On Ex. Momentum (August 15-23, 1953) he flew 18 sorties, 5 each on the 16th and 19th.

Experience in this era showed that RCAF Sabre pilots still lacked in instrument flying skills. To rectify this, the Air Division formed its Instrument Rating Flight under S/L Ken Lett at 3 (F) Wing in Zweibrucken. In January 1954 Al Robb, who earlier had done an instrument course at North Bay, was posted to the IRF with Ralph Annis, Rocky Paquette, Chuck Steacy, etc. He first flew there on January 5, 1954, going up with S/L Lett in 21018. Soon he was swamped, logging 66:45 hours on 48 sorties in August alone. The IRF pushed through every Sabre pilot in the Air Division. Little wonder that Canadians soon were touted as NATO's ace fighter pilots. Meanwhile, the capers continued, e.g. on May 7, 1954 the Air Division pulled one of its great flubs. That day a flypast was organized for the Chief of the Air Staff – 96 Sabres and 4 T-33s. Al Robb was in a T-bird with LAW Morin. Leading was a senior type who was a bit rusty. At some point he realized that his timing was off – the whole formation would be early. Solution? Without thinking, Lead called "Speed brakes". Wham … speed brakes popped all over the place, and aircraft began falling out of the sky. The CAS must have wondered what had happened to NATO's hottest pilots!

In November 1954 F/L Robb was posted to Chatham to instruct on Sabres and, in November 1956, began a ground tour as Chief AdminO at Foymount, a Pinetree Line station. From here he did his practice flying from Ottawa. To show how keen people used to be (forget about such skits in today's air force), on the weekend of May 23-25 F/L Robb with his CO, W/C Woolfenden, flew T-bird 21519 to Winnipeg (3:05 hours), Lethbridge (1:55), Vancouver (1:30), Cold Lake (1:50), Winnipeg (1:50), ending in Chatham (3:15). They were on duty at Foymount first thing Monday morning. In January 1961 Robb did a T-33 refresher at 3 AFS, Gimli. This led to CF-100 training (Course 100) at Cold Lake, where he first flew on March 21, then soloed next day. He and his nav, F/O Chuck Verge, were posted in July to 413 Squadron at Bagotville. But the CF-100 now was "over the hill" and on October 25 F/L Robb had his first Voodoo famil ride, Capt Rhonald D. Iverson (USMC) of the 75th FIS flying him at Dow AFB in 57-421.

On January 1, 1961, 413 Squadron became 416 under W/C Dean Kelly, whose boys began converting to Voodoos with 425 at Namao. F/L Robb flew initially on January 4 in 17478 with F/L Dave Hook. His OTU time was 28:05 hours, then he and F/O Verge joined 416 in Bagotville, where they first flew on February 5. That month Robb logged 15:30 Voodoo hours (trips averaged 1:35 hours), 5:25 on the T-bird. On October 14, 1961 416 flew in Ex. Skyshield III, with all North American airspace closed to civil traffic for a huge simulated war. On November 16, 1962, the squadron left Bagotville for Chatham, arriving there *en masse*.

All along, Al Robb had been requesting an exchange, but with no luck until December 1963, when he got the word. He flew his final 416 trip on July 2, 1964. Soon, Al and Shirley Robb and their three children left Canada by North Star. They landed in Grostenquin, then flew to the UK aboard an RCAF Bristol Freighter. F/L Robb joined Course 16 (Lightnings) at RAF Coltishall, flying first on August 31 in T.4 XM996 with F/L Harrison. After five hours dual, Robb soloed in a T.4 on September 22. Next day he flew single seat Mk.1 XM147. Total time for September was 13:55 hours in 20 sorties, plus 11 simulator sessions. F/L Robb now began a tour at the Central Fighter Establishment, Air Fighting Development Squadron at RAF Binbrook, flying initially on December 21 in a Lightning F. Mk.3.

CFE's Lightning trials unit had 4 RAF pilots, 1 RCAF and 1 USAF (Capt Dale Zimmerman, later Capt Bill Beardsley). Since the RAF kept posting its own pilots, the exchange types became development pilots for the Red Top IR missile, Firestreak's replacement. Trials almost exclusively involved supersonic flight. Pilots wore a standard G-suit and, for missions above 50,000 feet, a partial-pressure suit from neck to waist, and a Taylor pressure helmet. Typically, GCI would guide a Lightning towards its target which, at about 30 nm, a pilot would see on his scope. He would steer towards it, using the dot on the scope, while monitoring his flight instruments from the corner of an eye. Might such work have been easier with an AI navigator? Perhaps, but experience showed that solo Lightning pilots became very good in AI.

F/L Robb's log shows that Lightning flights were short until the F.6 appeared. Sorties of 40-45 minutes were usual, but afterburner shortened these further. A typical trip had the pursuing Lightning streaking towards its target (another Lightning) at Mach 1.3–1.8. The target (usually on-coming) also was supersonic. This scenario was aimed at perfecting Red Top as a weapon specifically to counter the new Tupolev Tu-22 Blinder, a Mach 1.5 Soviet bomber first flown in 1959 and much feared

A typical Tu-22 Blinder, the Soviet bomber most feared by NATO in the 1960s and, to counter which, the Red Top was especially designed. (CANAV Col.)

XP696 with Red Tops at RAF Finningley in September 1974. F/L Robb flew this F.3 on AFDS trials at RAF Binbrook. It had been delivered in 1963, as the Javelin was leaving service. (Roger Lindsay)

regular RAF/NATO exercises. During Ex. Embellish in early 1966 Robb flew against an F-100, F-4 and Vulcan. On January 10, 1966 he flew an F.6 for the first time, taking XR753 on a 1:50-hour single-engine endurance flight. With bigger ventral tanks, improved engine and cambered wings, the F.6 made a difference in Fighter Command. Besides Lightnings, AFDS flew Hunters; Robb checked out on this type at Chivenor in March 1965.

F/L Robb's most exciting time at AFDS came when he had his chance to launch a Firestreak. This was done from RAF Valley, starting on June 2, 1965. The missile would be fired low level in a 2-G manoeuvre (defence against low-flying Blinders had to be perfected). The target was a flare trailing a 23-foot, pilotless Jindivik drone (built in Australia to UK specs, first flown 1950). Ideally, the IR Firestreak would lock onto the flare. A Lightning cine camera would cover the event, as would a camera on the

by NATO. On a Red Top sortie, pursuer and target flew a profile across a 130-mile range. With closing speeds exceeding Mach 3, there was no room for error. For an IR lock on the target, Red Top used heat generated from the target's skin. If a missile failed to acquire IR lock, the pilot could sweep around for a stern attack, gaining a lock-on from jet pipe heat. If fuel permitted, a second run was tried. One or two sorties were flown each weekday. With every trip the program was refined and the Lightning fire control system was tweaked. On a typical intercept, F/L Robb would talk his way through each phase, recording his patter. The tape, along with cine film and various telemetry would be analyzed by the boffins. AFDS pilots would attend technical meetings along with MoD and Fighter Command personnel and contractors such as de Havilland and Ferranti.

On August 25, 1965, Robb flew Lightning F.3 XP695, his log entry reading: "Trial 360 M. 1.8 47,000". For November 2 he noted: "Firebrigade I, M. 1.5, Vulcan 55,000". Attacks on such overhead targets were launched in snap-ups from 36,000 feet (as with the Voodoo). Two days later Robb flew twice, logging 8 minutes at Mach 1.5, then 9 minutes at 1.5. AFDS also flew on

Major A.M. Robb: Flying Time	
Type	Hours
Harvard	226
Expeditor	107
Vampire	60
T-33	1927
F-86	845
CF-100	225
CF-101	1362
Lightning	421
Hunter	61

Al and Shirley Robb at home in Comox, BC in March 2002. (Larry Milberry)

Jindivik looking back at the flare. On June 2 Robb flew a 45-minute sortie in F.3 XP696, but the target was not acquired. Next day he flew 40 minutes, but did not fire due to "Insufficient G". There was no joy next day, due to "Poor control". Finally, came success later that day: "2.6G, fire, good missile", the Jindivik being at 100 feet, the Lightning firing from below 500 feet.

In February 1966 AFDS became the Fighter Command Trials Unit. Robb, by now a squadron leader and with his tour waning, was invited to extend for a year in the Red Top program. RCAF HQ concurred, then recanted. On June 6, 1967 Robb flew his last Lightning sortie, then returned to Canada. By this time he had 421:15 Lightning hours, 60:45 on the Hunter. On leaving FCTU, his CO, S/L John Vickery, inscribed Robb's log: "Many thanks, Al, for your excellent work." Simple RAF stuff, but that said it all. The Robbs, whose fourth child had been born in the UK, now spent four years on a NORAD posting in North Bay. Next, Al was base flight safety officer and test pilot at Comox. For his last flight, he took Voodoo 101012 aloft on July 30, 1971, then retired after more than 26 years in uniform. The Robbs settled in Comox, where Al worked in real estate. Subsequently, the Robbs were active in the Comox Officers Mess and 888 Wing RCAF Association, supported the Comox Air Force Museum, and operated the Levenvale bed and breakfast, famous worldwide for its quality. In 1988 Al teamed with a number of Comox area ex-Sabre pilots in founding SPAADS – the Sabre Pilots Association of the Air Division Squadrons.

With 111 Squadron

Raised in Sackville, NB, J. Robert Chisholm joined the RCAF in 1953 through the military college plan, which allowed a candidate to study through the school year and train in summer. Thus did Bob Chisholm find himself at Penhold for his first Harvard ride on July 18, 1955. He finished training the next summer, having 130 Harvard hours. Next came the T-33 at Portage-la-Prairie (February 5, 1957 to April 23). Jet instrument training followed at Saskatoon, then he got the ideal posting for any RCAF sprog, whose dream was to fly the Avro Arrow. On July 8, 1957 he took off with instructor F/L Abell in CF-100 18138 at 3 AW (F) OTU. Soon he crewed with F/O Gerry St-Arnaud. Later, they joined 432 Squadron at Bagotville, where Chisholm first flew on October 26. He would spend more than 5 years here before getting word of a Lightning exchange. His last 432 flight was with

F/L J.R. Chisholm (right) with S/L G. Black of 111 Squadron. (PL-144168 DND)

F/O Norm Grondin in CF-100 18640 on April 9, 1963.

F/L Chisholm commenced flying on the Hunter T.7 at 229 OCU at RAF Chivenor on May 22. Lasting to the 30th, this involved 11:20 flying hours, but the course was needed, since the Hunter was used by Lightning squadrons as an instrument trainer. Chisholm now was posted to 111 Squadron at Wattisham, where he had a familiarization flight in a Lightning T.4 on June 10. After three such flights he proceeded to 226 Conversion Squadron at Middleton, flying first in a T.4 on July 15. OCU totalled 8:05 hours on 11 sorties, plus 10 simulator exercises.

With a Lightning in its natural element (the faster the better), new pilots found it to be a dream, if not perfect. The Lightning had a small cockpit, the layout of which was not user friendly. Accustomed to the CF-100, Chisholm had to adjust to other Lightning traits. Approach to land was at 165-170 knots with power on all the way. Wheels touched at 150 knots (about 110 for a CF-100). With Wattisham having only 7000 feet of runway, landings were challenging in wet conditions, especially if the drag 'chute failed and full brakes were needed.

Chisholm returned to 111 Squadron on July 29, 1963 taking a T.4 flight that day with his OC, S/L Wirdnam. He soloed in the F.1A two days later, then got into daily routines, including GCIs on such targets as Canberras. Lightnings frequently would fight one on one, and affiliation with V-bombers offered Bomber Command the chance to practice fighter evasion and ECM. Mission planning was exacting, especially since (within 45 minutes of takeoff) pilots had to complete at least two intercepts, plus a GCA or an ILS approach. UK weather often being near limits and, because of short range, there always was a Lightning pilot in the Wattisham tower to monitor aerodrome status and weather, and advise lest diverting be prudent. Fortunately, Wattisham had three local USAFE bases. This permitted hand-overs from one GCA controller to another for a low fuel emergency. Nearby USAFE Weathersfield was 200 feet lower than Wattisham, which meant a higher cloud ceiling, should Wattisham go below limits.

Periodically, 111 refuelled from Valiant tankers. Chisholm flew his first such on February 3, 1964, remaining aloft for 1:35 hours. Next day he flew two more AR sorties. The squadron practiced night AR and even refuelled

The 111 Squadron Lightning demo team with the Red Arrows, flying Gnats, during a sortie from Wattisham of June 4, 1965. (Peter M. Warren/Chisholm Col.)

in cloud! There also were low-level, over-water intercepts, with targets down to 500 feet. Such intercepts (where Chisholm learned that the Lightning's Ferranti AI radar was superior to the CF-100's Hughes set) rarely lasted more than 30 minutes, due to fuel consumption.

On May 1, 1964 Chisholm had a famil ride in an F-100F from Weathersfield. In honour of the Queen's birthday, there was a fly-past of 16 Lightnings over Buckingham Palace on June 6. On this occasion Chisholm piloted XR713. In January 1965 the F.3 began reaching 111. With more power and a larger fin, it was a Mach 2 fighter, compared to Mach 1.7 for the F.1A. For January 15, 1965 Chisholm's log shows a 35-minute Mach 1.5 flight to 60,000 feet.

Firestreak-armed Lightning F.1A XM184 of 111 Squadron during an April 1964 photo shoot at Wattisham. This aircraft was damaged beyond repair in a landing accident at Coltishall on April 17, 1967. Corgi later produced a 1:72 scale diecast model of XM184, while Airfix offered a Lightning plastic kit with XM184 (111 Sqn decals). (PL-144174 DND)

F/L Chisholm does his walk-around before a Lightning T.4 sortie. (PL-144162 DND)

On the 18th he took an F.3 to Mach 2 on a 40-minute sortie. Another F.3 bonus was its more comfortable cockpit. One thing not practiced with the F.1A was firing the 30-mm Aden cannons. Word was that the airframe was not fully stressed for the Adens. Only after 111 converted to the F.3, did pilots do any firing with the F.1A (this was considered acceptable since the F.1A's were leaving frontline service). On January 30,

F/L Chisholm often flew F.3 XR713 (in the formation photo on page 114 he is flying it as No. 2 on Lead's starboard wing). Armed with Red Tops, XR713 is seen at Lakenheath on August 18, 1973. One of many preserved Lightnings, it sits today at RAF Leuchars. (P.J. Cooper via Roger Lindsay)

1965 four Lightnings (Chisholm included) flew overhead as the barge carrying the remains of Sir Winston Churchill passed down the Thames.

For April 23, 1965 Chisholm was in a 5-plane scramble with three Lightnings leading, closely followed by two others. For the month his log shows 23 flying hours, a bit low by RCAF standards, where longer Voodoo sorties prevailed. About this time the Valiant retired, being temporarily replaced by USAF KC-135s with refuelling booms modified to RAF "probe and drogue" configuration – a hose was fixed to the boom. To get fuel, a Lightning had to engage the basket at the end of the hose, pushing it forward to create a particular bend (only then would fuel flow). For April 27 Chisholm noted that, in trying to engage the basket, he had broken a probe. In May 1965 he was part of 111 Squadron's famous 9-plane diamond formation. On June 4 the Red Arrows, flying Gnats, formed up with 111's diamond. The squadron practiced its diamond for several days, then departed on June 15 for the Paris Airshow. On September 18 a 9-plane Battle of Britain formation was put up over Biggin Hill.

During Chisholm's exchange 111 Squadron deployed to Denmark and France, but the highlight was three trips to Akrotiri, Cyprus. For Chisholm this totalled five months and included much operational flying. In April 2002, however, he recalled

how policy restricted Lightnings on Cyprus. While alert aircraft would have their cannons armed, mechanically, they could not fire; neither could their Firestreaks. This was unknown to the Greeks and Turks. On July 19, 1966 F/L Chisholm strapped into a Lightning for the last time, then flew XR714 for 1:30 hours on an AR sortie in bad weather. With 621:55 Lightning hours, he was posted as Senior Staff Officer (Flight Safety) to ADC HQ in North Bay. Staff College in Toronto followed, then he took a new tack – helicopter flying. By July 1973 he commanded 403 (TacHel) Squadron in Gagetown. From September 1976 he worked under Col R.D. Schultz at the Directorate of Flight Safety in Ottawa, then succeeded his boss in 1977. Subsequently, Chisholm was Base Commander Comox, then Deputy Commander (later Commander) 10 TAG. In 1987 he was Deputy Commander AIRCOM in Winnipeg. MGen Bob Chisholm retired in 1990 to pursue a career in the aerospace industry.

Herb Karras

F/L Herb Karras, Bob Chisholm's replacement, flew Lightnings from April 1966 to July 1968. By the time he joined 111 he already had some 1400 jet hours, mainly on CF-100s at 409 Squadron. Nonetheless, converting to the Lightning, with its initial climb rate of 50,000 feet per minute, was a startling performance leap compared to a "Clunk". Karras recalled of the Lightning: "You could go supersonic in cold power by lowering the nose a bit to get there, then flying straight and level. Any manoeuvring at high speed required afterburners. I went Mach 2 once, just to say that I had gone 20 miles a minute. Normally we were restricted to Mach 1.6 on account of the refuelling probe that usually was fitted." Lightning operations were not without excitement. Karras, for example, had more than one undercarriage "situation":

Herb Karras while a junior RCAF flying officer. (PL-142144 DND)

In a wheels-up landing there was danger that a Lightning, with its high wing, might flip. Consequently, we took any unsafe gear indication seriously. When the undercarriage was down and locked, three green lights illuminated on the instrument panel. As the gear cycled down or up, three red lights appeared, indicating unsafe. When the gear was fully retracted, all lights were out. Should an unsafe indication occur, there would be enough fuel left for only one overshoot and, perhaps, a large circuit. In that time a pilot would keep the tower informed, while attempting to get the offending wheel down and locked.

Each time that I came in with an unsafe indication, I was met by a fire truck and ambulance. I would shut down my engines and climb down, leaving the ground crew to insert the safety pins (ejection seat, canopy, etc.) and tow the aircraft. On January 31, 1968, however, I had a more serious problem. After a night sortie, flying as target for F/L Bruce MacDonald, we returned to base, flew an overshoot, then set up for individual landings. When my speed got down to 250 knots, I lowered the gear. You normally could hear the wheels come down – three clunks. Not this time – I heard only two clunks, and the right gear was indicating red. With minimum fuel, I realized that the situation had to be resolved, or else I'd be bailing out. Our procedure was that, if possible, a pilot would eject over the English Channel, then the aircraft would fall into the water. But the thought of ejecting into the Channel on a windy night did nothing for my morale.

As I flew the first circuit, I recycled the gear, talked to Bruce and advised the tower. Recycling did no good, so the thought of ejecting came to mind – I tightened my parachute straps. Now I called the tower to say that I would be selecting emergency undercarriage. This worked – as I turned downwind, I was greatly relieved to see three greens, and soon was safe on the runway. I heard next day that, on selecting undercarriage "up", the right undercarriage door had closed before the gear had retracted. In that configuration, I was told, only by selecting "emergency" would the gear have dropped.

On April 18, 1967, Karras was returning from a scramble in XP762, when he had an unsafe brake pressure indication. Would there be enough pressure to stop? To play it safe, Wattisham diverted him to USAFE Bentwaters, which had a longer runway. To save fuel Karras shut down an engine and soon was on the runway, popping his drag 'chute, and braking normally. He parked, shut down, secured the cockpit, then slid down off a wing. At this point he spotted a hydraulic fluid leak, advised the Americans that he had live missiles on board, then headed to Base Ops to call Wattisham with an update. His CO, W/C Hall, would despatch a mobile repair party, so Karras headed into the Officers Club for beer call, planning to return to Wattisham with the repair crew. Other than having to sweat it out in his immersion suit, he had fun until summoned to the bar, where the officer "i/c repair party" announced that XP762 was ready to go! Karras called W/C Hall, who was delighted that he soon would have his Lightning back. But Karras had to stall, telling his boss that he had just ordered a steak, then heading off to find the coffee. By about 2200 hours he was strapping into XP762:

The Americans had a good relationship with the local population around Bentwaters. In part, this was maintained by keeping night flying to a minimum – noise abatement! On this occasion, however, I couldn't resist temptation. Normally, a Lightning takeoff was done in cold power, afterburners usually being reserved for scrambles. Tonight, as I lined up on the runway, I didn't just push the power up to 100% – I continued into full 'burners. Suddenly, XP762 shot down the runway, the booming noise "waking the dead", as exhaust flames lit up the 'drome. Up and away at 175 knots, I came out of 'burners and quickly levelled at 2000 feet in what was a murky sky.

When I changed channels to Wattisham radar, the response was intermittent and weak. My controller seemed to be miles away. Terrible thoughts flashed through my mind – little things can snowball, and an accident investigation board would have a field day if I blew this one. Suddenly, the controller came through. I flew a couple of GCAs and overshoots, gear down all the time. On the third GCA my weight was within limits, so down I came. On the tarmac was W/C Hall, happy to see us safely home. Soon I was cycling home, looking forward to getting out of my immersion suit after 17 hours!

Fighter Command annually checked the readiness of each Lightning squadron. On such occasions No. 1 and No. 2 Alert (armed) Lightnings, backed up by three groundcrew, sat a 5-minute alert. Here was the chance for a pilot to fire a Firestreak and on October 17, 1967 this fell to 111 Squadron. F/L Karras, No. 1 Alert for the day, was scrambled with vectors to the range at Valley, 35 minutes away. As the air weapons controller manoeuvred a target drone, Karras watched on his radar scope, while keeping half an eye on his fuel. As he chased down the drone at 34,000 feet, he realized that the target was above. At first he received an intermittent signal, but that increased to a strong, steady tone – good for a radar lock and a probable "kill":

Permission was received from the control officer to fire. I rolled level and squeezed the trigger. My first thought was that the missile was about to drop into the ocean, then it took off, leaving a trail of smoke. Within moments there was an explosion, as it hit a flare towed by the drone. I think I was lucky that day, for the flares only burned for 30 seconds, and I had eaten up most of that in manoeuvring and waiting for a solid tone. Had the flare fizzled, my missile would have hit the drone itself, making me unpopular with the drone crew. For security reasons I did not broadcast my "kill". Now, with fuel dwindling, I landed at Valley for a quick turn-around and return to Wattisham. On departure, I thought about the OTU student pilots on course at Valley. They rarely got to see a Lightning do an afterburner takeoff. Again, I couldn't resist – if the students didn't see my takeoff that day, they certainly heard it!

One of the great occasions in air force life is the mess dinner, an affair that usually features VIPs, speechifying, feasting, drinking and, in due course, singing, skits, pranks, sometimes worse. Certainly, in the "good old days", it was common for the partying to last until sun rise. In Herb Karras' opinion, his best mess dinner was at RAF Leuchars, Scotland, in 1967. At the time 111 was on detachment at this busy Lightning station, home to 11 and 23 squadrons. After a day on alert in the QRA (quick reaction area), Karras and a Rhodesian pilot, Rory Downes, started preparing for the mess dinner. First came a foray into Dundee, looking for water pistols. In 2003 Karras described what followed:

Normally, a Mess Dinner is quite proper, at least until after the toast to the Queen. Not this time for, as soon as the Mess President opened the dining room doors, all hell broke loose. As we proceeded to our seats, the Station band gave a dreadful rendition of the RAF March Past. Immediately, projectiles, fire crackers and streams of water came forth from the 23 Squadron tables – the fellows were well armed!

When this outburst subsided, each man stood behind his chair, as the padre said grace. Then we all sat, all except some 23 Squadron lads whose chairs earlier had been tied together by unknown saboteurs – 111 was suspected. After pulling against each other for a few seconds, the two young officers realized that they'd "been had". Now the Station Commander stood to warn that we had better start behaving like officers. Everyone complied and dinner proceeded with the basic decorum. The same can not be said for what followed in the bar, where water gun attacks continued and fellows periodically were doused with beer and gin. Dick Newman, one of our Flight Commanders, took a couple of drenchings.

Later came the highlight of the whole event. One Lightning pilot, who happened to be a decent musician, had a thing about pianos. A few days before the Mess Dinner he had purchased an old one for five pounds, and placed it in the storage room next to the bar. At about 0200 six rather intoxicated 111 pilots wheeled the piano into the lounge. As the playing began, a typical sing-along ensued. Predictably, however, the singing deteriorated into a shouting match.

Suddenly, out of the blue the piano player disappeared, then returned with a fire axe. We all stood back, knowing what was about to happen. With a mighty blow, the axe fell onto the keyboard. Ivories and wood splints flew everywhere. The Station Commander rushed in from the bar. Thinking that it was the Mess piano being trashed, he shouted for order, then announced, "Gentlemen, the bar is closed." When someone explained that our piano player had been wrecking his own piano, the "Groupie" would not be swayed, ordering that the fellow appear before him at 0800 Monday morning.

Other RCAF/CF pilots had tours on the Lightning. Roy Pashkiewich, who had joined the RCAF in 1955, served on 111 from 1970-73. Originally on Sabres, he later instructed at Moose Jaw, then flew Voodoos with 425. From Wattisham, he had deployments to Cyprus, including in the period when Israel took on the Arabs in October 1973. In a matter of days Israel, reportedly, shot down some 100 Syrian MiG-21s. An embarrassed Syria suggested that maybe it had been the RAF Lightnings on Cyprus that had done the deed! Those, however, had been grounded until the fireworks ceased.

Pashkiewich found the Lightning manoeuvrable and without great vices – nothing like the Voodoo's pitch-up. On the other hand, it was short-ranged and lacked nose-wheel steering – a pilot steered using differential main-wheel braking, something that was tricky on icy taxy strips. On transits to Cyprus, Pashkiewich recalled in May 2003 that three Lightnings would set off supported by three tankers, the fighters plugging into a tanker every 15–20 minutes. As the formation got over the Mediterranean, two tankers would offload their excess fuel into the third, and return to base. The third would proceed to Cyprus with its charges.

Pashkiewich logged some intercepts on Soviet Bison bombers. Photos were taken of the Bisons, so that the intel people could study them for antennae and other "bumps and bulges" that could reveal something new. Unfortunately, pilots couldn't keep copies of such routine photos. When Pashkiewich left 111, his place was taken by F/L Roger Ayotte. He returned to the Voodoo at 410 Squadron, then moved to 437 to fly 707s. He left the air force in 1980 to fly the 707 with Ontario World Air, then served Transport Canada in Toronto.

Nav to Pilot: An RAF Tour

Born in Jamaica, Brian Cluer lived in several countries in his youth. In February 1958 he came to Canada, sailing from Cape Town on a Norwegian tramp steamer. That August he joined the RCAF, his first flight (February 16, 1959) being a nav exer-

Brain Cluer during his career as an AI navigator on CF-100s. (PL-77988 DND)

cise from Winnipeg in an Expeditor. Next came AI training on CF-100s at Cold Lake. He crewed with John "Dutch" Stants, with whom he completed a tour at 410. This ended with a CF-101 sortie on September 5, 1963, soon after which F/L Cluer joined the RAF. Beginning in February 1964, he trained on the Jet Provost at Syerston, advanced to the Gnat at Valley, did a short Hunter course at Chivenor, then came the Lightning course at 226 OCU at Coltishall. Finally, he joined 111 Squadron at Wattisham, flying initially on June 27, 1966. In 1969 he completed the Interceptor Weapons Instructor's course, then instructed at 226. On promotion to squadron leader, in May 1970 he was posted as a flight commander to 11 Squadron at Leuchars.

Being so far north, 11 Squadron often intercepted Badgers and Bears, the latter on their way to Guinea, West Africa. His tour done in September 1972, S/L Cluer attended RAF Staff College at Bracknell. His last tour was as a staff officer at Strike Command. By this time there was a sense that the RAF was changing, and Cluer was much influenced by a lecture from Air Marshal "Mickey" Martin of Dam Buster fame. He told the young officers at Bracknell that if they felt things were bad in the RAF, they should wake up – things would be getting worse. With this warning in mind, in 1975 S/L Cluer left the RAF for British Aircraft Corporation to manage Royal Saudi Air Force pilot training for 3½ years in Riyadh and Dhahran.

In 1978 Cluer joined Cathay Pacific Airlines in Hong Kong, finishing there as general manager in Flight Operations. He then became the first Controller of the Government Flying Service in Hong Kong. This organization conducted SAR and police duties, co-operated with the Hong Kong fire brigade and flew VIPs and covert operations with the Blackhawk, S-76 and King Air. After retiring in 1996, Cluer returned to Canada. Others from 410 who followed the RCAF-to-RAF path were Rick McKnight (pilot, Lightnings) and Dave Mulinder (nav, Canberras, Buccaneers). As OC of the Buccaneer OCU at RAF Honington, Mulinder was awarded the AFC in 1974.

CHAPTER 13

Tornados Low and High

Tornado GR Exchange

After the demise by politics of Britain's TSR-2 strike aircraft in 1965, the RAF continued operating its aging Canberra, Victor and Vulcan bombers; Buccaneer, Harrier and Jaguar tactical fighters; and Lightning and Phantom II interceptors. To modernize, Britain co-operated with Germany and Italy in developing the multi-role Panavia Tornado, first flown in August 1974 and initially in service in 1979. Meanwhile, Canada was seeking a new fighter, eventually opting for the F/A-18 Hornet. RAF Tornados would serve well in the First Gulf War alongside those of Italy and Saudi Arabia, and in subsequent "no-fly zone" operations in Iraq, in the Kosovo campaign, and in the Second Gulf War.

Several Canadians have had Tornado exchanges on the GR.1 or GR.4 strike versions, and the F.3 interceptor. One slot over the years was instructing at 15 Squadron, Lossiemouth (the RAF insisted on a Canadian here, something perhaps connected to a general respect for Canadian aircrew and to the Canada-UK wartime experience). Canadians were viewed as superior instructors, and easily adapted to the RAF way of

Capt Mike Mirza while on RAF exchange. Then, Tornado "TA" of 15 Squadron scorching off from RAF Lossiemouth. (Mirza Col.)

doing business. Formed in 1915, the squadron operated some of the earliest military aircraft. It was prominent in WWII, finishing on Lancasters, then continued postwar in its traditional role with the Victor, Buccaneer and, since 1983, the Tornado. One 15 Squadron Canadian was Capt Mike "Mizer" Mirza, who flew a tour on the GR. Mk.4. Having joined the Army (Ontario Regiment) as a high school student in Oshawa, he bided his time as a recce driver, then joined the air force in 1988. He followed the usual training route from Musketeer to Tutor to Wings, then progressed to 419 and 410 at Cold Lake. In 1992 Mirza graduated from 410 and joined 441, there to spend five years. From 1997-99 he instructed at 410. In 1999 he was a CF-18 demo pilot, promoting the Canadian Forces at airshows across Canada. In December 1999 he was posted to 15 Squadron, replacing his CF predecessor, Capt Keith "Chirp" Moore.

Capt Mirza's first task was to learn the Tornado but, a fighter being a fighter, getting the hang of it was routine. What was really new to him, however, was the 2-crew concept, which Canada had not had since Voodoo days. Now, Mirza would be working with a back seater, whose job was managing the air-to-ground radar and weapons, while keeping a watch using the indispensable "Mark 1 Eyeball". Mirza also had to qualify as a navigator, before being cleared to instruct. He first flew the GR.1 on April 6, 2000, going on a famil flight with F/L Entwisle. Phase one was a 6-month basic conversion – getting the general feel of the GR.1, doing the standard formation and night flying, low-level sorties, getting to know the systems from radar and weapons to the HUD, ECM/ECCM, etc. After six months came phase two, where Mirza would qualify as an instructor. As he completed each stage, he was cleared for some basic instructing. He flew his first student trip on January 12, 2001 with F/L Bressani, a pipeline nav. Such a student, 60% of whom were pilots, the rest navigators, would finish training in six months.

Ultimately, Mirza was a qualified IP, good to train pilots and navs. By this time he had 160 Tornado hours, a further 20 in the simulator, and had completed all ground school requirements, and was enjoying the Tornado. In this period, upgrades were being added to the GR.1 to create the Mk.4: new cockpit displays, FLIR in the HUD, an electronics pod for precision-guided munition delivery, NVG kit, and an enhanced self-defence suite. Even so, the cockpit did not compare with the Hornet in design and comfort. "The Tornado has switches for its switches", Mirza noted in 2005. "While a Hornet has one weapons arming switch, a GR.4 has three."

The curriculum with which Capt Mirza now worked included everything from standard formation flying, attack profiles (2-ship, 4-ship, big packages, etc.), air combat tactics, weapons sorties, and EW. Low-level tactics (100') still were fundamental in the RAF, e.g. strafing with the 27-mm cannon. (In the 1998-99 Kosovo campaign, Canada had turned its thinking to high-level bombing, using PGMs, and low-level training was phased out at

Capt Brad Dolan while on his Voodoo tour with 416 Squadron. (all, Dolan Col.)

410 Squadron.) Mirza also trained for anti-shipping missions, had sorties to Italy and Germany, and the chance to represent the RAF in a prestigious month-long (March 1-28, 2002) multinational Tactical Leadership Program exercise in Belgium. On this he flew 14 missions for 25 hours. TLP sorties are noted for snap mission planning, intensive low-level flying and big packages. Flying Tornado ZA365 with S/L Eddie Middleton on one mission, Mirza lead a big TLP package that included fighters from Germany, Spain, Belgium, Italy, Greece, Turkey and the US. Mirza would spend more than three years on exchange. Eventually, he heard that several of his students had done operations in Iraq during "Northern Watch" and the Second Gulf War, e.g. suppressing Iraqi anti-aircraft sites with ALARM missiles. After more than three years, he joined 419 Squadron at Cold Lake to instruct on the Hawk. By then his log showed some 2600 flying hours, nearly all on high performance jets, 1500 being on Hornets, 550 on Tornados.

Tornado F.3 Exchange

One day Brad Dolan, then a boy living near Girvan, Saskatchewan, was thrilled when a helicopter landed at his grandfather's farm. The pilot was a local salesman keen to sell Brad's grandfather some new equipment. To seal the deal, grandfather got the salesman to take Brad and his brother on a helicopter ride. Naturally, the boys were thrilled. Some years later, Brad was enthralled when some Tutors passed over the farm. By then, the idea of being a pilot just wouldn't go away, and in 1978 he joined the Canadian Forces. After basic officer training, he made his first flight in a Musketeer at Portage-la-Prairie on May 14, 1979. He progressed quickly, going next to Moose Jaw for the Tutor course (f/f September 11), then 419 Squadron at Cold Lake for the CF-5 course (f/f September 9, 1980), to North Bay for IFR flying on the T-33, finally to 410 Squadron at Bagotville for the CF-101 Voodoo course (f/f September 4, 1981).

Qualified on the CF-101, Capt Dolan now spent an enjoyable 3½ years on the Voodoo with 416 Squadron. On April 24,

Capts Dolan and Peters ferrying Voodoos '056 and '064 to Cold Lake in January 1985.

the Tornado F.3. There he replaced Capt Dave Tower at 29 (F) Squadron, RAF Coningsby. First stop for Dolan was RAF Brawdy in Wales, where he commenced flying on January 10, 1989 on the Jet Provost T.4. This was a short famil course which Dolan recalled in 2006 as "a huge amount of fun" (amazingly, the "JP" remained in service more than 40 years after the first RCAF exchange officers instructed on it at Little Rissington). After a few "JP" hours, Dolan logged 35 hours on the Hawk 1A in 79 Tactical Weapons Unit at Brawdy, before moving to Coningsby. There he first flew the Tornado F.3 (ZE208/AK with S/L Rick Groombridge) at 229 OCU on May 25. Meanwhile, Brad, his wife, Barbara, and children, Jon and Jenna, settled into rental quarters in nearby Tattershall.

Following groundschool, simulator sessions and 27 sortie/30 flying hours on the F.3, Capt Dolan joined 29 Squadron. There, after a program reminiscent of that on a CF-18 squadron, on November 15 he attained combat ready status as a wingman. His training assured competency on the F.3s weapons – Skyflash AAM, AIM-9M Sidewinder AAM, 27mm Mauser cannon and related onboard systems. By this time Dolan's log book showed 150 hours on the F.3.

All the variety of life on a fighter squadron now ensued, the practice GCI intercepts, ACM and naval support exercises, NATO TacEvals, gunnery camps in Cyprus, etc. Dolan added to all this by working with the local Air Cadets, giving famil rides in the Chipmunk. By this time he knew the F.3 well, something that could make a fighter pilot long for his CF-18. The Tornado, after all, was a compromise, designed in the 1960s by a European consortium to perform one role too many. Fundamentally a low-level tactical fighter with a heavy, complicated swing wing, the F.3 had the air superiority role, but lacked the agility and performance of a modern fighter. Illustrating this, where two CF-18s would be tasked on a fighter sweep, the RAF would use four F.3s to ensure success.

When Iraq invaded Kuwait on August 2 1990 the West responded with Operation Desert Shield – a huge military build-

1982 he intercepted a Soviet Bear bomber over the Atlantic, this leading to his life-long call sign – "Bear". As the Voodoo came to the end of its NORAD days and 416 prepared to re-equip with the CF-18, Capt Dolan ferried several Voodoos to their final destinations: 101065 to Gander (museum), '064 to Cold Lake (ABDR), '006 to Shearwater (ABDR), '037 to Summerside (museum), '028 to Greenwood (museum in Hillsborough, NB), '050 to Bagotville (ABDR), finally '002 to North Bay (museum) with crewman MCpl Jim Trask on February 7, 1985.

Having logged 944 hours on the Voodoo, Dolan now was posted to 410 Squadron at Cold Lake for the CF-18 course (f/f May 13, 1985). Following this he instructed at 410 and qualified on the Fighter Weapons Instructor Course. With 1000+ CF-18 hours, late in 1988 he was posted on exchange to the UK to fly

Tornados of 29 Squadron over the North Sea in 1989.

Skud missiles. In-flight refuelling was part of every sortie.

Capt Dolan flew his 33rd and final Gulf War mission on March 8, 1991. On March 13 he ferried the last F.3 back to the UK routing via Decimomannu. His longest mission was that of January 14 – 6 hours. The routines of Coningsby now ensued, until Dolan's final F.3 flight on July 2, 1992. The Dolans now returned to Cold Lake, where Brad was promoted to major and flew the Hornet as OpsO

up in the region. One of the first signs of this saw 48 F-15s depart Langley AFB for Dhahran, Saudi Arabia on August 7, followed on the 11th by 29 Squadron deploying on Operation Granby from Akrotiri to Dhahran. As a participant, Capt Dolan became the first Canadian in the Gulf War theatre. With his navigator, F/L Ian "Bungle" Dearie, on the 13th he led the first F.3 "Desert Shield" CAP, a 2.1-hour, 4-ship mission. Henceforth, 29 Squadron flew nightly patrols, mainly protecting Allied AWACs from the threat of Iraqi MiG-25s. When the F.3s would land, USAF F-15s would take over to ensure 24-hour-a-day coverage.

Capt Dolan logged 10 CAP missions, including an abortive MiG-25 intercept on August 22. On the 26th the Iraqis launched a large, aggressive package of fighters and fighter bombers – 29 Squadron tracked them, but the Iraqis dispersed. On September 1 Dolan returned to Coningsby to check out on an upgraded F.3 (night vision goggles, improved avionics and air-to-air weapons). On September 15 he was part of the 168-strong Battle of Britain flypast over London. Nine more "Desert Shield" sorties followed for him. Then, on January 16, 1991, the Gulf scenario became "Desert Storm" and the Allies were at war full scale with Iraq. The F.3 now flew around the clock, missions ranging from escorts to sweeps, CAPs, recces and spotting for incoming Iraqi

at 416 Squadron, until posted to AIRCOM HQ in Winnipeg in July 1997. While there, Maj Brad Dolan and Capt Doug Carter, another former 29 Squadron exchange officer, spent six years as CF-5 test and demo pilots with Winnipeg-based Magellan Aerospace. Along the way, Dolan became an air reservist and joined Air Canada to fly the Airbus. On March 23, 2004 he (with Magellan tech Derek Kearney) and Carter ferried the last two Canadian Forces CF-5s (115833 and '839) from Winnipeg to Trenton via North Bay. By this time Dolan's log book showed total times of: CF-101 – 941 hours, CF-5 – 650, CF-18 – 2113, Tornado F.3 – 958, T-33 – 590, Hawk 1A – 35, CL-41 – 207. Meanwhile, the RAF announced that 29 Squadron would reform with the Eurofighter Typhoon II, an event that Dolan attended at Coningsby in September 2005. His old wingman from 1992, by then W/C Allistar McKay, now commanded 29 Squadron and it seemed likely that the exchange would resume. In 2006 Brad Dolan recalled:

Our exchange proved to be most enjoyable for me and my family. The children began their schooling in the English system and thrived. My wife was active in the community and we thoroughly enjoyed the local customs and characters. The RAF proved to be a stalwart organization, very flexible and skilled. While it was understood that the Tornado F.3 could not compete with the likes of the Hornet, the Eagle or the Viper, the RAF did their best with the machine, continuously upgrading the avionics and fire control, self-protection suite and weapons. They were innovative tacticians, always striving to get the best performance from man and machine.

My most vivid recollections (other than the Gulf War) were our flying exercises over the British Isles and surrounding waters. Whereas in Canada you would be lampooned and charged with low flying (even in the most remote pockets of the country), in England, Scotland and Wales low flying was an accepted and necessary thing. The beauty of low and fast flying through the fiords of Scotland, and over the green hedge rows of England and formidable granite of Wales is incomparable. The people of these islands have a remarkable appreciation for the RAF and accept all the noise as the cost of their freedoms. During our exchange we made many great friends with whom we remain close to this day.

Tornados in the UK and Saudi Arabia

Also on an RAF Tornado exchange was David Smith, call sign "Torch". Raised in Victoria, BC, he joined the Canadian Forces in 1979. Trained as a fighter pilot, he served initially on 421 Squadron at Baden-Soellingen. Between September 1989 and December 1992 he was on exchange with 45 Squadron at RAF Honington, instructing on the Tornado GR.1, 1A

"Torch" Smith in a typical hero shot at Honington in the spring of 1990. The crest of his shoulder signifies the Tornado Weapons Conversion Unit. (Shaun Hughes)

and 4. Having replaced Ron Dudley at 45 Squadron, Smith himself was replaced by Chris Chorney, by which time 45 Squadron had become 15 Squadron and moved to Lossiemouth. In 2006 Smith noted: "I learned much during my exchange, especially about flying a crewed aircraft in the air-to-ground role. The Tornado, on which I logged about 650 hours, proved most capable in the low-level environment for which it was designed."

Following his tour, Smith returned to instruct at 410 Squadron in Cold Lake.

In the 1990s there were many well-paid opportunities for aircrew and specialist ground trades to instruct overseas. A real magnet was the Kingdom of Saudi Arabia, which had been using ex-pats in a long-term project leading to self-sufficiency in running its modern air force. In 1985 the Royal Saudi Air Force ordered 48 IDS and 24 ADV Tornados. After deliveries began in February 1989, several ex-CanForces personnel, David Smith included, took advantage of a job offer from British Aerospace, which was recruiting Tornado pilots for the RSAF. In October 1995 Smith and his wife, Caroline, began their stay at Dhahran, the biggest RSAF fighter base. Accommodations were in modern British Aerospace compounds. Smith flew the Tornado IDS, first on 7 (Training) Squadron, then on 75 (Fighter) Squadron. Having been a FWIC instructor at Cold Lake and having a RAF QWI (qualified weapons instructor) ticket, he ultimately co-ordinated the development of the Saudi IDS weapons school, where he also was chief instructor. Among his various duties, Smith sometimes was asked to assist in evaluating tactical exercises. Meanwhile, other ex-pats from Canada and other Commonwealth nations were instructing on RSAF units flying the Ce.172, PC-9 and Hawk. The structure of these units tended to follow a USAF model.

In February 2001 the Smiths returned to Canada. By this time David's log book showed some 4000 jet hours including: Tutor – 400, CF-5 – 130, CF-18 – 1670, Hawk – 60 and Tornado – 1710. He now spent five years as a Reservist, flying the Bell 412 Griffon with 408 Squadron in Edmonton. In this period he flew operationally during the 2002 G8 Summit at Kananaskis, had a tour in Bosnia in 2004, and became a Transport Canada commercial and corporate aviation inspector.

CHAPTER 14

RAF Training Command

F/L Lloyd Hunt

Many postwar RCAF pilots instructed in the RAF and USAF. In 1956 F/L Robert C. Diamond was in the UK to observe the *ab initio* Hunting Jet Provost trials. Then, F/L Lloyd Hunt, a wartime Spitfire pilot from Allenford in Ontario's Lake Huron region, had a tour on the "JP". While teaching school in Timmins, Hunt accepted an invitation from AFHQ to return to flying. First, he attended FIS at Trenton, then taught on Harvards and T-33s, mainly at Portage-la-Prairie, all the time hoping for a more operational posting. One day his boss, G/C Chuck Burgess, said, "Lloyd, I've got a nice little slot for you – RAF Flying Training Command at Little Rissington." On June 1, 1956 F/L Hunt made his first flight at "Little Riz", going up with S/L D.L. Hughes in a Vampire T.11. His task now was to teach instructors and visit stations as a "trapper" – one of those at CFS who gave category upgrade rides to instructors or senior squadron pilots. The term referred to how these types liked to trap students into making mistakes. Pilots also might attend CFS for instrument and/or instructor category rides or ticket upgrades. Here they were put through the wringer in classroom and cockpit.

CFS also had Hunters, Jet Provosts and Meteor 7s. Besides flying all these, in July 1956 F/L Hunt visited Lossiemouth to check out on the RN's Sea Hawk. As to the Vampire, CFS policy was to fly to the limits. This was a change, for Hunt was used to RCAF CFS rules, which (officially) discouraged overly aggressive flying. He found the Vampire pleasant and more manoeuvrable at altitude than a T-33. Otherwise, RAF and

Several Canadians instructed on the Hunting Jet Provost. Early on was F/L Robert Hugh Dundas, an RCAF "retread", who flew the "JP" at RAF Syerston. Here he is with student P/O A.D. Jamieson of Glasgow, in April 1964. Then, Dundas aloft in XR673. (PL-144210, PL-144214 DND)

RCAF instructional techniques diverged. The RAF focused on handling, while the RCAF was bigger on nav skills. Thus, a T.11 routinely would take off on an instrument exercise and go to altitude in a spiral climb, often in the clag, which demanded great attention to IFR. Also a factor was that RAF airspace was limited, while the RCAF, in which instrument flying followed ground controlled procedures, had unlimited air space.

In July 1957 Princess Margaret visited Little Riz. CFS put on an airshow and F/L Hunt was honoured to meet the Royal guest. Between August 16-21, 1957 he was one of 12 pilots taking six Vampires through the Mediterranean. For this he was advised from the RCAF in London – should there be tension in the region, don't get involved. On October 8, 1957 Hunt took a Vampire to Kinloss to collect some fine salmon. He returned to Little Riz with the fish packed in his ammunition boxes. On landing he found that the salmon were partially cooked, the ammo boxes being so close to the engine! Another day, a "met" Spitfire visited. Hunt was offered a chance to fly it, but this fell through when the Spit was put on its nose. Hunt finished his

exchange on July 8, 1958 with a famil ride in a Javelin with F/L Stewart. His time totalled: Vampire – 378:45 hours, Meteor – 133:00, Hunter – 35:50, and Jet Provost – 23:00.

More of "Little Riz"

Having joined the RCAF in 1942, Douglas Rivoire of Ottawa earned his Wings at Camp Borden, then instructed at Brandon, Moncton and Weyburn. He left the air force in 1945, returning to his pre-war job at J.H. Connor, an Ottawa washing machine maker. Like Hunt, Rivoire received a letter from AFHQ, inviting him to re-enlist. Soon he was one of the many RCAF Cold War "retreads". Once he had his instructor's category from FIS, he was posted to Centralia, converted to T-33s at Chatham, then taught at Portage-la-Prairie and FIS. Out of the blue one day he was posted to Little Rissington to replace F/L Hunt. His first flight was a famil ride with F/L Bob Barnden in Meteor T.7 WL481 on August 8, 1958. On the 22nd he flew the Vampire T.11, then began teaching aspiring RAF instructors. At Little Riz at the same time were F/L Harry Molyneux (RCAF), Capt John A. Smitherman (USAF) and F/L J. Boast (RAAF). In one break in his routines Rivoire joined several CFS instructors touring Turkish Air Force bases. There also was the occasional nav exercise,

Lloyd Hunt (right) with Rayne D. "Joe" Schultz in a snapshot from July 31, 1998. Lloyd's exchange was on T.11s at Little Rissington 1956-58. When posted home, it was to 6 RD, Trenton. Next, he flew T-33s with 408 Squadron, followed by a tour at Mobile Command HQ. In 1969 he left the air force to resume his teaching career. (Larry Milberry)

(Below) WZ454, a typical D.H. Vampire T.11, while stationed at Sylt, West Germany in 1954. Delivered in November 1952, WZ454 was sold for scrap eight years later. (Brian Sharman via Roger Lindsay)

F/L Doug Rivoire (left) at "Little Riz". Having left the RCAF in 1964, he worked in sales with Corby's Distillery, then retired in Kingston, Ontario in 1984. He passed away in 2002. Here he is enjoying a tea break at Little Riz with his USAF counterpart in 2 Squadron, Capt John Smitherman. After graduating from the US Naval Academy, Smitherman trained in the USAF on the PA-18 Super Cub, T-6 Texan and T-33. Having earned his Wings in 1953, he instructed on the T-28 and T-33, then went on exchange in 1958. Later, he flew 186 F-4 combat missions from Danang, South Vietnam. Colonel Smitherman retired from the USAF in 1981. (Smitherman Col.)

(Right) The postwar years were highly spirited in all NATO air forces. Here, some of Doug Rivoire's sidekicks at Little Riz go at it in the Officers Mess. These days people barely have a clue about such esprit de corps – anyone having too good a time in the mess must beware lest he "put up a black" by offending one thin-skinned group or other. (Rivoire Col.)

F/L Morrice flew first at CFS in T.11 WZ551 on June 28, 1960. He took to the "Vamp" right away, although, like other RAF types, it was a tight squeeze. After all, it was a single-seater widened for two ejection seats. Morrice would have all sorts of students, including a couple of Iraqi MiG-15 pilots. Another memory was of the CFS Hunters at Kemble, a Little Riz satellite near Cirencester. Instructors and students flew these towards the end of their 3-month course. As to the T.11, even late in its career it still had mysterious quirks. In this period two or three were lost in spins – it seems that pilots could get disoriented, not realizing whether their spin was upright or inverted. Morrice flew in Vampire handling trials, which resulted in spin recovery recommendations.

CFS used to make a biennial examining trip to the Far East, doing check rides and category upgrades on

e.g. to Gibraltar or Malta. Rivoire finished his tour with a T.11 flight on July 21, 1960, then returned to an AFHQ slot in training. He had logged 373 hours on T.11s. Now, he recruited in Ottawa until retiring on November 9, 1964.

Ian Morrice, raised in Vernon BC, joined the RCAF in October 1951. Following FTS at Gimli and Sabre OTU at Chatham, he had a tour with 416 Squadron at 2 Wing, then instructed on T-33s at Portage la Prairie 1957-60. Towards the end of this, he heard from F/L Gerry Patterson in RCAF Postings and Careers in AFHQ, that there was something in the air about his future. This turned out to be a posting to Little Riz to replace F/L Rivoire and instruct on Gnats. But, by the time Morrice reached CFS, the Gnat program had slipped. With Aussies, Canucks, Kiwis, Pakistanis, Yanks and others, CFS was a mini United Nations. One joke was that these interlopers might overthrow the RAF! As many as 70 ex-RCAF pilots joined the RAF in this period, fellows who had responded to a RAF recruiting drive offering to recognize RCAF seniority and rank. Most later returned to Canada, some disgruntled about living conditions or poor pay.

The Morrice family on holiday in Rome during their Little Rissington tour: father Ian, mother Dorena and little ones Leigh and Jim. (Morrice Col.)

CFS staff during their wanderings from Little Riz to far off Butterworth, with many a stop en route. F/L Morrice is on the left. (Morrice Col.)

(Right) LCol Ian Morrice in a 1983 portrait. (EN83-469-1 DND)

down from 35,000 feet and lost control. They passed through various gyrations at either end of the G-load, perhaps as much as -4 to +10. Morrice took charge, recovered and landed. "Fortunately, we still had the wings on", he commented in 2002. When his student failed, the station commander quizzed Morrice about his decision, but Morrice held his ground. The CFS entourage returned to Little Riz on November 7.

New associations are made during any exchange, and earlier connections might be renewed. At Little Riz, for example, Morrice served with Peter Frame, RAF. Frame later had an exchange at CFS in Gimli, while Morrice was on staff. Upon finishing his tour, Morrice had a posting at CFS in Gimli and Winnipeg. Next came a desk job at NDHQ, followed by a CF-104 tour 1973-76 with 439 in Baden. He later instructed on CF-104s at Cold Lake, had a staff job at AIRCOM HQ in Winnipeg, was BAdminO in Comox and Base Commander CFB Penhold from where he retired in 1986.

instructional pilots with friendly air forces. On September 16, 1961 Morrice and 10 others departed in a Varsity to plod their way through "the Med" and Middle East. First stop for multi-engine and helicopter instruction was Ceylon. They pressed on to Mingaladon, near Rangoon, where category rides were given to Burmese pilots in the piston Provost. At Singapore, Morrice was invited by the Aussies to fly the Avon-powered Sabre at RAAF Butterworth. When he arrived, however, the runway was being upgraded, so there was no Sabre flying. All he flew after a sociable three weeks were some Vampire trips October 18-20, re-rating RAAF examiners. He then returned to Singapore to board the Varsity for Ceylon. This was an adventure for, mid-way over the Indian Ocean, the Varsity lost its radio and nav equipment. Happily, the nav knew his trade and got them to the obscure Indian Ocean island of Car Nicobar (south of the Andamans) for fuel and repairs. Now it was on to Ceylon, thence to Karachi. There, from October 25-31, Morrice did Pakistan Air Force T-33 rides. In one case his student was a squadron CO going for an instructor category. On a sortie to review the T-bird's Mach characteristics, Morrice had the CO demonstrate compressibility effects. The student immediately stuffed the nose straight

Fentiman, Charles and Wilson

Ron Fentiman also instructed at Little Riz. A West Coaster who had gotten his private pilot's licence on Cessna 140s at Vancouver U-Fly, he joined the RCAF in 1951. After a tour on Sabres, he instructed at CFS in Saskatoon on the Chipmunk, T-33 and Mitchell. From July 1962 he replaced Ian Morrice at Little Riz, beginning with six months on the Jet Provost, then converting to the Gnat. In 2002 he recalled, "You simply strapped on a Gnat and went flying." Unfortunately, in August 1963 Morrice was recalled to attend RCAF Staff College. He finished with 70:45 hours on "JPs", 85:40 on Gnats.

Paul Charles later instructed at CFS. Having joined the RCAF in 1950, he was an airframe tech, but remustered to pilot in 1953. His first tour was on Sabres, then he instructed at Portage-la-

Prairie and Moose Jaw. Later, he was in on the ground floor with Tutors at Moose Jaw. In July 1967 he went on RAF exchange, spending two typical years at Little Riz, and enjoying the highly manoeuvrable JP. One thing that struck Charles was how Little Riz and the JP, with its bare-bones nav aids, provided such a good combination for IFR instruction. Thus, one would take off on a sortie and navigate mainly by headings given by ATC. When it was time to descend, ATC again would assist. If needed, GCA was available on approach. Once home, Charles instructed in Winnipeg on Tutors and Dakotas. In 1977-79 he was with the Canadian High Commission in Dar es Salaam, working with the Tanzanian military and teaching IFR on the Cessna 310, even though there was little call for instrument ratings, since Tanzania's weather usually was CAVU. By the end of his flying days, Charles' time included: T-33 – 2350 hours, Tutor – 1155, F-86 – 814, Dakota – 800, Jet Provost – 650.

Fred Allport: JP Deadstick

Having grow up in Hamilton, Ontario, Fred Allport joined the RCAF in January 1943. He trained as a pilot at St. Catharines (Tiger Moths) and Dunnville (Harvards) in Ontario, then in the UK (Masters), then was posted to a Spitfire OTU in Palestine and on to 417 Squadron in Italy, just as the war in Europe ended. Once home he studied engineering at the University of Toronto, while flying Harvards and Mustangs with 424 Squadron (Aux) at Mount Hope, near Hamilton. Then, with Canada needing pilots for its NATO build-up, he returned to the regular RCAF, did the Sabre OTU at Chatham and flew a tour with 434 Squadron at Zweibrucken.

F/O Allport next spent three years instructing on T-33s at Gimli, then was in "postings and careers" at Training Command HQ

F/L Fred Allport on exchange at Little Riz. By tour's end he had logged 650 hours. He went home to a pilot training posting at RCAF HQ, later advised the Tanzanian Air Force, then retired from the military in 1971. (Allport Col.)

in Winnipeg, from where he requested a tour on Voodoos. In 2006, he recalled: "The RCAF in their wisdom saw this differently. They thought I would do better with an RAF exchange at Central Flying School. As a result, in July 1963 I was posted to Little Rissington to be a Flight Commander in the Basic School." There, F/L Allport, his wife and their two children settled into quarters on the station. Allport began flying on the Gnat but, after a few hours, converted to the JP, on which he would instruct until July 1965. All this was routine until a flight of February 27, 1964. Allport's sortie that day was to give his student the high level familiarization exercise. The RAF Flying Training Command "Good Show" report of what ensued explains:

During a dive to gain speed for a loop at FL280, severe vibration was felt, together with a sudden loss of thrust. Flt Lt Allport closed the throttle, whereupon, smoke filled the cockpit and he was left with no alternative but to shut down the engine by closing the HP cock (subsequent investigation showed a seized engine which could not be turned by hand). The student transmitted a MAYDAY call, which was answered by Uxbridge Centre. They in turn passed the emergency over to Pershore, who accepted the aircraft into a flame-out radar let-down.

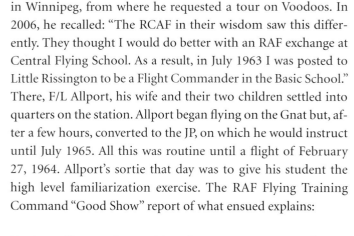

Throughout the subsequent let down in relatively poor weather conditions, Flt Lt Allport displayed exceptional qualities of airmanship coupled with a cool and calm approach towards an extremely unpleasant emergency. Were it not for his unerring decisions and judgment of the highest merit, this mechanical failure could have caused the loss of an aircraft. Flt Lt Allport has been awarded a Green Endorsement.

In 2006 Fred Allport added further to this story:

It would appear that the airman who did the preflight inspection on my aircraft had used a can he found in the hangar to top up the oil, not realizing that it contained cleaning fluid. This caused the oil to congeal and the engine to seize.

The cloud base that day was 1500 feet, which meant that the radar controller had to make sure I was in the right position relative to the runway, when I broke cloud. He did a marvellous job and I was able to make a perfect landing on the runway with no damage to the aircraft. My student and I were flown back to Little Riz for lunch, and I was back in the air with another student by 2 PM.

On July 14, 1965 F/L Allport submitted a detailed report to RCAF HQ covering his exchange. He described how his duties included responsibility for 30 students and a staff of 10 instructors. Besides all the on-going paper work, his duties included:

… testing the students at three stages throughout the course: progress check after 15 hours, intermediate handling test after 45 hours, and final handling test at the end of the course … the Flight Commander flies with as many students as possible during the course to obtain first hand knowledge of each student's capabilities. Normally [he] averages about 25-30 hours per month.

Late in 1964 Little Rissington hosted the RAF's annual CFS convention. F/L Allport reported how this brought together some 150 representative from the RAF, RN, MoD and Commonwealth nations. There were presentations illuminating areas of pilot training, e.g. aircrew selection and pre-basic flying at ITS. Allport commented how aircrew selection was similar in the RAF to the RCAF. Regarding flight training at the ITS level, he commented how the RAF was thinking of introducing it, while the RCAF was considering dropping it (i.e. the basic Chipmunk phase). Low flying seemed similar to the RCAF approach, i.e. a favourable view as per training pilots for the tactical role. Also much discussed were instruction techniques and how the RAF covered this every six months in a conference "to review various flying exercises in order to eliminate unnecessary and undesirable techniques." Attending these sessions were members of the Handling Squadron at Boscombe Down where pilots notes for all RAF aircraft types were produced.

F/L Allport also reported on exchange officer housing: "An agreement between the RCAF and the RAF for the allocation of housing for exchange officers should be pursued with renewed vigour. An officer cannot devote his full attention to his duties when he is concerned with finding proper accommodation for his family in a strange country … Fortunately, the Station Commander at RAF Little Rissington is most sympathetic to the

dilemma." He also suggested that an RCAF exchange officer at Little Rissington spend some time in Standards Flight, "where he would have the opportunity to see all aspects of flying training," adding how RAF exchange officers in RCAF Training Command spent their tours in Standards Flight. F/L Allport concluded: "The exchange position at CFS is at the hub of flying training in the RAF and the wealth of information available certainly justifies the retention of this position." Eight copies of his report were distributed among RCAF HQ, Canadian Joint Staff London, MoD, RAF HQ Flying Training Command, RAF CFS, and one copy to himself.

Baines Flies the JP

Stuart Baines, who joined the RCAF in September 1963, first flew at No. 1 PFS at Centralia, going up on April 10, 1964 in Chipmunk 18069 with F/O Wolfe. After 22:45 hours he graduated on October 16. Next stop was 4 FTS at Penhold for the final RCAF Harvard course, Baines flying first in Harvard 20225. He finished on May 21, 1965 with 164:25 hours dual/solo on the "Yellow Peril" and, on July 12, 1965, started on the last stage of Wings training – T-33s at AFS in Moose Jaw. Now he was posted to 3 AW (F) OTU at Bagotville, where flying began on December 7 in T-33 21387 (by this time the OTU had phased out CF-100s and was using T-33s to lead into the CF-101). OTU ended on April 24, 1966.

Early in May, Baines did some simulator training and, on May 8, flew CF-101 17472. As Bagotville's runway was being resurfaced, the OTU was at Chatham. "Crewed up" with F/L Bill Bland, he was posted to 409 Squadron, where flying commenced in August. This lasted to December 1969, when Baines was posted to Portage-la-Prairie for the FIS Course. Next, he joined 2 CFFTS at Moose Jaw to instruct on Tutors, beginning June 3, 1970. He enjoyed his tour at "The Big 2", where there was "never a dull moment", whether weekends on the road with a Tutor, or taking part in flypasts. One of these was on January 30, 1973 – 35 Tutors spelling "2 FTS" to commemorate the school. On July 9 Baines flew in a 37-plane formation spelling "RCMP" in honour of the force's 100th anniversary. On August 17 he was in a 24-plane formation spelling "OB" in honour of Col O.B. Philp, who was handing command of Moose Jaw to Col Ralph Annis.

In this period Baines was in touch with an RCAF mate, Graham Larke, flying Gnats at RAF Valley. He was interested in such a posting, so discussed the matter with Maj Don Williams, a 2 CFFTS flight commander. The paperwork done, Baines was posted to Little Riz. On May 10, 1974 he took a famil flight in a Jet Provost T.3 with F/L Nightengale. The transition was simple – Tutor and Jet Provost T.5 each were pressurized side-by-side trainers. Other general comparisons included:

Type	First Flown	Thrust	Max Weight	Max Speed
Tutor	1960	2950 lb	7400 lb	432 kt/28,500'
JP Mk.5	1967	2500 lb	9200 lb	382 kt/25000'

Maj Baines soon was teaching pilots being trained to instructor category. He found RAF and RCAF systems somewhat different. The RAF, for example, used an instructor-student patter technique. As a sortie progressed, the instructor talked more to his student, e.g. all the way through a loop, correcting his student as they went. On Tutors, Baines was used to giving a student more rope, letting him execute a manoeuvre, then doing the critique. For his first month at Little Riz (June) he logged 34:15 hours – fairly typical for the job (RAF flying time was logged from takeoff to touchdown. Taxying was not included, as in the CF). One break in

Baines' June routine was on the 28th, when he flew with Larke in the Gnat. Other famil flights would be in the Vampire and Lightning.

When Little Rissington closed, the JP school moved to Cranwell in April 1976. This was a period when some RAF fighter pilots were having trouble with spin recovery. A program was devised whereby CFS instructors visited stations to put F-4, Harrier and Lightning pilots through spin recognition and recovery exercises. The sorties, tailored to each fighter type, proved effective in broadening pilot skills and confidence. Stu Baines taught on many such "Spinex" sorties. He also was involved teaching a "pre-Gnat" course, readying students for supersonic training with its high washout rate. There also were refresher courses for senior people returning to flying, e.g. Air Commodore J.M.D. Sutton (Commandant, CFS), and A/V/M Roe (RAF Flying Training Command). On June 8, 1976 Baines flew the director of Finnish Air Force flight training. On November 16, 1976 he passed 1000 hours on the JP, then finished his tour 10 days later. Maj Baines returned to Canada to fly a desk until September 1980, then was posted to the CF-5.

Stuart Baines in T-bird days, then a true thing of beauty – the "2 FTS" Tutor formation in which he took part. (Baines Col.)

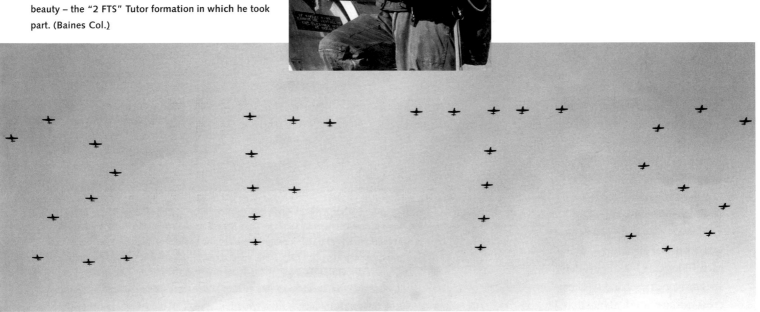

day 439 flew an impressive 25-plane formation then, on Op. Sal Siesta of November 5, delivered its Sabres to the breakers at Scottish Aviation in Prestwick. It had been a super time and F/O Schaan had 961 Sabre hours to prove it. Now he was posted to instruct at Gimli. While the job was to turn out new pilots and IPs, not everything was "routine". There were weekends on the road with a T-33, travelling pretty well anywhere in North America. An unusual assignment came July 21-23, 1964. The NRC was launching Black Brant research rockets at Churchill and needed a chase plane with a SARAH (search and rescue and homing) antenna. By chance, 3 AFS at Gimli had a SARAH T-bird, lest an aircraft become lost over the north. F/O Schaan and F/L Bob Dagenais were tasked to Churchill for the project. When a rocket's nose cone was inbound after a launch, the T-bird would home on its transmissions, then provide a fix for the recovery helicopter.

F/O Schaan now was posted on the first Tutor course, beginning at Portage-la-Prairie on November 13, 1964. Next came a short Tutor FIS at Moose Jaw – 22 trips December 1-10, then he returned to Gimli to teach on the first "direct entry" course (at the same time Moose Jaw was running a similar course). Schaan flew his first student (O/C Jim Rawlings) on January 25, 1965. He hoped to be the first to solo a Tutor student, but that honour went to S/L Don McNaughton, OC of the Tutor squadron. Schaan's log shows a typical flying rate during the course, e.g. April 1965 – 35:05 hours.

In this period 3 AFS comprised Apache, Bandit, Cobra and Demons flights. Training moved briskly, a new course starting every six weeks. Schaan especially enjoyed his RMC students, who seemed extra enthusiastic. Typical was Gord Diamond, who was good at cooking up projects, whether designing Bandit Flight's crest, or a "horse's ass" award (years later some of BGen (ret'd) Diamond's creations were on display in the RCAF Memorial Museum in Trenton). F/L Schaan flew his last 3 AFS trip on August 15, 1966, then began instructing at Portage-la-Prairie, his first student trip being on August 30 (about this time the FIS ceased being a unique formation, becoming a CFS detachment). On June 1, 1967, while up with F/O John Bagshaw in T-33 21243, Schaan hit his 3000th flying hour. On May 24, 1968 he was part of a T-33/Tutor "P" formation over Moose Jaw.

On the final weekend of November 1968 a historic Sabre stand-down party took place at Chatham. This explains what F/L Harvey Schaan and S/L Mark Sauder were doing that weekend. On November 27 they departed Portage-la-Prairie in Tutor '154, routing via Kincheloe AFB, Michigan and Bagotville. The partying done, they headed west on the 30th, this time via St. Hubert, North Bay and Thunder Bay. As his FIS tour waned in the spring of 1969, Capt Schaan learned that he would replace F/L Jim McCullough on the T-38 at the 3525th Pilot Training Squadron at Williams AFB. He first flew the T-38 on June 17 – an hour in 61-0890 with Capt Bill Wittenberg. He added some local trips to June 30 (16.5 hours), before going to Tyndall for the T-38 FIS at the 3250th Flying Training School. This lasted from July 30 to September 17, during which Schaan logged 51.2 hours. He returned to Williams, did some more practice flying, then flew his first student (Capt Doug Seeley, KIA in an O-2A in Laos on March 17, 1971) on October 13, 1969.

Williams was a booming place. Pilot candidates would arrive for screening on Cessna T-41s (Ce.172s). If selected, they did basic jet training in the T-37, then moved to the 6-month T-38 course. In one year alone Williams graduated some 625 pilots to Wings (annual CF pilot output in this period was about 100). Many a graduate could thank his Canadian instructor for, over the years, Williams also had a flock of "Helping Hand" T-37 and T-38 instructors. As did all Canadians on USAF exchanges F/L Schaan found the USAF training system regimented – micromanagement was the rule. Takeoffs were strictly at 3-minute intervals. Each flight was obliged to reserve its aircraft (for any given day) two weeks in advance. This was a headache for schedulers (a secondary duty for IPs). Should there be an accident in the circuit, all senior officers from the Wing Commander and Base Commander on down could expect to be fired within hours. In a day or two, new safety procedures would be published and implemented.

While airborne on July 30, 1970 with an Iranian student in T-38 61-0933, Capt Schaan passed his 4000th flying hour. On November 25 he and fellow Canadian Capt Chuck Reed took T-38 61-0935 to Ottawa via Tinker and Wright-Patterson AFBs. The mission was to consult with their career managers at NDHQ. They flew home on November 30, following a mechanical delay at "Wright-Pat". Another swan began on May 7, 1971, when Capts Schaan and Robertson took off in 61-0887, flying first to Peterson AFB, Colorado, then Winnipeg, from where they drove north to the huge Gimli close-down party. On July 9 they flew home via Ellsworth AFB, their legs being 1.2 and 1.9 hours. On July 16 Capt Schaan logged his final T-38 instructional exercise with 2Lt Hurd.

After tours in the intelligence world, in August 1977 Maj Schaan returned to flying, first to a refresher course at FIS in Moose Jaw. On October 4 he passed his 1000th hour on Tutors. On January 17, 1978 he was back instructing at Moose Jaw. In February 1979 he was in an Air Command party evaluating RAF trainers and syllabi. At RAF Leeming he flew Jet Provost T.3 XN477, while at RAF Valley he flew Hawk XX246. Back at Portage-la-Prairie on November 6-8 he flew Sia Marchetti SM260 N260CB four times (a possible Tutor lead-in type). February 19 to 21, 1980 he flew Pilatus PC-7 HB-HAD five times (possible Tutor replacement). Another break in routine came on April 3, 1981 when Maj Schaan and Capt John Thornton flew a Tutor to Edwards AFB. The Tutor was needed by the USAF Test Pilots School so that students could do some extra spin training. Killing time, Schaan enjoyed flights in a AT-37B, T-38 and two gliders. On April 13 he landed the Tutor on the famous Rogers Dry Lake. Next day he watched John Young and Robert Crippen land "Columbia" at Edwards, this being STS-1 – the first-ever Space Shuttle landing. Schaan and Thornton returned to Moose Jaw on April 15. On August 11, 1981 Schaan made his last flight in the military, a student trip in Tutor '014 with 2Lt Robin Camken. He had logged 2443.5 Tutor hours, 6225.6 overall. He now joined Transport Canada, where he would fly such types as the King Air, DC-3, Citation and Jetstar. Harvey Schaan left aviation on July 15, 1997, re-tiring in Ottawa with 7431.5 flying hours to his credit.

Helping Hand

As the war in Viet Nam expanded, the USAF urgently needed aircrew. Those were the days when valuable USA–Canada defence and diplomatic connections

Harvey Schaan reminiscing about old times at home in Ottawa in August 2002. (Larry Milberry)

In 1968-69 Capt Harv Kuszmaniuk was a "Helping Hand" instructor on the T-37/T-38 at Williams AFB, Arizona. In 2006 he recalled how he and fellow Canadians, Dave Cummings, Bobby Dahl and Jim McCullough, established the "Canada Cup" golf tournament there. In this 1970 photo are instructors Ted Taylor (CF), Harv Kuszmaniuk (CF), unknown USAF, Chuck Reed (CF), Dave Cummings (CF, kneeling), Harvey Schaan (CF), unknown USAF, and Bob Dahl (CF). With "Helping Hand", Canada made a much appreciated contribution to its best friend, the United States of America. (Cummings Col.)

could be made informally. Each year, for example, USAF "senior management" visited the RCAF's famous salmon fishing camp at Eagle River, Labrador. At other times Canadians were invited to golf with their USAF peers at places like Ramey AFB, Puerto Rico. In such a setting the topic of Viet Nam arose one year. Battle of Britain veteran LGen E.M. "Ed" Reyno, Chief of Personnel, was lamenting his surplus of fighter pilots – by 1970 many no longer would have airplanes to fly, due to Ottawa cutting back in NATO. LGen Reyno didn't want to release any of his pilots. Not for him to repeat the infamous 1964 mess, when AFHQ summarily fired the legendary "500". General George B. Simler, Commander of USAF Air Training Command, listened to Reyno, then his eyes lit up. "You have spare pilots, we need instructors. How about it!" From this friendly encounter arose "Helping Hand". Little paperwork was involved, but gung-ho decision-making got things moving. (Gen Simler died at Randolph AFB on September 9, 1972. Heading for a new posting to comsidered this his tour of a lifetime. The flying was great and the living easy – "All of Europe was at our feet in those days," is how he later put it. Back from "Zwei", F/L Allen recruited in London, then got into the Voodoo world with 416 Squadron 1966-68. From here he instructed with the 3500th PTS at Reese AFB. Of this tour he recalled in 2006:

An expensive fender-bender credited to one of Allen's less-than-swift students. The USAF ATC system, having a yearly quota for "wash-outs", kept this fellow around Reese for months after his classmates had graduated, trying to get him through. Finally, they had to admit that he didn't have the right stuff. (Allen Col.)

I was a bit surprised to see your long list of Canadian pilots who helped out with USAF pilot training in those days. I guess we were too busy down there to know what was happening elsewhere … My own tour began with the T-38 course at Tyndall in May 1968. In six weeks I logged 39 hours, then added a further 25 at Reese to complete my instructor checks (later, Canadians would go directly to their assigned bases to check out as instructors).

We found that the RCAF and USAF training systems had their differences, particularly the typical USAF instructor check ride. In the RCAF you would focus on three or four manoeuvres. In the USAF, however, you did it all, the basic instrument ride being especially demanding. You began with the pre-flight briefing, then flew and demoed every aspect of the flight from start to shut down, all at the pace of a tobacco auctioneer.

Maj Wesley B. Allen as a T-38 instructor at Reese AFB. (Allen Col.)

The undergraduate pilot training program at Reese ran for 53 weeks, beginning with a week of orientation, six weeks (30 flying hours) on the T-41 with civil instructors, 19 weeks (90 hours) on the T-37, then 27 weeks (120 hours) on the T-38. The 3500th PTS comprised eight training flights, each with about 30 students. Half the squadron reported for duty at 0500, the other half at 1400 with shifts alternating weekly. About once a month each instructor had a cross-country flight that gave his student five legs out and back from Friday to Sunday. This was instructional time, so required the usual briefings, debriefings and paperwork. On these trips we got to see a lot of the USA, even if mostly from 40,000 feet.

To illustrate the pace at Reese, in early 1969 we were so far behind because of bad weather that we worked seven days a week for seven

straight weeks. By the end of a typical week we instructors usually were so whipped that, after a couple of beers, our only wish was to go home and try to re-establish some sort of family life. Happily, the T-38 was a great airplane and being an instructor had its rewards, especially the satisfaction of watching a student progress. In two years at Reese I logged 1022 T-38 hours, 920 on student trips.

From Reese AFB, Maj Allen was posted to the CF Land Forces staff college course in Kingston, then was in flight safety at Mobile Command HQ, St. Hubert. In 1974 he returned to Voodoos, flying for four years at 409 Squadron, then came tours at Air Defence Group HQ, 22nd NORAD Region HQ, 21 Radar Squadron at St. Margarets, and NDHQ from where LCol Allen retired in 1989, having logged some 6800 hours, including: T-33 – 3000 hours, CF-101 – 1300, T-38 – 1022, CF-100 – 1000. Settled in St. George, Ontario, one of Wes Allen's pastimes was volunteering at the Canadian Warplane Heritage.

Claude Thibault

By the time he left Moose Jaw for Helping Hand at Williams AFB, Claude Thibault already had 1325 hours on the Tutor and T-33. He first flew the T-38 at Williams on May 18, 1970 then, in July and August, did the instructors course at Tyndall. With him were Mike Spooner and Al Robertson, who recently

Maj Claude Thibault does the walk-around on his CF-5, while 419 Squadron was deployed to Nellis AFB for Ex. Red Flag in January 1981. (EI81-41 DND)

had finished CF-104 tours at Baden-Soellingen. In September 1970 Thibault joined the staff of "Tipper Flight" in the 3525th FTS. The following July he was tested by the USAF Training Command Standards Evaluation Board, then was promoted to the Check Section, which did all student flight testing. In May 1972 Thibault again was evaluated, then joined Standards Evaluation, the highest level available for a USAF instructor. In September 2002 Thibault recalled: "I served there as a tester of instructors until my last flight on 11 April 1973. I returned to Canada with 1114.2 hours on the T-38. Not bad for two and a half years of flying. Helping Hand was a great flying experience and one where I made many good friends. I'm still in touch with some of them after 30 years."

Although instructors at Williams often put in 6-day weeks, there was time to play. Typical was the way T-37s and T-38s would fly away on Friday afternoons. This was done since the base was short of hangar space and the Wing Commander didn't want his airplanes sitting around in the open all weekend. The usual thing was that two planes and four pilots would head to Las Vegas to spend Friday night. About noon on Saturday they usually pushed on to Hamilton AFB, San Francisco. On Sunday it was usual to fly down to NAS Miramar, maybe for an after-noon in Tijuana. Crews would land back at Williams early on Monday morning. After such a road trip, one might wonder how a fellow would be ready for work!

The T-38: 40 Years On

Even though more than 40 years have passed since the first RCAF T-38 exchanges, Canadian Forces pilots still fly this great trainer, Capt Carl Cottrell included. Raised in Edmonton, as a boy he was a member of 504 Squadron, Royal Canadian Air Cadets.

There he earned his glider and powered flying licences. In 1989 he joined the Canadian Forces through the Officer Candidate Training Program. He first flew the Musketeer at Portage-la-Prairie on February 28, 1990, progressed to the Tutor at Moose Jaw and won his Wings in June 1991. His next posting was to 419 Squadron for the CF-5 fighter lead-in course. The Hornet followed then, beginning in January 1992, Capt Cottrell joined 416 Squadron. Among his many experiences with 416 was a de-ployment to Aviano, Italy, patrolling former Yugoslavia during Operation Mirador/Deliberate Guard.

In November 1997 Capt Cottrell began an instructional tour at Moose Jaw, and in April 1999 accepted the exchange slot at the 80th FTW at Sheppard AFB, Texas. Dedicated to training foreign students since 1967, Sheppard describes its *raison d'être*: "The Euro-NATO Joint Jet Training Program … [a] multi-nation-ally manned and managed flying training program chartered to produce combat pilots for NATO." At Sheppard, Capt Cottrell replaced Capt Jeff Butterworth, who had been instructing there on T-37s. Cottrell, his wife Karla and their two children reached Sheppard in April 1999, settling into a rental house in nearby Wichita Falls (the arrangement for housing had the exchange officer pay a set Canadian PMQ rate, with anything over that covered by Ottawa).

Flight students at Sheppard are about 50% American, 50% NATO. As were such bases in the 1960s, Sheppard is a huge op-eration. The 80th FTW annually trains some 250 students to Wings in the Undergraduate Pilot Training program, 120 new instructors in the Pilot Instructor Training program, while 150 pilots complete the Introduction to Fighter Fundamentals course. The wing operates more than 200 T-37s, T-6 Texan IIs, T-38Bs, T-38Cs and AT-38Bs. Capt Cottrell began his exchange with the PIT course, flying first on May 5, 1999 with CMDR "Bobo" Bodart of the Belgian Air Force , then joining the 90th FTS. He flew his first student trip there with "Jungle" Flight – an out-and-back to Vance AFB with 2Lt Alcorn on August 31.

During his tour Capt Cottrell would teach Americans, Belgians, Danes, Germans, Greeks, Italians, Norwegians, Portuguese, Turks and Spanish. Routines did not seem to have changed much since Canadians such as Wes Allen, Bob Endicott and Jim Gregory instructed on T-37s and T-38s decades ear-lier. The program being so vast at Sheppard, courses fly in two shifts, the first beginning at 0500, the second at 1100. As Cottrell

Helping Hand Pilots*

Base	Pilots		Base	Pilots		Base	Pilots	
Columbus	Charles Carrington-Smith	T-38	Laughlin	Marc Demers	T-38	Vance	Roger Arsenault	T-38
	Jim Gregory	T-37		Doug Fenton			Knobby Clark	T-38
	Bob Huxter	T-38		Al Luddington			Chris Colton	T-37
	Ted Kasprzak	T-37		Bill Perry	T-37		Tom Goodall	T-38
	Arnie MacLeish	T-38		Rob Porter	T-38		Gord Hatch	T-37
	Don Monk	T-38		Pete Presidente			Alec Raeside	T-38
	Larry Summers	T-37		Chuck Winegarden	T-37, T-38		Bob Reid	T-38
	Rick Wall	T-37	Randolph	Mike Adams	T-37, T-38		Mike Spooner	T-38
Craig	Tom Bugg	T-38		Kenn Doerksen	T-37	Webb	Wayne T. Foster	T-38
	Graham Hunter	T-38		Bob Endicott	T-37, T-38		Lou Glussich	T37, T-38
	Neil Kleinsteuber	T-37		Ron Jensen	T-38		Glen Heaton	T-37
	John Leross	T-38		Mal Joyce	T-37, T-38		Mike Krall	T-38
	Gary Liddiard	T-37		Pat Shamber	T-38		Bob Lake	T-38
	Mike Scott	T-38		Dave Trask	T-37		Terry Lyons	T-38
	Mike Weir	T-37		Chuck Vrana	T-38		Ian MacPherson	T-37
Laredo	Pete Argue	T-37	Reese	Wes Allen	T-38		Pat Moran	T-37, T-38
	Ron Coleman	T-37		Dick Brownfield	T-37, T-38		Mick Scromeda	T-38
	Guy Fabi	T-38		Al Currie	T-37		Chris Tuck	T-38
	Ian Graham	T-37		Norm Hartley	T-37, T-38	Williams	Dave Cummings	T-37, T-38
	Dave Kinsman	T-38		Stan Jones	T-38		Rick Debartoli	
	Mike Krall			Bill Kalbfleisch	T-37		Harvey Kuszmaniuk	T-37, T-38
	Al Robertson	T-38		Cliff Scott	T-37, T-38		Bobby Morris	T-37
	Don Sharkey	T-37		Gerry Walker	T-38		Chuck Reed	T-37, T-38
	Bob Swanson	T-38	Sheppard	Pat Ellison			Wayne Halladay	T-37
							Ted Taylor	T-37, T-38
							Claude Thibault	T-38

* Tentative 2007 data

learned, everything still runs strictly by the book. Students spend about six months on the T-37, advance to the T-38, then graduate after 55 weeks at Sheppard. As per the 1960s, besides routine missions in local flying areas, Capt Cottrell periodically would take a student on a weekend cross-country – 4, 5 or 6 hops pretty well anywhere, giving a student 5 or 6 hours of valuable experience. The occasional opportunity also arose for a "free" weekend. On one of these, in June 2000 Cottrell got as far as Bagotville for an airshow with fellow instructor, Capt "Panos" Patsavoudis of the Hellenic Air Force. Another time he attended the first North American "Tiger Meet", held at Buckley ANG Base near Denver in August 2001. The rational for that swan was that one of his flying mates for the trip was "Tiger Ecki", an instructor at the 80th who had flown Tornados in a Luftwaffe tiger squadron. Besides flying duties, exchange officers at the 80th also had the usual secondary duties, but these seemed less onerous in the 2000s than in RCAF exchange days.

Capt Cottrell's tour ended with a flight of May 31, 2002. For the occasion his T-38 was emblazoned with his call sign, "Sleepy", and Capt "Seigy" Seigmund, USAF, was in the back seat. On landing, he was met by his family and a crowd of other well-wishers. Cottrell had logged 1005 hours on the T-38 during his exchange, made many a life-long friend, and he and his wife had seen their family increase to four children. He now returned to Cold Lake to instruct on the Hawk at 419 Squadron. In 2007 Capt Cottrell was on staff in the Maple Flag planning office at Cold Lake and still was current on the Hawk. By October 2006 his log book showed 650 hours on the Tutor, 1005 – T-38, 1240 – CF-18, 760 – Hawk.

A typical Sheppard AFB T-38 touches down. This superb trainer has been in USAF service since 1961. Then, Capt Cottrell gets hosed down – a tradition when a pilot is "tour expired". For Cottrell's last mission, his T-38 carried his call sign "Sleepy" on one side, his wife's name on the other. At right, Capt Cottrell with wife, Karla, and little ones Aiden (in front), Noah (with dad), Isaac (with mom) and Saraiah still awaiting her appearance. (All, Cottrell Col.)

CHAPTER 16

RAF Coastal Command

The Shackleton

With much to share in the world of maritime aviation, it is not surprising that, for more than 50 years, RCAF/CF aircrew have had exchanges on the Shackleton and Nimrod in RAF Coastal Command. One of the earliest on Shackletons was F/L Douglas F. Robertson. Born in Sault Ste. Marie, Ontario, he was a millwright. Joining the RCAF, he trained at 15 EFTS, earned his wings at 4 SFTS, then flew ops on 426 Squadron. On March 15, 1944 he was on a raid to Stuttgart – 617 Lancasters, 230 Halifaxes and 16 Mosquitos. As the raid approached Stuttgart, fighters pounced, shooting down 37 bombers. Many others were shot up, including Robertson's Halifax, which was clobbered by flak. Despite fire on board, Robertson delivered his bombs. Mid-upper gunner F/O Sharer (an American in the RCAF) quelled the fire and Robertson flew to a safe landing in England. For their good

From the 1950s onwards, many RCAF/CF served on the Avro Shackleton and Hawker-Siddeley Nimrod maritime patrol aircraft. The Shackleton evolved from Avro's line which began pre-WWII with the Manchester. Lancaster, York and Lincoln followed, then came the Shackleton in 1949. Here are views of the Shackleton MR.3, with its trademark tricycle undercarriage and wingtip tanks. Powered by 2450-hp Rolls-Royce Griffons, it had an all-up weight of 100,000 lb, top speed of 260 mph and range of 3600+ nm. Length was 92'6", wing span 119'10". Details of the take-off view are unknown, but the second view is of 203 Squadron's MR.3 XF703 at the Turnhouse (Edinburgh) airshow of July 1, 1961. (via D. Peterson, Roger Lindsay)

The MR.1 Nimrod first flew in 1967. Since then the original fleet of 46 has been steadily upgraded. The basic Nimrod has a length of 126'9" and a wing span of 114'10". All-up weight in early days was 192,000 lb. In the 2000s several new Nimrods were on order, so the ancient de Havilland Comet "look" of the late 1940s soldiers on. XV232, seen in an early view, remained in service into 2007. (RAF)

show, he and Sharer received DFCs. Robertson remained in the RCAF at war's end. By 1950 he was chief flying instructor at No. 2 (M) OTU.

In 1956 Robertson was posted to 206 Squadron at St. Eval in Cornwall, a key Coastal Command station and home to four ASW squadrons. In one report he noted that a St. Eval Shackleton always was on 1-hour SAR readiness. On October 10, 1956 Robertson was airborne within 25 minutes of the alert, searching for a US Navy R6D (DC-6). The squadron flew 16 sorties/200 hours on this operation, but the result was distressing – the R6D had crashed off Land's End, killing all 59 aboard. Robertson also tested

S/L Douglas F. Robertson, DFC, while with Maritime Air Command in April 1961. (PL-142049 DND)

the Shackleton as a back-up transport, noting that 33 passengers could be squeezed in and that cargo was carried in as many as five panniers in the bomb bay. He comments that the Shackleton "proved itself a very valuable aircraft during the recent crisis in the Middle East as a non-bulk carrying aircraft." F/L Robertson reported about Shackleton "Autolycus" ASW trials, this system being used to locate submarines by flying very low to "sniff" for pockets of gaseous submarine emissions. One of his comments describes results as "poor" due to "lack of concrete technical knowledge concerning the formation and movement of the ionized particles on being emitted from the combustion source." For several years, sniffers were used on RCAF Neptunes and Argus, but operators rarely enjoyed success.

In 1957 Robertson was on Op. Grapple supporting UK atomic bomb trials in the Pacific. Eight Shackletons were based on Christmas Island, each allotted 280 flying hours for the mission. A trial was conducted to prove mission viability, much as had been done with the Singapores in 1934 with F/L Mawdesley. For "Grapple", two Shackletons left St. Eval on June 5, 1957, reached Christmas Island on the 18th, then returned home on July 14. The first of Op. Grapple's five Shackletons later staged from St. Eval to Christmas Island via Lajes, Bermuda, Charleston (South Carolina), Biggs (Texas), Travis (San Fransisco) and Honolulu. The others routed via Goose Bay and Winnipeg to Travis. Once on duty they were tasked with low- and medium-level weather recce, sea recce in advance of an explosion (making sure the blast area was clear of shipping), photo recce of post-blast cloud formations, and SAR. F/L Robertson also took part in test drops of the Mk.30 torpedo; and flew night photo recce trials. Douglas F. Robertson ended his RCAF days as a wing commander in AFHQ. He passed away in Ottawa on February 19, 2004.

RAF Ballykelly

Stuart Mohr, who joined the RCAF in Ottawa in 1954, was on the second of two RCAF Beech Mentor courses offered at Penhold. This began on October 25, 1954 – a flight with F/L Bob Ritchie in 24210. After Mohr had flown 71 hours, the program was cancelled, so he switched to Harvards, finishing FTS on June 24. He progressed to AFS at Portage-la-Prairie (T-33s from July to October 1955), completed the FIS course, then instructed on Harvards at Moose Jaw from February 1956 to May 1959. Next, he converted to the Neptune at Summerside (July to October 1959). This was a big step, considering that the Expeditor had been his largest type. The Argus Conversion Unit at Greenwood followed, Mohr flying initially on January 14, 1960. He joined 405 Squadron at Greenwood then, in October 1961, transferred to 415 at Summerside, serving until December 1963, by then having 2800 Argus hours.

Along the way Mohr had requested a RAF exchange. This came through and he replaced Tony Pascoe, a former RAF pilot in the RCAF. The Mohr family travelled to Lahr on a Yukon, got to the UK via Bristol Freighter, then went by train to Kinloss, where Stuart first flew in a Shackleton T.4 on February 21, 1964. The course

F/L Stuart Mohr whose exchange was on Shackletons in RAF Coastal Command. (PL-141373 DND)

ended in June, by when he was used to 4-engine "tail draggers" (it hadn't hurt that he had 2200 hours on another tail dragger – the Harvard). In July 1964 Mohr joined 206 Squadron at St. Mawgan, Cornwall. There he flew the Shackleton MR. Mk.3 until June 1965. In this period Coastal Command was using American nuclear depth bombs. Under the rules, RCAF HQ had to arrange with the US for Mohr's nuclear clearance. Meanwhile, 206 moved to Kinloss in the summer of 1965. Since his security clearance did not arrive in time, Mohr transferred to the Coastal Command Joint Anti Submarine Warfare School at Londonderry as a ground school instructor. He also flew on the Shackleton MR. Mk.2 with 210 Squadron based nearby at RAF Ballykelly. During his tour he crewed on a variety of ASW exercises from Bødo (Norway), Gibraltar, Greenwood, Machrihanish (Scotland) and Vaerløse (Denmark). On one flight he spotted a loitering Vulcan low over a Scottish loch. This was an opportunity – the Shackleton picked up speed in a dive and, just for fun, passed the Vulcan. Despite his short tour, Mohr logged 760 hours on Shackletons, then returned to Canada in July 1966 to Maritime Command HQ, Halifax. He checked out on the Tracker, then rejoined 415 in May 1970, flying the Argus until July 1972. He attended CF Staff College in Toronto, then spent three years in NDHQ. In 1976, following a Tutor refresher course and Cosmopolitan OTU at 426 Squadron, Mohr joined 412 Squadron at Uplands, serving to August 1979. From Colorado Springs he flew "Smoky 2", the NORAD Deputy Commander's "Cosmo", until August 1981. He then joined Transport Canada and the Air Reserve in Edmonton. As a reservist he flew Twin Otters at 418 Squadron until September 1992. At that time NDHQ realized that Mohr had hit age 56 – a year beyond compulsory retirement age.

Shackleton Navigators

A graduate of Toronto's Eastern High School of Commerce, W.D. "Don" Peterson had two brothers in the RCAF during the war. He joined the Army at 18, just as the war ended, but soon was back on Civvie Street. Once he finished school, he considered the RCAF. His choice was hastened by his father's death – his mother would be needing support, so in December 1948 Peterson enlisted. While hoping to be a pilot, he trained as a radio operator. First came an introductory course at the Radio and Communications School at Clinton (January to September 1949). Besides lectures, there were 14 RO exercises on 19 Dakota flights (49:25 hours) from nearby Centralia.

Peterson next attended the Ab Initio Gunnery Course at Trenton. This included 11:10 hours (15 sorties) on Venturas. Finishing with 79%, he was posted to 408 Squadron, flying first on February 1, 1950 in Lancaster FM216. On February 10 he was aboard FM212 under F/O John Sled, DFC, en route to Whitehorse to search for a missing C-54. From there they flew to Port Hardy searching for a USAF B-36 down on the 14th in the Queen Charlottes (next day other SAR resources saved 12 survivors of that crew). FM212 now flew to Vancouver, then left for home on the 18th carrying groundcrew and an RCAF pilot going on compassionate leave. Their departure was not auspicious,

RCAF maritime navigator F/L W.D. Peterson. He flew last on 120 Squadron on August 23, 1962 – a 6-hour night bombing exercise in WR971. By this time his Shackleton time totalled 736:40 hours. (PL-141431 DND)

for an inattentive air traffic controller nearly sent FM212 head on into an arriving TCA North Star!

En route, Peterson received hourly weather reports from Rockcliffe. Eventually, he got what supposedly was the latest report but, while passing Sault Ste. Marie in darkness, he got the true picture. Ottawa was "woxof" and the closest alternate was on the US east coast. FM212 had been airborne for more than nine hours as the FE announced that they were low on fuel. F/O Sled had little choice but to try Ottawa. Rockcliffe was just within limits, so an unsuccessful approach was made. On the second, they hit trees, damaging the nose, pitot head, VHF antennae, undercarriage, etc. They considered bailing out, but were one parachute short. Their final hope was Uplands, where flares were fired at the sound of the Lancaster approaching. F/O Sled, with co-pilot F/O Danny Kaye, spotted a flare and

Most RCAF personnel with Shackleton exchanges began at Greenwood on MR Lancasters and Neptunes. Here sits Neptune 24117 of 405 Squadron in a stock Ron Meush view. When accepted from Lockheed early in 1955, Canada's Neptunes were P2V-5s, i.e. *sans* jet booster engines. Upgraded with J34 jets, they became P2V-7s. RAF Coastal Command flew the P2V-5, while awaiting the Shackleton.

MR.3 Shackleton WR971 of 120 Squadron on which F/L Peterson crewed for the September-October 1961 trans-Atlantic trip. Roger Lindsay took this photo at RAF Acklington in September 1962.

landed in one piece. In time it came out that FM212's long-range belly tank was full, but a pump was u/s, and the FE had not noticed that fuel wasn't transferring to the main tanks. Later, Peterson heard that the met man at Rockcliffe had gone home before they arrived, leaving a junior man in charge, who was providing inaccurate reports.

Peterson resumed flying on March 15 then, on the 24th, was seconded to 414 Squadron for a summer on survey duties at Norman Wells. Many adventures ensued with 408, including much Arctic photo survey. On February 14, 1951, while on Ex. Sun Dog, Peterson was the navigator aboard FM120 (aircraft commander, F/O D.F. "Doug" Robertson, later on exchange). An engine caught fire, but Robertson blew out the flames by diving, then returned to Churchill. Of the 7:20 hours that they were aloft, 5:00 were on three engines. For June 1951 Peterson logged 82:20 from Churchill, Coral Harbour and Resolute Bay. The next month took him to Resolute Bay with F/O Sled and crew doing photo work as far afield as Arctic Bay.

In November 1951 Peterson was posted to 1 ANS in Summerside for the air navigation course, then remained there to instruct. One of his first duties was to navigate Expeditor 1527 on delivery to North Luffenham. This began with a dry run (done with North Star 17502). The delivery route was Trenton-Dorval (0:30 hours), Goose Bay (4:30), BW1 (5:10), Keflavik (5:45), Prestwick (6:45) and North Luffenham (2:30). Peterson

never forgot the sign in the Officers' Club at BW1 which read, "The ice in your drink is over one million years old." A more cryptic sign read, "Drive carefully. The man you kill may be your replacement."

Now on staff at 2 (M) OTU, Peterson taught navigation until posted in May 1954 to 405 at Greenwood. There he made his first Neptune trip on June 29, 1955, guiding 22110 to Argentia and back. The new aircraft was an improvement, not only with better nav equipment, but in crew comfort. Peterson seemed to be forever upgrading, even taking a US Navy ice reconnaissance course. In July 1957 he was posted to Maritime Air Command HQ to man a desk. He first crewed on the Argus on a trip to Lages in 20737 on December 14, 1959 (8:00 hours day, 9:45 night).

In June 1960 F/L Peterson was posted to the Shackleton. Conversion commenced on September 13 with a famil sortie from Kinloss under F/L Wimble. The course, which entailed 11 sorties for 78:15 hours day/night flying, concluded on November 9. By this time Peterson was used to the Shackleton, which seemed to be a good machine – more comfortable and better equipped than a Lancaster. A typical crew included two pilots, duty nav, tactical nav, FE, electronics officer and three signallers (radar, ECM and sonobuoys). From OTU Peterson was posted to 120 Squadron at Kinloss, where he and wife Jean settled in nearby Elgin. Later, however, they had a roomy PMQ at Kinloss (the CO preferred his crews living on station). Peterson commenced flying on December 5, 1960 under S/L Wightwick. Now came all the usual ASW exercises, listed in Peterson's log by sometimes long-forgotten codes – "CASEX", "JASSEX" (Joint Anti-Submarine School exercise), "MOBEX", "Pigeon", "SUBEX" (submarine exercise) and "Tiara".

In September 1961 Shackleton WR971 left Kinloss under S/L Newman with F/L Peterson navigating. They headed to Keflavik (4:25 hours) to overnight, then made Greenwood next day (11:10). On the 16th they proceeded to Norfolk (5:05), where little seemed to be on until the 18th. That day saw WR971 fly to Columbus, Ohio (2:15). Why so far from the sea? Coastal weather was going downhill as Hurricane Esther threatened. Aircraft that could not be hangared had to evacuate. WR971 returned to Norfolk (2:10 hours) on the 21st to prepare for a big NATO exercise – "Fishplay". This commenced on the 24th, Newman's crew logging 13:55 hours. On the 28th they flew in WR990 (11:50). According to Peterson's log there was no flying again until October 8 – a 30-minute air test in WR989. Next day they flew it to Torbay (6:10), then home on the 12th (9:45).

On two patrols between July 10-12, 1962 Peterson crewed on WR990 on "Special Operations" to shadow a Soviet flotilla in northern waters. The first day involved 13:50 hours on patrol, ending in Bødo, Norway. On the 12th WR990 resumed work. Officially, on such a patrol, a Shackleton was not to approach the Soviets closely but, when a new cruiser was identified, it was to press in for photos. As it flew by, anti-aircraft guns tracked it. On this patrol WR990 spotted a periscope, a rare event when seeking Soviet submarines. This prompted a full ASW training response and sonobuoys were dropped. The crew realized that there were several submarines in the area, one of which surfaced to retrieve a few RAF sonobuoys. The operation was a real opportunity for Peterson and crew to put their training to use. WR990 landed home after 16:10 hours.

Peterson usually found Coastal Command routines effective, but there were issues, e.g. the question of the "navigator captain". During exercises or operations, this crewman was the de facto aircraft commander. On occasion, one of these senior navs was known to give orders to the pilot-in-charge about flying the airplane – hardly a navigator's place. In another case, Peterson, as squadron nav leader, found his superior averse to the idea of certain maps:

The charts I ordered were for a new Loran chain covering our area of operations in the North Sea. The Coastal Command navigation officer, a wing commander, refused to fill my requisition, because the charts were from the US Navy. In my judgment, this was not a valid reason, as there were no other navigation aids covering most of that area, and Loran charts would be of great help. Consequently, I scrounged 25 sets from the USAF.

Peterson also recommended that the Shackletons be wired for VOR equipment:

VOR was necessary if you wanted to fly in North America. The Command navigation officer thought that the Shackletons could operate without difficulty, as they had TACAN. He could not have been more wrong. I recommended that they wire all the aircraft for VOR, and acquire 12 sets to permit up to two squadrons to visit Canada and/or the US at any time. The Command telecommunications officer (RCAF on exchange) supported my recommendation, but the Command navigation officer was adamant that there was no need.

Upon leaving Kinloss in 1962, F/L Peterson assumed a management engineering posting at Trenton, his duties entailing analysis of such things as the cost of moving service families around on NATO postings. The job allowed him to maintain flying status as an augmentee on North Stars, then Yukons. It was with regret that he flew his last trip, a July 14, 1967 Fredericton–Trenton hop in Yukon 15925. Don Peterson, who ended with 3911:55 flying hours, now joined the Management Study Unit at Lahr. Later he was with the MSU at Downsview, from where he retired in June 1971. In 2007 he remained an active member of the Aircrew Association in Toronto.

Shackleton Prang

Graduating from high school in Jasper, Alberta in 1949, John Hudson began his RCAF career as a student at Royal Roads in Victoria. Summers were spent training at the Air Navigation School in Summerside, although Hudson spent one summer at North Luffenham in the UK. This turned out to be a bit of a swan, and included meeting the girl whom he later would marry. In 1954 Hudson graduated from engineering from the University of British Columbia and was posted to 2 (M) OTU.

Shackleton XF710 on "the morning after". (Hudson Col.)

to MAC HQ, again specializing in ASW, often in co-operation with the RCN. In the summer of 1962 he requested an RAF exchange, a motivating factor being that his wife's family was in the UK. Accepted, he was posted to Kinloss to replace F/L Peterson. After his course at the Coastal Command Maritime Operational Training Unit, Hudson joined 120 Squadron. Unlike patrols from Greenwood or Summerside, when Soviet submarines were rarely seen, in this period 120 would photograph them passing through the North Sea.

While a usual MAC or Coastal Command tour was uneventful, S/L Hudson's included one big exclamation mark. On the night of January 10, 1964 his crew was on a sortie in Shackleton XF710. Suddenly, No. 3 engine suffered a catastrophic piston failure. Fire erupted and oil and fuel lines burst. Within two minutes the engine fell off, taking with it part of the tail. F/L Gladstone dove into the clear, breaking out near Inverness. In the darkness he spotted a farm field and did not waste a moment in crash landing. The 10 crew evacuated, then rushed to a nearby house, alerting the family to get clear, since the Shackleton was full of fuel and

Following this, he joined 405 in Greenwood. One deployment in this period was to the USNAS Guantanamo Bay, Cuba. There, for about a month in 1958, several 405 Neptunes flew local sorties, learning a new type of active ASW equipment dubbed "Julie". At the time, Fidel Castro was still a revolutionary in the mountains along Cuba's southeast coast, so 405 crews were briefed to skirt this region.

In 1958 Hudson was posted to Maritime Air Command HQ in Halifax, working with civilian scientists in the Defence Research Board's ASW Operational Research Team in the Joint Maritime Warfare School. Two years later he was re-assigned

"Crew 7" of 120 Squadron at Kinloss on January 14, 1964. Provost Alan Ross was visiting to thank them for having missed his town on the night of January 10. Seated are F/O Jim Lee (co-pilot), F/L John Gladstone (captain), Mr. Ross, F/L John Hudson (1st nav) and MWO Pete Lobb (2nd nav). Standing are MWO Bernie Hill (signaller), FSgt John Mepham (FE), FSgt Bill Hickman (signaller), FSgt Jim Hamilton (signaller), FSgt Robin Morrice (signaller) and F/O Dave Pierce (airborne electronics). (Hudson Col.)

pyrotechnics. Meanwhile, the Friday night dance was in progress in a hall a stone's throw away. Young people rushed to the scene. There was soon a tremendous explosion and, by morning, only a wing and part of the tail remained.

Later that summer S/L Hudson's exchange ended and he returned to Canada to attend RCAF Staff College. He joined the Directorate of International Plans at AFHQ, then worked in personnel. In 1967 he left the air force for an opportunity at the Defence Research Board. There he spent 20 years as a civilian scientist in the Operational Research and Analysis Establishment, finally retiring in 1987. While in the UK in 1994, Hudson visited Inverness, found his old crash site and, at a nearby country hotel, met some of those who were present the night of the crash. One woman had a photo of herself as a 4-year old, standing amid the wreck of XF710. John Hudson later joined the Shackleton Association, and reconnected with most of his old crew. On January 10, 1994 they held a 30th anniversary reunion in the same hotel.

F/L Denis Fillion – lost in the disaster of November 19, 1967. Here he receives his navigator's Wings at Moose Jaw from G/C G.H. Elms. (PL-65620 DND)

Sad Endings: Clack and Fillion

John Hudson's predecessor on 120 Squadron, F/L Philip G. Clack, also had an amazing escape. Born in St. Lambert, Quebec in 1929, he had been in Air Cadets during the war, in the Canadian Army Reserves 1947-50, then joined the RCAF. Having earned his Wings at Centralia in January 1951, he advanced through the system until posted in April 1951 to Greenwood. After converting to the Lancaster, he served with 405 Squadron until May 1954, then was posted to SAR Lancasters at 107 RU at Torbay. He later instructed at 2 (M) OTU then, on August 5, 1957, went on exchange to fly Shackletons at 206 Squadron, Kinloss. Clack's CO, W/C R.T. Billett, noted in an assessment of July 22, 1958: " … in his dealings with his crew, on the ground and in the air, he is firm and forceful and exercises good leadership … is mentally acute and discriminating, and can be depended on to reach sound conclusions." On April 13, 1958 Billett added that Clack was a "good all round officer … by his example and industry is an asset to his squadron and a credit to his service." Such were the comments earned by RCAF/CF exchange officers through the years.

WR964 ("Q" 204 Squadron from RAF Ballykelly) refuels at Summerside on October 8, 1963. In March of that year, "Q" completed the longest Shackleton flight, remaining aloft for 24 hours, 36 minutes. WR964 served from March 1954 until SOC in November 1971. (via D.C. Fletcher)

Sadly, F/L Clack's exchange was marred by disaster. While flying in cloud on January 10, 1958, his Shackleton VP259/Q crashed on a hillside near Kinloss. At that moment Clack, standing in the cockpit, was hurled from the aircraft. Pilots Emsden and Stastny died. With his exchange over in February 1960, Clack returned to join MP&EU at Summerside, was posted to Comox in November 1964, then joined 407 Squadron there in May 1967 flying Neptunes. All along, he was highly regarded by his peers and superiors. In August 1971 Capt Clack reluctantly accepted a posting to the RCC in Victoria, from where he retired from the military. By this time his log book showed: Lancaster – 2440 hours, Neptune – 905, Shackleton – 877, Argus -684, Dakota – 630, Expeditor – 554. Ironically, on August 2, 1974 Clack, then age 45, died in a crash similar to that of VP259. That day he and another renowned ex-RCAF pilot and ETPS graduate, Jimmy Fewell, were piloting Conair DC-6B water bomber CF-PWA on a forest fire near Kamloops, BC. Something went wrong and the plane flew into a mountain, killing the crew.

F/L Denis J.L.R. Fillion, born at St-Laurent d'Orleans, Quebec in 1932, joined the RCAF in August 1951. By July 1952 he was a student at No. 1 Radio and Communications School at Centralia. Following other duties, he was posted to No. 1 ANS at Winnipeg in April 1953. By year's ended he graduated as an air navigator and was commissioned. After training at 2 (M) OTU, he was with 404 Squadron at Greenwood from August 1954, then joined 107 RU in October 1958. He was a recruiting officer in Ottawa 1958-62, on staff at 2 (M) OTU, then flew on Neptunes at 407 to March 1966, when he was noted as on strength with CDLS London (to which all Canadians on UK exchanges were attached).

Fillion, with 120 Squadron at Kinloss, would be praised by his superiors for his "enthusiasm, intelligence and initiative." An assessment by S/L J.P. Wells noted, "I would endorse the manner in which this officer has converted ably to a strange aircraft, in a strange enjoinment, in a minimum time, throughout maintaining a co-operative and cheerful disposition for which

LCol John Bossons, who served on 120 Squadron, where he crewed on both Shackleton and Nimrod. (CSC94-133 DND)

he and his parent service may be justifiably proud." On November 19, 1967 F/L Denis Fillion was first navigator aboard Shackleton WR976 on detachment at RAF St. Mawgan for Ex. Midsummer. At 0815 local time WR976 engaged a friendly submarine. A Canadian report of February 14, 1968 explains:

At this time three seamen aboard HMS Brighton, an RN vessel participating in the exercise, sighted the aircraft flying in broken cloud … 700 feet to 800 feet above sea level in a descending turn to port. The aircraft suddenly appeared to level its wings and then crashed into the sea and disintegrated. Ships in the area recovered two survivors and three bodies, and a number of pieces of wreckage. However, F/L Fillion was not found [WR976 went down 180 nm off Land's End].

Nimrod Days: Bossons in Kinloss

Born in 1940, John E. Bossons was raised in Duncan, BC, where his father worked in forestry. After a year at university, in 1960 John decided to join the RCAF to learn a trade and earn some money. He first flew at the ANS at Winnipeg, going up in Expeditor 1536 on July 6, 1960. Selected for long-range navigation, he left the ANS in May 1961 with 143:05 hours on the Expeditor and Dakota. Posted to 2 (M) OTU at Summerside, he flew first on July 17, 1961 in Neptune 24104. Part of November was spent at the Argus Conversion Unit, then he joined 404 at Greenwood. This tour would be typical, with many ASW patrols throughout the Atlantic. October–November 1962 was a bit out of the ordinary, however, since Canada was on alert during the Cuban Missile Crisis. In this period Bossons' crew flew several patrols logged as "CUBEX", one of 16:15 hours on November 3, 1962 in Argus 20729. F/L Bossons next served at Summerside with 2 (M) OTU and the MP&EU, crewing on several missions evaluating improved nav/tactical equipment. He was posted in 1970 to 120 Squadron at RAF Kinloss, arriving on April 16 to replace Maj Al Kirkpatrick. The Bossons settled into an old farm house near the station.

Maj Iain Huddleston, aide-de-camp to Gen R.J. Hillier, Chief of Defence Staff. He's seen with Gordon Cooper at the Albany Club in Toronto, April 27, 2007. From 2002-06 Huddleston flew Nimrods on exchange at RAF Kinloss. In March 1994, Cooper had a mini-exchange on F-5s with the Turkish AF. (Larry Milberry)

Nimrod XV246, in which John Bossons flew his final sortie, passes over the Toronto waterfront on September 6, 1971. Then, a Soviet "Whiskey" Class submarine surprised by a Kinloss-based Nimrod between Iceland and the Faeroes in 1971. This widely-used diesel vessel evolved from the WWII German Type XXI U-boat. Catching a Soviet sub on the surface was rare for an ASW crew. (Larry Milberry, Bossons Col.)

Having formed late in WWI, 120 Squadron gained its fame in Coastal Command in WWII, flying Liberators over the North Atlantic. Disbanded at war's end, it reformed in 1946 with Lancasters, then re-equipped with Shackletons in 1951. Bossons' first duty with 120 Squadron was a surveillance mission of July 8 in WR982. Just off the Argus, he found the Shackleton cramped and obsolete (plotting still was done manually). Happily, 120 Squadron began re-equipping with the Nimrod MR.1 in October 1970. Now it was the Argus that looked obsolete. The Nimrod

greatly reduced transit times to patrol areas, and, not surprisingly, was more comfortable than an Argus. Capt Bossons first flew on the Nimrod on January 14, 1971 – a 236 OTU exercise in XV234. OTU ended on February 20. These were busy times for the UK, so Bossons and crew often were deployed. Exercises or operations could find a crew one month in Cyprus or Gibraltar, the next in distant Tengah, Singapore.

For a typical Far East deployment, on February 28, 1972 Bossons departed Kinloss with his crew aboard XV241. First stop was Akrotiri after six hours. They pressed on to Masirah in Muscat and Oman (4.8 hours) for fuel and to spend the night. Next day the first leg was to Gan in the Indian Ocean (4 hours), thence on to Tengah (4.5 hours). Their first patrol was on March 6, a 6.5-hour "Survex" mission. On the 10th came a patrol regarding Ex. Transitex (8.8 hours). A similar patrol came on the 13th (8 hours), then a "Subex" (training with an RN submarine) and Casex" (RN surface vessels) on the 16th for 6.3 hours. Next day there was a "Survex" for 8.2 hours. For a "Casex" of the 17th the crew co-operated with the surfaced submarine HMS *Ovens* for 5.3 hours. Ex. Genesis occupied XV241 on the 24th for 4 hours. There was crew training on the 27th and 28th totalling 9.3 hours. Capt Bossons flew eight sorties in April for 42 hours. For April 24 to 26 his crew was in the Philippines on R&R. They started home from Tengah on May 2, routing via Gan, Masirah and Akrotiri. Bossons flew his final mission in XV246 on October 4, 1972, then returned to Canada. His tour totalled 107 hours on the Shackleton, 942 on the Nimrod.

SAR, etc., plus some operations, appear in his log book in the following months. In February 1953 he was posted to the "SNIN" course, then joined 405 in May. In 1955 he spent almost a year at the Air Navigation School in Winnipeg, studying on the advanced "SPEC-N" course. From here he was posted to the Joint Maritime Warfare School at HMCS *Stadacona* in Halifax, working mainly in ASW tactics with military and Defence Research Board staff. From early 1956 he was involved in Neptune operational trials, especially relating to sonobuoys. In July 1957 he began a tour at Maritime Air Command HQ.

F/L Hicks had his first flight on the Argus on January 21, 1959, flying in 20723, the first trials Argus in what would become the Maritime Proving and Experimental Unit. The main task was evaluating ASW tactics and submarine detection systems, whether acoustic, MAD or radar. The newly-introduced "Julie" ASW system was big on the program. This involved Hicks in about 30 flying hours monthly. In April 1961, while Staff Officer Development

F/O Russell E. Hicks with F/O Dave Ives on a 1951 2 (M) OTU training exercise in Bermuda. Ives later was on exchange on C-141s. (PL-72315 DND, Ives Col.)

and Evaluation, he was promoted to squadron leader. Soon, he heard from G/C C. Burgess of MAC HQ that he was posted to VX-1, the US Navy experimental squadron at Key West, Florida. Hicks was the man for the job, since VX-1 was looking for a senior navigator who knew weapons and tactics, and had a test and development background, especially in acoustics. Hicks was the first RCAF aircrew at VX-1, which previously had only RCN exchange personnel. He reached VX-1 on September 21, 1961 and began flying on October 5 – a 4:35-hour mission in P2V-7 "29". On November 1 he flew in the S2F-3 Tracker and, on the 7th, in the HSS-2 Sea King. VX-1 also was doing trials with the new P3V-1.

One difference that Hicks noticed at VX-1 was that US Navy long range patrol planes carried no trained navigators. Instead, a third pilot acted as navigator, something unthinkable in the RCAF. Hicks also discovered that VX-1's aircraft needed their compasses swung, which he and S/L Spalding (RAF exchange) rectified. Meanwhile, VX-1 designated Hicks as "Jezebel" project officer. In 2002 he explained the basics of the sonobuoy and Jezebel:

A P-3 Orion, on which Canadians had USN, RAAF and RNAF exchanges over the decades. BurAero No. 150509 of the OTEF (NAS Norfolk) is seen at Charleston AFB on December 30, 1966. Today, it is on display at Moffitt Field, California. (Larry Milberry)

A sonobuoy is a device which is dropped into the ocean, then is powered by a salt water-activated battery. It includes a radio transmitter that transmits sounds detected by its underwater hydrophone. In the early days, the operator listened to the sounds and, with experience, could differentiate between undersea life and propelled vessels. If there were no targets nearby on radar, it might be assumed that the sounds were coming from a submarine, particularly if the submarine were snorkelling and, thus, using its diesel engine and making quite a bit of noise. The passive listening technique was prone to false alarms, until techniques were developed under Project Jezebel to give the operator a display of the frequencies emanating from the target. By this means target evaluation was much improved.

Passive sonobuoy techniques also suffered from a lack of range information. Under Project Julie, a small explosive charge was dropped near the sonobuoy and used as a sound source to get an echo from a submerged target. This would establish the range of the target from the sonobuoy. This was called making a passive buoy active ("Julie" was a stripper who was said to make passive boys active, and that's how the project got its name).

Since the Argus was at the height of development, MP&EU sometimes visited Key West. Argus '729 arrived on December 6, 1961 under F/L Phil Clack. Besides daily tasks, VX-1 also went on deployments. On July 5, 1962, for example, Hicks was on a Neptune headed for RAF Ballykelly. But, by far the most exciting time in this period came that fall — the Cuban Missile Crisis. On October 22 President Kennedy went on television to describe a looming crisis – the USSR was installing IRBMs in Cuba. Kennedy declared an embargo around the rogue nation and the world watched and waited. Meanwhile, Hicks and crew were in Pennsylvania under LCDR Carruth with P3V-1 "40". As the crisis worsened, on October 31 they deployed to NAS Norfolk, where they were armed and tasked to shadow Soviet submarines and freighters. At this time there were few P3Vs in service, so even VX-1's test aircraft was considered a national asset. Hicks' log shows the following November operations:

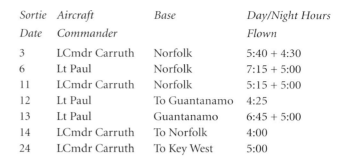

Sortie Date	Aircraft Commander	Base	Day/Night Hours Flown
3	LCmdr Carruth	Norfolk	5:40 + 4:30
6	Lt Paul	Norfolk	7:15 + 5:00
11	LCmdr Carruth	Norfolk	5:15 + 5:00
12	Lt Paul	To Guantanamo	4:25
13	Lt Paul	Guantanamo	6:45 + 5:00
14	LCmdr Carruth	To Norfolk	4:00
24	LCmdr Carruth	To Key West	5:00

From October to December 1962 S/L Hicks logged 102 flying hours. With the Cuban crisis resolved (the USSR withdrew its IRBMs) VX-1 returned to routines. On March 1963 Hicks was on a squadron exchange to Greenwood. This visit was the first there by a P3V. Hicks flew his last VX-1 mission on July 22, 1963, finishing with 730 hours on squadron. He returned to Canada and a year at RCAF Staff College. Upon graduation, he left the RCAF for a career in industry. He joined Computing Devises in Ottawa, working in the ASW field, then was with other firms in computer technology. He retired in Ottawa in 1990.

S/L Hicks whose VX-1 exchange led to unexpected operations during the Cuban Missile Crisis. (DND)

VP-56 NAS Jacksonville

From 1974-78 Canada sent five AESOps and three flight engineers on the US Navy P-3C exchange to VP-56 "Dragon" Squadron at NAS Jacksonville. One AESOp was Eric Welin, who had joined the RCAF in 1960. Having trained as a metal tech, he served from Saskatoon to Gimli, Marville and Lahr. For the latter two postings his main type was the Bristol Freighter at 109 (Comm) Flight. In 1970 he remustered to aircrew, training as an AESOp at the CF ANS in Winnipeg, and at 449 Squadron, the Argus OTU in Greenwood. Sgt Welin then had an Argus tour with 407 in Comox. In 1974 he and fellow AESOp Sgt Roy Chrapchynski were posted to VP-56. Initially, they spent several months at VP-30 (NAS Patuxent River), qualifying on P-3C ASW equipment, e.g. the AQA-7 acoustic system, a superior set compared to the Argus' AQA-5.

The Canadians joined VP-56 in January 1975. They now went by the US Navy job description "AW", i.e. airborne anti-submarine equipment operator. Although they were "in the navy", this didn't take a big adjustment. They settled into rented homes off

Sidewinders and a Matra R.530 IR-guided AAM. These missiles were early generation, so had limited performance (one Aussie referred to them as "Model T" missiles). As a bomber, the RAAF Mirage carried as many as ten 500-lb Mk.82 bombs.

While the flying was good at Williamtown and on deployment to such places as Darwin, Nesbitt felt that the RAAF was too self-centred of an operation. New ideas did not always seem welcomed. His superiors at OCU, for example, were not amused when he questioned the practice of fighters joining formation on the inside of a turn. Once he joined 77 Squadron, however, he found a more open atmosphere. In this period the RAAF's Mirages had interchangeable noses – a radar nose in fighter "config", or a recce nose with a 180-degrees panoramic camera. This camera, however, wasn't stereoscopic, so Nesbitt suggested two 70-mm Vinton cameras in the Mirage belly pack. Since there were some excellent photo techs at Williamtown (some with Vietnam experience) and lots of spare equipment, the techs came up with a belly pack mod and the Vinton system (normally used in the RAAF's Canberras) was installed.

Something else that Nesbitt learned about the Mirage was how, once it passed 30 degrees in a dive, its aerodynamic pressure centre moved back over the wing. This made the airplane dicey to control. He informed his CF-104 buddies in Germany about this – when jumped by a French or Belgian Mirage, if you have the altitude, just stuff your nose down and you'll lose a Mirage! The RAAF regularly sent squadrons overseas to places like Butterworth, Malaysia. Nesbitt, due to Canadian exchange regulations, could not participate in these deployments. In September 1975 his exchange ended. With 532 hours on the Mirage, he joined 419 Squadron at Cold Lake, instructing on CF-5s into 1980, then serving at NDHQ on the NFA project. Looking down the road, he began wondering about his future as a 40-year old fighter pilot, so moved into the "Herc" world at 435 Squadron. Although no other Canadian flew Mirages in the RAAF, to this day there is a Canadian F/A-18 slot at Williamtown.

(Right) Capt Bill Nesbitt during his tour at 419 Squadron. In 1985 he left the military for the airlines, spending several years flying 747s for Nationair and Air Atlanta. He retired from aviation in 1999 after logging some 13,000 hours. (Nesbitt Col.)

(Below) A superannuated RAAF Mirage III-O of the type flown by Bill Nesbitt. A3-55, which served 1967-87, is seen at RAAF Amberley in 76 Squadron markings in September 1998. The RAAF operated some 116 Mirages, some of which later flew in the Pakistan Air Force. (Larry Milberry)

CHAPTER 19

CAFE in Colour

RCAF personnel usually were posted on exchange based on their personal evaluation reports. "PERs" were written annually (usually by one's CO). Readers will see cases where a pilot or navigator served first on Lancasters with 408 Squadron. With a focus on the Arctic, 408 provided young aviators with many challenges, testing their abilities to the limit. From 408, aircrew could advance to Yukons, from whence an exchange might follow, perhaps to the Canberra. The RAF welcomed such experienced men. David Ives, who began on 408, photographed Lancaster 10AR KB839 at Resolute Bay in the Arctic on October 14, 1960. In September 1965, taking part in a formation of three Yukons at the Toronto air show, he photographed Yukon 15930. From 437 Maj Ives began a C-141 Starlifter exchange at Dover AFB. Here is a typical Starlifter 65-9408 at Charleston AFB on December 30, 1966. Back home Ives flew the C-130. Of the aircraft shown, KB839 is preserved with the Greenwood Military Aviation Museum in Nova Scotia. Yukon '930 served Canada 1961-71, then migrated to Zaire to fly for another decade. It was scrapped in 1985. Starlifter '9408 served the USAF for some 35 years, then went for scrap to Davis-Monthan AFB in 2001. (Ives Col., Larry Milberry)

RCAF pilots and radio operators crewed on the Hastings in RAF Transport Command. Leslie Corness photographed WD496 from A&AEE Boscombe Down at Frobisher Bay on September 11, 1958. This classic "propliner" eventually gave way to the Britannia.

RCAF members and "ex-pat" Canadians flew the Britannia. In its RAF years (1960-75) Britannia XM490 "Aldebaran" flew on 99 and 511 Squadrons at Lyneham. It later was a commercial freighter, then went for scrap in 1979. Leslie Corness photographed it at CFB Namao on August 1, 1974.

F/L T.E. "Ed" Dodd's exchange was with the Aircraft and Armament Experimental Establishment at Boscombe Down. He photographed A&AEE Comet XS235 "Canopus" at Kai Tak during a Hong Kong stopover. Ed Dodd left the air force in 1978 to work with Litton Industries, as Canada prepared to introduce the Aurora. Later, he operated a computer company franchise, before retiring in Berwick, Nova Scotia in 1993. As to XS235 it served the RAF 1963-95 and now is preserved at Bruntingthorpe, UK.

When F/L Doug Scott and crew of the 55th WRS faced a dire emergency during a weather patrol, WB-50D 49-0333 escorted them to Ladd Field. Scott photographed '0333 over Alaska's Brooks Range. At least one other RCAF officer, F/L George McCormick, served on the WB-50. (D.G. Scott Col.)

F/Ls Gordon Webb (pilot) and John Goldsmith (navigator) had USAF C-97 exchanges. Shown at Minneapolis on August 20, 1963 is C-97A 48-0412 of the 109th ATS, Minnesota ANG. (Larry Milberry)

"VP", or maritime patrol exchanges, have taken Canadians abroad on such types as the Shackleton, Nimrod, Neptune, Orion and Viking. Shown are Shackleton "B" of 120 Squadron at the Biggin Hill air show on May 13, 1965; Nimrod MR.2 XV240 at Abbotsford, BC on August 7, 1993; and an ex-RAAF Neptune. Having served until 1977, A89-273 later was restored by the Historical Aircraft Restoration Society of NSW and flies as VH-IOY. Here it arrives at the 1998 Scone, NSW airshow. (Leslie Corness, Larry Milberry)

Canberra PR.7 WJ821 over the Caribbean in 1962. Having joined the RAF in 1954, it served with 82 Squadron (Wyton), then was on 58 Squadron (Wyton) and 13 Squadron (Akrotiri and Luqa). After an engine failure on takeoff from Bedford on July 25, 1980, it became an instructional airframe and now is a gate guardian at Bassingbourn. (Funge Col.)

In 1951 Martin Aircraft of Baltimore signed an agreement with English Electric to build the B-57 version of the Canberra (first flown in July 1953). Martin built 403 B-57s in various configurations. Many later became EB-57s on which several RCAF EWOs served. EB-57E 55-4295 is seen at Kincheloe AFB, Michigan in August 1966. (Larry Milberry)

An extended-wing EB-57Ds (nine were converted from RB-57Ds) during F/L Ray Cutt's time at the 4677th DSES. One EB-57D survives at the USAF Museum in Ohio. (Ray Cutt)

IWS F-101F Voodoo 56-0274 along the Gulf Coast near Tyndall in May 1960. Then, below, F-106A 57-2476 on approach to Tyndall in February 1960. '2476 eventually became a QF-106A target drone. As such it was shot down by an AIM-120 on September 14, 1993. (Simkins Col.)

F/Ls Gary Naylor and Ping Green while on IWS exchange at Tyndall AFB 1965-67. (CANAV Col.)

F/L Gordon Joy shot F-100 Super Sabre 53-1583 at Nellis AFB *circa* 1956. Pilots in this era appreciated the limitations of such post-war fighters, so flew them accordingly. Some thought the F-100 was "a dog", others were more complimentary. This example ended with the Taiwanese Air Force.

B-57s from the Simkins/Harbarsher mission to Pakistan. (Simkins Col.)

(Below) A typical F-105D of the Vietnam War era. 61-0138 is shown at WPAFB on May 19, 1968. (Larry Milberry)

Unit patches are a big part of squadron spirit and heritage. This is the patch worn by F/L Tappy Carruthers during his F-105 tour at Nellis AFB. (via Nan Carruthers)

183

CF-5 116701 at Edwards AFB during 1968 trials. Then, below left, 434 "Bluenose" Squadron CF-5 116725 refuels from a US Navy KA-3B Skywarrior during a March 1981 squadron exchange. (Diller Col., Robert L. Lawson via 434 Sqn)

CF-5 squadrons spent about half of any year "on the road" doing exercises and exchanges. These 433 CF-5s were at Trenton on August 31, 1975 during one of their endless deployments. Following its career, CF-5 116733 became a museum display at Bagotville, while '742 was sold to Botswana. (Larry Milberry

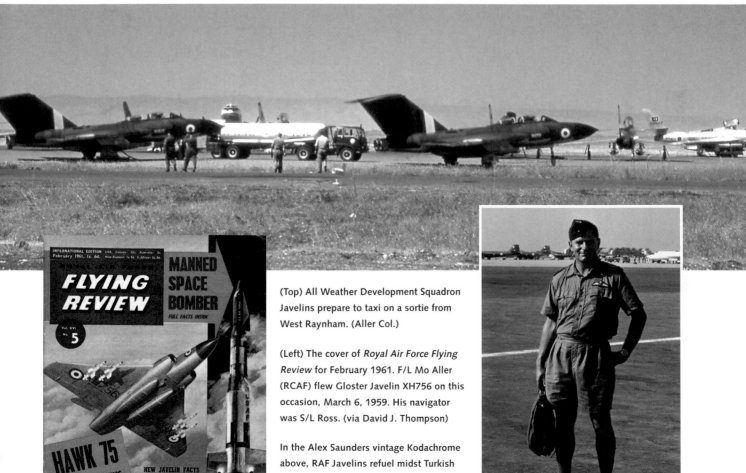

(Top) All Weather Development Squadron Javelins prepare to taxi on a sortie from West Raynham. (Aller Col.)

(Left) The cover of *Royal Air Force Flying Review* for February 1961. F/L Mo Aller (RCAF) flew Gloster Javelin XH756 on this occasion, March 6, 1959. His navigator was S/L Ross. (via David J. Thompson)

In the Alex Saunders vintage Kodachrome above, RAF Javelins refuel midst Turkish Air Force F-84s at Diyarbakir on July 28, 1961. Then, Saunders at Bahrain the following day.

Canadians had F-4 Phantom II tours with the USAF, USN, RAF and Luftwaffe. This RF-4C is seen at Wright Patterson AFB on May 22, 1966. (Larry Milberry)

Only F/Ls Don Elphick and Bob Worbets of the RCAF flew the F-106 Delta Dart operationally. Here, F-106A 58-0764 of their squadron, the 49th FIS, poses with a T-33 during a January 1985 NORAD training mission from Griffiss AFB. Retired in 1987, '0764 became a QF-106A drone and was shot down by an AIM-120 missile on September 19, 1994. (Larry Milberry)

A typical RF-4E Phantom II from Canadian exchange pilot Capt Gordon Zans' unit, No. 511 "Immelman" Squadron, based at Bremgarten. "35-40" is shown during a deployment to Beja, Portugal. (Zans Col.)

(Above) While on a NATO assignment on February 23, 1999, LCol Gordon Zans flew on a Czech AF intercept mission with Maj J. Hlava. Zans photographed MiG-21 No. 7802 after it had "shot down" their L.39 trainer.

(Right) LCol Zans at Rockcliffe on October 18, 2001 upon delivering CF-18 188901 to the national aeronautical collection. Zans finished his active fighter career with a July 8, 2002 mission in CF-18 118741. By then his log book showed 2875.4 hours, mainly on the Tutor, CF-104, CF-18 and RF-4E. (Zans Col.)

Mo Aller photographed AFDS Lightning F.1 XG336. TOS in August 1959, XG336 later was modified to F.3 standards and became a Red Top trials aircraft at A&AEE. It was scrapped in 1974.

(Right) Lightning sorties of January-February 1965 as logged by F/L J.R. Chisholm during his RAF exchange.

(Below) Wilf White's view of Lightning F.3 XP705. TOS in October 1963, it began on 74 Squadron, later served 56, 29 and 111 squadrons, then returned to 29 Squadron in July 1969. Following an in-flight fire on July 8, 1971, the pilot successfully ejected into the sea off Cyprus.

The RAF's durable Jet Provost was flown over the decades by RCAF/CF exchange pilots and "ex-pat" Canadians in the RAF. At Abingdon on September 16, 1967, Leslie Corness photographed Jet Provost T.3A XM470. This aircraft was flying privately in South Africa in 2007.

(Right) Canadians at a Little Rissington mess function *circa* 1960. On the left are Bill and Karen Mills, then Ian Morrice, Dorena Morrice (behind), Joan King, and Bernice and Jerry Thorneycroft. Bill and Jerry were ex-RCAF on RAF contracts. (Morrice Col.)

(Below) A typical Gloster Meteor T.7, the trainer flown by many Canadians in the 1950s-60s. WH166 is seen at Little Rissington in February 1969. In 2007 it was privately owned in the UK. (Turbo Tarling)

The Folland Gnat first flew in 1955 as a lightweight fighter project. In the RAF, however, it became the trainer onto which students advanced after the Vampire T.11 or Jet Provost. Various Canadians instructed on the Gnat, an example of which is shown in Red Arrows colours at Dulles Airport, Washington on May 25, 1972. (Larry Milberry)

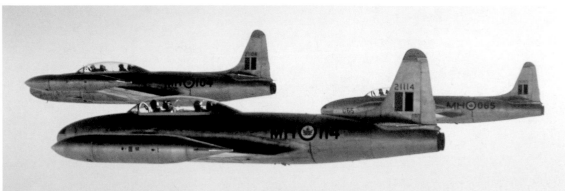

RCAF pilots on exchange postings invariably had trained/instructed on the T-33, a flight of which is seen on a 1956 mission from RCAF Station MacDonald. Many RAF and USAF exchange pilots enjoyed flying Canada's T-33s. (Don Carney)

(Above) The standard USAF jet trainers over the decades were the Cessna T-37 "Tweet" and Northrop T-38 Talon. More than a hundred Canadian pilots have had exchange tours on these types, especially with the Vietnam War era "Helping Hand" program. This T-37B was photographed by Larry Milberry at Griffiss AFB in July 1986, while with the 416th Bomb Wing as a B-52 pilot proficiency trainer. The T-38s above right were photographed by Capt Harvey Schaan during a November 1969 mission from Williams AFB, Arizona.

T-38 instructor F/O "Tex" Deagnon during his stint as the RCAF's "Red Knight". (PCN5140 DND)

Canadian pilots flew F-15 Eagles in Alaska, until the infamous "no foreign" rule kicked in, putting that exchange on ice. Canadians Seldon Doyle and Graham Sinclair had the F-15 exchange at Elmendorf AFB from 1989-93. Here is Sinclair in November 2003 with RCAF pilot Bill Stowe, who had flown P-40s in Alaska in WWII. Sinclair commissioned the painting showing him (in his fighter pilot dreams) shooting down an Su.27 Flanker over Alaska! (Larry Milberry)

Since the Berlin Wall came down, former-USSR aircraft from MiG-29 or Su-27 fighters to the impressive Bear bomber and six-engine An-225 freighter have visited Canada and the US. Here, 441 Squadron CF-18s escort a Russian MiG-29 heading for the Abbotsford air show on August 5, 1989. (CKC89-5682 DND)

Billie Flynn completes a Eurofighter test flight at Manching. In 2007 he was test flying F-16s for Lockheed Martin in Texas. (Larry Milberry)

Former 441 Squadron CO, Billie Flynn as a civilian Eurofighter Typhoon II test pilot at Manching, Germany in October 2002. While a CanForces pilot, he had spent five years at Edwards AFB testing exotic versions of such types as the F-16 and F/A-18. On the left is Bernhard Tantarn, designated CO of the first German Eurofighter squadron. Tantarn had flown CF-18s on exchange at 441 Squadron. (Larry Milberry)

In 2007, C-17 exchange pilot Maj Jeremy Reynolds commented about these photos: "Here is a C-17 on one of the very narrow taxiways in Bagram, Afghanistan. In the distance a C-17 is departing – a testament to how busy this forward operating base could be. Everybody came and went on slot times. The cockpit shot is of myself and my co-pilot, Capt Brian Hoffman, during a pause in Bagram, while on a night mission. The action shot demonstrates C-17 operational capability – taking off on a dirt runway. Finally, an Abrahms MBT is seen being loaded at Ramstein and bound for Iraq during the opening days of the war in 2003. We lifted 20 tanks into Iraq in less than 24 hours." (USAF)

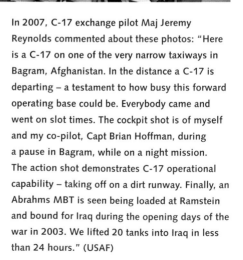

CHAPTER 20

USAF Fighter Exchanges

Early Days: F-86, F-89, F-94

America's technical progress after WWII made a healthy RCAF/USAF alliance essential. Once Canada chose the North American F-86 Sabre, for example, it sent personnel to train in the US on the new type. In 1949 there was a cadre of RCAF technical men at North American in Los Angeles. Headed by S/L Jim Hemsley, they constituted the RCAF Technical Services Unit, working with Canadair tech reps gathering data needed to service and maintain Sabres. The first RCAF Sabre pilot was F/L J.A. Omer Levesque. Checking out at the USAF F-86 conversion unit at Kirtland AFB, New Mexico in November 1950, he joined the 4th Fighter Wing, 334th Fighter Interceptor Squadron in Langley, Virginia. There his liaison turned into a combat posting, when the 334th moved to the Far East. F/L Levesque, the first of 22 RCAF Sabre pilots in Korean action, would be the first Commonwealth pilot to shoot down a MiG-15 (details of all RCAF Sabre pilots in Korea are in *The Canadair Sabre*).

Another Sabre course was attended by F/L Ray Greene of EP&E (Rockcliffe) and F/Os John Marion, Don Morrison and Grant Nichols of 410 Squadron. The latter three spent from November 22 to December 14, 1950 with the 92nd FIS at Larson AFB, Washington. There they each flew the F-86A for about 10 hours, but also spent hours in the classroom learning Sabre technical details. Of this experience Morrison recalled: "We returned to Canada to do the initial acceptance and pilot training on the F-86 produced by Canadair. The first 20 aircraft built had a 4-pound break-out force on the control column. These were difficult to fly in formation, but a modification to a reduced force with a built-in feel system improved later aircraft considerably. The original batch was updated by Canadair." On June 22, 1951 F/Os Bob Simmons and Willy Weeks of 410 were sent on a 10-week USAF Sabre gunnery course in Nevada. In August A/F/L Larry Spurr was off to fly Sabres with the 93rd FS at Kirtland AFB, New Mexico, following which he flew a tour in Korea.

While on secondment in Korea with the USAF (334th FIS), on March 31, 1951 F/L J.A. Omer Levesque became the first Commonwealth pilot to shoot down a MiG-15. Here, Col H.A. Sabastan presents Omer with the USAF DFC. Then, F/L Grant H. Nichols during his Korean Sabre tour (16th FIS). Nichols flew 50 combat missions from January to May, 1953 and was credited with one MiG-15 as a "probable". A chapter in *The Canadair Sabre* deals with 22 RCAF pilots who flew USAF Sabres in Korea. (PL-51603, PL-56431 DND)

All-Weather Jet Pioneers

Having joined the RCAF in November 1943, F/O James E. Hanna trained as a flight engineer in 1945, was commissioned, but was too late to get overseas. He remustered for pilot training, winning his wings at Centralia on August 25, 1949 as part of the initial RCAF University Air Training Plan course. In 1950 he earned an Aeronautical Engineering degree at the University of Toronto. Next came AAS at Trenton and No. 1 (F) OTU on Vampires, then Hanna flew Mustangs and Harvards with 416 Squadron at Uplands. By the time of his exchange he had 40 hours on Vampires, 90 on Mustangs.

On July 31, 1951 F/O Hanna reported to the Canadian Joint Liaison Staff in Washington, where he was briefed by W/C J.T. McCutcheson. Next day he reached Otis AFB, Massachusetts, home of the 33rd FIW. In 2005 he recalled: "On my arrival the base adjutant asked if I ranked the Base Commander. I resisted the opportunity to elevate the status of an RCAF flying officer." Defending the airspace from Boston to New York, the 33rd comprised the 58th FIS at Otis (F-86A Sabre), the 60th FIS at Westover, Maine (F-86E), and the 59th FIS at Grenier AFB, Massachusetts (F-47 Thunderbolt). Hanna began on the T-33 on August 6, 1951. This entailed 30 hours, 10 on instruments, but no aerobatics. He first flew a Sabre on October 9. Thereafter, his log notes formation flying, tail chases and GCI intercepts/let-downs: "My duties included standing alert after reaching combat ready status. Scrambles (my first was on October 13) could get interesting,

Jim Hanna, who flew the F-86A, F-94B and T-6 Texan on his USAF exchange. (PL-131578 DND)

since the Soviets were beginning their long-range reconnaissance flights over the pole. We sometimes intercepted commercial airliners over the Atlantic, but had to be careful not to be detected by them. GCI normally scrambled us once during an 8-hour alert period." Since all pilots in the 58th had some sort of secondary duties, F/O Hanna became squadron photo officer and T-6 pilot: "This was a true 'gofer' job that usually was relegated to the most junior pilot. A typical T-6 trip was July 11-13, 1952 when I flew SSgt Ballard to Kelly AFB, Texas, where he was needed to help repair one of our aircraft." Hanna was offered a check-out on the F-47, but scheduling kept him away from Grenier.

Hanna was impressed by his USAF peers, writing in his first report to RCAF HQ: "Generally speaking, the level of experience in the squadron is superior to that of a representative RCAF squadron. Most of the pilots have had previous combat experience and many are recent returnees from the Korean theatre." While agreeing that USAF and RCAF formation flying were similar, Hanna reported being "impressed by the manner in which inexperienced pilots

Sabre pilots of the 58th FIS in November 1951: Capt Ray Connolly (USMC), Lt Mudge (USAF), Capt Daniel "Chappie" James (USAF), Capt Ernest Craigwell, Jr. (USAF + Korean Air Force exchange) and F/O Jim Hanna (RCAF). (Hanna Col.)

are indoctrinated in tail chasing and formation aerobatics, a phase of fighter training which this observer feels has not yet been approached in the most effective manner by RCAF fighter squadrons and operational training units." F/O Hanna last flew the F-86A on January 20, 1952, by when he had 69 hours on type. Now the 58th prepared to convert to the F-94B Starfire all-weather fighter. In 2002 Hanna recalled:

We bade adieu to our Sabres and ferried them to Nellis AFB, Nevada. We departed in pairs, I on Capt Daniel "Chappie" James, Jr.'s wing. Chappie was already well-known and respected. While flying an F-51 Mustang in Korea, he had shot down a MiG-15. He was my first flight commander at the 58th and we became fast friends. For this mission we flight-planned via Andrews AFB, Washington; Shaw AFB, South Carolina; Wright-Patterson AFB, Ohio; Scott AFB, Missouri; Tinker AFB, Oklahoma, Carswell AFB, Texas; back to Tinker (with their nuclear weapons on base, SAC would not let us stay overnight); Reese AFB, Texas and Kirtland AFB, New Mexico. At Kirtland I overnighted with RCAF exchange officer Larry Spurr and his wife Nan. We reached Nellis on January 20. It was there that I learned about the politics of a "Jim Crow" state – Chappie could not go into Las Vegas with me. However, things had changed a lot by the time Chappie became the USAF's first African American 4-star general.

Back at Otis, F/O Hanna moved to the F-94B in order to gain all-weather experience at a time when the RCAF was introducing the CF-100:

Typical of the HQ approach to personnel management 50 years ago, I had not been consulted about my role in the 58th's shift to the F-94B. Instead, I had expected to be shipped out to joined the 4th FW in Korea. I was all pumped up about that, having been briefed by pilots recently back from there. Besides converting to the F-94B (which I flew first on January 30, 1952), I completed a 5-week course at the USAF All-Weather Instrument School at Moody AFB, Georgia. Training was in a Curtiss-Wright simulator and in T-28s and T-33s. Further all-weather training was on an OJT basis with the squadron.

F/O Hanna would log only 16 hours on the F-94B (not counting five missions as the RO in the back seat). The F-94B was a rudimentary fighter, sub-sonic and having only .50 machine guns: "The F-94B had a limiting Mach number of about 0.8. However, we determined that a sound similar to a sonic boom (which was such a big deal in the early 1950s) could be produced during a 'high speed' 350-knot low pass by extending the speed brakes while simultaneously lighting the afterburner." Hanna noted in his official report how the F-94B had a more "solid" feel to the controls than did a T-33: "The F-94B is well-equipped with attitude and navigational instruments … there is a Sperry Zero Reader, ILS receiver, radio compass and visual omni-range receiver. It handles well under instrument conditions … While it has a cruising endurance at altitude of approximately three hours (with 230-gallon tip tanks) … fuel consumption with afterburner is of the order of 42 gallons per minute at sea level."

One week a Sperry tech rep visited the 58th to demonstrate the "Zero Reader". F/O Hanna reported being impressed with this navigational aid during this demo and on later F-94B flights. He attended an F-94B systems course at Chanute AFB and a conference at MIT in Cambridge, Massachusetts, the topic being gun harmonization and weapons use. He studied and reported on a newly released USAF document about dead-stick landing procedures in jet fighters: "This observer has made half a dozen simulated flame-out approaches in the F-94 and has found the technique quite satisfactory." On another occasion he visited a USAF radar site, reporting later to RCAF HQ:

During this period [November 1, 1951 to April 15, 1952] squadron operations were somewhat curtailed due to shortage of aircraft, shortage or non-availability of parts, and inclement weather … In co-operation with the local Aircraft Control and Warning Unit, a pilot-controller cross-training program was in force during the latter part of the year. Groups of pilots … proceeded to the radar site at North Truro on Cape Cod to spend the day observing the operation of the early warning system and the ground control interceptions … Scanners report unknown aircraft to controllers, who may control several groups of interceptors at once … The unit is normally effective up to 200 miles and 40,000 feet altitude, although aircraft with functioning IFF equipment have been tracked and controlled at distances in excess of 300 miles. It is of interest to note that objects have been reported and tracked travelling at extreme altitude range and at speeds of the order of 2000 mph.

First flown in July 1949, the F-94 Starfire, the first USAF "all weather" jet interceptor, evolved from the wartime P-80. With machine guns, basic AI radar and a 4600-lb thrust Allison J-33 engine the F-94 filled a gap between the F-82 Twin Mustang and the anticipated F-89 in a time when the USSR had atomic bombs and the Tu-4 bombers to deliver them. The F-94A/B left service in 1958. (Lockheed-California Co.)

F/O Hanna's reports to RCAF HQ offered much detail about the radar establishment. The reference to high speed targets is not elaborated upon, although these were the days of countless UFO reports in North America. In late June 1952 Hanna left the 58th: "I received orders transferring me effective August 2 to 427 Squadron, flying F-86Es at RCAF Station St. Hubert. Meanwhile, the USAF sent me on TDY to join the 60th FIS for its annual air-to-air gunnery training at Eglin AFB, Florida. From June 20 to July 18 I flew 21 gunnery and 12 target tow missions, my best score on the flag being 36%."

In assessing F/O Hanna's exchange, G/C D.J. "Blackie" Williams wrote on July 25, 1952, thanking him for his reports, particularly regarding sighting and armament developments: "The difficulty in the past has always been in keeping up to date on the latest USAF tactics. In this field you can be of immense help." Following his 427 tour Hanna flew Sabres at Baden-Soellingen with 444, then instructed on T-33s, B-25s and CF-100s at North Bay and Cold Lake. Next, he

Jim Hanna at age 80 at the Canada Aviation Museum during the SPAADS reunion in August 2006. (Hanna Col.)

joined the CEPE Air Armament Evaluation Detachment at Cold Lake to fly the Otter, Sabre and CF-100. In 1956 he graduated from the Empire Test Pilots School at Farnborough, where he flew everything from the Tiger Moth and Anson to the Vampire, Meteor, Hunter, Canberra and Avro 707. He spent from 1957-61 with CEPE's Avro Canada detachment at Malton, and at Uplands. He later had a UNEF tour in the Gaza Strip, attended RCAF Staff College, instructed there, commanded CFB Rivers, got into the coming field of bilingualism in the DND, was defence attaché in Paris, commanded CF Air Defence Group and 22nd NORAD Region in North Bay, commanded CF Europe, then left the CF as MGen Hanna in 1981. From 1982-88 he directed government and military sales at De Havilland Canada, after which he consulted in government relations, before retiring in Ottawa in 1992.

Eglin Exchange

When Canada ordered an advanced fire control system for the CF-100 from Hughes in California, AFHQ was anxious to get some experience with it. Accordingly, in May 1952 F/L Bill Vincent and F/O Joe Clarke went to Eglin AFB, Florida, to fly the F-94C, which

Sgts W.H. "Bill" Vincent and Harold Rands having just received their wings at 10 SFTS, Dauphin, Manitoba on March 19, 1942. From Alliance, Alberta, Rands was shot down with his 426 Squadron Wellington crew on ops over Holland, February 26, 1943. As Bill said in 2006, "If you went to Bomber Command in 1942-43, your life span was very short." (PL-7945 DND)

(Below) W/C Vincent receives a NORAD achievement award in September 1963 at Northern NORAD HQ, North Bay. Presenting is A/V/M James B. Harvey, NORAD regional commander. Also being honoured is W/C Roy J. "Pop" Lawlor. Both "wingcos" were stationed at 25th NORAD Region, McChord AFB. (PL-151055 DND)

had a Hughes FCS in conjunction with its weapons (24 rockets in the nose, 12 each in two wing pods). Vincent and Clarke spent about a year at Eglin, then spent several weeks on cold weather trials in Maine. In February 2003 Bill Vincent recalled:

In 1952 AFHQ decided that the RCAF's all weather OTU at North Bay required a trained AI crew. This crew would proceed on 120-day exchange to the 3200th Fighter Test Unit at Eglin AFB to participate in proving the APG 40 fire control radar system in the latest USAF all-weather fighter, the Lockheed F-94C Starfire. The APG 40 would replace the APG 33 in our early CF-100s. I and my AI navigator, F/O Joe Clarke, accepted the posting to Eglin. In May 1952 we drove by car with our families to Florida.

Along with three USAF crews, we had a short time to check out on the aircraft, radar, and fire control system. I first flew the F-94C on August 5. Joe and I soon were assigned to test the APG 40 at high altitude in the head-on attack mode against SAC B-36s, B-47s and B-52s This was a bit hairy for the pilots, for we had to keep our heads in the cockpit to ensure that the steering dot on our radar scope was centred in the steering circle. This was essential, so that the correct information entered the data box (to be analyzed later by ground radar specialists). To ease our minds our AI navigators served as range safety officers, telling us to break off should a dangerous situa-

tion arise. Generally, our intercepts were at or above 40,000 feet.

The 3200th FTU also had to test the F-94C in cold weather – work usually done in Alaska during winter. This time, however, the trials were at Presque Isle, Maine. Since the RCAF routinely would be using the APG 40 in winter conditions, F/O Clarke and I flew the Presque Isle trials. Preliminary trials were begun in a cold weather hangar at Eglin, where aircraft could be tested down to -65°F. These could be started in the hangar, their exhausts being funnelled outside. All systems (flaps, dive brakes, undercarriage, canopy, radar, etc.) were checked to see how they functioned in extreme cold. It always seemed a little strange to enter the hangar, passing through three insulated doors, dressed in Arctic clothing, when outside it was typical Florida weather.

The F-94C in Eglin's "deep freeze" climate control hangar on August 7, 1952. The cold soaking was severe – note how the electronic and armament panels are open to get the full effect. (Vincent Col.)

NORAD's top all-weather interceptors *circa* 1955: the Avro CF-100, Northrop F-89 Scorpion and Convair F-102 Delta Dagger. F/L Norman and F/O Vaessen took part in F-89 trials in the US. Leading here is CF-100 Mk.5 18742 of 425 Squadron then at St. Hubert, F-89D 53-2663 and F-102A 56-1324. (PL-95877 DND)

F/L D.M. "Don" Norman, AFC, who crewed on the F-89 and F-94 during a USAF exchange. He was awarded an AFC in August 1945 for good service instructing at 7 OTU. (PL-147667 DND)

F/O C.L. "Chuck" Vaessen, DFC, who served on night fighters in WWII, then got early into the CF-100 game. His DFC dates to December 1944 when he was a 410 Squadron AI navigator on Mosquitos. (PL-36774 DND)

Before deploying to Presque Isle in December 1952, we shipped our families back to North Bay. Then we flew off for the Northeast. Our F-94C had the new UHF radios, but some ground stations en route could not receive us, so we had to lie a bit when filing our flight plans. While filing out of Nashville for Syracuse, we were in the room with some USAF crews. There were some quizzical (if not envious) looks from some of them upon seeing fellows wearing RCAF caps but wearing new-style USAF winter flying suits, and flying one of their new F-94Cs!

The Presque Isle trials went well, and even included manually firing the nose rockets over a range off Maine. Our program complete, in March 1953 we were cleared to fly to North Bay to show the F-94C and its radar to the OTU staff. Again, the lack of UHF facilities en routes was a bit of a pain, but we got in OK under the cloud, giving North Bay a blast of our afterburner as we beat up the station. I last flew the F-94C on March 13, 1953. In the end I logged about 100 hours during the Eglin-Presque Isle trials. As to the APG 40, it proved to be excellent equipment and served the RCAF well in the CF-100 Mk.4.

A report of March 1954 by F/L Donald M. Norman and F/O Charles L. Vaessen, also working at Eglin, is entitled "Operational Suitability Trials on the F-89D All-Weather Interceptor". It in-

cluded comments about the F-89 Scorpion's cockpit ("roomy and comfortable … instruments all well laid out"), but complained of complicated procedures and too much space between the radar operator's seat and his instruments. The report contained few comparisons with the CF-100, but did mention the F-89D's longer take-off run.

Norman and Vaessen studied the F-89D's 2.75-in folding fin rockets, looking ahead to CF-100 armament. They also noted F-89D tactics, which were like those of the CF-100. Thus, while a pursuit from the rear was still classic, the document noted, "The best attack from the safety standpoint, and for kill probability, is the beam attack." However, angle-on (i.e. "lead collision course"

– LCC) attacks also were used. Their report noted, "The psychological aspect generated by the lead collision course attack will impose problems which, to overcome, will require confidence in the equipment. This confidence is gained only though consistent and satisfactory performance of the lead collision course equipment." (For more about LCC see *The Avro CF-100*. Included is mention of at least one "perfect intercept", wherein a CF-100 collided with its target.) A fifth RCAF pilot at Eglin in this period was F/L Ray Green, who was evaluating the F-86D all-weather fighter.

W/C Kenneth B. Handley while CO of 423 Squadron then flying CF-100s. (PL-75965 DND)

In the late summer of 1952 S/L Kenneth B. "Butch" Handley was posted to the 25th Air Division at McChord AFB to study USAF air defence doctrine. He first took a 20-hour T-33 course at St. Hubert, then reported to McChord on September 1. He joined the 317th FIS, initially taking pre-flight examinations on USAF flying regulations. Next came a T-33 check, followed by the F-94, which he found impressive. He later reported that, even after graduating from the USAF All-Weather Interceptor School, a pilot would fly 40-50 hours in two or three months with the squadron, before being considered operational. "The average USAF fighter-interceptor pilot is well versed and extremely competent", he reported, adding that readiness training was "not a simulated condition – it is realistic".

Handley next spent a week at the 4704th Defensive Wing HQ, which did administration and planned training for units like the 317th. A visit followed to 25th Air Division HQ, which included a tour of Boeing in Seattle to see the B-52. The 25th itself co-ordinated flying with ground control units, and exuded professionalism. S/L Handley summarized that he was now better qualified to serve as an OpsO in RCAF Air Defence Command. He was dismayed, however,

that existing doctrine called for interceptions of enemy bombers by single fighters. This, he concluded, was unrealistic, especially in IFR weather, and he recommended co-ordinated interceptions by fighter pairs. In 1955-56 W/C Handley commanded 432 Squadron (CF-100s) at Bagotville.

In 1955-57 F/L Edgar J.R. Nourse was a Fighter Control Officer at Stewart AFB, New York. Looking at air defence from the controller's chair, and with added perspective from the US, his reports are enlightening. Describing Ex. Think Fast of October 13-14, 1955, he wrote: "SAC tactics employed were very impressive. The SAC effort, consisting of [B-47s], penetrated in a mass stream … between 35,000 and 40,000 feet. A heavy inversion extending over the strike route coupled with a heavy chaff drop and the weaving course of B-47s, proved very perplexing to the defending forces." In June 1956 Nourse noted how the USAF complimented the RCAF:

Reports from the ACW squadrons on a recent "Think Fast 20" mission invariably praised the early warning provided by RCAF GCIs. It was noted that RCAF CF-100 aircraft were utilized by the 766th ACW Squadron, Caswell, Maine, during this mission … "Excellent Early Warning resulted in early scrambles and intercepts taking place at a range of 100 to 150 miles from this station. The fighters from Bagotville made excellent intercepts, even though they had to fly 150 miles to the general track area. The CF-100s have a phenomenal range and endurance and were able to work at combat power and combat altitudes for periods in excess of 1 hour and 20 minutes. The Canadian crews were highly trained in our tactical doctrine and were extremely easy to control."

Tyndall AFB

In the late 1950s the Soviet strategic bomber threat included the Bear and Bison, which rendered the CF-100 obsolete. Canada countered with the Avro Arrow, first flown in 1958. By the time it should have been in production, however, the Arrow remained far from operational status – its Iroquois engine was behind schedule and the fire control system remained

Fighter controller F/L E.J.R. Nourse in January 1963. (PL-141336 DND)

The wreckage of the Russell-Simkins CF-100. Then, F/L Simkins bashed up but recuperating in his body cast. (via Frank Russell)

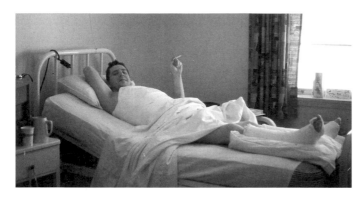

The Simkins over Christmas 1965: Ted and Mary with Mark, Lisa and Paul. (via Frank Russell)

not get out. He stopped in the midst of the sequence and decided to try a forced landing… The aircraft landed in a stubble field, skidded, struck a ditch, destroyed a small building and came to rest against a concrete-block barn.

The navigator extricated himself … removed the roof of the

building from the front cockpit, and rescued the semi-conscious pilot… On investigation it was revealed that all components [of the ejection seats] were serviceable, the correct type, properly installed, and tolerances within limits specified by the EOs. What went wrong? It was discovered that applicable EOs did not call for a functional test of the assembled seat in the aircraft.

Having recuperated, S/L Simkins converted to the Yukon. His final log book entry shows an 11.3 hour Lahr–Trenton flight on April 3, 1968. By this time he had flown 5790 flying hours. While holidaying near Peterborough, Ontario on July 25, 1970, Ted Simkins passed away suddenly. As to Jack Coates, he encountered health problems not long after leaving the RCAF. Like his navigator from Tyndall days, he passed on before his time.

Follow-on Tyndall Crews

F/L Ken Blackmore was to replace Jack Coates in 1961, but the exchange suddenly was terminated. It was February 1963 before the next RCAF crew arrived – F/Ls Don Carney and John Bradley would be IWS instructors. Carney from Brampton, Ontario, joined the RCAF in 1955. He trained at Moose Jaw on Harvards and did advance flying on T-33s at MacDonald and Saskatoon, before moving to CF-100s with 432 and 413 squadrons, then 3 AW (F) OTU. He converted to the CF-101 and instructed at 425 Squadron. Bradley was an RCAF Voodoo pioneer, having been in the original 425 cadre at Namao, where he occupied W/C Schultz's back seat.

At Tyndall, Carney started in the F-101 simulator on February 14, 1963. He flew the TF-102 on the 18th, the T-33 on the 20th, then had his first F-101 flight the night of the 22nd. Routine missions followed on IWS F-101s – early types with basic AI radar. The syllabus included ground school, GCI tactics training (high/low level) and live fire. Other trips were against ECM B-57s and supersonic B-58s. In June 1963 Carney was at Klamath Falls, Oregon to convert to the upgraded F-101 with an infra-red tracking system. Following Tyndall, he was at ADC HQ, flew Voodoos with 416 Squadron, and was on the TacEval team in North Bay. Later he served with the ICCS in Vietnam, attended Armed Forces Staff College in Norfolk, was BOpsO at Comox, and was in the Directorate of Defence Intelligence at NDHQ. He retired in 1985.

John A. Bradley, who joined the RCAF in February 1952, spent his first tour at 103 RU in Greenwood. A ground job in Ottawa followed, then he got into ADC in 1958. He converted to the F-101 at Hamilton AFB in 1961, before instructing at the OTU at Namao and Bagotville. At the IWS he and

F/Ls Don Carney and John Bradley at Tyndall. (via John Bradley)

Capt Pat Garvin (USAF) took a course at Hughes, covering the IRSTS (infra-red search and tracking system) being installed in F-101s. In February 2003 Bradley recalled: "After the course Pat and I returned to Tyndall to instruct on the 12-week IWS course. As well, we visited a few USAF squadrons, giving abbreviated IRSTS courses. When I got back to Canada in 1966 I gave the same lectures at our OTU in Bagotville." Bradley also was impressed by his Mach 2 F-106 flight with Capt Jimmy Rudisill on December 20, 1963. Another flight was less auspicious. On a visit to Lockbourne AFB, Ohio on October 16, 1964, Garvin and Bradley had a hairy arrival. Hydraulic trouble caused the right

main gear to lock up. Garvin tried for a cable engagement, but missed. Voodoo 56-0273 was written off without injuries (it went to the USAF Museum in Ohio and was on loan to the Air Museum in Chanute, Illinois in 2007).

Once home, Bradley served at ADC HQ 1965-66, attended RCAF Staff College, had a ground tour at AFHQ, then flew on Voodoos at 416 from April 1970. When he retired in June 1974, the Chatham base paper revealed another side to his personality: "He is known as possibly the best entertainer at any social function in the Command. His … interpretation of Shakespeare and other writers and poets have made him a sought-after lecturer and guest speaker." For the same occasion, a greeting arrived from friends at RMC Esquimalt: "We will miss your wisdom and guidance, and around the bar we will miss the re-telling of the works of Robert Service, made more memorable through your oration." In February 2003 Don Carney reminisced about Tyndall:

The Cuban Missile Crisis was still fresh in everyone's mind when, one noon in 1962 in Bagotville's Officers' Mess, I bumped into S/L Earl Reid from ADC HQ. Reid casually informed me that I and John Bradley had been selected for an exchange at the IWS at Tyndall AFB. To say that I was surprised would be an understatement, even

The single seat Convair F-102 Delta Dagger was flown daily at the IWS, but navigators often crewed in the side-by-side TF-102 "Tub". (via Don Carney)

involved in Southeast Asia, the feeling at Tyndall was gung-ho. The Canadians were impressed by the confidence and professionalism all around them. Nonetheless, they had no trouble holding their own. "We fit in well and had the respect of our USAF peers," Malcomson recalled in 2003. Home from Tyndall in August 1969, he cross-trained to pilot, flying the Chipmunk at Camp Borden, then progressing to the Tutor at Moose Jaw and the T-bird at Gimli. Posted to 409 Squadron in 1970, he flew the T-33 and CF-101. Later, he instructed on the Tutor at Moose Jaw 1976-80, flew a desk at AIRCOM HQ in Winnipeg, then left the military in 1987. By that time he had logged more than 1000 pilot hours on the Voodoo, plus some 3000 as a CF-100 and CF-101 AI navigator.

Fighter Controller

In 2005 Greg Vincent recalled his time at Tyndall:

During the 1950s the Soviet threat to North America was nuclear attack by bombers. As part of continental defence against this, the US and Canada established, funded and staffed the Pine Tree Line – 44 aircraft control and warning radar stations across the US-Canada border. These provided early warning of approaching aircraft, then controlled the fighters scrambled to intercept, identify and, if necessary, destroy them.

Pine Tree Line stations were staffed by Canadian and US controllers. The Canadians initially were trained at RAF Middle Wallop in the UK. Later, most were trained by the USAF at Tyndall AFB. In May 1956 I was on a 2-month course there. This included about 5 RCAF, 5 Japanese and 60 USAF. Some had an aircrew background, some had been commissioned from the ranks, others were recruited specifically for AC&W training. RCAF personnel at Tyndall usually included wartime "retreads", while most USAF and Japanese students had been WWII pilots.

Our course in radar and PPI (plan position indicators, i.e. scopes) was on

Greg Vincent (right) with fellow RCAF fighter controllers Paul Bordeau and Phylis Livingston at RCAF Station Parent, Quebec over Christmas 1956. (Vincent Col.)

US equipment such as the FPS-3 and the CPS-6B (the RCAF used similar equipment). We learned how to vector fighters for the lead collision course attack. During LCC, the interceptor would approach a target from abeam. Late in the attack the interceptor's fire control system would build in a small "lead." Then the rockets would fire and, theoretically, the interceptor might fly through the debris, should the target be hit. As an RCAF AI navigator, you always knew when you were successful at an LCC intercept, as you would fly through your target's wake turbulence. At Tyndall we also learned to direct fighters during an identification run. For this, an interceptor would be vectored behind the target, then slowly close to identify it. In combat an ID run would have been dangerous, since Soviet bombers had radar controlled tail guns.

As the key USAF all-weather fighter training base, Tyndall was busy. The school operated the single-seat F-86D, so a pilot had to fly his aircraft and operate the radar. Accidents were not uncommon. In one, a Tyndall-based F-86D flew into the B-29 target-towing aircraft, killing everyone. Other subjects were meteorology, radar theory, and armament. The instructors did a good job of integrating their Canadian and Japanese students. We would smile, however, when we were excluded from certain classified lectures.

The system of plotting aircraft that we had in Canada was a WWII hold over from the RAF. Using long sticks, plotters (mainly airwomen) would move colour-coded aircraft plots around a large horizontal map. At Tyndall we learned how the USAF plotted using vertical clear plastic maps that were edge-lit. Plotters (mainly airmen) wrote backwards from the rear of the map with coloured grease pencils.

In the Florida heat, classes started at 0700 and were done by noon. This gave us long afternoons at the beach, so no one complained. Meanwhile, we received an RCAF living allowance and, since we were on temporary duty from our Pine Tree Line stations, we also got a $25.00 monthly northern allowance. As to quarters, Bill Cann, Tom Winslow, a WWII RAF Typhoon pilot, and I shared a beach cottage at nearby Mexico Beach. At the end of our street was Roy's Gulf Gas Station. Roy was a hit with us, since he served beer along with oysters from Apalachicola Bay. Roy had much Canadian memorabilia in his station. I visited him in the early 1990s and he had many fond memories of his Canadian friends.

Otis AFB

Beginning in 1959 the 60th FIS at Otis AFB near Cape Cod was the first operational F-101 squadron. The original RCAF crew on exchange here (1959-60) was F/Ls Harvey Clark and Alec Faulkner, their tasks being to run the F-101 flight simulator and develop training syllabi. Clark and Faulkner were replaced in

the summer of 1960 by F/Ls Wilfred Lloyd Dobbin, DFC, and Michael V. Cromie, who had been on CF-100s at 413 Squadron. From Kamsack, Saskatchewan, where his father had taught school on an Indian reserve, Dobbin joined the RCAF in 1941. After EFTS at Prince Albert and SFTS at Saskatoon, he flew Wellingtons in Europe and the Mediterranean with RAAF and RAF squadrons. His DFC was gazetted in June 1943, while he was on 104 Squadron in Tunisia. Dobbin survived two prangs, then finished the war on Dakotas. He rejoined the RCAF in 1951, serving first at Air Armament School in Trenton.

Once at Otis, Dobbin and Cromie converted to the F-101, then came the daily routines of any ADC squadron (in this

F/Ls Clark and Faulkner on exchange with the 60th FIS at Otis AFB. Clark wears his "Ops Wing" showing that he had flown a wartime tour on operations. Note that even this early the "Voodoo Scope Wizard" patch, as on 1Lt Milton Meeher's right shoulder, was in use. (Dobbin Col.)

(Below) F-101Bs of the 60th FIS. 57-0377 later was CanForces 101041 and now is a historic display in Bangor, Maine. '0400 became 101052 and went to the Canadian Museum of Flight and Transportation in Langley, BC. (Dobbin Col.)

he was part owner of Cessna 172 C-GXJU, and a member of the Vancouver Soaring Association. Cromie's later postings included CF-104 mission planning/radar prediction at 4 Wing, CF Staff College, a Voodoo tour at 409, commanding the radar station at Dana, Saskatchewan, and a stint in NDHQ from where he retired in 1988.

SIZEABLE SHOULDERBOARDS--Recently promoted here was Royal Canadian Air Force Squadron Leader Ray Jolley (center), an exchange officer on duty with the 60th Fighter Interceptor Sq. at Otis. On hand to present a set of outsize shoulderboards significant of his promotion were Lt. Col. Thomas Wille (left), 60th Sq. commander, and Col. Norval K. Heath, commander, Boston Air Defense Sector (BOADS), visiting here briefly at the time. The informal ceremony took place in the squadron briefing room.   (USAF PHOTO)

A skit at the 60th FIS with Ray Jolley the centre of attraction. (USAF)

In April 1962 the 432 Squadron crew of pilot F/L Tom Wright, a wartime retread, and AI navigator F/L Mike Mahon replaced Dobbin and Cromie. About a year later Wright returned to Canada, F/L Ray Jolley replacing him. Jolley had joined the RCAF in 1949, flying first at Centralia on January 11, 1950. He won his Wings, then was posted to Chatham. There he flew a Vampire for the first time on December 8, 1950, joined 441 Squadron, and soon was overseas at North Luffenham. Later postings were at Downsview as Regular Support Officer with the auxiliary squadrons, at the radar site at Parent, Quebec, then he flew CF-100s at 409 Squadron. As the latter tour waned, Jolley's CO, W/C Hal Bridges, suggested the exchange slot at Otis. He accepted and in November 1962, Jolley, wife Yvonne and their six children began the trans-continental drive to Otis. There the action started with a T-33 famil flight on December 4.

On the 21st Jolley made his first Voodoo trip with Capt Drew. Since the USAF always admired the spirit and professionalism of the RCAF, Jolley soon was a flight commander, squadron test pilot and squadron instrument check pilot. A routine flying day (the basic schedule rarely changed) meant 12 hours of duty, while an alert crew was on for 25 hours. Personnel sometimes seemed to have permanent jobs, some staying for years with the 60th, compared to the RCAF's two-year postings. A couple of foreign

pilots on a USAF base was bound to attract attention – this Edward Jenner item, "Teaching Americans to Fly", appeared in the Boston *Globe* on May 23, 1965.

Newcomers and visitors to the 60th Fighter Interceptor Squadron at Otis Air Force Base are often startled when greeted by Squadron Leader John Jolley of the Royal Canadian Air Force. Jolley and Flight Lieutenant Michael Mahon are assigned to the 60th as exchange officers. United States officers also serve with the Canadian Air Force ... In answer to the inevitable question, "What are you doing here?" both gave the same answer: "Teaching the Americans to fly." This generally develops into a tongue-in-cheek discussion of the relative merits of two services ... Jolley, who lives in Falmouth with his wife and family, will leave shortly for assignment to the RCAF Staff College in Toronto ... He describes his two and a half years here as one long vacation. Mahon, on the other hand, misses skiing and curling. He has not let that keep him from having a good time, however ... Mahon has become an avid sailor, pushing the season into early December last year ...

Meanwhile, adjustments were in order for the Canadians. Otis was a SAC base with Bomarcs and tankers, so was on constant nuclear alert with high security. Something else that Canucks at Otis would note was the emphasis on climbing the USAF ladder – most officers were on career paths, so were very politically correct. In the RCAF the opposite was normal – get the job done, have fun, don't worry a lot about your career. After all, few RCAF aircrew were careerists. Instead, they were on short-term commissions and soon would be back on Civvie Street. Canadians at Otis also observed how senior pilots, right up to the base commander, kept current on the Voodoo. They also were impressed

"Peace Wings" Voodoos cram the hangar at Bristol Aircraft in Winnipeg. Two "old" RCAF Voodoos sit across the back windows awaiting return to the US, while "new" Voodoos fresh from the USAF undergo mods. From the far corner (centre) going clockwise are 57-0375 (CF 101042, ended as a range target at CFB Gagetown), '418 (CF 101053 now on display at Miramichi, NB), '305 (CF 101017 crashed from Bagotville on December 12, 1977), '286 (CF 101010 later for the RCAF Memorial Museum, but jettisoned into the Bay of Quinte on June 25, 1991 by the Chinook helicopter slinging it from nearby Mountain View), '323 (CF 101023 crashed at Comox on January 14, 1978), '444 (CF 101065 now in the North Atlantic Aviation Museum, Gander), 2 unknown. (Bristol Aerospace)

by the huge base infrastructure – there was never a shortage of anything. Something else that was very big was educational advancement. Most officers were taking university courses, getting degrees, then moving on to post-graduate studies, a brilliant approach that only came much later to Canada's military.

At some time in Jolley's tour ADC took over Otis. The first movie that he remembers seeing in the base theatre after that was "Dr. Strangelove". Critical of America's nuclear policy, it had been banned from Otis under SAC. Also of interest, President Kennedy often would arrive at Otis in "Air Force One" to vacation at Hyannis. Before he left the 60th in August 1965, Jolley one day scrounged a few circuits in the President's plane, while his crew was training.

To Mike Mahon the Voodoo was a comfortable fighter for a back seater, and well equipped, so good AI results were normal. He often crewed with Capt Denzil Boyd but, otherwise, the schedulers could crew a back seater with any pilot. In January 2003 Mahon recalled a few more differences in how USAF ADC operated. In 1961, for example, the RCAF formed a dedicated Voodoo OTU. In the USAF, however, crews assigned to the F-101 usually went directly to squadron for "on the job training". Each squadron had a Voodoo simulator, with professionals bringing along each man step by step. (Mike Cromie once made too much at the 60th about the RCAF all-weather crew concept, annoying his flight commander in the process.) Back in Canada in August 1965, Mahon spent four years instructing at 3 OTU/410 Squadron. An NDHQ tour followed, then he joined 409 on Voodoos until 1975. A UN Middle East tour came next. From 1976-78 he again was on Voodoos at 409, after which he left the air force. His career had totalled some 1200 hours on the CF-100, 2000 on the Voodoo. He settled in Comox, spent several years as a fisheries officer, then retired from the working world.

Capts Parkinson and Templeton while on the LTV detachment. They ferried Voodoos 57-0273, '0289, '0298, '0378 and '0424 from Winnipeg to Greenville. As well, Parkinson ferried two Voodoos solo – 56-260 and '324. They ferried Voodoos 101002, '009, '010, 018, '022, '024, '026, '032, '033, '036, '039, '053 and '054 from Greenville to Canada. Parkinson/Branter delivered 101049 and Parkinson/Serne crewed on February 25, 1972 on the last Voodoo delivery – 101001. (Templeton Col.)

Voodoo Test Crews

In 1961 the first batch of 66 RCAF Voodoos had been delivered under Op. Queen's Row. Then, in September 1970 Canada began exchanging those "old" Voodoos for 66 "new" ones. This was Op. Peace Wings under which USAF crews ferried Voodoos from storage at Davis-Monthan AFB to Bristol in Winnipeg for overhaul and to swap engines, ejection seats and oxygen equipment – Canada kept those systems from the older machines, but would regret this, when J57 engines began breaking down. The swapping done, crews ferried the "old" Voodoos to Davis-Monthan. In a letter to CANAV of March 1, 2003 F/L Jack Parkinson compared "old" and "new" aircraft: "The new Voodoos had IIP, which included better radar and an infra-red search and tracking system. They also had an upgraded auto pilot and a redundant limiter system replacing the horn-and-pusher pitch-up warnings in earlier Voodoos."

From Bristol, new Voodoos (still in USAF markings) flew to the Ling-Temco-Vought plant in Greenville, South Carolina for further work. As a Voodoo came off the LTV line, a 3-man Canadian team stood by: F/L Jack Parkinson (pilot), F/L Brodie Templeton (AI navigator) and F/L Bud Serne (engineering officer). Parkinson and Templeton were assigned for the duration to the Aeronautical Engineering and Test Establishment, HQ in Ottawa. While they did the flying, Serne ensured that aircraft were fit, did the engineering paperwork and signed the acceptance papers for each Voodoo.

F/L Parkinson had joined the RCAF in 1955. Following pilot training, he flew CF-100s with 419 Squadron at 4 Wing. Instructional tours came next (Harvards at Penhold, Tutors at Gimli), then he flew Voodoos with 416 at Chatham. F/L Templeton also had enlisted in 1955, serving first as a CF-100 navigator with 425 at St. Hubert. Later, he was an air weapons controller at Mont Apica and Senneterre, and had a DEW Line tour at Cape Dyer. After so much penance, he returned to Voodoos at 425. With "The 500 Cut" of 1964 Templeton was out of work but, by good fortune, heard that the RAF was recruiting. He enlisted in September

– PEACE WINGS –

UNITED STATES AIR FORCE - CANADIAN ARMED FORCES

ELECTROSYSTEMS LTV INC.
DONALDSON FACILITY
GREENVILLE, SOUTH CAROLINA

CF-101B serial number 101001, the final aircraft to be delivered by LTV ELECTROSYSTEMS, INC., DONALDSON FACILITY, on Project PEACE WINGS (Contract F4160B-70-A-4015-QP01), is formally accepted by the UNITED STATES AIR FORCE and delivered to the CANADIAN ARMED FORCES on this date, 24 February 1972.

JOHN W. DIXON
PRESIDENT
LTV ELECTROSYSTEMS, INC.

DONALD F. BLAKE
BRIGADIER GENERAL
USAF

D.W. GOSS
BRIGADIER GENERAL
CAF

A.B.C. JOHNSON
BRIGADIER GENERAL
CAF

A certificate commemorating the last "Peace Wings" Voodoo. (Joe F. Jordan)

the IWS course at Tyndall in 1968.

Parkinson and Templeton would fly all 66 "new" Voodoos, initially bringing a few to Greenville from Bristol, then test flying aircraft off the upgrade line. On a typical flight of about an hour Parkinson flew the test profiles, while Templeton monitored the equipment in the back and kept up the paperwork. Most aircraft were accepted by

1964 then, after training at Bassingbourn, spent the next 2½ years on Canberra B(I)8s with 3 Squadron at Geilenkirchen, Germany. The flying was all low-level – culture shock compared to Voodoos. His RAF contract finished, Templeton, who logged some 490 hours on Canberras, returned to Canada in March 1967. He re-enlisted, going to 409 Squadron in 1967, then did

F/L Serne after two or three flights. Voodoo 101033, however, took nine before the last bug was shaken out. Meanwhile, 29 of the "old" RCAF Voodoos were converted by LTV for the USAF as RF-101s. Templeton crewed on some of the test flights.

Later in the program F/Ls Mel Branter and John Blair were involved. Branter's main job was to ferry Voodoos be-

Voodoo 101015 on February 15, 1972 – stripped at Greenville and ready for test flying. Paint for '015 had been shipped from Canada but was lost en route! '015 is preserved in Levis, Quebec. With LCol Rhinehart Koehn of 410 Squadron, author Milberry flew in '015 on August 25, 1980. (Templeton Col.)

tween Winnipeg and Greenville. Parkinson recalled: "Mel often flew the southbound route solo. After all, the 'new' Voodoos had the IFF in the front cockpit and, since the radar usually wasn't working, he could fly without a navigator." Parkinson and Templeton flew their last LTV missions on February 22 and 24, 1972, respectively. For that month, Templeton's log shows 23 test flights for 17.8 hours. They now returned to Canada, Parkinson to ADC HQ in North Bay, Templeton to 410 in Bagotville. Each logged about 225 Voodoo hours during the LTV sojourn.

Nellis AFB

Following WWII, James Gordon Joy moved with his family from Newfoundland to Toronto, where he joined the RCAF. After winning his Wings, he trained on Vampires at Chatham, then flew Sabres at North Luffenham on 410 Squadron. In 1952-53 he completed an RAF weapons course on Meteors. Next came a tour at Chatham, from where he was posted in April 1956 to Nellis AFB to instruct on F-86Hs with the 3598th Combat Crew Training Squadron. In those days Nellis, a hot and dusty Nevada outpost, was where young men in the USAF went to become fighter pilots. It also was a dangerous place – in one year some 70 pilots would die there, mostly one at a time out in the desert. Someone once told a newcomer to Nellis, "If you see the flag at full staff, take a picture." That said, in the 1950s Nellis was *the* source for the best fighter pilots in the world. In June 1956 F/L Joy advanced to the North American F-100 Super Sabre at the 3594th CCTS.

The F-100, first flown on May 25, 1953, faced many development problems. These are detailed in the official US government publication, *Encyclopedia of US Air Force Aircraft and Missile Systems, Volume 1, Post-World War II Fighters 1945-1973*, e.g. "unsatisfactory yaw characteristics, structural failures induced by aerodynamic forces exceeding the airframe's limits, and malfunctions of the flight control system's hydraulic pump."

F/L Gord Joy in 1963 while on CF-104s at 427 Squadron, Zweibrucken. Gord enjoyed his time on the F-100, other pilots did not. In 2005 he recalled how, during a scissors manoeuvre, pilots were advised to keep their hand off the stick and steer by rudder. He noted that the USAF Thunderbirds flight demo team flew F-100s, suggesting that it couldn't have been that bad an airplane. Joy later was in flight safety at St. Hubert, converted to helicopters and finished his air force days with the Directorate of Flight Safety. In 1971 he retired to a farm near Lakefield, Ontario. (ZW8396-56 DND)

Nonetheless, in September 1954 the F-100 entered service with Tactical Air Command at George AFB, California.

Low F-100 serviceability delayed F/L Joy's progress, but he completed the 30-hour instructor's course by September 30. In February 1957 he was named "Instructor of the Month" at Nellis. On March 8 Col James C. McGehee, CO of the 3595th CCTW, noted in a Letter of Commendation:

Your efforts and enthusiasm have been of the highest example to all those with whom you have come in contact. As an instructor, the phase briefing guides which you have developed for all phases of training in the Combat Crew curricula have materially contributed to the effectiveness of your squadron. It is to be noted that you spent many non-duty hours compiling these phase briefings, which required extensive co-ordination between many organizations. Using your briefing guides, the most inexperienced instructor would be able to give a comprehensive briefing on any phase in the Combat Crew syllabus. The manner in which you have conducted yourself as an outstanding instructor reflects very favourably upon yourself, the 3594th Combat Crew Training Squadron, the United States Air Force and the Royal Canadian Air Force.

Joy now attended the Academic Session of the USAF Fighter Weapons School. In a class of 12 he attained the highest standing recorded to that date. In July 1957 he described one difficulty with his exchange: "The F-100F is now being phased into the combat crew training program. It is anticipated that in 1958 a new 110-hour syllabus will be flown and that the classified nature of a large portion of this syllabus will seriously restrict the activities of the next Canadian exchange officer." Joy had encountered this problem early on F-86Hs. His remarks led to some inter-service discussions, the most sensitive topic being nuclear data, as it pertained to Canadian involvement.

Following F/L Joy at Nellis was F/L Garth Cinnamon. Having joined the RCAF in 1949, he flew Sabres for five years at 410 Squadron, instructed at the Sabre OTU at Chatham and qualified on the fighter weapons leader course at Chatham before being posted to Nellis. On September 9, 1958 he began at Nellis with an F-100F famil flight. Showing him the ropes that day was one of Nellis' most accomplished and aggressive fighter pilots,

Capt John Boyd (with his unique philosophy Boyd later would re-write the USAF fighter weapons syllabus).

In 2006 Garth Cinnamon recalled how the F-100's ailerons produced a lot of adverse yaw, so rolls and turns mainly were controlled by rudder, especially in the landing pattern. After his 10-mission type check-out, he completed a weapons delivery course, which he found similar to what the RCAF was teaching at Chatham. Then, he instructed on the F-100 weapons course to March 1959, when he joined Nellis' R&D flight. Here, his initial duties were to qualify TAC squadrons on the Philco/GE GAR-8 Sidewinder air-to-air missile. Two other projects ensued.

First came the nuclear-armed, short-range (2 miles), air-to-surface Martin GAM-83B Bullpup missile. Cinnamon was one of three Nellis pilots on the GAM-83B project. The missile's guidance was controlled from launch to impact by the pilot in-putting electronic signals. Each pilot had 16 GAM-83Bs to fire, all this work resulting in two key conclusions: 1) that the GAM-83B functioned according to the manufacturer's claims 2) that the problem of protecting a pilot's eyes from "flash-blinding" from the nuclear warhead required further study. (In this period a CEPE Argus was at NAS Point Mugu, California test firing Bullpups. Likely due to the flash-blinding issue

Having delivered a Sabre to Turkey in 1954, F/O Gerald R.W. King was presented with ceremonial Turkish Air Force pilot Wings. His exchange tour on F-100s at Nellis AFB followed in 1957. (PL-81147 DND)

the RCAF did not acquire Bullpups.) F/L Cinnamon also was on a project to study the efficiency of the standard 750-lb and Mk.82 bombs. The weapons development staff tested versions of the Mk.82 that resulted in improved accuracy. The RCAF/CF would employ the Mk.82 on its CF-5s, CF-104s and CF-18s for decades to come.

Unlike F/L Joy, F/L Cinnamon was not so tightly restricted regarding nuclear weapons. It appears that the USAF had decided that anything an exchange pilot needed to know in the cockpit to deliver a nuclear weapon was approved. The re-stricted details of a weapon simply were not addressed. After logging 412 hours on the F-100, in August 1960 F/L Cinnamon was posted to CEPE at Cold Lake. There he helped plan the Primrose Lake Range, devised bombing tables for pilots flying the CF-104 (as yet there were no such tables, since the USAF did not use the F-104 tactically), etc. In this period he also completed a basic flying course on the F-104C at George AFB. He retired from the air force in 1973, by which time he had logged some 5050 flying hours, 1650 on the CF-104.

By late 1957 Canada–US affairs had improved through their NORAD bonds. Even so, three years later the US policy of playing some cards carefully was noted by F/L Gerald R.W. King, F/L Cinnamon's replacement at Nellis. Having joined the RCAF in 1943, King earned his Wings, then waited at "Y" Depot in

F/L Cinnamon during his Nellis exchange tour. Then, an F-100 in a typical AIM-9 launch scene during weapons development at Nellis. (USAF/Cinnamon Col.)

Montreal for his posting. By that time, however, there was little need for new aircrew in the UK, so King transferred to the RN Fleet Air Arm. He got to the UK, but the war ended and soon he was home in Powell River, BC. In 1951 he re-enlisted, trained on the Vampire and Sabre at Chatham, then had a NATO tour with 434 Squadron. He instructed at Chatham, then was posted to the 3597th CCTS at Nellis. He first flew the F-100 there on November 18, 1957.

In July 1958 Nellis switched from Training Command to Tactical Air Command. This involved changes in the syllabus to reflect TAC objectives. Early in 1960 King, now with the 4523rd CCTS, attended the Fighter Weapons Instructors Course, where he observed: "This course is similar to the Weapons Course at Chatham, NB, but is more up-to-date in its syllabus. It was unfortunate, but this officer could not attend all of the lectures. Such classified subjects as nuclear weapons … are restricted to foreign nationals." He enjoyed the course, which entailed 50 flying hours and 107 hours of lectures.

F/L King last flew at Nellis on June 7, 1960, having by then logged 801 F-100 hours. He now worked at AFHQ under G/C Bob Christie, who was managing the CF-104 program. King's duties involved writing the CF-104 OTU syllabus, making recommendations about the CF-104 bombing system, developing the Cold Lake range to accommodate the strike mission, even calculating the quantities of practice bombs needed by the OTU and forthcoming NATO squadrons. (In this period former "Golden Hawk" pilot, F/L Dave Tinson, joined W/C Christie's operation. Sent to the USAF nuclear weap-

ons centre in Albuquerque, he prepared three manuals, including one for the Mk.82 RE 2000-lb nuclear bomb, which RCAF CF-104s would carry.) F/L King later converted to the CF-104 at 6 OTU, flying initially with F/L Howie Rowe in 12647 on June 10, 1964. Following this, he was in the "recce shop" at No. 1 Air Division HQ in Metz, with 439 Squadron at Marville, and in flight safety at Lahr. Upon leaving the military in 1972, King joined Transport Canada in Vancouver, serving to 1992.

In 1961 several RCAF pilots did the F-100 low-level weapons delivery course at Nellis. This group constituted the first CF-104 cadre – those who would staff No. 6 (ST/R) OTU at Cold Lake, once the CF-104 entered service: W/C Ken Lett, S/L Bill Paisley and F/Ls John Hutt, Don McGowan, Jake Mulhall, Ernie Saunders, Don Weixl and Don Williamson. All met the basic AFHQ standard for CF-104 pilot – 1000 F-86 hours. F/L Saunders first flew the F-100F on May 31, 1961. Two more dual trips followed, then came several on the F-100C. These missions were on the range, getting instruction in and practicing lob-bombing (the "special weapons" delivery system planned for the CF-104). The course ended on June 19 when Saunders had 16 hours on F-100s. Next the Canadians visited Lockheed at Palmdale, California for ground school, then started flying the

Some of the original RCAF pilots on the F-104 at Palmdale in 1961 with Lockheed's Bob Gilliland (3rd from left): John Hutt, Ernie Saunders, Don McGowan, Jake Mulhall, Bill Paisley and Kenny Lett. Don Weixl and Don Williamson also were on this course, but were airborne when the photo was taken. (CANAV Col.)

CF-104. Saunders first flew the CF-104D on September 1 and would log 13 hours on 11 trips, the last on September 25.

From Wakaw, Saskatchewan, Don Weixl joined the RCAF in 1946, serving initially in ground transport, but remustering to pilot in 1949. His first postings were to Centralia and Gimli, instructing on Harvards. He converted to the Vampire at Chatham in 1952, instructed on the T-33, then had a Sabre tour at 413 Squadron 1955-57. He initially flew the F-100 at Nellis with 1Lt Goldberg on May 29, 1961, finishing on June 19 with 18:10 hours on F-100s. Weixl first flew an F-104 at Palmdale on September 1, 1961, going up with Lockheed pilot Tom Armstrong in F-104D "503". His course ended with a September 16 flight in the same aircraft. With only 12:45 hours on type he joined the instructing staff at 6 (ST/R) OTU at Cold Lake (still flying T-33s). On January 16, 1962 S/L Ken Lett, with S/L Bill Paisley in his back seat, delivered the first CF-104D to the OTU. In April 2006 Don Weixl recalled this:

Buster Kincaid, who began as a grunt in the PPCLIs, was wounded in Korea, then remustered to pilot. Here he is at Nellis with an F-100 as the backdrop. (Kincaid Col.)

I led a 5-plane section of T-33s and we rendezvoused with Ken a few miles south of the base, where we formed up in a "V". As it was dusk each aircraft had its nav lights burning, so it was a pretty sight as Ken led us low past the tower. The real show was how he then cut in his afterburner and climbed out, leaving the rest of us in his smoke. As he landed and taxied in, we T-birds did another low pass in salute. Once we were all on the ground, there were a few pops in the mess to signal a new era in high performance aircraft in the RCAF.

Super Sabre

Francis Graham "Buster" Kincaid's exchange tour was on the renowned F-100 Super Sabre. From Penticton, BC, as Cpl Kincaid he first had served with the Princess Patricia's Canadian Light Infantry. In Korea he was severely wounded on December 10, 1952 during a fire fight. He recuperated in Japan and returned to combat. In 1955 he enlisted in the RCAF, flying first at Claresholm on Monday May 30, 1955. That day he went up with F/O Gene Flewelling in Chipmunk 18003, then advanced to the Harvard, his first flight on July 7 also being with Flewelling. He next did the T-33 course at 3 AFS, Gimli and won his Wings. Chatham followed, then came a Sabre tour at 441 Squadron 1957-60, after which he instructed at Chatham. Early in 1962 he learned that he and Ed Stone were posted to Nellis.

In May 1962 Kincaid reported to the 4525th Fighter Weapons School. He did a brief F-100 course and started straight into instructing. Course members at the 4525th were experienced men training as fighter weapons specialists. Once graduated, they returned to their squadrons to pass on their knowledge. Kincaid usually would fly two F-100 missions a day. The syllabus was typical – air-to-air firing, ACM and air-to-ground exercises with cannons, rockets, bombs and napalm. Most missions took about an hour, but could be as long as three hours thanks to KC-135 tankers.

The F-100 was less manoeuvrable than a Sabre, but Kincaid found it a reasonable fighter. A nice feature was how it was supersonic in level flight but, like most "Fighters of the 50s", it had its bad habits (these are described in Robert Coram's book *Boyd: The Fighter Plot Who Changed the Art of War*). The F-100's worst quirk was falling into a flat spin in certain profiles. On June 6, 1962, Kincaid was air fighting with another F-100, when he found himself in such a jam. Nothing could remedy matters and the ground was rising fast. At 10,000 feet he ejected. Now came another crisis – his seat came tearing through his parachute, but enough of the 'chute remained for a safe landed. A rescue helicopter returned him to base. Kincaid later flew over the crash site. His F-100 had landed with no forward motion, so its black imprint lay in the desert sand. When F/L Myron Johnson took over the exchange slot at Nellis, Kincaid was posted to Cold Lake to instruct on the CF-104 from 1964-67. He later flew with 427 Squadron at Zweibrucken, then was OpsO at the air weapons

F/L Kincaid last flew at Nellis on an F-100 target tow mission of June 3, 1964. He had logged 462 hours on type. In this AAR scene the KC-135A at work served to retirement in 1992. F-100F 56-3927 later was in the Danish Air Force (1974-82), then joined the Danish national aviation museum. (Kincaid Col.)

The ruins of Buster Kincaid's F-100 that crashed on June 6, 1962. (Kincaid Col.)

training base at Decimomanu. Later postings were to NDHQ, then Portage, from where he retired in 1977 to settle with his wife, Donna, in Las Vegas.

Flying the Thud

In the early 1950s the USAF already had plans to replace the F-100. Proposals boiled down to North American's F-107 and Republic's F-105 Thunderchief. Prototypes were evaluated, each meeting the specs. But, when it came down to the wire, the F-105

won the day. Nicknamed "Thud", the F-105 was the last member of Republic's great fighter family. The pre-production YF-105A, flown in October 1955, was followed by the first F-105B in May 1956. Much development was crammed into the following months, e.g. fitting progressively more powerful P&W J75 engines, and the GE MA-18 automatic nav/FCS. In June 1959 the F-105D was introduced, and the 2-seat F-105F appeared in June 1963. More than 800 Thuds would be delivered, the "D" (600 built) being the chief model. From March 1961 to May 1964 RCAF F/Ls Raymond Eric "Tappy" Carruthers and Edward Henry "Ed" Stone were privileged to fly the F-105.

Born in Edmonton on December 23, 1930, Ray "Tappy" Carruthers joined the RCAF in 1951 (his nickname came from his fame on the dance floor). Carruthers commenced flying at 1 FTS in Centralia, going up on June 2 in Harvard 2996 with F/O Donnan. On July 23 he soloed, then completed his course on January 24, 1952. He left Centralia with 180:15 flying hours, then proceeded to 2 AFS and 1 PGS at MacDonald for the remainder of his training. Leaving there in July for OTU at Chatham, Carruthers' log showed 312:55 hours, all on Harvards. OTU commenced on July 16, 1952 with a flight in Harvard 3204, F/O Livingston touring Carruthers around the local area. Beginning on July 23 came 10 trips in the T-33. On August 14 Carruthers flew the Sabre (19359) for the first time. Many exercises ensued, as did a stint towing the drogue with the Mustang flight. This

Only two Canadians are known to have had tours on the legendary Republic F-105 Thunderchief. First flown in October 1955, the F-105 lineage dates from the XF-91 of 1949. This pair was photographed by a 439 Squadron CF-104 during a 1960s NATO Tiger Meet. (Huddleston Col.)

(Right) F/L Ray Carruthers (right) accepts a memento from his CO at Nellis AFB, LCol James E. Bean, on May 29, 1962. The USAF traditionally had superb leadership in this era. Bean, who had flown P-47s in WWII, established the USAF F-105 training organization at Nellis. He later flew in Southeast Asia, where he was shot down on January 3, 1968, then spent five years as a POW. This greatly admired leader passed away in Kentucky in January 2006. (via Nan Carruthers)

was a bit of "punishment", following a disagreement with his CFI, F/L Omer Levesque, over a recent accident – it didn't always pay for a junior flying officer to disagree with his boss!

Now Carruthers was posted to 422 in Ottawa, flying initially with F/O Rod Pritchard in T-33 14689 on April 1, then taking up Sabre 19289 the next day. Carruthers flew with his new "boss", S/L John Buzza, in a T-33 on April 23. On May 27, 1953 he was flying Sabre 19689, air fighting with F/O Dick Kiser, who was working hard to keep Carruthers off his tail. They fought from above 30,000 feet, down to the cloud tops at about 10,000, where Kiser lost radio contact. Carruthers suddenly was out of control and, with seconds to impact, ejected in cloud. He landed OK, phoned Uplands from a farm house and soon was back at squadron. Later that day he had a Link Trainer session, perhaps trying to understand what had happened to '689. Otherwise,

it was off to the mess, where a thrash ensued with all sorts of shenanigans, including Kiser boasting about how he had "shot down" his wing man, even though the accident was caused by a stuck leading edge slat that caused fatal asymmetric forces. Of the incident Carruthers reported in his log: "Battle formation, tail chases, 1:15. A/c out of control. Ejected. Quite a ride. Broken vertebrae in neck." Carruthers took time to recuperate, not flying the Sabre again until July 10. In August 1953 he married Nancy Lee, a Stratford girl whom he had met at Grand Bend in Centralia days.

In August, Carruthers joined Op. Leapfrog IV on which 422 flew the Atlantic to 4 Wing at Baden-Soellingen. November 18-23, 1954 he was on exchange to a French base. There in Sabre 23183, he made 10 sorties against Ouragan fighters. January 8-30, 1955 the squadron was at Rabat. There, he flew 26 times on

Young 1950s airmen followed magnificent leaders, any of whom would point a bright light towards an exchange opportunity. Typical was John Buzza, DFC, seen at home in Ottawa with his wife, Ruth, in August 1998. With a wartime tour on Lancasters, another on Typhoons, then postwar experience on the F-86 and CF-104, Buzza took pride in teaching and encouraging his charges. Ray Carruthers had the honour of learning from Buzza on 422 Squadron, then in CF-104 days at RCAF HQ in Metz. The Buzzas of the RCAF often ended with senior NORAD postings, where they usually could do some good non-operational flying. While Deputy Commander 24th NORAD Region at Malmstrom AFB, Montana, BGen Buzza did his proficiency flying on the B-57, F-106, T-33 and UH-1 "Huey". (Larry Milberry)

gunnery and towing. With F/O T.G. "Gerry" McDougall as his wingman, on February 1, 1955 F/O Carruthers set off in 23193 from Rabat for Istres. Before departing, someone wondered, "What's the temperature in the Med today?" F/O Carruthers jokingly replied, "Who cares … nobody's going swimming today." All went well for 1:20 hours, then Carruthers' day went down the drain – out of the blue McDougall called to warn that '193 was spewing smoke and flame. Right away Carruthers knew what to do – out he went. McDougall kept an eye, but ran low on fuel and landed at a Spanish base. Meanwhile, F/O Bill Weary had wished Carruthers good luck, to which Tappy coolly replied, "Don't worry. I've done this before."

As he splashed into the sea, Carruthers was dragged through 20-foot waves, struggled into his dinghy, but soon was sea sick. While S/L Buzza remained at Istres awaiting word, 422 pressed on to 4 Wing. By this time Nan Carruthers had heard from W/C Jack Allan that her husband was missing. Next morning Marge Allan let Nan know that he was safe. F/Os Weary and Fritz Belec flew to Istres in a T-33, then went down to dockside at Marseilles to await Carruthers. They must have been worried to see that the only welcoming party that the French had standing by was a hearse! Late at night the *Sahara*

docked. Carruthers was cheerful, if still shaky, having swallowed dye marker, shark repellent and too much of the Med. Weary and Carruthers returned to 4 Wing in T-bird 21051. After they landed, someone chewed them out for not waiting for the USAF ambulance that had been sent. Another great "survival" party was held that night. Tappy was back flying Sabres on February 28. His log entry summarizes this episode: "Engine failure near Valencia. Fire and bail out at 11:30 AM at 6000 feet. Thirteen hours in the water. Picked up by French cargo ship 'Sahara' 0045, 02 Feb."

In this period Hungary rebelled against Soviet rule. This was a worrisome time in NATO, with all squadrons on alert. Thus, the "Zulu" scrambles in which Carruthers took part October 25-30, 1956 must have been tense. In January 1957 he was back in Canada, instructing on the Weapons Flight at Chatham. On June 7, 1959 he surpassed 2000 hours. He continued at Chatham

F/L Carruthers' F-105 training certificate.

to June 6 a year later, then packed his bags, posted to the 4523rd "Hornet" CCTS (commanded by LCol Otto Kemp) at Nellis. Carruthers first flew on an F-100F familiarization mission with Capt Moser, soon was checked out and all the usual F-100 flying ensued. On August 15, 1960 he flew his first air-to-air refuelling, noting for the 3-hour flight, "5 hook-ups". He completed his first CPM (combat profile missions) on July 19. For October 25 he noted, "Nite rear seat check. Nite refuel, 4 dry hook-ups, 1:30" ("dry" meant no fuel taken).

A document of December 27, 1960 (authorized by Capt Don O. Quane) notes that Carruthers was qualified "non-nuclear" on the F-100 and designated him in the "Sharpshooter" category. By February 22 he was qualified "nuclear" in the categories "LHA", "RLB (TP)" and "RLB (L)". After logging 185 F-100 hours, he transferred to the 4526th "Cobra" CCTS (LCol James E. Bean commanding) to fly the F-105, going up initially on March 3, 1961 in F-105D No. 59-1738 (preserved today at Dyess AFB, Texas). On March 7 he flew his first F-105 CPM in 59-1757 (crashed March 3, 1966), then his first "NWD" (nuclear weapon delivery) on March 16 in 59-1770. For April 1962 Carruthers flew 37 sorties for 55:15 hours.

With F-105s steadily going back to Republic at Farmingdale, NY for overhaul and mods, F/L Carruthers got in some ferrying. On May 6, 1961 he took 60-0454 (shot down in Vietnam on May 7, 1967) from Farmingdale to Richards-Gebaur AFB (Kansas City) in 2:55 hours, then to Nellis in the same time. June 16 to 20, 1961 he put on two demo flights at the Air Force Academy in Colorado Springs, flying F-105D 59-1723 (shot down by a SAM in Vietnam on May 27, 1967). There were a few rumblings around Nellis at a Canadian getting this plum assignment. On June 21 Carruthers was thrilled to have a famil flight in F-104 57-1326. On the 35-minute flight he and Capt Gabrowski clocked Mach 1.2. Another "first" for Carruthers came on February 26, 1962, when he flew with Major Hogue in the back of what he noted as an "F-110" (original USAF designation for the F-4 Phantom). This 1:15-hour ride culminated in a Mach 2 run. April to June 1962 the 4526th named F/L Carruthers its outstanding instructor for the quarter, the base paper reporting:

Honored lately at his farewell party at Don French's Bonanza was Flight Lieutenant Raymond "Tappy" Carruthers of the Royal Canadian Air Force. He has been stationed at Nellis AFB for the past two years on exchange duty. At Nellis he has served as a flight commander of the 4526th Combat Crew Training Sq., better known as the Cobras … Originally from Edmonton, Alberta, he served from 1953-57 in … West Germany as part of the NATO alliance; and was a member of the 1961 Firepower Demonstration Team which performed for the Air Force Academy.

Tappy, formerly an instructor with the elite RCAF Fighter Weapons School at Chatham, New Brunswick, recently was nominated for the award "Instructor of the Quarter", which is a base-wide competition held quarterly at Nellis. Tappy's next assignment is to Metz, France, at the RCAF Air Division Headquarters. He will fly F-104 Starfighters. Tappy and his wife, Nancy, have a 2½ year old daughter, Alicia. The Cobra Squadron Commander, Lieut. Col. James E. Bean, said, "Flight Lieutenant Carruthers has been an outstanding instructor. His high standards are a credit to his service and his country. It has been a great pleasure to have Tappy as a member of our squadron."

On June 4, 1962 F/L Carruthers made his last F-105 flight, a 1:45-hour CPM in 59-1772 (it later recorded 2 MiG-17 kills, but was shot down by AAA January 27, 1970). He ended his exchange with 305:50 F-105 hours. Hereafter, the Carruthers moved to Metz, where Tappy was in the TacEval shop under two RCAF "greats", W/Cs Cam Mussells and John Buzza. On September 14, 1962 he began the CF-104 OTU, going up in 12635 with USAF exchange officer Capt Bill Leitch, then returned to Metz. On June 28, 1963 he had a famil trip with F/L Don Freeborn in the CL-41, then on a European demo tour. He finished at Metz with a flight in CF-104 12862 on July 26, 1966, then attended RCAF Staff College in Toronto. September 1967 to June 1969 he commanded 427 at Zweibrücken, a tour he considered to be the biggest feather in his RCAF cap. Subsequent tours were to 4 ATAF at Ramstein and the Air Warfare College at RAF Manby. In this period he had a famil ride in an F-111. An emergency developed, leading to someone wondering what a foreign national was doing in the USAF's top-secret F-111. From 1972-75 LCol Carruthers was in Military Plans and Operations at NDHQ. He was Canada's Military Attaché in Prague 1975-78, then was in NDHQ to 1983. A year followed at Fighter Group HQ, North Bay, then Carruthers returned to NDHQ in the Nuclear Planning Group and with the Permanent Joint Board on Defence. He retired from the Canadian Forces in 1987 to

While Air Attaché in Czechoslovakia, Maj Carruthers had a secondary role in the espionage world – such is the nature of an attaché's job. When a Soviet attaché and fighter pilot attended CANAV's *Canadair Sabre* book launching in Ottawa in 1986, the author was astonished. Then, someone explained how the Soviets went to any social event in Ottawa, if nothing else, to note who was present from NDHQ. Later, they filed a formal report. This was simple routine and "old hat" in the ambassadorial world. Fighter pilot that he was, Carruthers dove right into this role in Czechoslovakia, not just keeping his eyes open, but taking forbidden photos. Czech authorities soon were on to his game and one day ran his car off the road, putting him in hospital. From this selection of Carruthers' photos one can see how useful a hardworking attaché can be, but he does have to keep a step ahead of the locals. A MiG-21 "Fishbed" interceptor and MiG-23 "Flogger" fighter bomber are shown in the circuit. Then, Carruthers' quick shot of a Mil-24 "Hind" gunship over-flying an army base, and shoot-and-run snaps of Warsaw Pact armour on the move by road and rail. Finally, Maj Carruthers performing one of his official duties – attending a typical embassy social function in Prague. Carruthers' rank on this posting was Acting Colonel. (via Nan Carruthers)

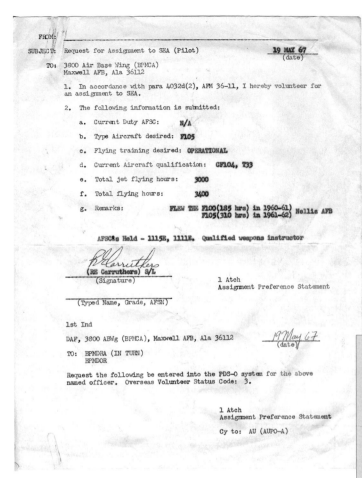

FROM:

SUBJECT: Request for Assignment to SEA (Pilot)   **19 MAY 67**
(date)

TO: 3800 Air Base Wing (BPMCA)
Maxwell AFB, Ala 36112

1. In accordance with para 4032d(2), AFM 36-11, I hereby volunteer for
an assignment to SEA.

2. The following information is submitted:

  a. Current Duty AFSC: **N/A**

  b. Type Aircraft desired: **F105**

  c. Flying training desired: **OPERATIONAL**

  d. Current Aircraft qualification: **CF104, T33**

  e. Total jet flying hours: **3000**

  f. Total flying hours: **3400**

  g. Remarks: **FLEW THE F100(185 hrs) in 1960-61)** Nellis AFB
           F105(310 hrs) in 1961-62)

    AFSCs Held - 1115E, 1111E. Qualified weapons instructor

(RE Carruthers) S/L
(Signature)
           1 Atch
           Assignment Preference Statement

(Typed Name, Grade, AFSN)

1st Ind

DAF, 3800 ABWg (BPMCA), Maxwell AFB, Ala 36112   19 May 67
(date)

TO: BPMDRA (IN TURN)
    BPMDOR

Request the following be entered into the PDS-O system for the above
named officer. Overseas Volunteer Status Code: 3.

           1 Atch
           Assignment Preference Statement

           Cy to: AU (AUPO-A)

The USAF form which S/L Carruthers used to apply for a Southeast Asia combat assignment. (via Nan Carruthers)

join Paramax, where his project was the EH-101 helicopter contract (which Prime Minister Chretien, seeking votes in the 1993 election, cancelled).

In March 2003 Nan Carruthers recalled that, while Tappy was at Staff College, his class visited the USAF War College at Maxwell AFB. At a BBQ there, he and Nan bumped into Bud Holman, a USAF friend from Nellis days. At some strategic point, Holman took the big bowl overflowing with salad and poured it over Tappy's head. "There, Carruthers," he said, "now you're officially off my back!" Nan recalled that Holman had been Tappy's boss regarding nuclear secrets. Harkening back to ferrying F-105s, she added: "Our squadron CO, Jim Bean, was a good looking bachelor. Always in demand, he often dated the stewardesses on the commercial flights between New York

and Las Vegas. Pilots returning after delivering a Thud were always greeted warmly by the airline cabin crews, even though they usually boarded carrying their helmets and parachutes. This led to many a comment and some concern amongst the other passengers. The parachutes, especially, made passengers a bit edgy. Eventually, the boys were asked to kindly check their 'chutes!"

During the Cuban Missile Crisis the 4526th deployed to Homestead AFB, Florida. Carruthers was keen to go with the squadron but, as Nan explained: "We had already been posted to 1 Air Division in Metz and, besides, the Canadian government said a very firm 'No' to Ray deploying into a combat setting." In 2003 several historic documents came to light. One, dated May 19, 1967, is Tappy's application (USAF "Form 90") for transfer to the USAF to fly a combat tour in Southeast Asia. This is addressed to the "3800 Air Base Wing (BPMCA)", Maxwell AFB, Alabama. Point No. 1 reads, "In accordance with para 4032d(2), AFM 36-11, I hereby volunteer for an assignment to SEA." Carruthers, then a major, requested a slot on F-105s, specifying the type of duty as "Operational". He listed his many qualifications plus his flying time of 3400 hours, 3000 on jets. All that is certain about this application is that Carruthers did not go to Southeast Asia.

S/L R.E. Carruthers Jet Flying Time, 1987	
Type	Hours
F-86	1428
T-33	901
CF-104	907
F-105	306
F-100	187
F-110	6
F-111	4
Vulcan	4.5
Nimrod	3
RF-4C	1.7
G.91	1
CL-41	1

LCol Carruthers receives Canada's Order of Military Merit from Governor General Jean Sauvé in a 1985 Ottawa investiture. (IS85-964 DND)

This early Northrop F-5A was at Glenview Naval Air Station, Chicago on August 28, 1966. The light-weight F-5 was supplied to many of America's allies. Resplendent in foreign flags, 63-8381 likely was a demo aircraft. Eventually, it flew with the Greeks. (Larry Milberry)

language, mainly evident when a student was getting a clearance from Phoenix terminal control.

The USAF F-5 was similar to a CF-5, although the cockpit was a bit simpler, e.g. no ADF. Its J85 engines were an earlier version – a CF-5 had a bit more kick in 'burner. Daily flying included air-to-air and air-to-ground training. On one mission a student got to deliver two 750-lb inert bombs. These were dropped singly to demonstrate the sudden effect of asymmetric aerodynamics, and how this was controlled. With such a program, Bergie had little time for much other than instructing, but one weekend he tried to book an F-5 to attend a CF-104 reunion at Cold Lake. Then he learned about TAC's "1000 mile rule" – an aircraft borrowed for the weekend couldn't venture more than 1000 miles from base. So fizzled the Cold Lake skit. Bergie finished at Williams on July 16, 1973. Through his tour he had averaged 24.6 flying hours and 22.4 sorties per month. Now he flew a desk at 10 TAG in St. Hubert, and served in weapons development at AETE until retiring in 1977. He and his wife then operated a dry cleaning business in Cold Lake, before settling in Arizona in 1994.

Replacing Capt Don Bergie at the 425th TFTS was Capt Wally Peel. A Manitoba farm boy, he joined the RCAF as an ROTP entrant in 1965. Earning his wings on the T-33 at Gimli in June 1969,

Don Bergie (centre) with 441 Squadron buddies H.A. Davidson and H.D. Klein at RCAF North Luffenham in December 1954. Davidson came to a sad end on May 2, 1957, following engine failure. He ejected too low and died when his 'chute failed to open. His Sabre crash-landed almost intact. (PL-63621 DND)

he was expecting CF-104s. But Ottawa was reducing its NATO commitment, so Peel became a CF-5 pipeliner half-way through his course at 434 Squadron. Suddenly he had nowhere to go.

Flying initially at 434 with Dave Mills on October 20, 1969, Lt Peel readily adapted to the CF-5, catching the eye of his CO, LCol Steve Gulyas. In an era when an operational fighter tour normally was required for a CF-5 instructor, Gulyas fingered Peel as IP material. Under the watchful eye of a few old-time IPs such as Don Bergie, Bernie Reid and John Swallow, he took to his new role and his CF-5 career was off and running. Notable events included a close-call with a tree on May 27, 1970, and winning "Overall Top Gun" at Ex. Open Challenge in September 1971. In 1972 Peel participated in Op. Canamigo, ferrying a CF-5 to Venezuela, and in June 1973 was part of Ex. Long Leap I, Canada's first trans-Atlantic aerial refuelling mission.

Capt Wally Peel during his USAF exchange at Williams AFB. (Peel Col.)

In July 1973 Capt Peel, already with some 1100 hours on CF-5s, was posted to Williams AFB on exchange. There he flew initially on August 18 with Maj Doug Lee in an F-5B and soon was into the daily instructing routines. As it happened, the advanced F-5E "Tiger II" was being introduced at the 425th. Peel became the first Canadian to fly one of these (F-5E 72-1393, later sold to Brazil) on September 27. The F-5E would leave an F-5A in its dust and out-manoeuvre pretty well any of the competition, especially with its 1500-foot turning radius, thanks to such improvements as leading edge wing extensions, manoeuvring flaps and 20% more power than an F-5A. In 2007 Wally Peel elucidated:

With such capabilities as sustained 6G at 10,000 feet and a radar-directed gun sight that made hitting the dart routine, the "E" was much of a surprise to us all. What really got our attention was its handling at max AOA in scissors, where it was always on the edge of departure, compared to an "A". Northrop had kept mum about this, not even advising the 425th pilots, who were evaluating the "E".

Then, one day, a South Vietnamese pilot, believing he was in an inverted spin, jumped out. Astoundingly, his "E" landed in one piece in the desert. Before long we were clued-in about a condition called "inverted pitch hang-up". When inverted with manoeuvre flaps down and with any negative G, the "E" will take over and fly itself, often with considerable yaw. Given the checklist procedure of holding the controls neutral for such a condition, the South Vietnamese pilot, unfortunately, had maintained the apparently out-of-control condition. On ejecting, his "E" said "Thank you very much", and recovered itself with the change in C of G. Northrop's fix for this condition was a simple note in the pilot operating instructions – select flaps up. No other "Es" found there way to the desert floor.

As had Don Bergie, Peel would train students from many nations. There were clear national traits – he rated the Malaysians as the top students, while other nations were not so hot (although they may have been the most polite) and the odd nation was pretty much hopeless in fighter pilot potential. With South Vietnam on the brink of collapse in 1973-74, most of its student pilots returned to the US in 1975 with the financial aid of IPs from the 425th.

While carrying out his daily training, Capt Peel also worked as Weapons Officer in curriculum development and gun-sight weapons assessment. Canada was asked to extend his tour to help develop the F-5E Fighter Weapons School Course. For this, a cadre of six pilots worked for several months developing double attack tactics and writing new syllabus for the F-5E, since it clearly was in a unique category that heralded the F-15, F-16 and F/A-18 era. In March 1974 and 1975, Peel was named to lead the select 4-ship mission to the Gila Bend range when the USAF TAC Inspector General made his annual visits. For these missions, upon which the reputation of the 425th rested, Capt Peel had the IG's representative with him as they briefed, flew their best possible mission on the range, landed and debriefed.

Life at the 425th was basically about Williams and environs – cross-country trips were uncommon. Once, however, Maj Peel

(Facing page) CF-104G prototype 60770 (later re-numbered as 12770) at Palmdale. It began as USAF F-104A 56-0770, then Lockheed turned it into a "G" with such mods as 25% more vertical tail area. First flight as such was on September 1, 1960. This "one off" F-104, in which LCol R.A. "Bud" White flew to 100,110 feet on December 14, 1967, is displayed in Canada's national aviation museum. In this view it heads a line of 7 F-104s plus NASARR DC-3 N18565. A development F-104G, FG-790 later was NASA "813" and "820" and today is with the NASA museum at Edwards AFB. FG-801 later was a chase plane on the ultra-secret A-12 interceptor program, then went to Pakistan. DA+101 served in Germany until scrapped in 1995. DA+102 today is in the Waffenmusem at Berlin/Gatow. Luftwaffe "103" went to West Germany in 1962. On June 30, 1976 it crashed on approach to Norwenich, killing the pilot. DC-3 N18565 began in 1942 as a USAAF C-53. It served TWA 1945-48, then joined Lockheed, eventually becoming the NASARR test bed in 1960. Later, it served the Luftwaffe, became N3101Q in 1969 then, apparently, was scrapped at Luqa *circa* 1983. (Lockheed 7856-4)

(Above) RCAF test pilots on secondment to Lockheed Palmdale and Edwards AFB flew some of the earliest F-104s. Jack Woodman and Alex Bowman are shown with Lockheed's Bob Schaefer. Woodman was the only RCAF pilot to fly the Avro CF-105. (Lockheed 2445-4)

(promoted in July 1975) did what Capt Bergie could not. February 13-15, 1976, just before leaving "Willy", he led two F-5Bs to Cold Lake. The official excuse was that he and Capt Ron Hintze (USAF) needed to "house hunt" in Cold Lake (Hintze soon would join 419 Squadron on exchange). On leaving the 425th at the end of February 1976, Peel had been instructing the first FWIC course with Iranian and Ethiopian students. His log showed 352 hours on the F-5A/B plus 383 on the F-5E. Replaced at the 425th by Capt Rick Savin, he returned to an NDHQ tour at DAR, where his duties revolved around the NFA project and development of the CRV-7 rocket. Other tours would follow, e.g. Maxwell AFB (USAF Air University), 441 Squadron (CF-104s) and Allied Air Forces Central Europe (NATO TacEval Team Chief). Col Peel retired from air force life in 1995 for a career in industry. In 2007 he was Senior Training Solutions Advisor at CAE in Montreal.

Also at Edwards in the 1950s was W/C R.G. "Bob" Middlemiss, shown (left) with Al D'Eon (both had been Honorary Colonels of 427 "Lion" Squadron and are seen at 427's "Gathering of the Lions" at CFB Petawawa, November 25, 2003). Bob, a veteran of Malta Spitfire days, commanded 427 when it stood up with CF-104s in 1962. His assignment in 1958 was to pair with Jack Woodman testing the Grumman F11F-1F Super Tiger and the F-104. He first flew the Super Tiger on June 18, 1958, the F-104 on January 15, 1959. He and Woodman eventually recommended the Super Tiger to RCAF HQ, so were a bit surprised when Ottawa chose the F-104. (Larry Milberry)

F-104 Starfighter

While Canada's CF-104 Starfighter years began in 1961, a few RCAF pilots got to fly this great fighter earlier, the pioneers being such men as Bob Ayres, Bob Middlemiss and Jack Woodman, who flew the F-104A, 'B and 'G at Palmdale and Edwards AFB, California. Middlemiss first flew an F-104 on January 15, 1959, continuing into June of that year. Woodman, the only RCAF pilot to fly the CF-105 Arrow, later was a test pilot with Lockheed in California, where his earlier projects included experimental F-104s. From July to October 1963 he made 38 NF-104A flights, reaching a top speed of 2.6M (August 21, aircraft 756 which crashed June 15, 1971) and a peak altitude of 97,500 feet (September 23, aircraft 760 – later crashed). Both these NF-104s today are on display at Edwards AFB, but as one machine comprising the wreckage of the two.

USN BurAero No. 138647 was one of the "two and only" Super Tigers. It survives as a display at the US Naval Museum of Armament and Technology at NAS China Lake, California. (Grumman History Centre)

In February 1957, after qualifying as a test pilot at the ETPS, F/L George R. "Bob" Ayres joined the CEPE (Climatic Flight), testing Canadian and British aircraft at Namao, Cold Lake and Churchill. In December 1959 he joined the AAED in Cold Lake. One of his special programs in this period involved firing the Bullpup anti-shipping missile from the Argus. In 1960 F/L Ayres became Canada's representative test pilot for the forthcoming F-104G Joint Test Force being established at Edwards. Since he would need some time on the airplane, in 1960 he checked out at Westover, Mass. with the 337th FIS, commanded by LCol James Jabara. Ayres first flew on May 5, then continued to June 10, by when he had 30 F-104s hours. Since the 337th was an interceptor squadron, he had the rare chance (for an RCAF pilot) to practice supersonic intercepts. F-104s at the 337th had downward-firing ejection seats, not a great pilot morale booster. While Ayres was at Westover, a crew had an emergency on takeoff. They ejected unsuccessfully (the USAF soon installed upward-firing seats). In this period F/L Ayres and USAF Capt George Schulestad brought two F-104s to Ottawa (Uplands) to show the aircraft to AFHQ, some NATO reps and the media. Of this occasion Ayres recalled in 2006:

The weather was poor for the demonstration – low ceiling, low visibility, high humidity, not ideal for showing off a high-performance fighter. Even so, George decided to give it a try. Once airborne, he set up for some passes. On the second one he got a bit wide on his turn-in to come down across the flightline. To keep his speed up, he plugged in the afterburner, but he left it in too long. As he came by the crowd, he was just supersonic and the shock wave broke every window in the new control tower! Repairs totalled three-quarters of a million dollars. Ottawa paid the bills and George went on to become a general.

On January 2, 1961 Ayres arrived at Edwards, where his chief task (as a "Category 1A" test pilot) would be to prove all CF-104 and F-104G armament configurations. He joined other F-104 test pilots working on the NATO re-equipment program: Maj Heinz Birkenbeil and Lt Erhard Goedert (Germany), Maj Etienne Cailleu (Belgium), Capt Mathias G. Janssen (Netherlands), Capt Franco Bonazzi (Italy) and Capt A. Crews (USAF). These constituted the pilots of the F-104G Joint Test Force, commanded by Col W.A. Kruge, USAF. Each NATO nation also had engineers and technicians in the JTF to support the aircraft and weapons, process data and write reports that the program would generate. The RCAF component had test pilot Jack Woodman, who did Category 1 (production) test flying at Palmdale, supported by RCAF engineers S/L J.A. Tarzwell, S/L H.E. Bjornstad, F/L Blezard, F/L I.R. Atkins and F/L Bell.

F/L Ayres was stationed at Palmdale until June 1962, where he flew some 235 hours on various F-104s (the program would use 23 F-104Gs). Ayres would specialize in weapons – bombs, rockets, guns, as well as inertial navigation systems, air-to-air/air-to-ground radars and ground mapping/terrain avoidance applications. The main task was to evaluate how each weapon or system functioned and how it influenced performance, utilization and flexibility. Missions were flown from Edwards over the ranges at NAS China Lake, with operations dictated by diurnal temperatures. In 2006 Bob Ayres recalled, "It made sense to get the flying done before it got too hot, so we normally started work at 5 AM."

For his 17 months with JTF, Ayres found no serious flaw with any equipment. On one mission, however, he had some excitement: "I was to launch a Sidewinder infrared missile at high speed and altitude. First I fired a 4-inch rocket from one of the underwing hardpoints (the rocket became my IR target). I fired the Sidewinder, but it promptly exploded in front of me. In an instant I saw pieces of debris flashing past on either side of the cockpit, but I got lucky, landing unscathed. On March 22, 1962 F/L Ayres delivered an F-104G from Palmdale via Hill AFB to Cold Lake for trials. In June, he, his wife and son left California, Bob assuming CF-104 test pilot duties with CEPE at Cold Lake. He also did CF-104 acceptance flying with Canadair at Cartierville. In August 1963 he was posted to the RCAF Detachment in Bonn, West Germany, on secondment to the fighter-bomber wing at Norvenich, assisting the Luftwaffe with F-104G trials. The Luftwaffe, however, was not ready to proceed, so Ayres found work at 3 (F) Wing in Zweibrucken, testing new CF-104s delivered by RCAF C-130s. Ayres spent 10 years at 3 Wing as maintenance test pilot and wing flight safety officer.

In time F/L Ayres' log showed flights in 200 of the RCAF's 225 Starfighters and a total of some 2300 hours on type. On March 7, 1969 he received a message from 1 CAG commander, MGen R.J. Lane, DSO, DFC, congratulating him of having logged his 2000th F-104 hour. MGen Lane noted how this represented "a wealth of experience which has benefited all who fly the CF-104 and constitutes an unusual individual contribution to the introduction and subsequent field development of a combat aircraft." In Ayres' Performance Evaluation Report for May 1968 to April 1969 his assessor noted: "On many occasions he has used his position as Maintenance Test Pilot to further understand and appreciate the many characteristics of the high performance CF-104 … His enthusiasm is continuously displayed by the thorough way he performs and reports on his test flights … he has established a relationship with the groundcrew that has

become SOP for all aircrew, which contributes much to the harmony at 3 Wing."

In 1969 Maj Ayres returned to Canada as CO of 129 Test and Ferry Flight at Trenton. In his PER for May 1971 to April 1972 he was commended for running a productive, high-spirited operation. That year his pilots and other crew tested and ferried 13 different aircraft types, logging 4276 hours (Ayres flew 815 hours that year). Next, he returned to Cold Lake for a final AETE tour. He left the air force in 1972, then had many years with Transport Canada and such northern air carriers as Superior Airways of Thunder Bay, Aerotrades of Winnipeg and Norcanair of Saskatoon. In 1990 Bob Ayres and his wife Mary retired to Blind Bay, BC, where he flew bush planes. With some 32,000 flying hours, he finally left aviation in 1997. In 2006 he noted, "I had two flying careers – 30 years in the military, 30 in civil aviation. No serious accidents, but lots of thrills. I got to fly more than 100 aircraft types and never found a one that I didn't enjoy."

F-104 Instructor
In 1966 Larry "Zoot" Sutton began an F-104 exchange at Luke AFB, Arizona. His interest in aviation had begun with 176 Squadron Royal Canadian Air Cadets in Winnipeg. On a flying scholarship he earned his pilot's licence at the Winnipeg Flying Club, then joined the RCAF. After FTS at Claresholm and AFS in Gimli, he won his Wings in June 1956. Next came OTU at Chatham, where he flew a Sabre on September 4. From here he joined 441 Squadron at Marville. This would have been routine had it not been for March 24, 1956. That day F/O Sutton was air fighting with other Sabres, when his oil pressure began falling. RCAF Yellow Jack control in Metz gave him a course to Rhein Main. Meanwhile, Sutton shut off all but essential electric power, but to no avail – his engine seized, so he ejected at 15,000 feet. He escaped hitting some high tension wires,

JTF test pilots at Edwards: Lt Erhard Goedert (Belgian AF), Capt Armstrong (USAF), F/L Ayres (RCAF), Maj Etienne Cailleu (Belgian AF) and Capt Mathias Janssen (RNethAF). (Ayres Col.)

Larry Sutton (left) and a fellow pilot at Luke AB receive commemorative plaques from a Lockheed rep. Sutton liked his exclusive situation at Luke – being an RCAF pilot flying Luftwaffe F-104s in USAF markings. In a bit of Cold War trickery, these aircraft bear spurious USAF serial numbers – 61-2746 actually was a Titan II ICBM, while '3275 and '3276 down the line have the serials of Bullpup cruise missiles that were never built. (Sutton Col.)

then plunked into a river and swam ashore near Kelsterbach. A lad on the river bank took him to his farm, poured him a glass of cognac, ran a hot bath and got him dry clothes. A USAF helicopter ferried Sutton to Rhein Main from where he returned to Marville via T-33.

From 1960-63 Sutton instructed at Chatham. With 1218:45 hours on Sabres he moved to the CF-104 at Cold Lake, flying initially on July 6, 1963 with Capt Mark Cook (USAF exchange). He soloed on July 24 in 12785, graduated, then flew his first student trip with F/L Myron Filyk on January 16, 1964. In this period, Sutton was at Canadair with Len Fitzsimmons evaluating CL-41R NASARR trainer CF-LTX-X, e.g. using the advanced NASARR. He flew 'LTX four times with test pilot S/L Alex Bowman. CEPE found that the CL-41R, with fuel for only an hour, was unsuitable, so the OTU stuck to its NASARR "DC-104" Dakotas.

In 1966 Sutton heard of an exchange instructing Luftwaffe pilots on the TF-104G at Luke. He submitted a memo mentioning his interest and, to his surprise, got the job. His final OTU flight was in T-33 21150 with F/L Buster Kincaid on June 21. Sutton left Cold Lake with 555:45 hours on the CF-104. With the war in Southeast Asia raging, Sutton found Luke busy with F-100, F-104, F-5 and T-33 units. The count for F-100s was some 400, for F-104s, 120. Assigned to the 4518th CCTS, he made his first flight in TF-104 63-8457 with Capt Henderson on July 21,

1966. (Aircraft '457 later went to the Taiwanese AF.) His CO quickly deemed Sutton qualified and gave him his first student, Sgt Lieneman, on October 8. Sutton first flew the F-104G on August 16. An odd thing about Luke was that the F-104s were Luftwaffe aircraft in USAF colours. This was the period when the Luftwaffe was rapidly building its F-104G force, so contracted with the US to do much of its training. Luke was in the wide-open southwest with limitless air space, ranges, etc., and good year 'round weather, while Germany was small with congested air space and changeable weather.

F/L Sutton noted differences in Luke's F-104s, such as their Vulcan 20mm rotary cannon, which CF-104s lacked (in the cannon bay CF-104s carried extra fuel). Also, Luke's F-104s didn't have the same type of ENCS – emergency nozzle closing system. On the CF-104 this was an explosive devise to close the afterburner nozzle, should it stick open. US aircraft had a mechanical system. While a CF-104 pilot could only use the ENCS once, in an F-104 it could be operated any time. When taxiing out, it was simple to leave the throttle at idle, then pull the ENCS handle to close the nozzle to get more than adequate power for a brake check. The ENCS then could return to "open", with taxi speed maintained by throttle. (Several RCAF/CF pilots had ENCS problems, one being F/L L.G. Van Vliet. While flying 104858 from Lahr on January 27, 1964, his nozzle would not close and he had to get out in a hurry. On May 1, 1964 F/L D.E. Wilson was on a sortie from Zweibrucken in 104809 when his nozzle failed. The ENCS was engaged, but the nozzle slowly opened again, obliging Wilson to eject.)

The training syllabus at Luke had different emphases than Cold Lake. The basics were similar – conversion, formation, night and instrument flying, but Luke focused more on ACM tactics and conventional weapons delivery. These were less important in the RCAF, where CF-104s flew level on the deck in the nuclear strike role, then sped home, hoping to evade MiGs and SAMs. At Luke cannons and AIM-9B Sidewinders were fired daily at aerial targets, and 2.75-inch rockets, skip-bombs and napalm were used against ground targets. Due to the push to graduate pilots and fighter weapons instructors, ranges were busy night and day. At night they were lit by flares dropped

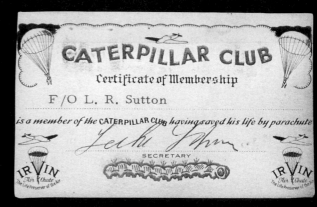

From Larry Sutton's log book during exchange days at Luke AFB: Larry on the left with three fellow pilots, typical log book entries, then his Caterpillar Club ID card harkening back to the day he ejected over Germany. (Sutton Col.)

(Below) Larry Sutton at home in Kanata, Ontario in 2002. (Larry Milberry)

CATERPILLAR CLUB
Certificate of Membership
F/O L. R. Sutton
is a member of the CATERPILLAR CLUB, having saved his life by parachute
SECRETARY
IRVIN Air Chute — The Life Preserver of the Air

YEAR 1967		AIRCRAFT		PILOT, OR 1ST PILOT	2ND PILOT, PUPIL OR PASSENGER	DUTY (Including Results and Remarks)	SINGLE-ENGINE DAY	
MONTH	DATE	Type	No.			TOTALS BROUGHT FORWARD	DUAL (1)	PILOT (2)
							271:35	2441:10
Jan	3	TF-104	084	Self	Grewert	A/A R #1		1:10
"	4	TF-104	458	Self	Kowarik	A/A Radar #1		1:15
"	4	TF-104	457	Self	Joerges	A/A " #1		1:20
"	5	TF-104	469	Self	Autenreith	A/A " #2		1:20
"	5	TF-104	082	Self	Kowarik	A/A " 2		1:15
"	6	TF-104	458	Self	Joerges	A/A " 2		1:25
"	9	TF-104	084	Self	Huff	A/A " 3		1:20
"	9	TF-104	455	Self	Grewert	A/A " 4		:55
"	10	TF-104	025	Maj Sweet	Self	'60-1 (Local IF)		1:20
"	10	TF-104	455	Self	Roesch	A/A #4		:50
"	11	TF-104	083	Self	Joerges	A/A #7		1:15
"	11	TF-104	083	Self	Eickstaedt	A/A #3		1:15
"	12	TF-104	458	Self	Betz	R&B Nite Nav 22		
"	13	TF-104	079	Self	Schwann	A/A #6		1:30
"	16	TF-104	073	Self	Juerges	A/A #6		1:20
"	17	TF-104	463	Self	Eickstaedt	A/A 5-5 HVAR-AIM 98		:6
"	18	TF-104	455	Self	Huff	A/A 5-5 HVAR-AIM 90		:5
"	18	104 G	273	Self	— Capt	A/A Radar & Chase		1:2
"	19	TF-104	452	Self	Tanschror Lt	N/S Tac Range V out		1:10
"	20	TF-104	466	Self	Kowarik	A/A R #6		1:1
"	20	TF-104	081	Capt Larry / Self Knox	Self	Luf-Las (Nellis)		1:3
"	21	TF-104	081	Capt Knox	Self Lt	Las-Luf		1:3
"	29	TF-104	078	Self	Thueringer	R&B #2		1:1

GRAND TOTAL [Cols. (1) to (10)]   TOTALS CARRIED FORWARD
_____ Hrs. _____ Mins.   271:35 / 246...

by the fighters or by an orbitting C-130. After a run-in, a pilot would pull out to go around, but he had to be careful. Blinding magnesium flares would affect night vision, making it tricky to see others in the circuit.

Firing AIM-9 Sidewinders was great fun. The routine was to launch a 5-in. unguided rocket. Once it got ahead about two miles, it became the Sidewinder's target, its IR signature enhanced by a flare. Sutton's first launch was on January 17, 1968. His log notes, "A/A#5 – 5" HVAR, AIM-9B". Further launches were on January 18 and March 3. On the first date he also passed 1000 Starfighter hours. On the latter, his second flight was listed as "M2.05". In August, he had three Sidewinder missions. (Meanwhile, the RCAF still had no operational air-to-air missiles. Only the RCN had used such weapons – Sidewinders for its long-retired Banshees.) Also of interest at Luke were low-level nav trips and nuclear weapons practice delivery. For the latter the standard "bomb tossing" manoeuvre was used – a steep pull-up short of target and an escape manoeuvre as the practice bomb described an upward arch, then descended by parachute. F-104 missions averaged 1.5 hours, the aircraft usually flying "clean".

Sutton also had secondary duties at Luke. All pilots spent certain days in the mobile tower at the end of the runway, controlling traffic. Sutton was amazed at how busy the circuit was – on a typical day there were hundreds of fighter launches. With such action, there were emergencies. The crash alarm sounded at least once a day, but accidents were few. Pilots also served as safety officers on the air-to-ground ranges.

One day in the spring of 1968 Sutton bumped into several Canadians. Led by O.B. Philp these were the first RCAF pilots taking T-38/F-5 conversion and soon would constitute 434 Squadron at Cold Lake. Sutton expressed an interest in 434 and "OB" was agreeable. On June 25, 1968 Sutton flew his final Luke mission – in TF-104 63-8452 (later to Taiwan) with Lt Reinert. He lead four F-104s on a ground attack exercise (logged as "skip and strafe"). His total time on the Starfighter by now was 1149 hours. He now joined 434, flying there on July 31 (434, still without CF-5s, was flying T-birds). He flew the CF-5 first on February 21, 1969. His next slot was in ground training at No. 1 PFS at Portage-la-Prairie, but he also flew Chipmunks and Musketeers here. Then came a tour on Trackers at 880 Squadron. This was a busy time, even though ASW was no longer an 880 role. On a May 1974 mission Sutton's crew photographed the Soviet satellite tracking ship *Yuri Gagarin*. Subsequent postings were to NDHQ, UNMO in the Golan Heights, Base Ops at Portage-la-Prairie, then back to NDHQ to the Directorate of Cartography. He retired in 1985, worked in the Air Cadet gliding program, then returned to "DCart" until re-retiring in 1989. In April 2004 "Zoot" Sutton died suddenly in Kanata, Ontario.

Other Canadians at Luke

Several other Canadians would fly the F-104G at Luke. This was driven in the mid-1970s by 1 Canadian Air Group seeking to upgrade its fighter weapons skills. To get the ball rolling, such pilots as Dave Bashow (439 Sqn) and Clive Caton (421 Sqn) trained in fighter weapons at Luke. Bashow's course (March 6 to June 2, 1975) included all current fighter tactics, e.g. air-to-ground with bombs and rockets, air-to-air with AIM-9s and delivery of tactical nuclear weapons (even though Canada had relinquished that role). He then returned to 439 as one of 1 CAG's first FWIC graduates. Later, Capts David Bartram (1974-77), Ron Doyle (1977-80) and David Bashow (1980-83) instructed at Luke. In 2006 LCol Bashow (ret'd) recalled of this era:

The course at Luke in the 1970s had career ramifications for any Canadian fighter pilot – for starters it got me an extra 1½ years with 439 Squadron. Otherwise, chances are I would have left Germany after the normal 3-year tour, likely to instruct basic students at Moose Jaw. Instead, keen on setting up our own FWIC, in the mid-70s we moved our new fighter weapons expertise back to Cold Lake. There I again joined 417 Squadron, instructing at the CF-104 OTU, but also helping plan, run and instruct on the earliest Canadian FWIC courses and Maple Flag exercises.

Later, while instructing at Luke, I would fly less than on a Canadian squadron (180 compared to 240 hours annually), but the missions were more sophisticated, challenging and 'cutting edge'. This was an incomparable opportunity for any pilot on exchange.

I had flown in Maple Flag I in April-May 1978. The Spring of 2008 will mark the 30th anniversary of this very enduring, successful, international event, so I'm proud to have been involved from the beginning. We watched "The Flag" evolve year-by-year until today, when it embraces all aspects of modern aerial warfare. This success can be traced to 1 CAG days and the experience gained by Canadians at Luke AFB. In the end, instead of flying the normal 800 hours in the CF-104, I logged nearly 2400 and what a blast it all was!

Capt Dave Bashow during CF-104 days at 439 "Tiger" Squadron. Then, some 439 "Tigers": Guy Dutil, Dave Bashow, Marty Abbott, "Miss Canada 1975" Terry Lynne Meyer, Bernie Reid and the CO, Peter Desmedt. (via 439 Sqn/ Richard Girouard)

Capt Dave Bartram served at Luke in a Luftwaffe flight within the 418th Tactical Flying Training Squadron. Here he receives a memento after logging his 2000th F-104 hour, flown from Luke AFB on January 5, 1977 in F-104G No. 753. Then, to highlight the occasion, his buddies douse him in champagne. (Bartram Col.)

In 2006 Dave Bartram recalled of his time at Luke:

From June 1974 to June 1977 I flew 478 hours in the F-104G at Luke. Most flights were short ACMs missions of .7–.8 hours. I used to go through two frozen bottles of water between start and takeoff – I kept one in each of my G-suit pockets to combat the heat on the tarmac.

I think that the most memorable trips for me were towing the dart (target) in the summer heat. You taxied with a full pylon tank under the left wing, and the dart with all its attachments under the right wing. Take-off speed was close to 220 knots with a tire-fail speed of 230 knots. On top of that you had to get the flaps up by 260, or the dart would twist off. Needless to say, you were hanging on afterburner. I often said, "If this engine even hiccups, I'm outa here!"

All in all it was a great exchange tour where I learned a lot about flying the "104" and met some great USAF and GAF pilots. I've kept in touch with many of them over the years.

"The Six" – As Fast as It Gets

Only two RCAF/CF pilots had operational tours on the Convair F-106 Delta Dart, by far the hottest "Fighter of the Fifties". Both flew with the 49th FIS at Griffiss AFB, near Rome, New York. First to serve was Donald Gary Elphick. Born on March 30, 1942, his decision to join the RCAF at age 19 likely was influenced by his brother Len, 12 year's his senior. An RCAF Sabre pilot, Len had lost his life in a road accident in September 1954, while on duty in Europe. Don Elphick first flew on July 12, 1961 at PFS at Centralia in Chipmunk 18054, F/O Donovan instructing. His course finished on August 16, by when he had 18:30 hours (dual) plus 9:00 (solo). He progressed to Moose Jaw, beginning in Harvard 20427 with F/L Grip in September, finishing on March 14, 1962 with 164:20 hours on the Harvard. Next came the Wings course on T-33s at 2 AFS, starting on May 15 with a flight in 21520 with F/O Bernet. Upon graduation Elphick was posted to FIS at Portage-la-Prairie – the system had decreed that he would instruct. He first flew here with F/L Erlenson on January 21, 1963, progressed to course end on March 8, then joined "Crowbar" Flight, taking up his first student (F/C Levring) on March 14. A Danish NATO student, Levring would finish on April 18, taking the course flying trophy.

On June 12, 1964 Elphick passed 1000 hours while in T-bird 21311 en route Portage-la-Prairie to Edmonton (he was one to keep note of such highlights in the margins of his log). In June and July he had an Army support T-33 deployment to Gagetown. Missions involved close air support, and "attacking" ground targets. On others he would have an Army forward air controller in the back seat, directing artillery fire. All along, Elphick, like any sharp young pilot, was establishing important connections. At AFS, for example, he had the respected F/L Bob Brinkhurst as an instructor. At Portage-la-Prairie, one of his students was O/C Jeff Brace, later to command Air Transport Group.

From Moose Jaw on January 7, 1965 Elphick logged his 1000th T-33 hour. Now began a posting to 3 (F) AW OTU at Bagotville, where the T-33 was the lead-in for pilots going on Voodoos. He began on the T-bird with F/L Borden on May 17. Next came a Voodoo famil ride – he went up in 17472 with S/L Pike, noting that they reached Mach 1.2. To the summer of 1968

Elphick logged a further 600 T-bird hours, while completing the Unit Instrument Check Pilot course at Central Flying School, Winnipeg. He now began the Voodoo OTU at 410 Squadron, starting with 12 simulator sessions supervised by Capt Bob Merrick. He first flew with Capt Lapointe in 17487 on July 29. The course ended on September 30 by when Elphick had 65.7 Voodoo hours. He was posted to 409 Squadron, where flying began on October 21. Henceforth, his log is filled with entries showing various missions, mostly flown with AI navigator Lt Hammerschmidt. The entry "Cudgel Capers" ("Cudgel" being 409's call sign) occurred randomly, although the meaning is not explained. "HL-AI" refers to high level, airborne intercept, "ECM-AEW" meant electronic countermeasures-airborne early warning. But the details of many exercises and their cryptic acronyms are only vaguely recalled.

For a mission of February 10, 1969 Elphick commented, "Nite AI, very rough weather." For April 29, 1969 he entered, "Emergency, Pitch-Up" – a dire event in the Voodoo world. Happily, this was a simulator exercise, so all was well. A mission of January 19, 1970 with Capt Munro in the back seat was entered as "ADEX, 3 destroyers, fun." On an ADEX (air defence exercise) Voodoos, T-33s or CF-100s played targets for the Navy, sneaking in at low level to let shipboard radar operators and gunners practice. January 21 was less fun. After takeoff there was a landing gear "unsafe" warning light. Elphick and nav Lt Karl Hammerschmidt returned to Comox. On approach, their nose wheels fell off, but a safe landing resulted. For May 13, 1970 Elphick and Hammerschmidt were aloft in '469 when things got dicey: "HL-AI. Snap up. Pitch up. Too close!" (That bugaboo, pitch-up, would keep crews twitchy to the last Voodoo flight in the mid-1980s.) On February 1, 1971 Elphick scrambled from the QRA for a low-level ECM mission. On February 18 he noted, "HL-AI. 440 blew up this AM " (when 17440 caught fire, Capts Doug Stuart and Lynn Wager ejected). On May 9 Elphick logged his 3000th flying hour. On August 3, 1971, while on a mission with Capt Peter Dunda (USAF) in Voodoo '396, they nearly collided with a 407 Squadron Argus. A mission of December 21 with Capt Hank Dielwart in '017 was on a high-flying target 200 miles out. En route they hit Mach 1.5.

Don Elphick's last flight at 409 was on April 26, 1972 with Maj Mike Cromie. For the occasion he pushed Voodoo 101030 past Mach 1. Having asked in this period for an overseas posting,

Capt Elphick's "personal" F-106 was 58-0787, the most famous of all F-106s. Before joining the 49th FIS, it was on a February 2, 1970 mission with the 71st FIS from Selfridge AFB. Michigan. Somehow Capt Gary Faust got into a flat spin from which he could not escape. He ejected, then '787 descended in a series of falling leaf manoeuvres until gently belly-landing in a farm field. Here '787 sits at Griffiss on July 10, 1986, about the time that the 49th disbanded. In August 1986, it joined the USAF Museum at WPAFB. (Larry Milberry)

he had been promised something at Tyndall, then Voodoos at Minot, North Dakota. In the end he was posted to the F-106 with the 49th FIS at Griffiss AFB. He, his wife Ann, and children aged 2, 4 and 5 reached Griffiss in April 1972. After settling into their new home on base, Don left for the F-106 "transition course" at Tyndall with the 4756th CCTS. On June 30 he made the first of several T-33 famil flights, going up with 1Lt Snyder. Then came five F-106 simulator sessions and, on July 3, his first flight in F-106B 57-2532 with Capt Henderson. The course totalled 9.1 hours on F-106s, 6.9 on T-birds.

Maj Elphick now returned to Griffiss. He was to fly with Maj Parker on July 25, 1972, but their trip was logged as "Ground abort". Finally, he flew with Capt Hall on August 8, taking 59-0161 to Mach 1.7. Hereafter came all the routines of an ADC squadron, missions briefly alluded to in Elphick's log as "Snaps", "Sterns", "Clean Aircraft", "Clean, LL Intercepts", etc. A mission in 59-0028 of August 30, 1973 was listed as "Intercepts. Super Snaps" (i.e. supersonic snap-ups). One of March 2, 1973, however, wasn't so routine: "Air abort, smoke in cockpit". He and Capt Hall logged five minutes. By this time the local media had noticed Elphick's presence at Griffiss. On July 23, 1973 the Syracuse *Herald-Journal* reported: "When he arrived at Griffiss in June 1972, Capt Elphick was the first foreign national to fly the F-106 at the squadron level. Since then just about any first concerning the F-106 and Canadian pilots has been done by him … [he] is now an Alpha Flight commander."

Generally, missions in "the Six" lasted 2 to 2.5 hours, so a lot could be done. "Clean" trips (i.e. without underwing tanks) were shorter (on April 25, 1974 Elphick took up 59-0081 "clean" on a low-level mission, but was back on the ground in 1.4 hours). In contrast, using air-to-air refuelling, the F-106 flew and flew. On an April 17, 1974 AAR mission, Elphick was up for 3.2 hours. Relative to the days of the CF-100 or Voodoo at 1.5 to 2 hours, the F-106 was a huge NORAD asset. In June 1973 Maj Elphick was assigned his own aircraft – 58-0787. He flew it first for 2.8 hours on June 27, noting, "My aircraft, beautiful!"

The Elphicks returned to Canada in July 1974. Don next spent until 1977 in the Directorate of Aircraft Requirements at NDHQ. In that time he had several famil flights in the F-15, then being considered by Canada's New Fighter Aircraft committee. The Elphicks were in Toronto for 1977-78, while Don attended Staff College; then he was posted to Trackers at 880 Squadron in Shearwater. After a year, however, he lost his medical and was grounded. He transferred to Base Ops at Shearwater, then returned to Ottawa for care at the National Defence Medical Centre. Postings followed – intelligence at NDHQ, in Ramstein, then back in Ottawa. Then a sudden heart attack felled Don Elphick in March 1996. and he passed away on July 9.

Following Don Elphick at the 49th was Capt R.W. "Bob" Worbets. From Lamont, Alberta, he joined the RCAF in 1964 to train as a long-range navigator in Winnipeg. He served on the Argus at Greenwood from November 1965 to June 1968, flying

MOHAWK FLYER

49th pilot

JULY 11, 1973

Canadian qualifies for F-106 refueling

A Canadian pilot assigned to the 49th Fighter Interceptor Squadron recently became the first member of the Canadian Armed Forces to qualify in inflight refueling with the F-106 Delta Dart.

Capt. Donald G. Elphick, a native of Victoria, British Columbia, Canada, is assigned to the Griffiss interceptor unit under the U.S.-Canadian exchange program.

The aerial refueling first is just another of a long string of firsts accredited to the captain. When he arrived at Griffiss in June 1972, Captain Elphick was the first foreign national to fly the F-106 at the squadron level. As such, just about any first concerning the F-106 and Canadian pilots was done by Captain Elphick.

About halfway through his two-year tour with the 49th, the captain is the "A" Flight commander for the 49th. While a Canadian flying to defend the U.S. may seem a little unusual, it has been the story of the captain's 12 year career.

The 49th is part of the North American Air Defense Command (NORAD), a unified command consisting of the armed forces of Canada and the United States.

Units of NORAD provide the air defense for both Canada and the U.S.

Inflight refueling means connecting up to a tanker aircraft to refueling while in flying. Inflight refueling provides extended range for aircraft operations.

Captain Elphick joined the 49th after a two-month check out program at the Aerospace Defense Command Combat Crew Training School at Tyndall AFB, Fla.

FIRST FLYER --- A member of the Canadian Armed Forces and the 49th Fighter Interceptor Squadron, Capt. Donald G. Elphick is the first Canadian to qualify in inflight refueling. (U.S. Air Force Photo)

Maj Don Elphick: Flying Hours	
T-33	2786
CF-101	659
F-106	443
Harvard	164
Tracker	120
Tutor	6
F-15	3

which he ferried to Winnipeg on June 16, 1971. On June 18 he and Capt Dick Borys flew 56-304 (later CF 101005) from Bristol to LTV in South Carolina via Wurtsmith AFB, Michigan. Then, on June 23 they ferried 101017 from LTV to Bagotville via Griffiss.

In March 1974 Worbets left 416 with some 800 Voodoo hours. About this time he was considering leaving the military for an airline job. He had an interview with Eastern Provincial Airlines, then career manager Capt Dave Koski made him an offer – Griffiss. This was tempting, since Worbets always wanted to fly single seat fighters. He accepted and soon was at the 4756th in Tyndall, where he flew the F-106 with Capt Rex Riley on April 23, 1974. The course was short (10 hours), ending on May 16, then Worbets joined the 49th. He flew his first KC-135 AAR mission (3.5 hours) on December 9, 1974. On February 26, 1975 he took part in a NORAD regional OpEval. Scrambled from Griffiss in F-106 58-0787, he was vectored north, handed over to NORAD in North Bay, then proceeded into the Hudson Bay area before swinging south to Wurtsmith. There he refuelled and departed eastward.

on typical exercises and operations with 404 Squadron. On May 31 and June 2, 4, 6 and 7, 1968 his crew was on a SAR mission in the Cape Verdes, searching for traces of the nuclear submarine USS *Scorpion* (later found to have sunk with all hands). In 1968 Worbets remustered to pilot, flying initially in Chipmunk 18077 with Capt Jim Godfrey at Borden on August 6. Tutor and T-33 training followed, then he earned his Wings and was posted to Voodoos. Training began with an advanced T-bird course at Chatham. On August 3, 1970 Worbets flew the Voodoo, going up at Bagotville in 17407 with Capt John Rose of 410 Squadron. In October 1970 he joined 416 for an enjoyable tour, whether on alert at Gander, on the first Voodoo Fighter Weapons Course at Bagotville, or on Op. Peace Wings. Worbets' last flight in one of the original RCAF Voodoos was in 17461,

Off Nova Scotia the chase was on for some F-111 bogies heading towards New York City. The next turn-around was at Otis AFB, then the third stage of the exercise was flown, Worbets finally landing home after six flying hours.

A highlight of Worbets' exchange was flying DACT (dissimilar air combat training) missions. After initial work-ups, in September 1975 there was DACT with USN F-4s at Andrews AFB (Washington, DC), where the "Sixes" had the upper hand. In January 1976 the 49th sent six jets to Luke AFB to fight F-15As. With this the "Six" pilots knew that they had met their match. Later that spring they fought USN F-8 Crusaders at Griffiss and USMC F-4s at Tyndall. Also in the "highlights" category, Worbets had the chance to fire the F-106 weapons. Flying F-106 59-0081 on July 15, 1975, he fired a Genie at a low-level drone. Flying 59-0074 on November 15 that year, he fired an AIM-4D against a low-level infrared drone.

The big difference between the F-106 and F-101 was that there was no back-seater, so a "Six" pilot was busy from take off to touch down. On the other hand, the aircraft was highly manoeuvrable. Failing all else, a pilot up against a superior adversary could play his last-ditch card – a diving spiral: stick back, full rudder either direction, pull to the stall, then plummet like a rock in a vertical spiral. No enemy could follow. Another asset was speed – Mach 2 was easy, although a pilot had to monitor leading edge heat, for which there was a "go slow" warning light. Depending on outside air temperature, at something above 750 KIAS, the light would illuminate, warning a pilot to slow.

With a 3.5-hour AAR mission in 59-0135 on May 24, 1976, Bob Worbets ended his tour. He had flown 450.1 hours on type, but now had another good job – at the Directorate of Flight Safety under Col R.D. "Joe" Schultz. Next, he joined on 409 Squadron. He led the

(Above) F/O Bob Worbets in his days as a maritime navigator. (PL-99416 DND)

Capts Elphick and Worbets would have been fascinated by the layout of the F-106F-106 at the 49th FIS. The tapes flank the flight director (attitude director indicator and horizontal situation indicator). From the left on the first tape the pilot read AOA (angle of attack), Mach number, then airspeed in knots. On the right tape are vertical speed, altitude, then the target's altitude. F-106 pilot Grant Bruckmeier explains, "The toggles beneath the Mach, airspeed and altitude tapes indicate that you can set an index so you can quickly scan to see if you have met the specified parameters." Atop the dash sits a radar scope for target tracking. Between the pilot's legs is the tactical situation display. (G. Bruckmeier)

squadron to Tyndall for the 1982 William Tell meet, where he and back-seater Capt Bill Ricketts won the F-101 Top Gun trophy. Worbets now spent nine years in Europe, mainly in operations with 4 ATAF in Heidelberg. A NORAD tour in Colorado Springs followed, then he was posted to 1 CAD HQ in Winnipeg, helping to co-ordinate such operations as the deployment of CF-18s to Aviano for the Kosovo crisis. Worbets retired from the CF in 1997. In October 2002 he reminisced about F-106 days:

When looking back at this exchange, three aspects stand out. First was the opportunity to work with many fine officers in the USAF. The professional bonds formed during that two-year period continued, and were beneficial during my later posting to 4 ATAF. There many squadron mates were, by then, unit commanders or operations officers on NATO F-15 and F-16 squadrons. Fortunately, this camaraderie continues to this day.

Second, the opportunity to fly and fight one of the best fighters of that era is memorable. In weather the F-106, with its state-of-the-art cockpit (vertical tape vs. "round eye" instruments), and its stable flying characteristics, made the aircraft a pleasure to fly. It gave one a sense of confidence in his ability to handle the worst weather. Conversely, its power and agility in the clear air environment made one think of a sports car.

Third, the exchange permitted me to study how the USAF was looking to the future. While Canada's air force has a unique character of its own, upon reflection, many aspects of Canadian air operations mirrored those I had experienced during my tour, but at a point approximately five years later. This is not to say that the CF was behind. Rather, because of technology and demography, both air forces were meeting new societal challenges. Canadian society at large, was following the lead of our neighbour.

CHAPTER 21

USAF Exchanges in Canada, EW Exchanges

USAF Exchanges in Canada

While RCAF men flew USAF F-101s, some American and British crews flew the CF-101. The pioneers at this were Capts Perrin Gower, Jr. (pilot) and Ernie Throne (radar operator), who were at 425 Squadron from its inception at Namao in 1961, then at 3 AW (F) OTU in Bagotville. Gower returned to the US after his allotted two years, while Throne took a 1-year extension. Born in September 1928, Perrin Gower, Jr. was raised in Raleigh, North Carolina. In 1951 he joined the USAF, training on the T-6 at Bainbridge, Georgia. He advanced to the T-28 and T-33 at Bryan, Texas, fighter conversion at Nellis AFB on F-80s, then was posted to Korea, where he flew 80 F-86 missions with the 35th FBS. From 1954-56 he instructed at Moody AFB with the 3554th CCTW on the all-weather course (F-94C, F-86D), then joined the 444th FIS at Charleston on the F-86D. In 1960 the 444th converted to the F-101, this being done on squadron. Everyone was happy to see the last of the F-86D – as Gower put it in February 2003, "We just loved the F-101 with its two beautiful, big J57s. That beat the hell out of flying away out over the Atlantic Ocean in a single-engine F-86D."

While visiting the personnel bureau in the Pentagon in 1960, Gower had heard of an exchange at 425 Squadron. This interested him, since he had the right qualifications – he was an all-weather pilot, a graduate of the USAF instructors school and even had some French language training. After a successful tour with 425, Gower attended the Naval War College Command & Staff Course at Newport, Rhode Island. In 1965 he volunteered for service in Southeast Asia. There he joined the 602nd FS at Bien Hoa, Vietnam to fly some 350 A-1 Skyraider missions. Back home he was a director with the Air Force Studies and Analysis branch in the Pentagon, then attended the National War College. From 1971-72 he was with the 379th

Bomb Wing (B-52s) at Wurtsmith AFB, finishing there as the Wing Commander. Following a US Embassy tour in Saigon, Col Gower served in the Pentagon, from where he retired in 1979.

Replacing Gower at 425 was Capt John Foote. A farm boy from Virginia, he had joined the USAF in 1957. He trained on T-34s and T-28s at Bainsbridge, Georgia, then got his Wings on T-33s at Vance AFB, Oklahoma. Next came Interceptor School at Moody AFB flying the F-86L, a Sabre with AI radar, afterburner, and armament of 24 FFARs. 1Lt Foote then joined the 444th FIS, initially on the F-86L, then the F-101. One day in 1962 Foote's Ops officer asked him a favour. A visiting ADC major needed some time in the circuit to get re-qualified on the Voodoo. Foote put in an hour or so letting the major "do his thing" in the front seat. Back on the ground, he was careful to document the mission as instructional, even though he was not a qualified Voodoo IP. About a year later ADC was looking for a replacement for Capt Gower. When the computer spat out all the names of available Voodoo IPs, by good fortune Capt Foote's was included. True,

Flying alone at night in terrible weather in a single engine F-86D or 'L was no pilot's idea of fun. This Nebraska ANG "L" was at WPAFB, Ohio on August 28, 1964. (Larry Milberry)

his IP time totalled 1.5 hours, but the rest of his file looked just right. Before long he was packing for Canada.

At Bagotville, Capt Foote crewed with Capt Throne for the first year, but sometimes would fly with Throne's replacement Capt Roger Maltbie. In this period Foote checked out on the CF-100, logging about 20 pleasant hours, especially liking the "Clunk's" power. When his first students graduated, he liked to tell them how a Voodoo "IP" with 1.5 instructing hours had come to be their mentor and role model. As Foote related in 2003: "At the graduation of my first students I told the whole story of becoming a 'qualified' IP. Everyone got a real charge out of it, even my fellow instructors. They, after all, viewed the USAF as overburdened with rules and restrictions. They were delighted to hear that one fellow at least had fallen through the cracks." In 1965 Foote returned home. He flew F-101s with the 84th FIS at Hamilton AFB and the 62nd at K.I. Sawyer AFB, then converted to the tactical recce world, spending a year on operations from Saigon, logging 125 RF-101 combat missions. An RF-4 tour followed with the 32nd TRS at Alconbury, UK, after which Foote spent much of his time in aircraft maintenance, finishing in 1987 at Seymour-Johnson AFB, where he flew the F-4E. By this time he had more than 2000 hours on F-101s, 1000+ on F-4s. In May 2003 John Foote recalled some exchange anecdotes:

USAF exchange officers with the CF-101 OTU at Bagotville in the early 1960s: Capt Roger Maltbie (right) with F/L Don Elphick. Then, Capt John Foote with F/L Syd Rennick. (via Ann Elphick)

One beautiful afternoon in 1963 Ernie Throne and I were in Ottawa, preparing for our return to Bagotville. Out of nowhere we suddenly heard the "snapping and snarling" of Rolls-Royce Merlins. I had an instant mental image of a flight of Mustangs in the pattern. So we rushed outside, there to observe a lone North Start on downwind, having made a fighter-type pitch-out into the landing pattern. That was my introduction to the North Star, before which I had no idea that it had Merlins.

Ernie Throne was a nav with quite a bit of stick time. In fact, he was right good at aircraft handling. Back at 3 OTU I had noticed that he occasionally mentioned to the CFI, S/L Hal Pike, that he was way overdue for a front seat ride in the T-33. His comment was always accepted with good humour, nothing more. Well, on that beautiful day in Ottawa we had a T-33. As we walked across the tarmac, I commented, "Hey Ern, isn't it your turn to fly the front seat?" Ernie just grinned. Yes, he flew the entire trip front seat to Bagotville. I never touched the controls, from brake release to landing roll-out. Ernie Throne is the only nav I know who ever did this in a T-33. Naturally, we kept this quiet around 3 OTU. Was Ernie ever proud of his accomplishment, and was I ever proud of him!

My tour with the RCAF was a most pleasant and rewarding and part of my career. I was treated well and learned a lot about aviation and military operations. In turn, I am satisfied that my efforts as an instructor were appreciated by Canada. My hero and, to some degree, my mentor, was S/L Hal Pike. Hal, who died later of a brain tumour, taught me a lot about integrity as a life value. My best friend at Bagotville was Karl Robinson. Sadly, last summer he was killed in a gliding accident in Nova Scotia. In closing, let me say that I was on parade at Bagotville for the first raising of the new Canadian flag, I was there at the beginning of the integration of the Canadian armed forces, and I was there on May 31, 1965 when the first "nukes" (Genie rockets) were delivered to Bagotville.

Life at 3 OTU/410 Squadron was mainly routine for USAF exchange officers. Not so routine was the time spent in the mess. Those were the days when the rule in any RCAF mess was pretty well "anything goes". Besides all the fun of regular TGIFs, mess dinners, etc. there was one great annual affair – "Sap Sucking". This was when Bagotville invited NORAD friends to a first-class weekend bash. By Friday beer-call, the flightline would be lined with Voodoos, F-106s, CF-100s, T-33s, B-57s and who knows what else. Drinking, feasting, speechifying, manly games of crud, and other local "cultural" events would go on non-stop. A famous potent beverage, "moose milk", would be downed by the gallon. Some time on Sunday afternoon the first crews would climb groggily back into their cockpits, fire up, then, after a beat-up or two (seeing who could fly fastest and lowest), turn for home.

This grand event was not without casualties. There is the story of a certain USAF nav from the IWS at Tyndall being invited to Sap Sucking but, unable to get transportation, he despaired. Then the OC 425 stepped in – W/C Mike Dooher sent a Voodoo from Bagotville to collect his crony. As the party progressed, so did the shenanigans. In the midst of some skit our USAF nav "pitched up" at the bar, ending on his face with a broken nose. The party roared on but, come Monday morning, there was a snag. With his "war wound" the nav couldn't get his oxygen mask on without great pain. How to get home? No sweat, for W/C Dooher again had the solution – a T-33 was produced to fly the nav home below 10,000 feet, where oxygen was not needed.

With 409 Squadron

Having grown up in Pueblo, Colorado, Peter Dunda joined the USAF in November 1960, hoping to be a pilot. Instead, he entered the Aviation Cadet Navigator Training Program at Harlingen AFB, Texas. He received his navigator Wings and was commissioned a 2nd Lieutenant in September 1961. Radar Intercept Officer (AI) training followed at Connelly AFB in Waco, Texas. This combined ground school with about 40 F-89J Scorpion missions, each of about 1.5 hours. 2Lt Dunda came away with a good respect for the Scorpion. "I loved it," is how he summed

up his feelings decades later. Dunda now looked forward to a posting to F-101s. Instead, in 1962 he went to the 965th AEW Squadron, flying EC-121s at McClellan AFB, in Sacramento (in the early 1960s the EC-121 was a key NORAD asset, patrolling the coasts for intruding aircraft). In this period Dunda had some interesting deployments, as during the Cuban Missile Crisis, when his crew was on alert in Florida.

In January 1966 Dunda finally got his F-101 posting. First he joined the 13th FIS at Glasgow, Montana, then moved to the 62nd FIS at K.I. Sawyer AFB in 1967. In this period numerous F-101 AI navs were being selected for F-4 back seat slots in Vietnam, so Dunda expected to end there. However, the USAF was facing a pilot training backlog, and had to put F-4 assignments on the back burner. So it was that Dunda got notification of his exchange to 409 AW (F) Squadron at RCAF Station Comox. This reminded him how, as a junior EC-121 lieutenant, he had noted on some career "dream sheet" that he eventually would like a foreign exchange tour. His career manager made note of this and granted Dunda his wish years later. By this time Capt Dunda was married with two children, so moving to Comox would be an adventure in more ways than one. In June 1969 the family set out from K.I. Sawyer to drive to Comox. There they arrived to temporary quarters in a motel. On checking in, Dunda found a note from Capt Doug Munro: "Welcome to the 409th. You are no longer in the USAF, so relax. We work hard and play hard without any of the USAF requirements to 'fill squares'. We'll pick you up at 4:30 for happy hour in the mess."

A great party ensued, then Capt Dunda settled in to squadron life. There were a few things to get used to, including how 409's older CF-101Bs lacked the IR radar and ECM equipment of the USAF's "IIP" Voodoos. On his first few AI intercepts, Dunda was disappointed at his results, but things improved as he got used to the

Capt Pete Dunda in a hero shot from June 1970 when 409 was competing at Tyndall AFB in Ex. William Tell. (Dunda Col.)

The 409 "Blackhawk" Squadron team that took Ex. Call Shot at Bagotville before "Willy Tell 70": Brodie Templeton, Ernie Poole, Pete Dunda, George McCaffer, Don Marion, Pete Armour, Doug Munro, Fred Williams, Gordon "Mo" Morrison, Doug Stuart, Lynn Wagar and Rhinehart Koehn. The crew of Munro and Wagar earlier had gone down in flames near Comox, but ejected safely. None of the RCAF in this photo had exchange or such postings other than Brodie Templeton, although Ernie Poole was in the original RCAF Voodoo cadre. In 1961 he did the Voodoo ground school at Otis AFB, then converted to type at Hamilton AFB. (BN70-530 DND)

older technology. There were also a few operational differences, including how 409 generally flew Voodoos "clean", making for shorter missions than on USAF squadrons, which always flew tanked.

Dunda served on Canada's 1970 William Tell team. To begin, 409 had to compete that year at Bagotville with Canada's other Voodoo squadrons on Ex. Call Shot, the winner advancing to "Willy Tell". For several days at Tyndall, 409 led the pack but, on the final day, its four Voodoos scored zeroes in the missile shoot. The team suspected electrical snags caused by their aircraft getting drenched in a sudden downpour. Whatever the cause, 409 settled for second place. Embarrassingly, the Comox base newspaper, the *Totem Times*, had heard such good reports from Willy Tell, that it jumped the gun went to press announcing how 409 had cleaned up at Tyndall!

Dunda usually crewed with Doug Stuart, but one day there was a crew change. Capt Lynn Wagar asked Dunda for his seat

on a mission to McChord AFB, Washington, where Wagar wanted to do some shopping in the Base Exchange. Dunda agreed and watched as the two blasted off in Voodoo 101440. Instantly, however, the scene went wrong and the Voodoo crashed into the water. Happily, the crew punched out and a 442 Squadron Labrador rescued them from the water. Stuart was uninjured, but Wagar suffered burns after ejecting through a fireball. It later was determined that the accident happened after compressor blades failed in the right engine. Shrapnel disabled the left engine and '440 exploded.

Towards the end of his exchange, Capt Dunda asked for a year's extension. This coincided with the CF converting to IIP Voodoos. Knowing that Dunda was qualified on type, 409 needed him to guide them through the transition. Finally, however, it was time to head home. The Dundas had enjoyed their three years, so packed regretfully. The great camaraderie would be missed, as would be the wonderful salmon and trout fishing that Peter enjoyed. He also had become a local musician of note, often entertaining on the accordion (on occasion the accordion even flew around in the weapons bay of a Voodoo). In 2005 retired LtCol Dunda looked back at his exchange:

My wife, Susan, and I consider our CF/USAF exchange tour with 409 AW (F) Squadron to be the all-round highlight of our military career. It was an exceptionally rewarding experience for our family. It also was a pleasure to fly and work with the professional officers and enlisted personnel of the Canadian Armed Forces. The many friendships that we made with 409 members and their families remain close and strong today. We always look forward to attending the Canadian all-weather reunions where we can renew the camaraderie of old friends. Upon returning to the United States, on the first day of school, when our six-year old son's first grade class rose to sing the US National Anthem, he began signing "Oh Canada" instead, as that was the only anthem he knew! Yes, we had become totally immersed in the "Canuck" culture and still consider ourselves to be half Canadian.

Capt Dunda now was assigned to the Air Force Institute of Technology at Wright-Patterson AFB, Ohio, receiving there a BSc in laser technology (1972-74). Next came a tour on F-4Ds at Kusan, Korea with the 80th TAC Fighter Squadron. In 1976 he was home again, this time to the Airborne Laser Laboratory research program at Kirtland AFB. In June 1985 he retired, but continued in laser technology until October 1997. Retired for good in Colorado, he now focused on golf, fishing, skiing and playing in his own polka band, including gigs at Harmel's Ranch Resort. By the time he had left flying LCol Dunda had logged some 5400 hours, including 1500 in the F-101.

Americans on the CF-104

Pilots from Australia, Germany, the United States and the United Kingdom enjoyed CF-104 exchanges, the earliest being Capts Mark D. Cook and Bill Leitch, who instructed at 6 (ST/R) OTU at Cold Lake from 1961-63. In 2005 Cook recalled:

While working in 1961 as an F-105 test pilot with the USAF Fighter Weapons School at Nellis AFB, W/C K.C. Lett, S/L Bill Paisley, F/L Ernie Saunders and other RCAF officers on course at Nellis asked if I'd like to come to Cold Lake to help set up the CF-104 training

program. This sounded like a great idea, wheels were put in motion, and all the arrangements made. One morning I made an F-104 flight at George AFB (preparing for my RCAF tour). I then drove back to Nellis and test flew an F-105 that afternoon. To the best of my knowledge I'm the only one to have flown those two types on the same day. Cold Lake was a highlight in my career and I will always treasure the generous hospitality and camaraderie of the Royal Canadian Air Force. As to the F-104 and F-105, I much preferred the F-104 "Zipper".

Also on exchange in Cold Lake was Donald Gerlinger, USAF. Raised in Chicago, he graduated in 1953 from the University of Montana, where he was an ROTC student. In January 1954 Gerlinger began his USAF service. After flight training he instructed on T-33s at Webb AFB (Big Spring, Texas), then flew F-100s with the 36th TFW in Bitburg, Germany to 1961. Next, he was assigned to the 401st TFW in Alexandria, Louisiana. For

Don Gerlinger (standing, left) with his 6 (ST/R) OTU Starfighter buddies, who astounded air show crowds from coast to coast. The boss (standing, right) was G.N. "Gin" Smith. In front are Pogo Hamilton, Grant Baker and Buster Kincaid. Pogo and Buster had earlier exchanges at Nellis. (Gerlinger Col.)

Don and Nola Gerlinger with Reen and Bud Jameson, the USAF reps at 6 (ST/R) OTU in 1966-67. (Gerlinger Col.)

OTU was second-to-none. In the summer of 1966 we put together an OTU display team for the Canadian International Air Show in Toronto. With five CF-104s we impressed the crowd with our diamond formation, then a high-speed trail flypast with a vertical climb-out and rejoin.

Major Gerlinger left Cold Lake in June 1967 having flown 640 hours in the CF-104. He moved to TAC HQ at Langley AFB, then returned in 1969 to Vietnam to fly 227 F-100 combat missions (later postings – 2nd Aircraft Delivery Unit at McClellan AFB, California, 354th TFW at Myrtle Beach, South Carolina, 5th Air Force HQ Yakota, Japan). LCol Gerlinger retired in 1976, returned to university, earned his teacher's qualifications, then taught high school in Texas until 1993.

"Red Indian" CF-104 Exchange

While most CF-104 exchange slots were at Cold Lake, a few were operational. One American with one such was Maj W.B. "Bill" Sparks. Born in Hardyville, Kentucky on December 7, 1934, Sparks was an ROTC student at Indiana State University. Commissioned from there in 1957, he did basic flight training at Malden, Missouri on the T-34 and T-28, then earned his Wings on the T-33 at Webb AFB in November 1958. From here he trained on the F-100 at Luke AFB, then did weapons training at Nellis, the "hard polish" part of F-100 conversion.

In 1959 1Lt Sparks was assigned to the 49th TFW at Spangdahlem, West Germany. He flew the F-100 (which he considered a typical "dog" of its day), then was two years on the F-105, the main role with each being "tactical nuke". Those were the days when the RCAF "ruled the roost" with its Sabre 6 day fighters and the boys at the 49th would have more than their share of run-ins with the Canucks. As Sparks said in 2005, "On more than one occasion I was the star of the Canadian film festival," meaning that a Sabre had good cine film shot from his "six".

From 1964-67 Capt Sparks was on F-105s with the 563rd TFS at McConnell AFB, Wichita. In this period he flew 63 combat missions

five months he flew operations from Danang, Vietnam, then was assigned to 6 (ST/R) OTU in Cold Lake, where he, his wife Nola and two children arrived in June 1965. Now began a memorable tour that would include the birth of a third child. For Don the flying was superb and lifelong friendships resulted. In 2005 he recalled:

From Day 1 the RCAF went overboard to welcome us to Cold Lake. When our furniture was delayed in transit, our neighbours pitched in, donating what was needed for us to get a comfortable start. Family life ran smoothly, Nola and I taking an active part in the social scene, while our daughter attended the base school. We even got into curling. We may not have been great at it, but sure got a lot of good exercise sweeping. Nola wasn't too thrilled with Friday night stags in the mess, where we officers whooped it up to the extreme, but enjoyed the frequent women's socials, and the mixed affairs where we all turned out in our finest.

Instructing on the CF-104 was a great thrill and the comradeship on the

Canadian International Air Show 6 (ST/R) OTU Demo Team*		
Date	Route	Time
28 August	Cold Lake–Winnipeg	1:30 hrs.
	Winnipeg–Trenton	2:00
31 August	Trenton–CIAS–Trenton	1:40
1 September	Trenton–CIAS–Trenton	1:40
2 September	Trenton–CIAS–Trenton	1:40
5 September	Trenton–Winnipeg	2:15
	Winnipeg–Cold Lake	1:40

*From the log book of team member F/L G.N. "Gin" Smith

Maj Sparks with some 421 Squadron mates. Standing are Cecil Hume, John Bagshaw, Bill Sparks, Don Harrington, Jack McLean, Clive Caton and Ron Swaizland. In front are Frank Thorne and "the boss" – Chops Viger. (Sparks Col.)

Maj Sparks quickly adapted to the situation, making all sorts of new friends and being impressed at what a bunch of gung-ho types the Canadians were. His course finished, Sparks got wind that an NDHQ exchange awaited. This was not the best of news, but the only option was just as bad – flying a desk in the Pentagon. Then, course mate LCol Fern Villeneuve, former CO of the Golden Hawks aerobatics team, suggested that Sparks talk to LCol Ben Oxholm, CO of 421 Squadron at CFB Baden-Soellingen. Oxholm wanted someone on exchange with recent combat experience, so created a new exchange slot for a USAF major. "Don't kid a guy", was Sparks initial reaction

in Southeast Asia. In that period, pilots of the 563rd could see the North Vietnamese installing SAM sites, but the USAF ROE was that these could not be attacked. One day Sparks observed the first North Vietnamese SAM launch. The missile rose through a cloud layer to clobber a flight of four F-4s, one of which was a kill. Four days later he took part in the first SAM site attack of the war. In 1966 Capt Sparks was on the third course at the Weapons School at Nellis, then was the Wing standards and evaluation officer back at McConnell. In 1967 he got into the "Wild Weasel" world (today's "SEAD" – suppression of enemy air defences). This led him back to Thailand with the 357th TFS. On November 5, 1967, while piloting F-105D 61-0173, he was shot down by 57mm fire while flying low near Hanoi. He punched out and within three hours was picked up by an HH-3 "Jolly Green Giant" rescue chopper.

In 1968 Sparks returned to Nellis as a Weapons School instructor on F-105s. The following summer, while anticipating a US Navy exchange on A-4s, he was surprised when posted instead to Canadian Forces Staff College in Toronto. Soon he, his wife Dell and their two children were in their new home.

about this, but was delighted when it turned out to be true. Soon he was in Gimli doing T-33 jet re-currency, then Cold Lake for the CF-104 "short course". He took to the CF-104 automatically, and judged the Canadian low-level training system better than anything at Nellis. In September 1970 Sparks joined 421, receiving a huge welcome and getting right down to flying, 421's DCO, Maj John England, leading him around initially. Sparks soon took over as "A" Flight Commander.

At this period Canada was bowing out of its NATO nuclear role, and 4 Wing was starting to change tactics for the switch to conventional warfare. That was going to be a bare bones operation, using a former nuclear hit-and-run "bomber" to deliver small loads of rockets and bombs. Sparks' early missions were single-ship as per the nuke role – one aircraft at a time going out to train to kill one target. By late 1970, however, 421 was practicing 2- and 4-ship missions, and polishing its skills on such ranges as Suippes and Siegenberg. Recalled Sparks, "All this really was a piece of cake and it didn't take long to appreciate that the CF-104 was by far the best weapons platform I'd flown."

As yet the CF-104 didn't have a gun (Sparks looked on the

bright side of that – no gun, more gas). The aircraft had no jammers and no radar warning equipment, but would depend on pilot skill, low-level tactics, its small profile and great speed to survive WWIII. Otherwise, Sparks found that any CF-104 equipment shortages were more than covered by the superb mission planning skills at 4 Wing, and the unsurpassable spirit of the Canadians, pilots like Dave Bagshaw and Roy Riley, who endlessly were bouncing ideas off each other, then roaring off to prove their theories. "It was a bit scary some days," Sparks recalled in 2005. "We'd talk about something that was pretty ropy, then go out and try it!"

Sparks would assist 421 in developing the equivalent of the USAF "Air Force 3-1" fighter pilot handbook. Such progress was only possible under 421's leadership: "The best CO I ever worked for was LCol Ben Oxholm", Sparks emphasized. In-house mini weapons competitions were organized, and a great skit was bouncing neighbouring NATO bases. Of those missions Sparks recalled, "They never laid a glove on us." Baden-Soellingen base commander, Col "AJ" Bauer, supported all such efforts to turn 4 Wing into NATO's best conventional fighter outfit. Besides making a precision low-level/pop-up attack

Capt Bill Sparks with his HH-3E "Jolly Green Giant 37" rescuer, Harry Walker. That day seven Americans parachuted over North Vietnam, but only Sparks, down near Hanoi, was rescued. Years later he recalled: "I managed to slip my 'chute down the river and land in what I thought was elephant grass, only to come down in 75-foot high bamboo... when Harry Walker came to hover over my position, 4 MiG-17s showed up. The low Sandy [Skyraider] was calling Harry to get out of the area, but his answer was, 'FU ... just keep them off my butt. I got a job to do.' Harry stayed in the hover with all but three feet of cable out, and hauled my worthless butt out from under a very tall tree. I had 17 birds in my CAP at the time and they chased the MiGs off." LCol Sparks left the USAF in 1977 to work in industry, then retired in Nevada. He and his wife, Dell, celebrated their 50th wedding anniversary in the Nellis AFB Officers Club on July 16, 2005. (Sparks Col.)

Exchange Officers on the CF-104*

Name	Affiliation	Canadian Unit	Period
Barton, C.D. "Doug"	USAF	441 Sqn	1977-80
Blake, Gary R.	USAF	439 Sqn	1972-75
Blatter, W.H. "Burt	USAF	NDHQ	1973-75
Brooks, William	USAF	AETE	1978-81
Cook, Mark D.	USAF	6 (ST/R) OTU	1961-63
Cordle, Robert	USAF	6 (ST/R) OTU	1963-65
Cotner, Keith L.	USAF	417 Sqn	1977-80
Denard, Jamie	USAF	417 Sqn	
Fiorelli, James	USAF	417 Sqn	1971-72
Gerlinger, Donald	USAF	6 (ST/R) OTU	1965-67
Goodson, C.W. "Bill"	US Army	421 Sqn	1982-85
Habersky, C.	USAF	417 Sqn	
Hammond, Thomas	RAF	441 Sqn	1982-84
Heston, R.A. "Al"	USAF	417 Sqn	1969-71
Horn, C.V. "Van"	USAF	NDHQ	1981-83
Jameson, Roy W,	USAF	6 (ST/R) OTU	1966-67
Jennings, Gary L.	USAF	AETE	1976-78
Judd, John A.	USAF	NDHQ	1977-79
Larsen, D.A. "Dud"	USAF	417 Sqn	1980-82
Leach, David	RAAF	417 Sqn	1973-75
Leitch, William	USAF	6 (ST/R) OTU	1961-63
Major, Michael	USAF	441 Sqn	1975-77
McCarthy, Michael	USAF	417 Sqn	1972-74
Mincey, W. "Will"	USAF	NDHQ	1975-77
Navarro, Michael	USAF	NDHQ	1979-81
Nicholas, Michael C.	USAF	441 Sqn	1964-66
Noack, Robert	USAF	6 (ST/R) OTU	1963-65
Paine, Merv	RAF	417 Sqn	1972-74
Pierce, Jon W.	RAF	439 Sqn	1978-80
Pollock, Elton	USAF	AETE	1981-83
Reed, James W.	USAF	AETE	1966-69
Riedel, Harald	Luftwaffe	417 Sqn	1979-83
Sargent, R.H. "Rob"	RAF	439 Sqn	1980-82
Sellers, John	USAF	417 Sqn	1974-77
Sparks, W.R. "Billy"	USAF	421 Sqn	1970-72
Summers, C.F.	US Army	1 Wing	1964-66
Washburn, F.D.	USAF	421 Sqn	1980-83
West, Gene	USAF	NDHQ	1967-69
Wholey, R.	RAF	417 Sqn	1974-77

*As known to 2007

each time, it was vital for the CF-104s to get out of a threat area ASAP, and this too was perfected. It also was great fun training with NATO forces flying F-104s – the Belgians, Danes, Dutch, Italians, etc. Much was learned from them, as 421 made the transition from the tactical nuke role and developed its unique "bag of tricks". When 421 faced its first conventional "TacEval", it aced this demanding requirement. On that occasion 421 bounced a West German base, pounding it with 20 CF-104s in 18 seconds.

On the social side, besides enjoying another great European tour, Sparks was introduced to the wonders of the fighter pilot's favourite mess game – crud. In due course crud was adopted by the USAF and perfected to the point that Nellis had a dedicated "crud pit". (As its military prowess faded in the coming years, the CanForces "powers that be" began looking askance at crud as "violent", hence, politically incorrect. Along with other former hallmarks of a fighter squadron, by the 2000s crud was barely tolerated in the Canadian air force). In September 1972 the Sparks family again was on the move. Bill (promoted to lieutenant colonel) recalled of this: "We had never been treated so royally." His replacement at 421 was Maj Gary Blake. The Sparks returned to Nellis, where Bill headed academics at the Fighter Weapons School. In 1974 he commanded the 35th TFS (F-4Ds) in South Korea, then returned to Nellis to head a research project involving the F-5, F-14 and F-15, the mission being to test IR seeker heads and their usefulness in close-in air-to-air combat.

The EW World

From the mid-1950s the RCAF was developing electronic warfare (EW) training tactics and equipment. At first 104 KU Dakotas and C-119s were used in radar jamming against ground-based aircraft warning and control radar units. This was done by filling the sky with chaff (developed in WWII, chaff was a mass of aluminum strips dropped to cloud enemy radar). In 1956 the first RCAF electronic warfare CF-100 was developed. From this project evolved the Electronic Warfare Unit, flying CF-100s at St.

F/O W.I. "Walt" Suttie was on exchange as a "Scope Wizzard" on EB-57s. Here he receives his nav wings on May 13, 1955 from Air Commodore G.A. Walker, Station Commander Winnipeg. (PL-89580 DND)

Hubert in April 1959. The EWU eventually became 414 Squadron at Uplands, then North Bay. This unit would roam North American skies, making life difficult for NORAD ground radar sites and interceptors. USAF defence system evaluation squadrons did similar work with Martin EB-57E Canberras.

Several RCAF "Scope Wizards", or "Wizzos", as ECM back-seaters were called, had EB-57 exchanges with the 4677th Defense System Evaluation Squadron, based first at Hill AFB near Salt Lake City, Utah, then at Malmstrom AFB near Great Falls, Montana. The first Canadian on exchange was F/L Punch Walker, then came F/Ls H. Ray Cutt, Lyle Hall, Walt Suttie at Hill; and Bill Bland and Doug Mathias at Malmstrom.

Raised in Goderich, Ontario, Ray Cutt joined the RCAF in 1951. Trained at Clinton as a radio officer, he spent four years in Winnipeg, mainly on SAR duty with 111 C&R Flight. Next, he instructed for three years at the Air Navigation School in Winnipeg. In 1962 he was posted to the USAF electronic warfare school at Mather AFB near Sacramento, California. This intensive 1-year course already had been attended by several RCAF officers. Besides lectures and demonstrations, there were airborne exercises – Cutt's log shows 14 C-54 missions for 94 flying hours. Finished at Mather, he was posted to the EWU at St.

F/O Ray Cutt. Upon retiring in 1976, he and his wife settled in Roseneath, Ontario. Since 1951 Ray had flown 6813 hours, including 1645 in CF-100s and 506 in EB-57s. (DND)

Hubert. There he first flew on April 21, 1963 on "EC-119" 22122. In this period the EWU used EC-119s mainly to drop chaff and to electronically jam ground radars along the Mid Canada and Pine Tree early warning lines. On a typical sortie Cutt crewed from Goose Bay to Gander for what was called a "demonstration" to the radar site at Gander, a 6:30-hour mission.

About this time, under an ADC HQ project spearheaded by EWU F/L Jim Palmer, the first EW CF-100s came on strength. At first all they could do was drop chaff from underwing tanks, but electronic equipment was added that allowed the jamming of ground radar. Finally, CF-100s were modified for air-to-air jamming against CF-101s. F/L Cutt's first CF-100 mission was in 18673 with F/L Wayne Foster on March 31, 1964. Henceforth, he was logging about 30 hours a month on CF-100s.

In 1967 Cutt was posted to EB-57s at the 4677th DSES. After a brief course, beginning with a famil flight of August 15, he assumed his EWO duties. Coming from the EWU, he was not surprised to find that much of the next two years were spent "on the road", mainly working with ground radar sites. In this period, the 4677th also had three extended wing EB-57s. Able to cruise at 49,000 feet, these had J57s with 12,000 lb thrust, compared to the J65s of 7200 lb in a standard EB-57. Cutt would crew in the extended-wing EB-57 nine times, the longest trip being 4:20 hours on May 5, 1968. On such missions they worked with interceptors needing practice on a high flying target. With B-57s returning from Southeast Asia for EW conversion, F/L Cutt and Maj Gus Von Wolfradt one day found themselves on an exotic mission – on a commercial flight to Clark Air Base in the Philippines. There they collected B-57 53-3856 for the flight east:

From	To	Time
Clark Air Base	Andersen AFB, Guam	4:00
Andersen AFB	Wake Island	3:25
Wake Island	Hickam AFB, Hawaii	4:40
Hickam AFB	McClellan AFB, California	4:55
McClellan AFB	Hill AFB	1:15

From Hill the B-57 continued to Homestead AFB, Florida for overhaul and mods, but someone decided that it would be "illegal" to land at Homestead with foreign crew. F/L Cutt, thereby, did not get to navigate the final leg (EB-57 '856 would serve until sent for

scrap to Davis-Monthan AFB in December 1981). In 1969 Cutt returned to Canada, replaced at the 4677th by Capt Lyle Hall. He cross-trained to long-range navigator at the ANS in Winnipeg, then served on the Argus at Summerside. In 1973 he returned to the EW CF-100 at North Bay. On August 10, 1976 he logged his last mission, flying in 100476 with Capt Anderson. This tour had totalled 616.70 hours. In April 2003 he summarized his EW years:

The role of either the EWU/414 Sqn or any USAF EW unit was very much the same. Both trained ground and airborne radars in electronic jamming and deception techniques. Yes, the platforms were different, the B-57 being larger and roomier than the Clunk. To me, however, the CF-100 had better manoeuvrability. Both types had adequate jammers and chaff capability for confusing radars.

The elevation at Hill AFB was 4788 feet, meaning that we used a lot more runway on takeoff (we had 13,000 feet). An advantage with the EB-57 was in starting. Instead of using an external energizer plugged into the CF-100, the EB-57 was started by firing explosive charges in the front of each engine. This is how the starters were engaged. Well, the 4677th was an excellent tour and I enjoyed every minute of it.

F/O Bill Bland's first RCAF tour began in 1957 on CF-100s at 416 Squadron. GCI postings followed at Senneterre and Barrington then, in April 1964, he was let out of the RCAF in "The 500 Cut". While most of "The 500" found something to do on Civvie Street, Bland opted for an inter-service transfer, biding his time in the Army for two years. In 1966 he returned to the

RCAF, converting to the Voodoo at Bagotville, then serving with 409. Next came a stint with AETE in Ottawa, followed by an EWO posting to 414. That meant doing the course at Mather, where the flying was now on ET-29s. Back at 414 Capt Bland plied his trade on the EW CF-100 and T-33 until named

Capt Bill Bland in 1980 during his final EW tour at 414 Squadron, North Bay. (NB80-1392 DND)

EB-57C 53-3840 of the 134th DSES during a photo mission over Vermont on March 17, 1980. '3840 retired for scrapping in December 1981. (Larry Milberry)

in 1974 to replace Capt Walt Suttie at the 4677th (about this time the squadron became the 17th DSES). In 2003 Bland called this posting "as good a flying job as I could have." For two years he operated through the "Lower 48", Alaska, Canada and Europe. Deployments might include a lone EB-57 or a flock – the squadron had some 18 EB-57s and 6 B-57 "dual" trainers (by Bland's time, the EB-57s were gone). When the DSES at Stewart AFB, NY disbanded, its former USAFE EW training commitment was inherited by the 17th. A 1976 USAFE deployment with five EB-57s became a memorable opportunity for Bland. This was a NATO exercise, which explains why he was allowed to participate (had it been a USAFE show, the "no foreign" rule would have applied). His positioning flight to Bitburg, Germany (EB-57E 55-4242, pilot – LCol J.T. Stanley, Deputy OpsO) routed:

Date	Route	Time
April 13	Malmstrom–Sawyer AFB, Michigan	2.7 hours
	Loring AFB, Maine	2.3
April 14	Goose Bay	1.6
	Sondrestrom, Greenland	2.5
April 15	Keflavik	2.0
	Upper Heyford, UK	2.7
April 16	Bitburg	1.6

From Bitburg there were exercises involving ground radar sites and "enemy" aircraft. The EB-57 proved its worth, taking on all comers, staying in the fight for 2.5 to 3 hours and challenging interceptor crews more than in previous years, for the EB-57 now had RWR – radar warning receivers, to warn an EW crew if it was being tracked by an interceptor. This alerted the EWO, who could chaff or jam his pursuer, direct evasion action, etc. On April 28 the EB-57s repositioned to Alconbury for three days, then returned to Bitburg. On May 2 they moved to Aviano, then to Gioia del Colle, in Italy. On the 13th they returned to Bitburg, proceeded to Mildenhall to clear customs, then flew to Leuchars, Scotland to overnight. By the 15th the EW gypsies were overnighting at Griffiss AFB from where they flew home next day via Fargo, North Dakota. Capt Bland and his pilot each logged 60 hours on this exercise.

A more routine exercise was a quarterly deployment to Elmendorf. Four aircraft were involved, giving ground radars and fighters the chance to match their wits against chaff and jammers. On a special deployment in April 1975, Bland and LCol Stanley operated EB-57E 55-4295 from Langley AFB on missions connected with the development of the Boeing E-3 AWACS. In 1976, by then with 584 hours on the EB-57, he was posted to the 22nd NORAD Region in North Bay. In 1980 he rejoined 414 on the CF-100, Falcon and ET-33. He left military life in 1985 to work at Canadair in special projects, one such being development of the abortive EW Challenger. In June 1990 he took his retirement on the West Coast.

CHAPTER 22

Classic Fighter – The F-4 Phantom

Pogo Hamilton

Canadians also flew the McDonnell F-4 Phantom II, one of aviation's greatest fighters. First flown in 1958 as the US Navy's XF4H-1, F-4s soon equipped USN, USMC and USAF units and were making a huge reputation in the Vietnam War. The next phase saw F-4s equipping US Allies from Japan to West Germany. In the 1960s the RCAF seriously considered the F-4. In the end, however, budget sense prevailed and Canada got the CF-5 instead. The last of 5211 F-4s rolled off a Japanese line in 1981. Although retired from US service, F-4s remain in use with such nations as Israel, Japan and Turkey.

One Canadian on an F-4 exchange was John "Pogo" Hamilton, born in Perth, Ontario on February 23, 1933. In the summer of 1952 he visited the Canadian National Exhibition in Toronto with some buddies. While on their big adventure, they heard that Avro was hiring for CF-100 production. They had interviews, but only Hamilton took Avro's offer. He spent the next three years at Avro, earning a peak of $1.69. Then, strolling along Toronto's St. Clair Avenue one day, he spotted the RCAF recruiting centre. Air force life sounded like a good deal, certainly an escape from the mundane 9-to-5 grind at Avro. In May 1955 he enlisted and by July was in Moose Jaw for Harvard training. AFS at Gimli followed, then came Chatham and a 421 Squadron tour from May 1957 to October 1960. F/O Hamilton returned to Chatham to instruct in Weapons Flight and later at the STU, moved to Cold Lake for the CF-104 course, then instructed there 1963-67. Finally came his exchange at Nellis' Tactical Fighter Weapons Center. There he replaced F/L Myron "Johnny" Johnson, who had just finished an F-100 tour.

Arrived at Nellis in May 1967, F/L Hamilton first converted to type at Davis-Monthan AFB near Tucson. He earned his certificate on June 23, the scroll noting that he had "successfully completed the F-4C Category IV checkout". By now he was at home with the Phantom, although he had one quarrel

Over the decades many Canadians crewed on the McDonnell F-4 Phantom II. Here, F-4C 64-749 (Missouri ANG) taxies at RAF Leeming in July 1982, where Roger Lindsay and Larry Milberry were busy that day recording the proceedings on film. '749 eventually became a ground training aid, but was wrecked at Homestead AFB when Hurricane Andrew swept through in August 1992.

with its cockpit layout. The control stick was quite a reach for a small fellow such as he. On long flights, he found this tiresome. Otherwise, like most fighters of the Fifties, the Phantom had its handling quirks, e.g. in a high-G turn, the turn could only be tightened by using rudder. Pulling back on the stick was a recipe for trouble – a Phantom would stall and flick. At low level this could be deadly.

Hamilton returned to Nellis for the fighter weapons instructor course, qualifying on September 22, 1967. In this period a USAF F-4 crew comprised two pilots, the "GIB", or "guy in the back", being a junior type. Naturally, his dream was to get into the front seat, so there was a sense that pilot GIBs were not the most dedicated back seaters. Yet, their job was crucial – extra eyes during do-or-die ACM, entering data into the weapons system, weapons release, etc. About this time the USAF decided to try navigator GIBs, hoping that they would be more committed. Pogo Hamilton was assigned one of these navs, Capt Gary L. Hughes. On December 19, 1967 they were at Davis-Monthan where Hughes was in the simulator.

At day's end they strapped in to return to Nellis. Hamilton's section of three taxied, rolled for takeoff, rotated and climbed out. Normal, except that just as Hamilton came out of 'burner, both engines died. To the GIB it was a case of "flame out, bale out" – he was gone! Hamilton hung in to make a quick assessment, hoping for a relight, but nothing went right. When the Phantom shuddered in a stall, he punched out. As he went up the rail, he thought to himself, "Boy, did that ever hurt!" A moment before he would have thundered into the ground, his 'chute partially opened. Splash, down he came into a backyard swimming pool – a life saver. At the same instant the F-4C slammed into a shopping plaza and some nearby homes, killing four people.

The pool owner assisted Hamilton and even offered him a drink. "No, thanks", replied the pilot, who didn't want alcohol on his breath when the USAF arrived. Soon an air force MP showed, then an ambulance, which led to a bit of a farce – the ambulance pooped out and had to be jump started! Hamilton eventually got to hospital, where he was assessed with three crushed vertebrae. He would be weeks recuperating. Hughes suffered no ill effects. In this period USAF policy was to ground back injury aircrew for a year, but Hamilton soon was fit. He put his case to return to flying, the USAF surgeon general agreed, and he

went back to his FWIC job, much of which involved weapons – dropping bombs (up to 1000 lb) and napalm, firing rockets on the air-to-ground range, air fighting with F-4s and F-100s, firing the Vulcan cannon at towed targets, and AIM-9s at flares. On one occasion he launched a Bullpup, a wire-guided rocket used to destroy hard targets. Nuclear weapons bomb toss also was on the syllabus. This was LADD – low altitude drogue delivery, and involved a run-in to target at 540 knots, a steep pull-up, bomb release and downward escape manoeuvre. Upon release, a drogue parachute would retard the bomb, letting the pilot get away. Should the drogue fail, however, he might collide with his bomb. Thus would he do a visual check to ensure that he wasn't in formation with his bomb! At Nellis, LADD involved a dedicated spotter aircraft to let the bombing crew know whether or not their drogue deployed

Hamilton was extra careful during night range exercises for which F-4s provided their own illumination. As each made a run and pulled out, it would drop a flare for the following Phantom. Such missions kept a crew busy and sharp, especially during something like a 60-degree dive bombing manoeuvre. Something else that Hamilton had to get used to was aerial refuelling. At his first AR briefing, Lead simply assumed that everyone knew what was going on. When he spotted a look of concern on Hamilton's face, he enquired. No, Hamilton admitted … he had never done AR. "Not to worry", Lead reassured him, "there's nothing to it." Away they went. Hamilton felt his way through the mission, then was "qualified". Meanwhile, he did secondary duty in scheduling. This involved all aircraft and crews being organized days in advance. Hamilton handled this so well that the servicing echelon made him an honorary maintainer.

When hauling 16 500-lb bombs, the Phantom was what Hamilton called a "brute force" airplane. It would fly as advertised, perform no miracles and it was unforgiving if abused. F/L Hamilton's tour ended after 2½ years and 376 flying hours. Back in Canada he flew a desk at 10 TAG in St. Hubert, then was posted to 434 Squadron at Cold Lake on CF-5s. A stint at DFS followed, working under Col R.D. Schultz and Col Bob Chisholm. Finally, he joined 414 Squadron on the EW Falcon, his first flight being with Capt Bill Turnbull on November 19, 1979. About this time his health deteriorated. The solution recommended by National Defence Medical Centre in Ottawa was surgery. Hamilton flew last on January 24, 1980, then began a series of operations at

NDMC, which result in a leg being amputated. Thereafter, he retired, settling with his family in Munster Hamlet, near Ottawa.

Bill Ross

Raised in Kirkland Lake in Northern Ontario, W.J.C. "Bill" Ross joined the RCAF in 1954. He made his first flight in a Harvard (before he had a driver's licence) at Moose Jaw on October 6 of that year. His course proceeded to Gimli, where the students won their Wings off the T-33. Following gunnery school at MacDonald, Ross did the Sabre OTU at Chatham, from where he joined 422 Squadron at Baden-Soellingen, serving there from 1956-59. Like most "Air Div" pilots finished a first tour, F/O Ross next instructed on T-33s (Portage-la-Prairie), then took the CF-104 OTU at Cold Lake. Another tour at 422 followed, after which he remained in the CF-104 world, spending 1965-67 as the weapons training officer at Decimomannou. With lots of great flying, this Mediterranean posting was a dream. Living as they did pretty well right on the beach, Bill, his wife Betty and their children, Michael and Charlayne, had few complaints.

From "Deci" the family returned to Cold Lake, where Bill instructed at 417. He now was posted to the 414th Fighter Weapons Squadron at Nellis AFB to instruct on the F-4E. He flew first with Maj Billie "The Axe" Wilson in aircraft 66-0303 on September 10, 1969, completed the basic F-4E transition, did the gunnery course at George AFB, then flew his first instructional trip on January 22, 1970. His student that day was Capt "Peanuts" Pennachio who, typically, had several hundred F-4 hours plus a Vietnam combat tour. The objective at Nellis was to teach such "post grad" students the latest fighter weapons tactics, then send them back to their squadrons to pass on the good word.

Life at Nellis never was dull. Besides routine instructing, Maj Ross also would go "on the road", visiting F-4 squadrons around the country, teaching pilots the latest BFM and ACM concepts. Sometimes the "No Foreign" rule would be in effect, but this never seemed a problem. On occa-

sion, Ross would be lecturing on matters that were "No Foreign", but the show went on, as it did one day at NAS Miramar. He and the RAF and RAAF exchange pilots even made up a "No Foreign" shoulder patch, which they wore on their flight suits for a bit of a laugh. Other cross-country flying included a trip to Cold Lake in April 1972 to attend the 10th anniversary of the CF-104 in service there, and trips to North Bay on family related matters. May 7-9, 1970, Ross took part in a fire power display on the Indian Springs Range at Nellis.

In this period the F-15 was in development and one of the innumerable projects was to evaluate the sight for its gun. This task fell to Maj Ross who, from April 20 to 27, 1972 flew four

Instructors at the 414th, Nellis AFB, in 1969. On the lower rung of the ladder is F/L Bill Ross, RCAF, all the rest being his American cousins. Standing second from the left is F/L Trevor Richardson, RAAF. On his right is Capt Les Alford, wearing an F-4 "100 Missions" patch from the war in Southeast Asia. (via Bill Ross)

RCAF men with WS-10 at Oldenburg in 1959. On the wing are S/L Amos Pudsey (CTechO), Jim McComb (pilot) and Pete Caws (pilot). Standing are Pete Lenton (Air Traffic Control), R.J. "Pinky" Flynn (pilot), Arnie Leiter (pilot), Bill Krantz (ATC), Merv Esch (pilot), S/L Duke Warren, Con Platz (pilot), Bill Van Oene (pilot), Walt Moore (pilot, who later took over from S/L Warren) and Bob Longhouse (pilot). In front are Glen Hollingshead (pilot, KIFA in OTU CF-104 June 19, 1963), Roy Gummeson, John Taylor, Myron Filyk (pilot) and Warner Unruh (Adj). (via Stella Krantz)

(Left) The (as usual) wild and crazy Canadians whoop it up in the mess at "Oldie". Pete Lenton and Bill Van Oene are front and centre. (Van Oene Col.)

Bill Krantz with his Luftwaffe counterpart in air traffic control, Lt Haack. (via Stella Krantz)

1971-75. He retired from the military in 1976 for the life of a fruit farmer in the BC interior.

Life at Oldenburg

In November 1944 P/O William T. "Bill" Krantz of 419 Squadron was awarded the DFC for good service on Lancasters with 419 Squadron. The war over, he went home to Saskatchewan, but air force life beckoned and he rejoined. First he trained as an aero engine tech, then remustered to air traffic control. In 1953 he was serving in Moose Jaw, when he met a young English girl, Stella. They soon married. As a respected ATC officer, F/L Krantz, then at Marville, accepted an offer to join WS-10 in 1958.

From Oldenburg, the Krantzs had postings at Trenton, Goose Bay and Moose Jaw. Bill retired in the early 1970s, he and Stella settling on Warner St. in Moose Jaw. Bill passed away in 2003. In September 2005 Stella shared a few "Oldie" memories:

Oldenburg had been in the British sector after the war. Upon settling into our new situation there, we, the Bells, Flynns, Fylicks, Leiters, Lentons and Unruhs all were allotted homes previously occupied by senior British officers. German officers didn't want these houses, since they were charged rent based on square footage. What stands out most in my mind from those early days was trying to furnish these large houses. Since they had been vacant for some time, all

Canadian wives at Oldenburg in June 1960: Betty Lenton, Grace Reiffer, Minnie Taylor, Anita Unruh, Corky Hollingshead, Marion Moore, Les Heard, Sue Caws, Mary MacDonnell, Pauline Bordeleaux, Merrilyn Flynn, Melba Warren, Stella Krantz, Lou Anne Sherwin, Sylvia Bell and Flo Van Oene. (via Stella Krantz)

Duke Warren with his boys in June 1960: Red Reiffer, Bill Van Oene, Con Platz, Alex Leslie, Al Sherwin, Bill Krantz, Jack MacDonnell (Canadair tech rep), S/L Warren, Jim McComb, Oberst Wehnelt, Walt Moore, Lew Mann, Padre Chuck Jenks, Reg Heard, Warner Unruh (Admin), Pete Caws, Glen Hollingshead, Brian Bell, Pete Lenton (ATC), Bob Flynn and Andy Bordeleaux (EO). Besides their RCAF Wing, the Canadian pilots also wear that of the Luftwaffe. Oberst Wehnelt had joined the Luftwaffe in 1936 and fought in the Battle of Britain and on the Eastern Front, ending with 36 victories. In the postwar Luftwaffe he rose to the rank of general. (via Stella Krantz)

the carpets and drapes had been stored in warehouses. We wives were taken out by truck to pick out what we wanted. This was quite a job, and a dirty one! Our place was large for the two of us, but I was happy, since there was a big garden. After living in an upstairs apartment at our last posting, it was wonderful to walk outside to a lawn, flowers, vegetable garden and my strawberry patch.

Each house had two furnaces, one for winter, one for summer, and there was an elderly German who looked after these. I had a young local girl, Lise, to help with the housework. Meanwhile, I hoped to learn German, but I didn't get very far. Even when I tried my little bit of German in the local stores, I always was answered in English

In 1959 our daughter Jean was born. That was quite an event taking place as it did on a foggy February night with the baby in a hurry to be born. I was supposed to go to the RAF hospital in Jever, but that was an hour's drive over a cobblestone road. We arranged for an ambulance (which had to be paid for in advance) to take me to Frauenklinik in Oldenburg. On the way we were held up by a passing train at a railway crossing. All the time Bill was following in his car, not having a clue where he was going. We made it just in time – they showed Bill into one room, me into another and, before Bill got to sit down, they showed him his daughter!

Social life at Oldenburg was excellent. There were the usual Mess functions and lots of house parties. I liked how polite the average

German officer was when arriving at a house party. After greeting his host and hostess (often with a flower for her), he would go around shaking hands with everyone, the same when leaving. This all was quite different for the Canadians and our casual way of doing things.

There was lots of other great fun for us during our Oldenburg days. We enjoyed touring around the local area and, being so close to Scandinavia, were able to holiday in Norway, Denmark and Sweden. The RAF had a fine recreational facility for family activities of all sorts, and we could shop in the American PX in Bremerhaven. Even such simple things as watching the chimney sweeps at work, or the storks nesting atop barns, was fun.

German RF-4 Exchange

Since RCAF Advisory Group days, several CF aircrew had Luftwaffe exchanges (RF-4, then Tornado), while Germans served in Canada (CF-5, then CF-18). The first Canadian on the RF-4 was Gordon Zans, who had been born to German immigrant parents in Hamilton, Ontario in 1958. In 1972 the family returned to Germany. Low-flying fighters operated in their area, and any time one roared over, Gordon would dream about being a fighter pilot. In 1979 he enlisted in the Canadian Forces at Lahr. Gradually, he moved through the training system, until

Capt Gordon Zans following an RF-4 mission. A squadron tech services the recce equipment. (All, Zans Col.)

Capt Zans is towed around the tarmac at Bremgarten following his last flight with 511 Squadron. His buddies have smeared his face with crud from his RF-4 tail pipe! Then, Zans receives a presentation from Maj Karl Nickel of 511.

qualifying for his Wings at Moose Jaw February 17, 1982. By that time he was on track for fighters, so was posted to 419 Squadron at Cold Lake on the CF-5 fighter lead-in course. Proceeding to the CF-104 OTU, he topped his course.

Posted to 441 Squadron at Baden-Soellingen, Zans first flew in CF-104D '661 with Capt Gerry Bayles on May 17, 1983. Henceforth, his tour was typical. There were exercises on various ranges, squadron exchanges, airshows, TacEvals, etc. August

12 to 18, 1983, for example, Zans was on exchange with the Norwegians at Oerland. That was a good month – 27.6 hours in the CF-104, 1.5 in the T-33. Another exercise was "Ample Gain", when a CF-104 section could be re-routed without notice to land away from base. The goal was to train NATO techs in refuelling and re-arming someone else's fighters. For October 17, 1983 Capt Zans was at Furstenfeldbruck for such an "inter-operability" exercise. Also fun were exchanges with 441's sister squadron at Schleswig, 1 Marinefliegergeschwader (1 Sqn/1 Naval Air Wing with F-104Gs).

The life of a 1 CAG pilot was never dull. In May 1984 Zans was on exchange to RAF Leuchars and RAF Binbrook then, in June, he was in Rimini, Italy with 102º Gruppo, also a Starfighter squadron. From June 12-28 Zans logged eight sorties. Meanwhile, 102º Gruppo went overboard to keep the social calendar filled. The occasional exercise saw 441 suiting up in NBCW kit. For pilots this meant climbing into their bulky "AR5" chemical suits. Zans' log shows him doing this on March 13, 1985. On April 19 he passed his annual TacEval, this time in AR5 kit. For October 1984, 441 sojourned in Tanagra, Greece, although there were no missions with Greek fighters, which were on alert due to some regional tensions. Instead, 441 made its own fun, bombing on the Abalone Range and flying ACM missions. The squadron flew home via Rimini – a social call. By late 1985, 441 was getting ready to stand-down. A reunion was held, the final fly-by going off without a hitch on March 1, 1986. On March 12-13 Zans joined in the rush to deliver the last of 54 1CAG CF-104s to the Turks, flying 104735 to Diyarbakir. A local flight from Baden on April 14 was Zan's last in the CF-104 – he had logged 804.6 hours on type.

No sooner had 441 folded than a Luftwaffe RF-4E recce exchange opened up. This was ideal for Zans, a German-speaking Canadian current on low level fighter ops. He applied, was accepted and slid straight into the job. There was no OTU – he went straight into training with his new unit, 511 Immelman at Bremgarten, south of Lahr. First came four sessions in the operational flight trainer, then Zans flew on August 27, 1986. His crew solo came on September 29 in RF-4E "35-38". As with Jensen and Huddleston, the move from CF-104 to RF-4 took some adjusting. Now there was that "guy in the back" to talk and listen to. He knew that a good back-seater was an asset, taking care of flight planning, navigating and operating the recce gear. But not all were equal – to play it safe, Zans carried route maps. Then there was equipment. No more cannon, bombs and rockets, but a load of electronics from cameras to IR line scan (for low-level recce) and SLAR – side-looking radar used higher up to record such things as armour situated miles behind the Iron Curtain.

One of 511's annual deployments was to the Coca low-level range near Beja, Portugal. There it trained in its secondary air-to-ground role. For training in the wide open spaces, there was Goose Bay, where Zans had a deployment September 28–October 13, 1987, flying 11 sorties. On the 14th he left for home in Phantom "35 + 52", a 6.3-hour transit using multiple air refuellings from USAF KC-135s. Another exchange was in Strasbourg, where 511 trained with the Armée de l'Air recce Mirage F.1s. Once at Strasbourg, Zans made five test sorties in NBCW gear (to profit from his AR5 knowledge, 511 made Zans its NBCW officer).

Maj Zans made his last flight with 511 on October 28, 1988. His two years had streaked by and he had flown 458.2 hours on the RF-4E. Replaced by Capt Ron Huzarik, he now moved into the CF-18 world. He instructed at 410 Squadron from 1993-96, then had four years as a NATO exercise planner in Ramstein. Since the Berlin Wall was down, he visited several former Warsaw Pact countries, occasionally scrounging a famil flight, as in the L-39 jet trainer. Following a brief CF-18 refresher course in May 2000, LCol Zans commanded 410 Squadron. On March 22, 2001 he was honoured to fly one of 410's most famous night fighter pilots (8 kills), G/C R.D. "Joe" Schultz, DFC and Bar. In August 4 Wing hosted some B-1Bs on exchange from the 128th "Georgia Bones" Bomb Squadron. When some B-1B crew got Hornet rides, their CO, Col Doehling, offered a ride to LCol Zans. On August 6 they climbed aboard B-1B 86-0124, Zans being offered the aircraft commander's seat. What followed was the full B-1B treatment, from low-level at 600 knots, to mountain flying, touch-and-goes – 3.4 hours of fighter pilot heaven in a bomber. From August 8-13, 2001 LCol Zans led 410 to victory at the inaugural "Tiger Meet of the Americas" at Buckley ANG Base. There, the Cougars pitted their athletic, flying and social skills against the opposition.

Another opportunity was delivering the oldest CF-18 (188901) from Cold Lake to the national aeronautical collection in Ottawa. On October 18, 2001, with LGen Al Dequetteville in his back seat, LCol Zans landed '901 on Rockcliffe's 3100-foot runway, equipped for the occasion with a mobile arrester cable system. Other noteworthy log book entries followed. During the June 2002 G-8 Summit in Alberta, LCol Zans flew two Op. Grizzly sorties, CAP missions covering the G-8 site (9-11 still was fresh in everyone's mind). On July 9, 2002 he flew his final sortie as 410 CO, taking up '741. Upon making up his log book after the mission, LCol Zans noted his total air force time as 2875.4 hours, including 1177.4 on CF-18s.

Tornados in Germany

When Canada retired the CF-104 and re-equipped with the CF-18, the former Luftwaffe CF-5 exchange at 419 Squadron moved to the CF-18 at 416 Squadron. About the same time, the Canadian Forces RF-4 exchange at Bremgarten became a Tornado exchange at Lechfeld. The first Canadian on the Lechfeld exchange was Capt Harry A. Mueller. The son of German parents, who had emigrated to Canada in 1952, Harry grew up in Chilliwack. During the war, his father had worked in the shipyards in Kiel, then had been ground crew on an Me.109 unit. After relatives sponsored the family to settle in Canada, Herr Mueller made his living in Chilliwack, BC as a welder.

When he was only 18 years old and just out of high school in 1980, Harry joined the Canadian Forces. He followed the standard route for a future fighter pilot – CFB Chilliwack for officer training, then Portage-la-Prairie on the Musketeer, Moose Jaw on the Tutor, Cold Lake on the CF-5 and CF-104. For the latter, Mueller's was the final course at 417 Squadron, which disbanded in July 1983 (the last German exchange officer there had been HPTM Riedel). Mueller, only 21 years of age and by then christened with the call-sign "Chimp", joined 421 Squadron at Baden-Soellingen, where his father had laboured as a young man after WWII. When 421 stood down, he flew with its sister squadron, 441. Finally, come March 1986 and it was "lights out" for the CF-104 in Canadian service. Capt Mueller got in on the last operation, ferrying two CF-104s to Turkey, then he was posted to 434 Squadron at CFB Chatham. There he flew CF-5s into 1988, when 434 stood down. Next came two years instructing on the CF-5, still flying with 419 Squadron as the CF-18 lead-in fighter trainer.

In 1990 Capt Mueller was selected for the first Canadian Forces Tornado exchange at Lechfeld. His record in the fighter world and his facility with the German language made him an ideal choice for this slot. Meanwhile, HPTM Roland Gakenholz became the first German on the CF-18 exchange at Cold Lake. His conversion to the IDS Tornado began on Course 156 at RAF Cottesmore with the Tri-National Tornado Training Establishment, which produced IDS (interdictor/strike) Tornado crews for the UK, Germany and Italy. Capt Mueller flew there first on February 12, 1991. Along with ground school and 14 simulator sessions, his course would entail 60 flying hours. Something new for him was the 2-man crew concept, but he soon adapted to the "guy in the back", whose tasks included managing the weapons and radar, deploying self-defence equipment, and updating the nav system as a mission progressed. Mueller also was impressed by the Tornado's advanced HUD and INS, and by its sophisticated terrain-following radar, which could fly a mission more effectively than the crew itself.

Finished at TTTE with a mission of May 16, Capt Mueller joined 322 "Flying Monsters" Squadron at Lechfeld, where he was one of 27 crews. Flying the IDS Tornado, 322 specialized in low-level operations as Germany's ACE Mobile Force squadron. IDS used a wide range of weapons from cluster bombs, to the German-developed multi-purpose MW-1 weapons carrier, to a pair of 27-mm cannons. For self-defence there was chaff, flares, a jamming pod and AIM-9L missiles. Mueller flew first at Lechfeld on May 28, 1991, beginning a busy three years, whether on routine missions to such bombing ranges as Pampa, Siegenburg or Stetten; on NATO squadron exchanges; or on trans-Atlantic trips to Goose Bay. While Germany was limited by noise abatement rules to 1000 feet, at "Goose" the tree tops were the limit for low-level training. (The IDS Tornado had been tailored for the low level environment, but flew unimpressively above 20,000. In all his time on it, Chimp only once would fly supersonic.)

Before long, Mueller was a designated *Einsetzer* (OpsO) at 322, a rare honour for an exchange officer. As such, he would be in charge should the CO be absent. As *Einsetzer*, Mueller was the detachment commander on deployments to Turkey, or to "Red Flag" at Nellis AFB. In Turkey, as on "Display Determination 92", missions were with Turkish F-16s and USAF F-15s. Being a typical Canadian fighter pilot, Mueller got onto as many such trips as possible.

While Canadians were used to logging 180 to 210 hours

yearly on the CF-18, in the Luftwaffe 130 hours was more usual and few were the pilots who logged more, as extra flying was limited. For example, when 322 was offered slots for two crews to attend the coveted Tactical Leadership Program course at Florennes, Belgium, no Germans rushed to snag it, since they already had been to TLP, or were too inexperienced to be selected. Those who qualified had one reason or another why they couldn't attend. Capt Mueller, however, put up his hand. The CO argued that the German taxpayer would be footing the bill for the TLP, so how could he justify sending a foreigner? Before long, however, Mueller had the TLP slot and led the 322 Squadron 2-ship to Florennes. Since this was a long-range TLP at a time when the Gulf War was in full swing, it looked like the normal support for USAF tankers would be in jeopardy. Anticipating this, Mueller laid some groundwork, e.g. visiting the RAF tanker facility at Brize Norton to organize training on RAF tankers, with the hope of securing approval from the Luft Flotte in Cologne to tank off RAF L.1011s, VC-10s or Victors. Between August 9, 1993 and September 1, Mueller flew 16 TLP missions using RAF tankers. During a deployment to Red Flag (January 25 to February 4, 1993) he ended

From <www.flyingmonsters.de> here are views of Lechfeld-based "Flying Monsters" Tornados. Canadian Harry Mueller flew Tornados while on exchange at Lechfeld 1991-1994.

as the Warlord for the last of his eight missions, planning and leading a package of 70 aircraft ranging from the F-16 to the B-1B.

On July 14, 1994 Capt Mueller flew the Tornado for the last time, taking up PA200-624 on a 1:40 mission. He had logged 497 hours on type, just short of where he had wanted, since he had plans for a personalized 500-hour patch. Undeterred, he turned out a 497-hour patch! Mueller headed back to Canada, while his replacement, Capt Oliver Baus, arrived to join 321 Squadron at Lechfeld on the ECR Tornado (electronic/combat reconnaissance). Mueller's new posting was to 5 Wing Goose Bay as the Military Coordination Centre Officer, supervising all the low-level NATO missions being flown there in the mid-1990s. From 1997-2000 he was on 416 Squadron at 4 Wing Cold Lake, where he finished as DCO in May 2000. Next, he was Deputy OpsO at 4 Wing. In 2004 he joined 419 Squadron to instruct on the Hawk. In December 2006 he was DCO at 419. By this time his total flying time was 3540 hours including Musketeer – 33 hours, Tutor – 234, T-33 – 60, CF-104 – 725, CF-5 – 1047, CF-18 – 426, Tornado – 497. Maj Mueller left 419 in July 2007 for Dubai, there to assume FLIT instructing duties on the Hawk.

instrumented there for flight testing. Once the whole program was complete, No. 1 RQU Det was reduced to myself and Sgt Wilbur. My job then was to provide on-site technical support to DSS staff on the CF-5 and NF-5 (Canadair F-5s for Holland), and handle miscellaneous issues with Northrop and our HQ support office in Ottawa. Meanwhile 116701 was reconfigured as the prototype NF-5, e.g. with leading edge slats and 275-gallon underwing tanks. The NF-5A began its flight test period in February 1969. This also was a success, except that on the last flight Capt Ton Okkerman (RNAF) had a double flameout and had to eject. We also used CF-5A 116715 in trials at Edwards. While there, we also had some involvement with the CC-109 "Cosmo" re-engining program at PacAero.

In hindsight, it can be argued that, strictly as a peacetime fighter, the CF-5 was a fair choice, certainly as far as Hellyer's "industrial offsets" went. Even the claims of Northrop's 1960s sales brochures would pan out and … ask any experienced CF-5 pilot and he'll have nothing but praise for his "fun" CF-5 in close air support, recce, rapid deployment and fighter lead-in training. Naturally, he'll also admit that few enjoyed the prospect of ever going to war in a CF-5. In the end, Canada got nearly 30 years of service from the CF-5, the fighter that provoked almost as much controversy as the Avro Arrow. (For a detailed explanation of this story, read "Cold War Air Power Choices for the RCAF: Paul Hellyer and the Selection of the CF-5 Freedom Fighter" by Dr. Ray Stouffer in Vol. 7 No. 3 of *Canadian Military Journal*.)

A tight squeeze as the CF-5 116701 goes aboard RCAF Hercules 130122 for the trip from Cartierville to Edwards AFB. Then, members of the CF-5 detachment at Edwards: J. Fielding, E.A. "Gene" Skinner, Gordon Diller, Russ Bush, Don Linneborn and Mars Godin.

Discussing the day's affairs at Edwards: F/L Gordon Diller, S/L Barry Gartner, S/L Bob Smith, G/C R.G. "Bob" Christie (standing) and Mr. Wilf Langlois (DDP). Gartner was a seasoned test pilot, as had been Bob Christie, a 1951 graduate of the USAF Experimental Test Pilot School at Wright Field, Ohio and Edwards.

YF-5B 63-8445 served as a "Northrop-Canadair" demo plane in spurious RCAF markings. It later was an F-5F prototype (2-seat version of the F-5E Tiger II). (CANAV Col.)

Dutch Exchanges

Since they operated the Canadair CF-5 and NF-5 it was natural that Canada and the Netherlands co-operate in exchanges. Over the years, Canadians would fly the NF-5 in Holland, while Dutch pilots would enjoy CF-5 exchanges. The first Canadian on such a posting was Capt Ken Kee. Having joined the RCAF in 1955, he flew Sabres on 422 Squadron, then instructed on T-33s at Gimli and had a posting in personnel at Winnipeg. In September 1968 he joined 434 Squadron then flying T-33s, but in January 1969 the first CF-5s arrived and 434 was back in the fighter game. By 1970 the squadron had its own exchange pilots – Capt Steve Netto (RNAF) and Capt Tom Tillman (USAF), and had checked out the first five Dutch pilots on the CF-5.

Word now filtered down that the NDHQ was looking for an experienced CF-5 instructor who did not have any school-age children (thinking that foreign children might not adapt to Dutch schools). Ken Kee, by then with some 300 CF-5 hours, immediately jumped at this chance and, supported by his CO, LCol Steve Gulyas, received the posting. He, his wife and pre-school son soon were moving into quarters near the Dutch fighter base of Twenthe (they later settled in a home in Lonneker, a village near Twenthe).

Capt Kee flew first the NF-5 on April 13, 1970, going up with Capt Renus Kamphius of 315 Squadron in aircraft 3006. He quickly adapted to life on 315 Squadron, finding his fellow instructors to be experienced men off such types as the F-84 and F-104. His CO, Maj Fred DeJong (later RNAF Chief of Air Staff), realizing that Kee had more F-5 time than most 315 Squadron

IPs, sent him solo to CFB Baden-Soellingen. Kee then went to work instructing his pipeline students. On average, he found that the NF-5 syllabus mirrored that at Cold Lake. Besides its OTU role, 315 Squadron had a secondary tactical operational role (air fighting was not as high a priority compared to 434). Weapons were as per Cold Lake, e.g. 2.75" rockets, Mk. 82 bombs, cluster bomb canisters, cannons.

Since the Dutch automatically were promoted according to experience,

F/L Ken Kee during his Dutch exchange. (Kee Col.)

Capt Kee could not hold any executive position on squadron, e.g. flight commander. His job was simply instructing and that spelled one thing – lots of flying. In his first month (May) he logged 30.7 hours. The work day began routinely at 0830, something different from Cold Lake, where 434 usually was on the job by 0700, then pushed until the day's work was done. At Twenthe, however, the work ethic was different and the base was pretty well done for the day by 1630. This was driven by the RNAF non-flying trades, who operated a bit like a union.

Daily NF-5 missions usually sent instructors and students into German air space. Whereas navigation around Cold Lake depended on lakes, rivers and contours, below a pilot in this part of Europe was a maze of roads, a dazzling pattern of farmland, countless villages, canals, etc. As to squadron life, Capt Kee was enthusiastically welcomed by his new squadron mates and strong friendships quickly formed. His exchange ended after 2 years and 3 months, by which time he had logged 850 hours on the NF-5. He and his family had thoroughly enjoyed this opportunity. His son had reached school age and, contrary to official doubts, readily adapted and soon was speaking Dutch. There had been some special moments as well. Being Canadians, the Kees were well treated by the Dutch, who revere Canada for how it liberated much of Holland in 1944. On a melancholic occasion, Capt Kee would visit the grave of his brother, WO2 Robert James Kee, a WOpAG. While on operations with 61 Squadron on January 3, 1943, he and his crew were lost over Holland in their Lancaster and lie today in the renowned War Cemetery at Bergen-Op-Zoom. On another occasion, Governor General Roland Mitchener visited Twenthe. Part of his tour included an NF-5 cockpit briefing. Later that week the CBC national news back home featured the great man seated in an NF-5 with "some unknown Canadian pilot" answering his questions.

Maj Kee now attended Army Staff College, then wrote Army/Air Force doctrine (e.g. "The Tactical Fighter Squadron in Battle") at FMC HQ in St. Hubert. Although he did a CF-5 refresher course in 1977, LCol Kee now became CO at 424 Squadron in Trenton. His "office" now was the cockpit of a Buffalo. Later postings were to CF Training System HQ and CF Staff College. He spent his final six years with CDLS London as Air Adviser to the Canadian High Commissioner. From here he retired in 1993. Col Ken Key then became involved with the RCAF Memorial Museum in Trenton, first as Executive Director, later as Chairman of the Board, then as fund raiser.

Fred Mueller

Born in Bavaria in 1944, Fred Mueller emigrated to Canada in 1958. Once finished high school in Toronto, he joined the RCN in 1962. Through the ROTP he attended Carleton University, studying history and German. In 1967 he trained on Chipmunks at Camp Borden, then on Tutors and T-33s at Gimli, from where he earned his Wings a year later. Subsequently, he instructed at Gimli and Cold Lake. In January 1972 Capt Mueller joined 434 Squadron, from where he was posted to The Netherlands in the summer of 1974, replacing Maj Larry Hill at 313 Squadron.

Capt Mueller first flew in Holland with 315 Squadron on July 10, 1974 in NF-5 4027. In September he joined 313 Squadron, the NF-5 OTU (until recently, 313 had been a joint Dutch-Belgian T-33 fighter OTU). Mueller soon came to appreciate the NF-5 over the CF-5, improvements being its manoeuvring flaps, which improved the turn rate (the CF-5 had selectable leading edge flaps), and a Doppler rolling map, which provided position data. Students came well prepared, whether off Tutors, T-birds and CF-5s in Canada, or T-38s at Sheppard AFB. They advanced through the syllabus one exercise at a time. Included were frequent trips to the Dutch weapons ranges at Vlieland and Terschelling, and to a Germany range at Nordhorn. This being an OTU, there were some tactical exercises that normally terminate in Belgium, Germany or Denmark. When runway repairs were scheduled for Twenthe, 313 deployed for three months to Hopsten AB, Germany. An exchange with a USAF F-4 unit at RAF Bentwaters was a welcomed bit of variety. All things considered, there was plenty of flying for Capt Mueller – he would log 654.5 hours in two years. His tour was normal in most ways, exceptional in others. High on the list was the birth in Holland of the Muellers' second child. Also, from Twenthe the whole of Western Europe was there to enjoy on leave. Otherwise, the family enjoyed the excellent mess life and established life-long friendships.

Promoted while overseas and replaced at 313 Squadron by Capt Don Matthews, Maj Mueller last flew at Twenthe on July 15, 1976. On that occasion, his wife Karen and son Christopher were in the tower for his recovery. "Karen cleared me to land on this final trip," he recalled in 2007. Mueller now was posted to Winnipeg for the Aerospace Systems Course. Two years in AIRCOM HQ followed, then came CF Staff College. Finally, Mueller returned to the fighter world. After a CF-5 refresher at 419 Squadron, he converted to the CF-104 at 417 Squadron, then served with 439 Squadron at Baden from 1981-84. A tour ensued as 1 CAG TacEval Officer, near the end of which he delivered CF-104 No. 841 to Turkey. LCol Mueller spent 1986-88 at Lahr as Senior Air Staff Officer, had a year in Fighter Group HQ, North Bay, then commanded 419 Squadron 1989-91. In this period, having 37 CF-5s, 419 was Canada's largest fighter

NF-5A K-3061 on a typical low-level mission. The badge on the tail is that of 313 Squadron, which had the motto "Ex Umbra In Umbras". In 1967 the Dutch ordered 75 NF-5As and 30 NF-5Bs to replace their aging F-84 Thunderstreaks. The first NF-5 flew at Cartierville in March 1969, and the last left Dutch service on May 1, 1991. By then, the Dutch were flying F-16s, which Canadian exchange pilots also would fly. Meanwhile, Greece, Turkey and Venezuela were happy to add superannuated NF-5s, taking 11, 60 and 7, respectively. (Mueller Col.)

(Right) Maj Fred Mueller following the last NF-5 mission of his Dutch tour. He's being greeted by his son, Christopher. (Mueller Col.)

squadron. LCol Mueller completed his air force career in NDHQ, retiring in September 1994. He then joined Bombardier for the planning, implementation and marketing of the NATO Flying Training in Canada program. NFTC was inaugurated in 2000 and continues to operate at Moose Jaw and Cold Lake, producing fighter pilots for Canada, Denmark, Hungary, Italy, Singapore and the UK.

Dave Penney

Having joined the RCAF in 1964, Capt Dave Penney trained first as a maritime navigator, then flew on the Argus with 405 Squadron from 1966-69. Next, he cross-trained to pilot in 1970. Penney then resisted efforts to get him back into the maritime world by taking a CF-5 posting. After his OTU at 434 Squadron he joined 433 in Bagotville, one of the choice postings in the Canadian fighter world. Many great times ensued, as when 433 led the first CF-5 trans-Atlantic aerial refuelling mission (Op. Long Leap I to Andoya, Norway, June 9, 1973). Ex. Red Flag at Nellis AFB and Ex. Maple Flag at Cold Lake also appear in Penney's log book.

In 1974 Capt Penney was posted to instruct in Moose Jaw. This was not good news. While on Ex. Open Challenge (where 433 and 434 competed in tactical flying) he grumbled about this to LCol Glen Younghusband, 434's CO. Shortly afterwards, Penney was delighted to hear that his posting had magically been changed to 434. When 419 Squadron stood up in 1976, he was part of its original instructing cadre, remaining on staff until posted on exchange to 313 Squadron in 1978.

On July 18, 1978 Capt Penney strapped into NF-5 4015 for his initial famil flight at 313 Squadron (Twenthe being under construction, 313 temporarily was deployed to Gilze Rijen). Penney's "tour guide" this day was Capt Don Matthews, whom he was replacing. After a few more famil trips, he flew his first student mission on July 26, leading a 3-ship to the range. Now it was down to two years of good flying, whether instructing or doing operational missions. Besides IP duties, Penney also was 313's weapons officer. On September 6, 1979 he logged his 2000th F-5 hour.

Capt Penney would find his NF-5 students a competent bunch. After all, most had been through Moose Jaw, then had 60 hours on CF-5s with 419 Squadron, so there was a low washout rate at 313. As did all Canadians on the NF-5, he also enjoyed social and family life. The squadron had its own bar where, at day's end, pilots could enjoy a beer and "recap" their missions before heading home. The Penneys sent their children to a local school, where they thrived and learned the language readily. The Penneys also enjoyed touring Europe and on one leave spent a month tenting up as far as Norway. There they visited Capt Stu Holdsworth, then holding the

Capt Dave Penney during 433 days at Bagotville in 1972. (Penney Col.)

September 6, 1979 and a scruffy-looking Capt Penney accepts a congratulatory drink from his CO at 313 Squadron, Rob Buffart. The occasion was Penney's hitting his 2000th hour in the CF-5/NF-5. (Penney Col.)

Norwegian F-5 exchange, and Hans Lei, a Norwegian who had had a CF-5 exchange in Cold Lake. Hans was delighted when the Penneys arrived bearing gifts – bottles of booze which, in Norway, would have cost him a small fortune.

Often on a Friday, Capt Penney would lead a 4-ship to Baden-Soellingen for TGIF shenanigans. Otherwise, the pilots would

shop, especially for the cheap booze in the CanEx. In this era the Dutch military was infamous for its long-haired look. Penney adopted this style, but it backfired on him one TGIF at Baden-Soellingen. Spotting Penney at the bar, base commander Col Tony Bosman, himself a Dutch-Canadian, reacted by turfing the scruffy-looking pilot out of the mess!

With its operational role, 313 had its share of NATO exchanges. One on which Capt Penney took part was in December 1978 with the RAF Buccaneer wing (15 and 16 squadrons) at Laarbruch, West Germany, close to the Dutch border. There was a bit of cockpit trading, with Penney taking a back-seat Buccaneer ride. Ruefully, however, he found the navigator's office most unpleasant. As they scorched along at 50 feet, he kept groping for the stick, but it wasn't there. Happy to be back on the ground, he didn't even enter this wretched trip in his log book. On a sortie of May 28, 1979 Penney flew newspaper reporter Ria Straathof, who hacked her first "fast jet" flight and reported glowingly about her Canadian pilot.

Tour-expired in the summer of 1980, Maj Penney was replaced by Capt Cliff Patterson. The Penneys now returned to Canada, Dave to run the Maple Flag office in Cold Lake. In 1983 he was sent to fly a desk at HMCS *Stadacona* in Halifax, attended CF Staff College in 1985-86, then was grabbed by LCol Tom Henry, CO of 434 Squadron in Chatham. Henry was looking for a senior CF-5 pilot and the timing was perfect. Maj Penney now enjoyed his last flying tour on the CF-5. On June 11, 1986, as 434 prepared to stand down, LCol Henry and Maj Penney led a CF-5 9-ship over-flying several local communities. This was Penney's last CF-5 flight and the final entry in his log book. Of his 3600 hours, some 3000 had been on CF-5s. LCol Penney now spent five years with AAFCEN at Ramstein. At a function there one evening, he again met reporter Straathof, who by then was married to a Dutch officer. Penney now got to pick his final tour. From 1993-97 he served with the Canadian NORAD contingent at Tyndall AFB, then retired to life in Nova Scotia. (Following Cliff Patterson's tour, the Dutch fighter exchange switched to the F-16, a slot that continues to this day.)

Norwegian F-5 Exchange

Don Fair joined the Canadian Forces as an RMC cadet in 1968. As such his flying training was squeezed into summer sessions between academic terms. He graduated with Wings from 1CFFTS at Cold Lake in October 1973 (Course 7204), then joined 434 Squadron on the CF-5 in January 1974. About two years later word reached 434 that a Norwegian exchange slot, then held by Capt Les Koski, was coming up. Normally, some experienced pilot would leap at such an opportunity, but the posting went instead to a junior fellow – Capt Don Fair (as he light-heartedly put it in 2007, "They must have been scraping the bottom of the barrel.")

Capt Fair reached Sola (on the south coast of Norway near Stavanger) in June 1976. His first flight was with Capt Koski in F-5 No. 243, After his type check, in September-October there was a 1-month northern deployment to Banak. In this period Fair came to understand 718's role as they flew daily low-level sovereignty sorties close along the Finnish and USSR borders. He now joined 718 to instruct, his first student trip be-

F-5 exchange pilots Don Fair and Don Matthews, with 434 Squadron CF-5B 116815. They had just survived a dicey mission in '815, when their left aileron jammed down. To keep control, both pilots had to exert full left pressure on their sticks. With great support from their controller, they landed back at Cold Lake. In 2007 Don Fair recalled, "This was shortly before Don left for Twenthe and I for Sola." (Fair Col.)

ing on November 18 with Lt Bogen. Now followed a routine of student trips reminiscent of life at Cold Lake, a monthly flying rate of about 25 hours being normal.

Typically, NATO OTUs held some secondary operational roles. With an RNoAF F-5 unit this could be tactical/anti-shipping or air superiority. One mission that put an F-5 pilot to the test was low-level night flying, not a usual CF-5 requirement. Before the days of NVGs, or even of strip lighting, RNoAF F-5s would fly 2-ship, low-level nav trips in the fiords and mountains (without radar or radar altimeters). Navigation was facilitated using special gray and white "night maps" in a blackened cockpit. To stay current, two missions in one night were the norm over the winter months. Pilots also did night practice bombing on the Halkavarre range near Banak, which was lit by flares dropped by F-5s.

In July 1978 Capt Fair completed his Norwegian tour. Having logged 550 hours with 718 Squadron, he was replaced by Capt Stu Holdsworth. He now spent a year instructing at 419 Squadron, then left the air force. He flew briefly with Canadian Airlines then, in 1985, joined Conair of Abbotsford as an air tanker pilot, first on the A-26, then the DC-6. Meanwhile, he re-joined the military as an air reserve pilot, flying Trackers at 420 Squadron at Summerside and VU-33 at Comox. When the Tracker retired, in 1990 he became the first reserve pilot on the Sea King. In 2007 Don Fair still was flying the DC-6 (usually summers at Conair's Dawson City base) and Sea Kings with 443 (MH) Squadron at Victoria. With 443 he had served 10 straight years at sea, including with HMCS *Provider* on the UN embargo of Haiti in 1993-94, and with HMCS *Vancouver* on Op. Apollo

An RNoAF F-5 above typical Norwegian terrain. Note that it is armed with AIM-9 Sidewinder missiles. Canada's CF-5s never carried this specialized weapon. (Fair Col.)

from October 2001 to April 2002. By January 2007 Don Fair's log book showed a total flying time of 9400 hours, including: CF-5/F-5 – 1710 hours, Tracker – 1200, Sea King – 2250 and DC-6 – 2490.

Down in Maracay
In another CF-5 episode Canadian Forces personnel were seconded to the Venezuelan Air Force when Ottawa OK'd Canadair's sale to the VAF of 20 CF-5s. This caused a flap, Northrop rapping Canadair's knuckles, since their licensing agreement approved business with the Netherlands only. Now, instead of selling new "VF-5s" to Venezuela, Ottawa provided 18 surplus CanForces CF-5s, took delivery of 20 new CF-5Ds to off-set Canadair's potential loss in the deal, then allowed Canadair to sell Venezuela two new CF-5Ds. Northrop later won a settlement from Ottawa, so everyone got something out of these odd shenanigans.

In January 1972 three VAF pilots and 29 techs checked out on the CF-5 with 434 Squadron, while three CanForces CF-5 pilots and thirteen 434 Squadron technical people prepared for a 6-month tour in Venezuela. Among the pilots was Henry "Hank" Morris of 433 Squadron. He first heard of the posting when called from NDHQ by LCol Steve Gulyas, who was looking for a Spanish-speaking CF-5 pilot. Having spent his early years in Barcelona and having worked in the oil industry in Venezuela,

Morris fit the bill and was delighted to accept this offer. (Morris had emigrated to Canada from the UK in 1957. He joined the RCAF in 1959, training as a maritime navigator and serving on the Argus with 415 and 404 squadrons. In 1966 he remustered to pilot, serving initially on CF-5s at 433.)

The first VF-5s left Trenton on Operation Canamigo in February 1972. Pilots Barry Krall, Hank Morris and Doug Pickering routed through Myrtle Beach AFB, South Carolina, Homestead AFB, Florida and Roosevelt Roads Naval Station, Puerto Rico to the VAF base at Maracay. The Canadians quickly organized a VF-5 ground school, then commenced flying. This included all phases, e.g. low level navigation, recce, basic fighter manoeuvres, weapons training. The initial student cadre proved fairly capable, most having some experience on the F-86, Vampire, etc. Meanwhile, CWO "Slim" Stranks headed the 434 techs in maintaining the VF-5s and training techs. Stranks' team proved almost obsessive about keeping the VF-5s in top condition.

In April 1972 eight more VF-5s left Trenton for Venezuela, piloted by Denis Gauthier, Hank Morris, Val Pattee, and Daryl LaRoche of 433, and Ron Clayton, Pete Howe (CO 434), Jock Mackay and Pat Pattison of 434. In 2007 Denis Gauthier, pilot of VF-5 No. 3274, recalled how from Myrtle Beach they covered the 1.5-hour leg to Homestead by following the coast at sight-seeing level. With triple external "jugs" there was no shortage of fuel for this pleasant trip. The leg next day to "Rosie Roads" took 2.2 hours, which left the pilots sweating it for fuel, but they landed OK after disregarding ATC's round-about course headings. The flight to Maracay next day was in 1.8 hours, so total flying time was about 7.0 hours. The final batch of VF-5s left Trenton on June 5 with pilots Romeo Lalonde, Rénault Préfontaine and Jean-Guy Beaumont of 433 and Bob Dahl, Leo O'Donovan and Wally Peel of 434. The familiar route was followed, the aircraft reaching Maracay on the 11th. Approaching on the final leg, the Canadians were met by Hank Morris and friends, then they formed up for an arrival fly-by.

In July, Maj Charlie Leake replaced Maj Pickering, who was posted home to CF Staff College. In August 1972 the Canadians finished their secondment, but just before he left for Bagotville, Capt Morris scrounged a flight in one of the VAF's classic F-86Fs. All in all, the Canadians came home with a sense of satisfaction, even though they had not been able to raise their students to

CF-5s to Venezuela
CanForces No. with VAF No. in brackets:
116767 (6719), 116773 (7200), 116774 (6539),
116775 (9124), 116776 (6323), 116777 (6018),
116778 (5276), 116779 (3318), 116780 (3274),
116781 (2950), 116782 (9538), 116783 (9456),
116786 (9348), 116787 (8792), 116788 (9215),
116789 (8707), 116803 (1269), 116808 (2327),
116827 (2985), 116828 (5618)

the standards required at Cold Lake. It also had been culturally enlightening to see another dimension to air force life, where fighter pilots were generally from the upper classes and where something so taken-for-granted in Canada as military discipline could take a back seat to other priorities.

From 1973-78 Maj Morris flew CF-104s with 421 Squadron and later was the 1 CAG TacEval Officer. Next came two years in intel at NDHQ, followed by a USAF exchange at TAC HQ at Langley AFB. Although desk-bound there, he took the chance to fly the T-39 Sabreliner. LCol Morris next served at SHAPE HQ, then transferred to the Air Reserve in 1986, serving at MAG HQ. In 1989-92 he was 32 months on UN peacekeeping in Nicaragua, El Salvador and Guatemala. When he retired in 1992, UN HQ asked him to establish an air logistic support operation regarding Angola's first national elections. On this, Morris managed a fleet of 60 Russian aircraft. UN duties in Central America followed, before Morris retired in Florida in 1999. He then set up a security business serving Latin America'a oil and mining

Op. Canamigo pilots Maj Jock Mackay, Capt Denis Gauthier, Capt Hank Morris, Capt Pat Pattison, LCol R.P Pattee (CO 433 Sqn), Pete Howe (CO 434), Daryl LaRoche and Ron Clayton at Trenton prior to their delivery mission. These were top fighter pilots, who would advance in their careers. Denis Gauthier would command the Snowbirds, while Pete Howe would finish as Base Commander North Bay. Jock Mackay had begun in the RAF, then emigrated to Canada in 1954. He completed a tour on Sabres with 444 Squadron. CF-5 days followed, then he served at 10 TAG HQ and was OC Base Flight Cold Lake. After leaving the military in 1980, he spent 20 years flying A-26 water bombers with Airspray and in 2007 was flying commercial helicopters in the Yukon. (DND)

Hank Morris had a dream career as a fighter pilot, then on USAF exchange, on UN duties in and out of uniform, etc. Top left he is as a youthful CF-5 pilot with 433 Squadron, then ready to fly a VAF F-86E Sabre. Note the VF-5 beyond. (all, Morris Col.)

(Left) Maj Hank Morris by a T-39 Sabreliner during his USAF exchange at Langley AFB. Many RCAF/CF pilots had the privilege of flying the T-39 while on USAF postings since the early 1960s.

(Below left) One of Hank Morris' UN tours was in Central America while the Sandinistas were being demobilized. In this period he investigated the crash of this Mil Mi-17 helicopter in Nicaragua.

(Below) LCol Morris is awarded the Order of Military Merit by Governor General Ray Hnatyshyn in Ottawa on November 21, 1990.

industries. On a visit to Venezuela, he met an old flying compatriot, MGen Freddie Yanes (Ret'd), who had risen to command the Venezuelan Air Force. Yanes commented how some VF-5s remained in inventory. With a maintenance contract in the wind between Venezuela and Iran, it seemed that the VF-5 era was not yet over.

Turko-Canadian CF-5 Visit

In 1994 policy-makers in Ottawa were scheming to get rid of Canada's CF-5s, then serving 419 Squadron so efficiently in the fighter lead-in training (FLIT) role. No sooner had Ottawa begun thinking evil thoughts about the CF-5, than Turkey got wind of events. Having operated the F-5 for decades, the Turks knew its worth, so began angling to acquire Canada's recently upgraded fleet of 39 aircraft, and even proposed that Turkey take over training Canadian Forces pilots at the FLIT stage.

With a potential deal brewing, AIRCOM and Fighter Group sent representatives to Turkey to appraise possibilities. An AIRCOM memo succinctly painted the picture: "The mission is to examine the feasibility of conducting safe and effective F-5 FLIT with the TUAF." Five CanForces officers were tasked, including Maj H.M. "Marty" Tate and Capt G.V. "Gordo" Cooper, two experienced CF-5 pilots. The team formulated its "to do" list, e.g. outlining how a FLIT course in Turkey would work for Canadians: ground school, all phases of flying, length of course, students per course, quality of instructing, language and cultural factors, and the likelihood of Canadian instructors holding Turkish exchange slots.

On March 4, 1994 the Canadians departed Toronto on Air Canada to Frankfurt, then proceeded next day on Turkish Airlines to Ankara. Since the group would be returning to Frankfurt on March 11, everyone got to work. Tate and Cooper did interviews, toured facilities and worked on reports. In some ways they found the Turkish syllabus similar to 419's, but there were too many question marks. They would point these out to the Turks, who were eager to implement any such recommendations.

In one case Tate and Cooper analyzed Turkish F-5 BFM (basic fighter manoeuvres). On a standard exercise these involved two students, one the attacker, one the defender, but no instructor. At 419, however, an instructor was always in the fray to guide his students. In another case, the Canadians were amazed to see how

the Turks briefed very generally, and debriefed in flight. They had no ACMI (air combat manoeuvring instrumentation) or video tape, and could only conduct a fuzzy post-exercise debrief depending on memory. On the air-to-ground range, which the Canadians deemed to be decent, Tate and Cooper saw how the Turks used a steep angle for bombing, compared to the 419's low-angle. In summary, their report suggested that a graduate from the Turkish F-5 FLIT would have only about 30% the skills acquired by a 419 graduate. All things considered, they were not great supporters of moving Canada's FLIT to Turkey. If this did transpire, however, they suggested that only Canadian instructors teach Canadian students. According to plan, the team landed back in Toronto on March 11. In 2006 "Gordo" Cooper, by then a pilot with Air Canada, looked back at his Turkish sojourn:

In 1994 government cutbacks meant that yet another Canadian fighter squadron would have to close. Initially, a CF-18 squadron was proposed, but another scapegoat was quickly targeted. The budget barons in Ottawa suddenly declared our newly-modified CF-5s to be more expensive to operate than a CF-18 – according to these "experts" it was costing the taxpayers $25,000 per hour to fly a CF-5. This was news to us, but the fix was in and 419 Squadron had to go.

Somehow, the Turks learned of 419's dilemma. A few years earlier (to howls of protest from the Greeks), Canada had given Turkey 54 CF-104s, so now they jumped in, offering to kindly take the CF-5s off our hands. In return, they would train our FLIT students, using our former aircraft but, as I was to later learn, there was a hidden agenda behind all this.

After some false starts, a Canadian team was assembled to evaluate the Turkish proposal. Major Marty Tate from NDHQ, and myself, CF-5 Standards Officer from Fighter Group HQ in North Bay, travelled to Turkey, where Col J.E. Miller, the Canadian Military Attaché, briefed us on Turkish history and customs, the latter including the Turkish custom of giving you the shirts off their backs if you asked. In the next few days we would visit FLIT bases at Izmir and Konya, and TAF HQ in Ankara.

The Turks were amazing hosts. We were wined and dined, driven everywhere in limos with fender flags, and even assigned body guards. I guess the Turks really wanted our CF-5s. At the first formal dinner of the week I met a Turkish fighter pilot colonel. He asked if we preferred wine or the local Turkish drink called "Raki". We won him over by asking to try both. The Colonel eventually would take care of all our needs. You name it and he would get on the phone and things would happen. On account of this, we started calling him "El Presidente".

As dinner progressed, the topic of CF-104s and F-100s arose. I was dreaming of flying them this week, but El Presidente advised that both recently had been retired. However, he spoke highly of the ex-Canadian CF-104s, of how well they flew and how well they bombed. As the Raki was clouding my thinking by then, it took me a while to realize that he was talking about bombing the Kurds! So that's what the body guards were all about – El Presidente didn't want us getting bumped off by Kurdish rebels and embarrassing the Turkish government in the process.

During dinner, one of our Admin Officers happened to admire the ring worn by El Presidente. Without any hesitation, he took it off and presented it to the Canadian! Hadn't we just had a briefing about what not to say in a situation like this? We felt badly that the Colonel had just given up his Air Force graduation ring, so arrangements were made to return it to him later. Our next faux pas came after a meeting with the Commander of the TAF, Col Miller commented how it was unfortunate that we did not have time to visit any of Ankara's great museums. Our host's ears went up, commands were yelled and orderlies went running down the hall. The curator of a great museum was summoned, a private tour was set up, and our flight to Izmir re-scheduled. When our limo pulled up in front of the museum, fender flags flying, the curator was waiting at the door. After an amazing tour, which included King Midas' tomb, we departed for Izmir four hours late.

On another occasion, Major Tate commented that he would like to see some of Turkey's famous religious sites. Faux pas No. 3 … before we could say "get the shirt off his back", El Presidente had organized a tour that included visiting that last house of Mary, the mother of Jesus Christ. At Izmir we did our inspections and briefings, then had some time to shop. The previous day I had asked El Presidente about shopping for a silk carpet for my wife. As we lunched in a café by the water, imagine my surprise when several cars pulled up and out came all the local carpet dealers ready to show me their finest products.

Konya is the Cold Lake of Turkey, a booming fighter base with operational and training squadrons, including two with F-5s. On March 8 Marty and I were able to fly here. As I strapped in, I was surprised to find that it was a Canadair-built NF-5, sold originally to the Dutch, who later passed it on to the Turks. We found a great bombing range and in one mission overflew mountains, desert,

Capt Gordon Cooper, 419 Squadron's demo pilot, at Moose Jaw on July 12, 1992. Then, Turkish F-5 14017 with Maj Marty Tate aboard for the sortie of March 8, 1994. (Larry Milberry, Gordon Cooper)

the Mediterranean, cities, ancient ruins and forests. I was flying a double attack with a Turkish pilot. We flew lower and lower, trying to size each other up. I won that one by flying lowest, thereby earning the unspoken respect – the "right stuff" that writers try to describe, but which can only be truly understood within the fighter community. The Turks did get one on me, though. As we approached a large city, flying low level in combat formation, I zoom-climbed and came out of afterburner. I glided across the city before descending clear of it. That's how we did it in Cold Lake – to avoid noise complaints. Meanwhile, the Turks had kept up at 480 knots low-level straight across the city. I later was told that noise complaints in Turkey are unknown so … straight ahead at full throttle is the way to go. For the rest of the mission we flew low level across Mediterranean beaches and down city streets!

Our flight this day had been with the Turkish Stars, Turkey's F-5 flight demo team. The Stars had visited Moose Jaw a few years earlier, had adopted the Snowbird aerobatic model, and still revered the Canadian team. At Konya we also attended mission briefings/ debriefings, and toured the F-5 FLIT facilities and simulators. In the end, however, it was clear that the Turkish FLIT was not up to Canadian standards. In a later discussion with a Turkish commander at TAF HQ, I realized that there was another side to the Turkish proposal. Yes, the TAF wanted the CF-5s, but they didn't exactly want to train our pilots. The Turkish officer, who had trained in Canada years earlier, was intent on getting my opinions about TAF training. He acknowledged that the TAF was having trouble meeting NATO training standards, and that pilots flying Turkey's new F-16s had much to learn. It was the Turkish officer's dream to take our jets, build a first-class training facility, and have Canadian and Turkish instructors train students from both nations. So … they get our CF-5s and a greatly improved training standard; we get a free facility and get to fly the CF-5s that, apparently, we could no longer afford to operate ourselves! This man had true vision and I respected his frankness in opening the conversation.

Back home I reported on the Turkish "hidden agenda", but other forces were at work and the sale of CF-5s to Turkey was nixed. In the summer of 1995, 419 Squadron closed. Students now went directly onto the CF-18 from the Tutor and the failure rate soared. However, once the military accepted that it really did need a high performance FLIT, in July 2000 419 was reactivated using the Hawk trainer.

By the summer of 1996 I was an A320 First Officer with Skyservice. We had just dropped off our passengers in Cypress and were returning to Belfast. After a while our radio went quiet … too quiet. I looked at our map and suddenly realized what was happening. "We're in Turkey", I exclaimed, as I got on the radio to a Greek controller. I asked why they hadn't handed us over to the Turks, to which he replied, "We have not talked to the Turks in years and you are on your own. Goodnight." We quickly raised a Turkish controller. He was raving mad, saying that they were just about to launch a fighter to intercept us. Turkish control wanted all our particulars, emphasizing what trouble we were in. My captain looked worried as I said, "Let me handle this."

"So very sorry," I informed the controller. "By the way, I used to fly with the Turkish Stars. How are they doing?"

"You know the Turkish Stars? replied the controller in disbelief.

"Yes, I flew with them in Konya, and please pass along a hello from me to your Chief of the Air Force." Well, by the end of this conversation and by the time we had exited Turkish air space, the controller was like a long lost friend, inviting us to "Come back soon". I grinned as I looked over at the Captain, "How was that?"

"No one will ever believe me if I tell this story. We fly half way around the world, get knee deep in shit, and only you would know somebody to get us out of it!"

"Ah, that was nothing. Let me tell you about El Presidente"…

All the details about the Turkish CF-5 deal falling through are not yet out, but the reason likely was pure politics. Ottawa publicly was dissatisfied with Turkey's human rights record. Activists made their views known and won support from back-benchers on Parliament Hill. One news report of the day stated: "Turkey has been criticized by Canada for its human rights violations, which include the bombing of civilians and the violent suppression of advocates of Kurdish independence."

The Edmonton Journal, ignoring a 1986 deal between "peacekeeping" Ottawa and Turkey for 54 CF-104s, naively opined: "Prime Minister Jean Chretien seems to think that foreign policy is all about selling things. Well, we shouldn't sell any fighter planes to Turkey … We can either abandon our principles for the price of 39 refitted CF-5 jets, or we can keep our credibility as international peace keepers and mediators." In the end, instead of selling CF-5s to its NATO partner, Ottawa approved a deal with a Third World African state – CF-5s were sold to Botswana, which needed them a lot less than it needed educational and health care assistance (A small southern African nation, Botswana's economy depends on diamonds and beef. In 2007 some 350,000 of Botswana's 1,600,000 citizens were HIV positive). If one wanted an example of a country with a muddled foreign policy, Canada might be a fair choice.

Botswana Interlude

In 1996 Bristol Aerospace of Winnipeg was completing the avionics update program (AUP) on a run of 39 CF-5s. The final product was a superb, HUD-equipped trainer for 419 Squadron. Co-incidentally, however, "the powers that be" at NDHQ decided that Canada should get out of the FLIT world and, instead, start sending fighter pilot candidates straight from Tutor to CF-18. Bristol was tasked to dispose of the AUP CF-5s. Capt Ron "VeeDee" Van der Voort and Capt Dave "Stoner" Stone were seconded there to test fly and deliver CF-5s still coming off the AUP line, and to fly "demos" for interested parties.

A native of Holland, Van der Voort had joined the Royal Netherlands Air Force in 1978. After his pilot selection course on the Saab Safir trainer, he completed training in Canada through the existing NATO plan. This included the usual path through Portage la Prairie (Musketeer), Moose Jaw (Tutor) and Cold Lake (CF-5). He then returned to Holland in early 1981 to complete the Tactical Conversion Course on the NF-5 at 313 Squadron. Next came three years on the NF-5 at 315 Squadron.

In 1984 Capt Van der Voort was posted to the NATO air training base at Sheppard AFB, Texas. There he spent almost eight years instructing on T-38s, on which he would accumulate some 3500 hours. With this tour wending, he had the offer of F-16s

in Holland but, instead, decided to emigrate to Canada. There, through the auspices of LGen David Huddleston, he enlisted in the Canadian Forces. By November 1991 he was instructing on CF-5s at 419 Squadron. There he remained until 419 stood down on June 24, 1995. As he put it in 2006, when 419 closed its doors, "I was the one doing most of the paper shredding." He recalled his last operational mission on the CF-5 on February 21, 1996. That day, with Capt Brent "Sparky" Sparks in the back seat, he piloted 116833 on something that he laughingly recalled as a single-ship CF-5 "mass attack" on the base in aid of an Army air defence exercise.

Van der Voort and Stone now returned to duty at Bristol, ferrying CF-5s into storage at Trenton, thence to nearby Mountain View. Before long only two demo AUP CF-5s remained at Bristol. Several parties visited to view them, watch a demo and maybe scrounge a ride. There were tire-kickers from Botswana, Malaysia, Turkey, the US Navy and the Philippines. In the end Ottawa would sell 13 AUP CF-5s to the Botswana Defence Force Air Arm, which desired a small fighter force to bolster its regional prowess. A rumoured price per CF-5 was $1.5 million. The deal included air and ground training, a flight simulator and some spares at little or no charge. Eventually three more CF-5s were added and all "BF-5s" were attached to Z28 Squadron. By this time Van der Voort and another ex-CanForces CF-5 pilot, Bill "Bronco" Brown (a former 419 pilot who had retired from the military in 1995), had signed 18-month contracts with Botswana to train prospective pilots. Van der Voort re-checked Brown out on type on August 22, 1996, then flew his last CF-5 mission as

Some of Canada's retired AUP CF-5s stored at Trenton in 1997. (Van der Voort Col.)

a CanForces pilot on August 29, 1996. He and Brown departed for Botswana, as Capts Brad "Bear" Dolan and Doug "Dog" Carter took over as Bristol's CF-5 pilots.

Van der Voort and Brown travelled to the BDF base at Thebe Phatshwa near Botswana's capital, Gaborone. At first they lived in hotels, then tried base accommodations, before settling for local rental properties. Thebe Phatshwa was a new military airfield being completed by French contractors under what was referred to as the "Eagle Project". PC-7s, Strikemasters, CASA transports and a few helicopters were stationed here. The first CF-5s soon began arriving, three at a time aboard An-124 freighters. They were assembled by technical personnel from Bristol and on November 13,

Capt Ron Van der Voort served with 419 Squadron at Cold Lake from November 1991 to June 1996, and later instructed in Botswana. (Van der Voort Col.)

1996, Ron Van der Voort took the first ("OJ-21") on a shakedown flight. In the process he completed the first supersonic flight over Botswana. Meanwhile, the Bristol tech reps were busy training their BDF counterparts in every aspect of maintaining and repairing BF-5s.

Besides their basic equipment, the CF-5s were fitted by the BDF with VOR, VHF radio, and GPS. Meanwhile, Van der Voort and Brown were devising a basic CF-5 ground school and flying training syllabus. Three pilots comprised their initial student cadre – Capts "Fergi" Ferguson, Dijeng and Conrad "Big Boy" Solomon. The initial 13 aircraft proved typically reliable, so training commenced, but the Canadians found that accomplishing their goals would not be a piece of cake. Their students, although keen and well educated, had only a limited knowledge of flying high performance aircraft, and the CF-5 was no toy. Transmitting their concerns to officialdom proved difficult, and support from Ottawa or Winnipeg was scarce.

The initial student cadre proved to be the most experienced and promising, but future pilots identified by the BDF for BF-5 train-

CF-5s to Botswana

CanForces Nos. 116705, 116716, 116719, 116723, 116727, 116732, 116734, 116742, 116754, 116764, 116765, 116784, 116801, 116802, 116811, 116829, 116830

ing had only rudimentary training on the PC-7, and were hardly suitable for the BF-5. Van der Voort and Brown pushed for CanForces involvement, i.e. providing a basic pilot training course for follow-up students. Ottawa and the BDF were reluctant to accept, although Ottawa agreed that some BDF students do a jet famil course in Moose Jaw. This was tried, but with only marginal benefits – no BDF student achieved solo status on the Tutor. Also frustrating for the Canadian IPs was a shortage of CF-5 fuel, liquid oxygen and lubricants. Basic logistics infrastructure was non-existent. There were no plans for search and rescue, nor survival equipment, even though missions were flown over the vast Kalahari Desert. As the team leader, Van der Voort spent hours attempting to convince the BDF of the need to have suitable fire fighting equipment, training, and emergency response plans.

Besides official duties, the Canadians also provided some entertainment (fly-bys and aerobatics) during official Botswana functions. Van der Voort had been a Canadian Forces CF-5 demo pilot in 1994, flying 116721 at airshows in such places as Abbotsford, Reno and Toronto. This experience proved useful, showing off the BF-5 to local and foreign dignitaries. Ron Van der Voort last flew in Botswana on August 17, 1998. His tour amounted to only about 200 flying hours. By this time the BDF still had no BF-5 QFI's of its own. It also had suffered its first CF-5 crash, when a BDF pilot made an inadvertent gear-up landing. The aircraft was only lightly damaged, but there was no fire fighting equipment, so it was lost in the ensuing fire. In another case, the BDF's "hottest stick", Capt "Big Boy" Solomon, wrote himself off while attempting aerobatics, trying to emulate his Canadian tutors. After Van der Voort and Brown left Botswana, a third ex-CanForces CF-5 pilot, Riamo "Kujo" Kujala, had a short BDF tour. He arrived in Botswana via there was a delay for advanced Kiowa training at 403 (H) Operational Training Squadron in Gagetown. Capitalizing on this, Gosden logged plenty of "OJT" flying time at 427. When he reached 403 in February 1974, that totalled nearly 400 hours, so his course was smooth sailing.

Back again at 427 Capt Gosden settled into the routines of a Kiowa recce pilot until August 1976, when he was posted to 444 Squadron at Lahr. With field exercises from squadron level to the huge NATO "Reforger" exercise held each fall, this was heaven for a diehard TacHel pilot. Much work was done with US Army attack helicopter units, which would seek out 444 on account of its gung-ho spirit, professionalism and ability to gain them high kill scores as assessed by exercise umpires. Capt Gosden served 444 until February 1978, then was posted to the Scout at 665 Squadron, Army Air Corps in Colchester Garrison. OTU flying commenced on March 13 at the Army Air Corps Centre, Middle Wallop. The course continued to April 27, by which time Gosden had flown the Scout for 31.9 hours dual, 9.7 hours solo. Now he joined 665, flying initially on May 3. This exchange would prove ideal for both services. Canada wanted experience on the anti-armour helicopter, while the British Army benefitted from the experience for which

A typical Scout AH.1 at Topcliffe on July 8, 1972. XR628 suffered a mishap on June 8, 1982. Its remains supposedly survived into the 2000s. This type originated in 1956 as the Saunders-Roe P.531. Once Westland absorbed "Saro", the P.531 became the AH.1 Scout general-purpose helicopter. In this configuration, XR628 has an casevac litter attached. From 1963-1994 the army operated 150 Scouts. Eventually, these were replaced by the multi-role Lynx, which Canadians also flew. (Roger Lindsay)

444 was renowned (by this time Capt Gosden had more than 2600 rotary wing hours, much more than a typical Scout pilot). Soon, 665 moved to Oakington, where it became 657 Squadron. In this period, Army Air Corps TOW squadrons were suffering from a bit of neglect, mainly due to frequent Northern Ireland rotations. Capt Gosden, however, was straight from NATO's "front line" and had fresh ideas to offer. Soon training picked up and, on the live-fire range in June 1980, 657 recorded the best SS.11 scores of the three UK-based squadrons.

While on exchange Gosden was promoted to major. In June 1980 his tour ended and Capt Michel Legault, an experienced TacHel pilot from 430 Squadron, took over the Scout exchange slot. The experience had proved valuable for the CF, as Gosden would go on to hold key staff and command appointments in the TacHel world, where he was able to share his knowledge of

Capt Ed Gosden while serving with 427 Squadron at Petawawa. (Gosden Col.)

Scout vs Kiowa

	UK Army AH.1Scout	CanForces CH-136 Kiowa
First flight	1958	1966
Crew	2	2
Power	1050 shp R-R Nimbus	371 shp Allison 250 C-18
Cruise speed	106 knots	102 knots
AUW	5300 lb	3200 lb
Armament	4 × Nord SS.11 missiles	1 × 7.62 minigun (optional)
No. in service	150	66
Status	Retired from AAC service	Retired from CF service

Since the 1970s any CF helicopter pilot on exchange went to their new postings with solid experience on the Bell CH-136 Kiowa. This 444 Squadron Kiowa is seen along the Rhine in West Germany on July 22, 1988. (Larry Milberry)

(Left) Capt Michel Legault followed Maj Gosden on the Scout exchange. Here he is (left) in June 1982 with Capt Alan Paul, a fellow pilot on 657 Squadron. Legault last flew the Scout on June 4, 1982 by when he had 610 hours on type. Legault returned to a staff job at 5th Mechanized Brigade Group at CFB Valcartier, serving into 1985. Next came Gagetown, instructing at the Air Ground Operations School. Promoted to major, he attended CF Staff College in 1987, then spent to 1991 as Director of Studies there. Next he was DCO at 430, then was promoted and had three years at 10 TAG HQ in St-Hubert. For 1996-97 LCol Legault commanded 430. In this period 430 did the OpEval on the CH-146 Griffon (Bell 412). In March 1997 Legault led 430 to Haiti on a 6-month peacekeeping mission. There, 430's night missions exclusively used NVGs. From 1998 to 2000 LCol Legault headed CF Directorate of Flight Safety. He then was chief of liaison with the MFO in the Sinai, after which he was the CF Air Advisor at CDLS London. He had a year at the CF Language School, before becoming Canadian Defence Attaché to Hungary in August 2005. (Legault Col.)